THE CHRISTIAN'S PRESENT FOR ALL SEASONS

IDENTITY OF MEN ON THE COVER

Archbishop Robert Leighton

Timothy Dwight

William Jay

Joseph Hall

John Owen

John Bunyan

Isaac Watts

THE CHRISTIAN'S PRESENT FOR ALL SEASONS

CONTAINING

DEVOTIONAL THOUGHTS

OF

EMINENT DIVINES

FROM

JOSEPH HALL TO WILLIAM JAY

SELECTED AND EDITED BY

D.A. HARSHA

WITH AN

INTRODUCTORY ESSAY ON DEVOTION

BY

W.B. SPRAGUE

"O God, raise my spirits more and more
to that heavenly employment."
Bishop Patrick

Solid Ground Christian Books
Birmingham, Alabama USA
August 2008

Solid Ground Christian Books
PO Box 660132
Vestavia Hills AL 35266
205-443-0311
sgcb@charter.net
www.solid-ground-books.com

THE CHRISTIAN'S PRESENT FOR ALL SEASONS
Containing Devotional Thoughts from Eminent Divines

Selected and Edited by David A. Harsha (1827-1896)

Taken from the 1866 edition published by the American Tract Society, New York, NY

SPECIAL THANKS: Solid Ground owes a great debt to Pastor Keith Doster of Pine Grove Mills, PA for letting us know about this buried gem and for being willing to send it to us so that we might use it in this project. It is an honor for us to dedicate this book to Pastor Doster.

Cover image is taken from frontispiece of the original book, and engraved by F. Halpin, NY

Cover design by Borgo Design
Contact them at borgogirl@bellsouth.net

ISBN- 978-159925-187-5

INTRODUCTORY ESSAY.

Devotion may be considered in reference either to the act performed, or the spirit in which the act originates. Between the act and the spirit there is an indissoluble connection—the latter could not long exist without manifesting itself in the former—the former without the latter would be simple hypocrisy. As the heart, being the fountain of all moral action, gives complexion to the life, so the devotional habits of an individual will be determined by his devotional feelings. There may indeed be the appearance of devotion where there is not the reality; but insincerity even towards God will be almost sure to betray itself to the observation of men.

But while all devotion recognizes a God, or at least a being who is called God, it is obvious that the devotion must assume a type corresponding with the character of the being who is the object of it. The Pagan bows before an image of wood or stone;

but the homage that he renders, is an offence not only against the living and true God, but against the dignity of his own nature. The Deist professedly acknowledges the God who is revealed by the light of nature; and he ascribes to Him infinite perfection; and owns himself dependent upon his bounty and his care; but he forgets that he has to approach Him as a sinner, and that God is of purer eyes than to behold iniquity, and therefore cannot be approached except in the new and living way which He hath himself ordained. It is Christianity alone that puts us into legitimate communion with the Father of our spirits. This shows us that the only way to the throne of mercy leads by the Cross; that it is only through the gracious intercession of the Lord Jesus, founded on the merit of his atoning sacrifice, that our prayers, offered in humility and faith, can find acceptance.

The spirit of devotion may be regarded as an epitome of the Christian graces — these graces are combined in the exercise of this spirit; and more than that, they react with a quickening power upon the spirit itself. The truly devout Christian bows with reverence before the Divine perfections; takes counsel of the word and providence of God for intimations of the Divine will; laments the prevalence of indwelling sin; relies on the merits of Christ and the power and grace of the Holy Spirit; and prays for an increasing conformity to the precepts of the Gospel, and for the universal prevalence of truth and righteousness. And with these exercises are identified humility, trust, submission, charity, zeal in doing good,—every thing that elevates human character, and constitutes the appropriate preparation for Heaven.

If then the spirit of devotion is so important in its exercises and results, if it is that with which the tone of Christian character is pre-eminently identified, surely it is not less the interest than the duty of every Christian to guard against all those influences by which its exercise is impeded. And what *are* some of those influences?

There is the influence of a low state of religion in the heart. The process of sanctification, though on the whole progressive, is marked by great irregularity and inconstancy, and sometimes even seems to assume a retrograde course. There are times, in the experience of many Christians at least, when most of the graces seem to have passed into an eclipse, and the world triumphantly inquire in respect to them,—"What do they more than others?" The sense of Christian obligation has been greatly lowered; the estimate of God's word and ordinances has sunk proportionally; and the atmosphere which they breathe most freely is not that which is sanctified by the presence of the Holy Spirit. In such a heart surely the spirit of devotion cannot but languish; and the waking up of that spirit is to be looked for only in a return to all the duties of the Christian life.

Closely connected with the preceding, and even identified with it, is the prevalence of ungodly passion, which forms so large an element in our corrupt nature. As men differ in their original constitutions,— some possessing one quality in a higher degree, and some another,— so the evil passions and propensities that remain in the heart, after the regenerating work is performed, exist in different individuals in various degrees of strength. Here there is an undue appreciation of worldly honour, and corresponding efforts to attain it. There deceitful riches play upon the imagination and the heart with a power that proves irresistible. And yonder is another who indulges in covetousness, or envy, or who even suffers the viper revenge, under some misnomer, to linger in his bosom. But can any thing be more hostile than these ungodly passions to the spirit of devotion? Is it not manifest that, just in proportion as they prevail in the soul, there must be a disinclination, an absolute disability, for communion with God?

And there is an influence from the *outer* world, co-operating with that from the inner, tending to the same result. Here we have, for the present, our home,— our place of residence, our field of labour. Such has been the ordering of our lot that we are kept, at various points, in contact with the world; and, in yielding to this arrangement and acting in accordance with it, we only obey a divinely ordained necessity of our earthly condition. Nor is there any thing in this arrangement that necessarily interferes with the exercise of a devotional spirit — on the contrary, there is much, which, if viewed aright, is fitted to encourage and cherish it; and yet all experience proves that, by perversion, it becomes a powerful means of counteracting the soul's upward tendencies, and sometimes of absolutely chaining it down to earth. So long as we can plead that we are obeying the Divine mandate in attending to our secular concerns, and that to "be diligent in business" is required by the same authority as to "pray without ceasing," there is danger, great danger, that we shall suffer the world to gain an undue dominion over us; and, as a consequence, that a proportional irregularity and formality will pervade our devotions. But while this effect may be produced by the mere want of watchfulness in our necessary worldly engagements, let it be remembered that the world is little less than "a show-box of temptations;" that the wealth of the world, and the pomp and show of the world, and the official stations of the world, have each their respective attractions; while the world itself is full of "evil men and seducers who wax worse and worse." Now, when it is remembered that these varied influences for evil have to act upon hearts in which the love of evil has been only partially removed, and in which there is still more or less of sympathy with surrounding temptation, who does not perceive that there is imminent danger lest the principle of the new life should languish, involving of course the vigorous actings of the spirit of devotion? What observing Christian is there, whose memory is not the depository of many sad cases in which the world has so far triumphed in the heart of the professed disciple of Christ, that prayer, which had once been his vital breath, has come to seem indifferent, if not positively distasteful?

But if it is important that we watch against those influences which tend to deaden the spirit of devotion, equally necessary is it that we avail ourselves of all the helps within our reach for its exercise and culture.

One of these is to be found in the careful keeping of the heart. He who keeps his heart with all diligence will not only be secure against the inroads of temptation, but will be sure also to keep a conscience in a good degree void of offence; and this will render an approach to the throne of grace easy and pleasant to him. So too there will be associated with this a deep sense of dependence; for it is impossible that one should explore diligently and habitually his own heart, without realizing that the sanctifying work that is to be carried forward there, can never proceed independently of an influence from on high,— an influence not to be hoped for except in answer to fervent prayer. Indeed, the very exercise of keeping the heart not only serves to keep alive a devotional spirit, by direct ministration, but that spirit may be regarded as its primary element — the two essentially coexist, and inhere in each other.

A religious observance of the dispensations of Providence, whether in respect to ourselves or others, tends to the same result. Notwithstanding the order of events proceeds according to fixed laws, and in this very uniformity the Atheist finds an argument against the existence of a God, still every religious observer of what is passing must see evidences the most conclusive of the movements of a Divine hand. And if God is always present with me to supply my wants and crown me with his goodness, shall I not be drawn near to Him in acts of devout thanksgiving? If I become forgetful of his benefits or remiss in my duty, and He administers a gracious chastisement with a view to humble and reform me, shall I not betake myself at once to the throne of mercy, there to humble myself for my sin, and to accept reverently the Divine correction? And so, when I look around me and notice the various ways in which my fellow-creatures are led; when I see blessings crowding upon the footsteps of some, and fearful calamities accumulating in the path of others; when I extend my view and take in the nation or the world, and mark the wonderful changes that are going forward everywhere — here perplexity and disaster, there success and triumph; here the reign of the deepest moral darkness, and there the clouds passing off as the Sun of Righteousness breaks forth;— I say, when I take such a broad view as this, can I fail to find material for devotion every where? Must I not adore the hand that can work such changes? Must I not praise the hand that can pour forth such blessings? Must I not tremble before the hand that can inflict such terrible evils? Must I not be more than ever desirous to dwell in the secret place of the Most High?

There is that also in frequent and intimate Christian intercourse, that is fitted to strengthen the habit of devotion. By communing frequently with each other, Christians come to know more not only of one another's hearts but of their own; and thus they come to the throne of grace, sharing one another's burdens, and supplicating more intelligently as well as more earnestly for themselves. Let a company of Christian friends be assembled to take counsel of each other in respect to their trials, or duties, or prospects, or any thing pertaining to the Christian life, and while they will almost of course crown the interview with united prayer, they will carry away with them a spirit that will make their closets more dear to them, and render them fellow helpers there unto the kingdom of God.

Yet another aid to the spirit of devotion is found in the diligent study of God's word, and other books of spiritual tendency. As the Bible is an immediate revelation from God, containing a record of his doings in the past and predictions of what He will do hereafter; as it illustrates the great principles of his government, and teaches us all that it is necessary we should know in respect to the economy of our salvation; as it brings us in contact with truths and facts, bearing not upon individuals merely, but upon the race, and as not a small portion of its contents actually take on the form of confession, supplication and praise,— it cannot otherwise be, in view of all these considerations, than that the earnest student of the Bible,— admitting that he approaches it with a proper spirit,— should, at the same time, possess, in large measure, the spirit of prayer. It certainly is not to be denied that the Bible may be studied, and that too with great zeal and carefulness, for the mere gratification of curiosity, or for the still worse purpose of disproving its Divine authority; and in every such case of course nothing but evil can be expected as the result; but let it be studied *as* the word of God, with a sincere desire to find out and digest its precious meaning, and the effect will be that the individual concerned will be sensible of constantly growing attractions in the throne of grace, and with the increase of his scriptural knowledge there will be a corresponding growth of his devotional fervour.

And though the Bible is *the* Book above all

others, yet it is by no means the only book, from which the spirit of devotion is to be inhaled — the world is full of books which have drawn their materials substantially from the Bible; some of which are designed simply to explain its meaning; others to enforce and impress its blessed truths; and not a few, like the Psalms of David, bring the soul into direct communion with its God. We are obliged indeed to admit that in this almost endless variety of books, purporting to bear a religious character, there are not a few that are worse than useless; while some strike at the very roots of that religion of which they profess to appear as advocates. But, notwithstanding the deluge of trash that has come in under the assumed character of religious literature, the world abounds with works that reflect the truths of the Bible in sunbeams, and that bring these truths in direct contact with the conscience and the heart. Such works, judiciously selected, it is desirable that every Christian should avail himself of, in the prosecution of his religious course; and in so doing, while the general tone of his spiritual life will be quickened, he will secure to himself a larger measure of that dependent, grateful, confiding spirit that loves to breathe out its offerings at the throne of the Heavenly grace.

Among the many excellent works adapted especially to help the Christian in his devotions, that to which this brief Essay is designed as an introduction, holds a prominent place. The Compiler seems to have ranged through almost the whole field of devotional literature, and to have gathered up all the brightest gems that came in his way; and so successful has he been that one may open the book at random, as often as he will, and will never find his eye resting upon any thing that he can afford to pass over, or that does not supply the elements of rich devotional thought. It is difficult to say which is most to be admired, the Compiler's good judgment and taste, or his extraordinary patience in research, that has brought to us the heavenly thoughts of so many saints and sages. Of all the contributions that Mr. Harsha has made to our Christian literature, it may reasonably be doubted whether there is one for which posterity will hold him in more grateful remembrance, than this beautiful compilation of "DEVOTIONAL THOUGHTS."

W. B. S.

ALPHABETICAL LIST OF DIVINES.

ADAM, THOMAS	PAGE 392	HOWE, JOHN	312
BARROW, ISAAC	298	JAY, WILLIAM	547
BATES, WILLIAM	208	JENKS, BENJAMIN	344
BAXTER, RICHARD	153	KEN, THOMAS	335
BICKERSTETH, EDWARD	533	LEIGHTON, ROBERT	125
BUNYAN, JOHN	279	LOGAN, JOHN	475
CHALMERS, THOMAS	519	MASON, JOHN M.	514
CHARNOCK, STEPHEN	251	NEVINS, WILLIAM	539
COMBER, THOMAS	341	NEWTON, JOHN	456
DAVIES, SAMUEL	445	OWEN, JOHN	189
DODDRIDGE, PHILIP	396	PATRICK, SYMON	216
DWIGHT, TIMOTHY	481	ROMAINE, WILLIAM	431
EDWARDS, JONATHAN	411	SCOTT, THOMAS	465
FLAVEL, JOHN	225	SIBBES, RICHARD	86
FULLER, ANDREW	495	TAYLOR, JEREMY	102
HALL, JOSEPH	27	TILLOTSON, JOHN	291
HALL, ROBERT	500	WALKER, ROBERT	439
HEBER, REGINALD	529	WATTS, ISAAC	369
HENRY, MATTHEW	355	WESLEY, JOHN	425
HOPKINS, EZEKIEL	328	WILSON, THOMAS	363

Oh that I felt my soul upborne
  On pure devotion's wings,
Far above earth's deceitful joys
  And sublunary things.

Where Thou, bless'd Saviour sit'st enthroned
  In everlasting light,
The glory of the angelic host,
  The source of their delight.

There, in Thy blissful presence, reigns
  Immortal joy serene;
No wintry storms are heard to roar,
  Nor desolation seen.

Around Thee flow unmix'd delights,
  Like rivers deep and wide;
While from the ocean of Thy love,
  Proceeds an endless tide.

My soul thirsteth for God, for the living God; when shall I come and appear before God? PSALM xlii. 2.

Devotion is the life of religion; the very soul of piety; the highest employment of grace; and no other than the prepossession of heaven by the saints of God here upon earth: every improvement whereof is of more advantage and value to the Christian soul, than all the profit and contentment which this world can afford it.—BISHOP HALL.

Devotion is one of the first and last things which the eye of God discerns, in every day, of a truly upright and good man.—DR. DODDRIDGE.

PREFACE.

It is more than ten years since the preparation of the present volume was commenced. During all this time, the selection of these beautiful passages has been slowly but steadily carried on. The work was undertaken in connection with the editing of a *Library of Christian Authors*, embracing Memoirs of Eminent Divines, and their choice works—a series whose preparation is not yet completed. In performing this long and arduous labor, and while carefully perusing the works of our best authors, from the 17th century to the present time, passages in each author, which the editor regarded as among the finest specimens of devotional and practical writing, were selected for the present volume. In this manner have these 'calm and holy thoughts' of those who have shone as stars in the firmament of the Christian Church, been brought together; and it is believed that in the following pages will be found some of the choicest gems of English sacred literature—gems which 'within small compass, and in purest gold, will preserve their lustre for ages.'

The selections are from forty writers, whose names are given in chronological order, with the dates of their birth and death. By far the most copious selections are from the works of Bishop Hall, one of the most devotional, and at the same time, most evangelical of our Christian authors. Among the others, a large space is also given to Archbishop Leighton, who exhibits a truly devotional spirit, and of whom Coleridge has justly remarked: 'If there could be an intermediate space between inspired and uninspired writings, that space would be occupied by Leighton.'

The selections are made from the latest or best editions of the works of the various authors, in the editor's private library; and the most of the following specimens of devotional and practical writings, are from volumes not easily accessible to the general reader.

'There are *remains* of great and good men,' says Matthew Henry, 'which, like Elijah's mantle, ought to be gathered up and preserved by the survivors; their sayings, their writings, their examples; that as their works follow them in the reward of them, they may stay behind in the benefit of them.' And here are some of those 'remains,' gathered from the writings of some of the excellent of the earth, which are fitted to fill the mind of the Christian with delightful thoughts of the Saviour, and of His glorious work of redemption;

to excite devotional feelings, and to raise the affections to that better land,—

'Where beauty smiles eternally,
And pleasure never dies.'

It has been well remarked by Bishop Hall, that 'the soul that is rightly affected to God, is never void of a holy devotion. Whereever it is, whatever it doth, it is still lifted up to God, and fastened upon Him, and converses with Him; ever serving the Lord in fear and rejoicing in Him with trembling.' Most gladly would the editor of this volume say to the Christian reader, in the words of the same excellent divine: 'If I have given your devotions any light, it is well; the least glimpse of this knowledge is worth all the full gleams of human and earthly skill.'

In the sincere hope of assisting the believer in Jesus in the heavenly exercise of devotion, and of solacing his mind amidst the various trials, conflicts, sorrows and bereavements of life, the present manual is now offered to the Christian public.

May the precious thoughts in this volume soothe and cheer the Christian in his pilgrimage through a vale of tears, endearing the Saviour in His personal excellencies, and in His mediatorial work, more and more to his heart, till fully prepared by divine grace for the joys of heaven, his sanctified soul is carried at the hour of death, by ministering angels, to the realms of bliss, there to be ever with the Lord, and to praise Him in those 'many mansions' of our Father's house, where God wipes away the last tear of sorrow. O happy close of life's weary pilgrimage, to depart and to be with Christ! What Christian, as he thinks of the glory reserved for him in heaven, does not now feel like breathing the prayer of the Christian poet:—

'Oh, when life's sunset draws around me,
Closing my eventful day,
Let Thy love, O Christ, upon me
Shed its pure and spirit ray.
Up the starry steeps of even,
Let Thy Spirit be my guide,
Till in the deathless light of heaven,
Lost to earth, my spirit glide.

'There, where daylight ever lingers,
O'er the vernal, flower-clad plains,—
There, where morning's rosy fingers
Wreathe with light the azure main,—
There, where all we dream of brightness,
Joy or peace, to make us blest,
May the wrapt soul on wings of lightness
Find rest, ah, yes: eternal rest.'

ARGYLE, N. Y., *Jan.* 1867.   D. A. H.

CONTENTS.

Joseph Hall, D. D.:   Page.

The Saviour in Gethsemane	27
Christ the Smitten Rock	30
Blessedness of Salvation	31
Meditation on Death	32
The Divine Mercy in Redemption	36
Pardon for the Most Guilty	38
The Fear of Death	41
Behold God as Really Present	42
Thoughts of God in the Devout Person	43
Thoughts at the Communion Table	44
Do this in Remembrance of Me	46
Thoughts after the Communion	47
True Repentance	48
Mercy for the Vilest	48
All are Pilgrims	50
Death but a Sleep	51
Prayer	52
Redemption	53
The Christian in his Devotion	54
The Christian in his Death	55
The Christian's Home	56
Heavenly and Earthly Things	57
Humility	58
Eternity	59
The Celestial City	59
The True Christian Happy	60
The Saviour's Agony	61
The Night of Death	63
Heavenly Joys	63
Honey from the Rock	64
The Heavenly Manna	66
The Happy Return Home	67
The Felicity of Heaven	68
God Manifest in the Flesh	70
The Saviour received up into Glory	71
Heavenly Mindedness	72
Heavenly Recognition	73
The Glory of Heaven	75
The Saviour's Sufferings and Glories	76
Paradise	77
Unchangeable Duration	79
Rest in God	80
Life a Pilgrimage	81
On the Length of the Way	82
The Divine Love	83

Richard Sibbes, D. D.:

Grace	86
The Holy Spirit our Guide	87
Beholding of Christ, a Transforming Sight	89

Comfort in Distress	90
Pardoning Mercy	90
Prayer and Praise	91
Praising God	93
God our Refuge	96
Spiritual Desertion	97
God our Portion	98
Comfort in the Hour of Death	100

JEREMY TAYLOR, D. D.:

Prayers, I.	102
" II.	103
" III.	104
" IV.	105
" V.	106
" VI.	107
" VII.	108
" VIII.	109
Evening Prayers, I.	109
" " II.	110
Prayer for one in Trouble	111
Prayer for one in Sickness	112
Prayer before a Journey	113
Prayers on receiving the Sacrament, I.	114
" " " II.	115
Prayers for Pardon of Sins, I.	115
" " " II.	116
On Prayer	117
Advantages of Prayer	119
The Righteous Safe	120
Consolation	121
God's Mercy	123
The Repenting Sinner	124

ROBERT LEIGHTON, D. D.:

Salvation	125
Free Grace	126
Redemption the Admiration of Angels	127
The Scriptures	128
Prayer	129
True Rest	131
The Christian Warfare	131
Communion with Christ in Suffering	133
The Believer's Joy at the Revelation of Christ	134
Glory of Christ at the Last Day	135
Steadfastness in the Faith	135
Eternal Glory	136
Meditation on the Eighth Psalm	137
Spiritual Desire of Death	138
Come to the Saviour	139
Christ the Light of the Christian	140
Happiness of the Life to Come	140
Prayers, I.	143
" II.	144
" III.	145
" IV.	146
" V.	147
" VI.	148
" VII.	149
" VIII.	151

RICHARD BAXTER:

Walking with God	153
Prayer in the Hour of Death	155
Language and Power of Faith	156

CONTENTS.

Second Coming of Christ 158
The Saints' Joy 161
The Word of God 163
Love of God 164
Everlasting Joys of Heaven 165
Repose of the Soul 166
How to Live a Pleasant Life 167
Thanksgiving and Praise 169
The Redeemed in Glory 171
Heavenly Recognition 173
Love to Saints in Heaven 175
Loss of Pious Friends 176
Live by Faith 177
Comtemplation of God 178
Solitude 180
Infinite Goodness of God 181
The Saviour's Condescension and Love 183
Heavenly Aspirations 185
Prayer for the Penitent 186
Crucified to the World 187
Now or Never 187

JOHN OWEN, D. D.:

Prayer to Christ in Seasons of Distress 189
Communion of Believers in Heavenly Worship 190
Visions of Celestial Glory 192
The Saints' Rest 193
The Word of God 195
A Hiding Place from the Wind 196
A Covert from the Tempest 197
Faith Triumphant in the Hour of Death 198
Fulness of Christ 198
Beholding the Glory of Christ 199
Saving Grace 200
Flourishing of the Righteous 200
Spiritual Decays in the Christian 202
Recovery from Backsliding 203
How to Die Comfortably 204
The Departing Soul 205
True Pleasures 207

WILLIAM BATES, D. D.:

Heavenly Joy 208
Heavenly Conversation 209
The Music of Heaven 210
Death and Heaven 211
Death of Pious Friends 212
Perpetuity of Bliss 213
Ever with the Lord 214

SYMON PATRICK, D. D.:

Prayers, I. 216
"   II. 218
"   III. 220
"   IV. 223

JOHN FLAVEL, B. A.:

Efficacy of the Blood of the Cross 225
Fountain of Life 227
The Study of Christ 228
Vision of God in Glory 228
Divine Care 230
Faith in God's Unchangeableness 232
Walking with God 233
Rest in God 233

CONTENTS.

Communion with God 234
Christ's Love manifest from the Cross 335
Free Grace 236
Grace of God 237
Pardon for the most Heinous Sins 237
Peace to the Soul 238
Joy in the Holy Ghost 239
Foretastes of Heaven 241
The Longing Soul's Reflection 243
Reflection of a Growing Christian 244
Lost and Found 245
The Ocean of Divine Mercy 245
Joy of the Redeemed 246
Assurance 247
Constancy of Christ's Love 248
Maturity of Grace 249
End of the Christian's Trials 250

STEPHEN CHARNOCK, B. D.:
Meditation on the Glory of Christ 251
Christ our Advocate 254
Christ Presenting the Memorials of his Death 257
Perpetuity of Christ's Intercession 259
Efficacy of Christ's Intercession 261
Love to Christ as our Advocate 262
The Glorified Redeemer 263
The Substance of the Gospel 264
Love of God 265
Our Access to God 265
The Covenant of Redemption 266
Christ Filled with the Spirit 267
Infinite Compassion of God 268
The Saviour's Agony 269
Christ's Love as Manifested in His Death 271
God Spared not His Son 271
Our Acceptance in Christ 272
The Gospel 275
Comfort against Death 276
God to be Praised in Reconciliation 277

JOHN BUNYAN:
On Prayer 279
Grace of Christ 280
Christ made Sin for us 281
Coming to God by Christ 282
Christ's Intercession 282
Giving Glory to Christ 283
Church Fellowship 284
Grace 285
The Pilgrims Entering the Celestial City 285
Last Words of Mr. Standfast 287
Comfort in Christ's Intercession 288
The New Song in Glory 289

JOHN TILLOTSON, D. D.:
Eternal Happiness 291
Glorified Bodies of the Righteous 293
Earthly and Heavenly Joys 294
Resurrection of Christ 295
Excellency of Heavenly Things 296

ISAAC BARROW, D. D.:
Duty of Thanksgiving 298
Imitation of Christ 300
Consolation in Affliction 302
Our Life 303

CONTENTS.

Incarnation of Christ	305
The Great Physician	306
Resurrection of Christ	307
Our Saviour's Ascension and Glorification	308
The Life Everlasting	310

JOHN HOWE, M. A.:

Anticipation of the Joys of Heaven	312
Humility	314
The Righteous willing to Die	315
Christian Hope	317
Meditation on Heavenly Things	319
The Saint's Delight in God	321
Live with Eternity in View	327

EZEKIEL HOPKINS, D. D.:

The Christian's Joy	328
Inconstancy of Earthly Enjoyments	329
Pardon of Sin	329
Grace Opposing Sin	331
Heavenly Rest	331
Heavenly Hope	331
The Work of Grace and Sanctification	332
Comfort in the Death of Pious Friends	333

THOMAS KEN, D. D.:

A Prayer for Spiritualized Affections	335
On Communion with God	336
On the Love of the Saviour	337
On the Joys of Heaven	337
A Prayer for One in Affliction	338
The Righteous Eternally Secure	340

THOMAS COMBER, D. D.:

Meditations on the Lord's Supper, I.	341
" " " " II.	342
" " " " III.	343

BENJAMIN JENKS:

A Morning Prayer	344
An Evening Prayer	346
A Prayer on Going Abroad	348
A Prayer for Faith and Trust in God	349
A Prayer for Increase of Grace	350
A Prayer for God's Gracious Presence	351
A Prayer on Preparation for Death	352

MATTHEW HENRY:

Pleasures of Communion with God	355
Exercise of Holy Joy and Praise	356
Meditations on the Heavenly Rest	357
The Bible	359
Pious Ejaculations	359
A Life of Communion with God	360
The Soul's Triumph over Death	360
Divine Knowledge	361
A Sacramental Petition	362

THOMAS WILSON, D. D.:

Afflictions	363
The Saviour's Patience	364
A Prayer for Submission of Spirit	364
A Morning Prayer	365
An Evening Prayer	367

ISAAC WATTS, D. D.:

Holy Breathing	369
Holy Fortitude	370

CONTENTS.

Fly to the Mercy Seat ... 372
Uncertainty of Life ... 372
Awake to God ... 373
Heavenly Rest ... 375
No Sorrow in Heaven ... 376
Our Pious Departed Friends ... 377
The Lord's Supper ... 379
The End of Time ... 380
No Pain among the Blessed ... 380
No Night in Heaven ... 381
Joy at the Resurrection ... 383
Death of a Pious Youth ... 385
Death of Christian Relatives ... 385
The Believer's Possessions ... 388
The Christian's Hidden Life in Heaven ... 389
All-sufficiency of God ... 390

Thomas Adam:
The Man of Prayer ... 392
Prayers, I. ... 393
" II. ... 393
" III. ... 394
" IV. ... 395

Philip Doddridge, D. D.:
Praising the Lord ... 396
The Water of Life ... 397
A Devout Meditation ... 398
Our Great Intercessor ... 3 9
A Prayer for Gospel Blessings ... 401
My Father's House ... 402
Heaven our Home ... 402
Death to the Believer ... 404
A Prayer on Committing the Soul to Jesus ... 404
Safe in Jesus ... 405
Advice to the Afflicted ... 405
Mutual Joy of Christ and Believers in Heaven ... 406
A Model of Devotion for the Evening ... 408
Salvation Near ... 409

Jonathan Edwards, A. M.:
On Religious Affections ... 411
The Saint's Love to God ... 412
Christ's Invitations ... 413
Spiritual Light ... 416
Pardon for the Greatest Sinner ... 418
Attractions in the Saviour ... 420
Our Journey towards Heaven ... 423

John Wesley, A. M.:
Religion in the Heart ... 425
Walking by Faith ... 426
Our Redemption Near ... 427
Second Coming of Christ ... 428
Felicity of Heaven ... 429
The Poor in Spirit ... 430

William Romaine, A. M.:
Privileges of Prayer ... 431
Prayers, I. ... 432
" II. ... 433
Praise and Prayer ... 435
Institution and Benefits of the Lord's Supper ... 436
The Full Vision and Enjoyment of Christ ... 437

Robert Walker:
On Prayer ... 439

CONTENTS.

The Believing Soul's Address to Christ ... 439
The Heavy Laden Invited to Christ ... 441
Grace ... 442
Resignation to the Divine Will ... 442
Christ's Presence with Believers at Death ... 443

Samuel Davies, A. M.:
Excellency of the Divine Being ... 445
Love of God in the Gift of His Son ... 446
The Saint's Happiness at the Judgment Day ... 447
The Preciousness of Christ ... 448
Christ the only Foundation ... 449
The Saviour in His Exaltation ... 450
Hope of the Righteous in Death ... 451
Hope of a Happy Immortality ... 453
Christ Precious in His Instructions ... 453
Eternity ... 455

John Newton:
Trials ... 456
Devotion to Christ ... 456
The Believer Safe ... 457
Assurance ... 458
The Christian Soldier ... 458
Happy State of the Believer ... 459
Intercourse with Heaven ... 459
Prayer and Reading the Scriptures ... 461
Faith's View of Christ Crucified ... 461
The Sabbath an Earnest of Heaven ... 462
Divine Guidance ... 463
Blessed Fruits of Affliction ... 463

Thomas Scott, D. D.:
Morning Prayers for a Family, I. ... 465
" " " " II. ... 468
A Family Prayer for Saturday Evening ... 471

John Logan, F. R. S.:
The Message which Jesus Brings ... 475
The Christian's Victory over Death ... 477
Passing Away ... 480

Timothy Dwight, D. D., LL. D.:
The Blessings to which the Saviour invites us ... 481
Without an Interest in Christ ... 482
The Love of Christ ... 483
The Saviour's Goodness to the Believer ... 484
The Sinner Invited to Return to God ... 485
Advantages of Affliction ... 486
Consolation for the Afflicted ... 487
The Desire of Immortality ... 488
Blessings of Prayer ... 489
On Prayer for Revivals of Religion ... 490
Heaven our Home ... 491
Heaven in View ... 492
Our Father's House ... 492
Heaven and Earth Compared ... 493
Christ the Light of Heaven ... 494

Andrew Fuller:
Life of Faith ... 495
Christ Crucified ... 496
Progressive Character of Heavenly Bliss ... 497
Blessedness of Heaven ... 498

Robert Hall, A. M.:
Reunion of Good Men in Heaven ... 500
Friendship Founded on Religion ... 501

CONTENTS.

How a Minister should Preach ---- 502
The Pursuit of Salvation ---- 502
Funeral Obsequies of a Lost Soul ---- 503
A Penitent on his Knees ---- 504
Preparation for Judgment and Eternity ---- 504
The Lamb of God ---- 505
The Eye of Faith ---- 506
The Divine Promises ---- 506
Continual Virtue of Christ's Blood ---- 507
Importance of the Christian Ministry ---- 508
Salvation to the Uttermost ---- 509
Gratitude to the Saviour ---- 510
Come to the Saviour Now ---- 511
A Prayer ---- 511

JOHN M. MASON, D. D.:
Redemption through the Blood of Christ ---- 514
Death to a Child of God ---- 515
Blessed Effects of the Gospel ---- 516
Forgiveness of Sins Final ---- 516
Contemplation of the Love of Christ ---- 517
Our Duty and Happiness ---- 518

THOMAS CHALMERS, D. D., LL. D.:
Choose Christ ---- 519
Human Life Perishable ---- 520
Hope of Immortality ---- 521
Come to Christ ---- 522
Death Will Come ---- 523
A Christian's Love for the Sabbath ---- 524
Our Great High Priest ---- 525
Omnipresence of God ---- 526
Prayers, I. ---- 527
    " II. ---- 528

REGINALD HEBER, D. D.:
Life like a River ---- 529
Heaven and Earth ---- 530
Christ is Ours ---- 530
Fear of Death Removed ---- 530
Our Salvation of Grace ---- 531
Hymn Before the Sacrament ---- 532

EDWARD BICKERSTETH:
Meditations and Prayers on the Lord's Supper, I. ---- 533
    " " " " " II. ---- 534
    " " " " " III. ---- 536
    " " " " " IV. ---- 536
    " " " " " V. ---- 537
    " " " " " VI. ---- 538

WILLIAM NEVINS, D. D.:
Heaven ---- 539
Heaven's Attractions ---- 540
The Saint near to Heaven ---- 545
Christ's Love and that of the Christian ---- 545
Sympathy of Christ for the Believer ---- 546

WILLIAM JAY:
The Bible ---- 547
Death of Christian Friends ---- 548
On Prayer ---- 549
A Family Prayer for the Morning ---- 550
A Family Prayer for the Evening ---- 553
A Family Prayer for Sabbath Morning ---- 556
A Family Prayer for Sabbath Evening ---- 559

DEVOTIONAL THOUGHTS.

JOSEPH HALL, D. D.
1574-1656.

THE SAVIOUR IN GETHSEMANE.

Y soul is exceeding sorrowful, even unto death. Matt. xxvi. 38. What was it, what could it be, O Saviour, that lay thus heavy upon Thy Divine Soul? Was it the fear of death? Was it the forefelt pain, shame, torment of Thine ensuing crucifixion? O poor and base thoughts of the narrow hearts of cowardly and impotent mortality! How many thousands of Thy blessed martyrs have welcomed no less tortures, with smiles and gratulations; and have made a sport of those exquisite cruelties, which their very tyrants thought unsufferable! Whence had they this strength but from Thee? If their weakness were thus undaunted and prevalent, what was Thy power? No, no; it was the sad weight of the sin of mankind; it was the heavy burden of Thy

Father's wrath for our sin, that thus pressed Thy soul, and wrung from Thee these bitter expressions.

What can it avail Thee, O Saviour, to tell Thy grief to men? Who can ease Thee, but He of whom thou saidst, *My Father is greater than I?* Lo, to Him Thou turnest; *O Father, if it be possible, let this cup pass from me.*

While Thy mind was in this fearful agitation, it is no marvel; if Thy feet were not fixed. Thy place is more changed than Thy thoughts. One while, Thou walkest to Thy drowsy attendants, and stirrest up their needful vigilancy; then Thou returnest to Thy passionate devotions, Thou fallest again upon Thy face.

If Thy body be humbled down to the earth, Thy soul is yet lower; Thy prayers are so much more vehement, as Thy pangs are: *And being in an agony, He prayed more earnestly, and His sweat was as it were great drops of blood falling down to the ground.*

O my Saviour, what an agony I am in, while I think of Thine! What pain, what fear, what strife, what horror was in Thy sacred Breast! How didst Thou struggle under the weight of our sins, that Thou thus sweatest, that Thou thus bleedest! All was peace with Thee: Thou wert one with Thy co-eternal and co-essential Father; all the angels worshiped Thee; all the powers of heaven and earth awfully acknowledged Thine infiniteness. It was our person that feoffed Thee in this misery and torment: in that, Thou sustainedst Thy Father's wrath and our curse. If eternal death be unsufferable, if every sin deserve eternal death, what, Oh! what was it for Thy soul, in this short time of Thy bitter passion, to answer those millions of eternal deaths, which all the sins of all mankind had deserved from the just hand of Thy Godhead? I marvel not, if Thou bleedest a sweat, if Thou sweatest blood. If the moisture of that sweat be from the body, the tincture of it is from the soul. As there never was such another sweat, so neither can there be ever such a suffering. It is no wonder, if the sweat were more than natural, when the suffering was more than human. O Saviour, so willing was that precious blood of Thine to be let forth for us, that it was ready to prevent Thy persecutors; and issued forth in those pores, before Thy wounds were opened by Thy tormenters. Oh that my heart could bleed unto Thee, with true inward compunction for those sins of mine, which are guilty of this Thine agony; and have drawn blood of Thee, both in the garden and on the cross. Woe is me: I had been in hell, if Thou hadst not been in Thine agony; I had scorched, if Thou hadst not sweat. Oh let me abhor my own wickedness, and admire and bless Thy mercy.

But, O ye blessed spirits, which came to comfort my conflicted Saviour, how did ye look upon the Son of God, when ye saw Him laboring for life under these violent temptations! With what astonishment, did ye behold Him bleeding whom ye adored! In the Wilderness, after His duel with

Satan, ye came and ministered unto Him; and now in the Garden, while He is in a harder combat, ye appear to strengthen Him. O the wise and marvelous dispensation of the Almighty! Whom God will afflict, an angel shall relieve; the Son shall suffer, the servant shall comfort Him; the God of angels droopeth, the angel of God strengthens Him.

Blessed Jesus, if as man Thou wouldst be *made a little lower than the angels,* how can it disparage Thee to be attended and cheered up by an angel? Thine humiliation would not disdain comfort from meaner hands. How free was it for Thy Father, to convey seasonable consolations to Thine humbled soul, by whatsoever means! Behold, though Thy cup shall not pass, yet it shall be sweetened. What if Thou see not, for the time, Thy Father's face? yet, Thou shalt feel His hand. What could that spirit have done, without the God of Spirits? O Father of Mercies, Thou mayest bring Thine into agonies, but Thou wilt never leave them there. *In the midst of the sorrows of my heart, Thy comforts shall refresh my soul.* Whatsoever be the means of my supportation, I know and adore the Author.

CHRIST THE SMITTEN ROCK.

BEHOLD the Rock, which was smitten, and the waters of life gushed forth. Behold *the fountain, that is set open to the house of David, for sin and for uncleanness:* a fountain, not of water only, but of blood too. O Saviour, by Thy water we are washed; by Thy blood we are redeemed. Those two sacraments, which Thou didst institute alive, flow also from Thee dead, as the last memorials of Thy love to Thy Church: the water of baptism; *the blood of the New Testament shed for remission of sins:* and these, together with the Spirit that gives life to them both, are the three witnesses on earth, whose attestation cannot fail us. O precious and sovereign wound, by which our souls are healed! Into this cleft of the Rock, let my Dove fly and enter; and there safely hide herself from the talons of all the birds of prey.*

BLESSEDNESS OF SALVATION.

DAVID saith, *Oh taste, and see how sweet the Lord is.* In meditation we do both see and taste; but we see before we taste: sight, is of the understanding; taste, of the affection: neither can we see, but we must taste, we cannot know aright, but we must needs be affected. Let the heart, therefore, first conceive and feel in itself the sweetness or bitterness of the matter meditated: which is never done, without some passion; nor expressed, without some hearty exclamation.

'O blessed estate of the saints! O glory not to be expressed, even by those which are glorified! *O incomprehensible salvation!* What savour hath this earth to thee? Who can regard the world, that

---

* What Christian that reads these solemn and impressive words, does not think of the tender and beautiful lines of Toplady,—
 'Rock of Ages! cleft for me'!

believeth Thee? Who can think of Thee, and not be ravished with wonder and desire? Who can hope for Thee, and not rejoice? Who can know Thee, and not be swallowed up with admiration at the mercy of Him that bestoweth Thee? O blessedness, worthy of Christ's blood to purchase Thee! worthy of the continual songs of Saints and Angels to celebrate Thee! How should I magnify Thee! How should I long for Thee! How should I hate all this world for Thee!

Meditation on Death.

HE, that is the Lord of Life, and tried what it was to die, hath proclaimed them blessed that die in the Lord. Those are blessed, I know, that live in Him; but they rest not from their labors: toil, and sorrow, is between them and a perfect enjoying of that blessedness, which they now possess only in hope and inchoation: when death hath added rest, their happiness is finished.

O death, how sweet is that rest, wherewith thou refreshest the weary pilgrims of this vale of mortality! How pleasant is thy face to those eyes, that have acquainted themselves with the sight of it, which to strangers is grim and ghastly! How worthy art thou to be welcome, unto those, that know whence thou art, and whither thou tendest! Who that knows thee, can fear thee? Who, that is not all nature, would rather hide himself amongst the baggage of this vile life, than follow thee to a crown? What indifferent judge, that should see life painted over with vain semblances of pleasures, attended with troops of sorrows on the one side, and on the other with uncertainty of continuance and certainty of dissolution; and then should turn his eyes unto death, and see her black, but comely, attended on the one hand with a momentary pain, with eternity of glory on the other, would not say, out of choice, that which the prophet said out of passion, *It is better for me to die than to live?*

But, O my soul, what ails thee to be thus suddenly backward and fearful? No heart hath more freely discoursed of death, in speculation: no tongue hath more extolled it, in absence. And now, that it is come to thy bed's side, and hath drawn thy curtains, and takes thee by the hand, and offers thee service, thou shrinkest inward; and, by the paleness of thy face and wildness of thine eye bewrayest an amazement at the presence of such a guest. That face, which was so familiar to thy thoughts, is now unwelcome to thine eyes. I am ashamed of this weak irresolution. Whitherto have tended all thy serious meditations? What hath Christianity done to thee, if thy fears be still heathenish? Is this thine imitation of so many worthy saints of God, whom thou hast seen entertain the violentest deaths with smiles and songs? Is this the fruit of thy long and frequent instruction? Didst thou think death would have been content with words? didst thou hope it would suffice thee to talk, while all others suffer? Where is thy faith? Yea, where art thou thyself, O my soul? Is heaven worthy of no more thanks; no more joy? Shall heretics, shall pagans give death a better welcome than thou? Hath thy Maker, thy Redeemer sent for thee; and art thou loth to go? hath He sent for thee to put thee in possession of that glorious inheritance, which thy wardship hath cheerfully expected; and art thou loth to go? Hath God, with this sergeant of His, sent His angels to fetch thee; and art thou loth to go? Rouse up thyself for shame, O my soul; and, if ever thou hast truly believed, shake off this unchristian diffidence; and address thyself joyfully for thy glory.

Yea, O my Lord, it is Thou, that must raise up this faint and drooping heart of mine: Thou only canst rid me of this weak and cowardly distrust: Thou that sendest for my soul, canst prepare it for Thyself: Thou only canst make Thy messenger welcome to me. Oh, that I could but see Thy face through death! Oh, that I could see death, not as it was, but as Thou hast made it! Oh, that I could heartily pledge Thee, my Saviour, in this cup; that so I might drink new wine with Thee, in Thy Father's kingdom!

But alas, O my God, nature is strong and weak in me, at once! I cannot wish to welcome death, as it is worthy: when I look for most courage, I find strongest temptations: I see and confess, that when I am myself, Thou hast no such coward as I. Let me alone, and I shall shame that name of Thine, which I have professed: every secure wordling shall laugh at my feebleness. O God, were Thy martyrs thus haled to their stakes? might they not have been loosed from their racks, and choose to die in those torments? Let it be no shame, for Thy servant to take up that complaint, which Thou madest of Thy better attendants: *The spirit is willing but the flesh is weak.*

O Thou God of spirits, that hast coupled these two together, unite them in a desire of their dissolution: weaken this flesh to receive, and encourage this spirit either to desire or to contemn death; and now, as I grow nearer to my home, let me increase in the sense of my joys. I am Thine, save me, O Lord. It was Thou that didst put such courage into Thine ancient and late witnesses, that they either invited or challenged death; and held their persecutors their best friends, for letting them loose from these gives of flesh. I know Thy hand is not shortened; neither any of them hath received more proofs of Thy former mercies. Oh, let Thy goodness enable me to reach them, in the comfortable steadiness of my passage. Do but draw this veil a little, that I may see my glory; and I cannot but be enflamed with the desire of it. It was not I, that either made this body for the earth, or this soul for my body, or this heaven for my soul, or this glory of heaven, or this entrance into glory: all is Thine own work. Oh, perfect what Thou hast begun; that Thy praise and my happiness may be consummate at once.

Yea, O my soul, what needest thou wish the God of Mercies to be tender of His own honor? Art thou not a member of that body, whereof Thy Saviour is the Head? Canst thou drown, when thy Head is above? Was it not for thee that He triumphed over death? Is there any fear in a foiled adversary? O my Redeemer, I have already overcome in Thee: how can I miscarry in myself? O my soul, thou hast marched valiantly! Behold, the damsels of that Heavenly Jerusalem come forth with timbrels and harps to meet thee, and to applaud thy success: and now, there remains nothing for thee but *a crown of righteousness, which that righteous Judge shall give thee, at that day: O death, where is thy sting? O grave, where is thy victory?*

Return now unto thy rest, O my soul; for the Lord hath been beneficial unto thee. O Lord God, *the strength of my salvation, Thou hast covered my head in the day of battle:* O my God and *King, I will extol Thee, and will bless Thy name for ever and ever. I will bless Thee daily, and praise Thy Name for ever and ever. Great is the Lord, and most worthy to be praised, and His greatness is incomprehensible: I will meditate of the beauty of Thy glorious Majesty, and thy wonderful works:* Hosanna, *Thou that dwellest in the highest heavens.* Amen.

The Divine Mercy in Redemption.

GREAT *is Thy mercy, that Thou mayest be feared*, saith the sweet singer of Israel. Lo, power doth not more command this holy fear, than mercy doth; though both here meet together: for as there was infinite mercy mixed with power, in thus creating us; so also, there is a no less mighty power mixed with infinite mercy, in our redemption. What heart can but awfully adore Thy sovereign mercy, O Blessed God, the Father of our Lord Jesus Christ, in sending Thine only and coequal Son, the Son of Thy love, the Son of Thine eternal essence, out of Thy bosom, down from the height of celestial glory, into this vale of tears and death, to abase Himself, in the susception of our nature; to clothe Himself with the rags of our humanity; to endure temptation, shame, death, for us? O Blessed Jesus, the Redeemer of Mankind, what soul can be capable of a sufficient adoration of Thine inconceivable mercy, in Thy mean and despicable incarnation; in Thy miserable and toilsome life; in Thy bloody agony; in Thine ignominious and tormenting passion; in Thy woeful sense of Thy Father's wrath, in our stead; and lastly, in Thy bitter and painful death? Thou, that knewest no sin, wert made sin for us: Thou that art Omnipotent, wouldest die; and, by Thy death, hast victoriously triumphed over death and hell. It is enough, O Saviour, it is more than enough to ravish our hearts with love, and to bruise them with a loving fear. O Blessed Spirit, the God of Comfort, who but Thou only, can make our souls sensible of Thy unspeakable mercy, in applying to us the wonderful benefit of this our dear redemption; in the great work of our inchoate regeneration; in the mortifying of our evil and corrupt affections; in raising us to the life of grace, and preparing us for the life of glory? O God, if mercy be proper to attract fear, how must our hearts, in all these respects, needs be filled with an awful regard unto Thy divine bounty! *Oh, how great is the goodness, that Thou hast laid up for those that fear Thee, even before the sons of men!* Psalm xxxi. 20.

Pardon for the most Guilty.

HEAR this then, thou drooping soul: thou art dismayed with the heinousness of thy sins, and the sense of God's anger for them; dost thou know with whom thou hast to do? hast thou heard Him proclaim His own style? *The Lord, the Lord merciful and gracious; long-suffering and abundant in goodness and truth; keeping mercy for thousands; forgiving iniquities, and transgressions, and sins:* Exod. xxxiv. 6, 7; and canst thou distrust that infinite goodness? Lo, if there were no mercy in heaven, thou couldst not be otherwise affected. Look up and see that glorious light, that shines about thee: *With the Lord there is mercy, and with Him is plenteous redemption:* Psalm cxxx. 7. And is there plenteous redemption for all, and none for thee? Because thou hast wronged God in His justice, wilt thou more wrong Him in His mercy? and, because thou hast wronged Him in both, wilt thou wrong thyself in Him? Know, O thou weak man, in what hands thou art. He that said, *Thy mercy, O Lord, is in the heavens, and Thy faithfulness reacheth unto the clouds:* Psalm xxxvi. 5: said also, *Thy mercy is great above the heavens, and Thy truth reacheth unto the clouds:* Psalm cviii. 4. It is a sure comfort to thee, that He cannot fail in His faithfulness and truth. Thou art upon earth, and these reach above thee to the clouds; but if thy sins could be so great and high, as to over-look the clouds, yet His mercy is beyond them, for it reacheth unto heaven: and, if they could, in a hellish presumption, reach so high as heaven; yet His mercy is great above the heavens; higher than this they cannot. If now thy heinous sins could sink thee to the bottom of hell, yet that mercy, which is above the heavens, can fetch thee up again.

Thou art a grievous sinner: we know one, that said he was *the chief of sinners*, who is now one of the prime saints in heaven. Look upon those, whom thou must confess worse than thyself. Cast back thine eyes but upon Manasseh, the lewd son of a holy parent: see him, rearing up altars to Baal; worshipping all the host of heaven; building altars for his new gods in the very courts of the house of the Lord; causing his sons to pass through the fire; trading with witches and wicked spirits; seducing God's people to more than Amoritish wickedness; filling the streets of Jerusalem with innocent blood: 2 Kings xxi. 3, 4, 5, 6, 7, 9, 11, 16: say if thy sin can be thus crimson; yet, behold this man a no less famous example of mercy than wickedness: and what? *Is the hand of God shortened, that He cannot now save? Or, hath the Lord cast off for ever? and will He be favorable no more? Is His mercy clean gone for ever? hath God forgotten to be gracious? hath He in anger shut up His tender mercies?* Psalm lxxvii. 7—10. O man, say justly, *No: This is mine infirmity:* thine infirmity, sure enough; and take heed, if thou persist to distrust, that it be not worse. These misprisions* of God are dangerous. The honor of His mercy is justly dear to Him: no marvel if He cannot endure it to be questioned. When the temptation is blown over, hear what the same tongue says: *The Lord is merciful and gracious, slow to anger, and plenteous in mercy. He will not always chide, neither will He keep his anger for ever. He hath not dealt with us after our sins; nor rewarded us after our iniquities: for, as the heaven is high above the earth, so great is His mercy towards them that fear Him:* Psalm ciii. 8—11. Oh, then lay hold on the large and illimited mercy of thy God, and thou art safe. What cares the debtor, for the length of a bill that is crossed? what cares the condemned person, for the sentence of death, while he hath his pardon sealed in his bosom?

Thou art a heinous sinner: wherefore came thy Saviour? wherefore suffered He? If thy sin remain, wherefore serves His blood? If thy debt be still called for, wherefore was thine obligation cancelled? If thou be still captive to sin and death, wherefore was that dear ransom paid? why did He stretch forth His blessed hands upon the cross, but to receive thee? why did He bow down His head, but to invite thee? why was His precious side opened, but that He might take thee into His heart? Thou depisest Him, if

---

* MISPRISION: the act of misprizing, misapprehension; misconception; mistake. [Obsolete or rare.] *Webster.*

thou trustest Him not. Judas and thou shall sin more in despairing, than in betraying Him. Oh, then gather heart to thyself, from the merits, from the mercies of thine All-sufficient Redeemer, against all thy sinfulness: for, who is it, that shall be once thy Judge? before what tribunal shalt thou appear to receive thy sentence? Is it not thy Saviour, that sits there? He, that died for thee, that He might rescue thee from death; shall He, can He doom thee to that death, from which He came to save thee? Comfort thyself then with these words: and, if thou wouldest keep thy soul in an equal temper, as thou hast two eyes, fix the one of them upon God's justice, to keep thee low and humble, and to quit thee from presumption; fix the other upon His transcendent mercy, to keep thee from the depth of sorrow and desperation.

The Fear of Death.

THOU fearest death: is it not that, thy Saviour underwent for thee? Did thy Blessed Redeemer drink of this cup; and art thou unwilling to pledge him? His was a bitter one, in respect of thine; for it was besides, spiced with the wrath of His Father due to our sins: yet He drank it up to the very dregs, for thee; and wilt thou shrink at an ordinary draught, from His hand? And why did He yield to death, but to overcome him? Why was death suffered to seize upon that Lord of Life, but that, by dying, He might pull out the sting of death? *The sting of death is sin:* 1 Cor. xv. 56. So then, death has lost his sting: now thou mayest carry it in thy bosom: it may cool thee; it cannot hurt thee. Temper then thy fear with these thoughts; and that thou mayest not be too much troubled with the sight of death, acquaint thyself with him, beforehand: present him to thy thoughts; entertain him, in thy holy and resolute discourses.

Behold God as Really Present.

NEITHER doth the devout heart see his God aloof off, as dwelling above, in the circle of heaven, but BEHOLDS THAT INFINITE SPIRIT REALLY PRESENT WITH HIM.

The Lord is upon thy right hand: saith the Psalmist. Our bodily eye doth not more certainly see our own flesh, than the spiritual eye sees God, close by us; yea, in us. A man's own soul is not so intimate to himself as God is to his soul: neither do we move by Him only, but in Him.

What a sweet conversation therefore, hath the holy soul with his God! What heavenly conferences have they two, which the world is not privy to; while God entertains the soul with the divine motions of His Spirit, the soul entertains God with gracious compliances!

Is the heart heavy with the grievous pressures of affliction? the soul goes in to his God and pours out itself before Him, in earnest bemoanings and supplications: the God of Mercy answers the soul again with seasonable refreshings of comfort.

Is the heart secretly wounded and bleeding with

the conscience of some sin? it speedily betakes itself to the great Physician of the Soul; who, forthwith, applies the balm of Gilead, for an unfailing and present cure.

Is the heart distracted with doubts? the soul retires to that inward oracle of God, for counsel: He returns to the soul a happy settlement of just resolution.

Is the heart deeply affected with the sense of some special favor from his God? the soul breaks forth into the passionate voice of praise and thanksgiving: God returns the pleasing testimony of a cheerful acceptation.

O blessed soul, that hath a God to go unto, upon all occasions! O infinite mercy of a God, that vouchsafes to stoop to such entireness with dust and ashes! It was a gracious speech of a worthy divine* upon his death-bed, now breathing towards heaven: That he should change his place, not his company. His conversation was now, beforehand, with his God and His holy angels: the only difference was, that he was now going to a more free and full fruition of the Lord of Life, in that region of glory above; whom he had truly, though with weakness and imperfection, enjoyed in this vale of tears.

Thoughts of God in the Devout Person.

THERE is nothing that he sees which doth not BRING GOD TO HIS THOUGHTS.

Indeed, there is no creature, wherein there are not

* Dr. Preston.

manifest footsteps of Omnipotence; yea, which hath not a tongue to tell us of its Maker. *The heavens declare the glory of God, and the firmament sheweth His handy work: one day telleth another, and one night certifieth another:* Psalm xix. 1, 2. *Yea, O Lord, how manifold are Thy works! in wisdom hast Thou made them all. The earth is full of Thy riches: so is the great and wide sea, where are things creeping innumerable, both small and great beasts:* Psalm civ. 24, 25. Every herb, flower, spire of grass, every twig and leaf, every worm and fly, every scale and feather, every billow and meteor, speaks the power and wisdom of their Infinite Creator. Solomon sends the sluggard to the ant: Isaiah sends the Jews to the ox and the ass: our Saviour sends His disciples to the ravens, and to the lilies of the field. There is no creature, of whom we may not learn something. We shall have spent our time ill in this great school of the world, if, in such store of lessons, we be non-proficients in devotion.

Thoughts at the Communion Table.

WHAT intention of holy thoughts, what fervor of spirit, what depth of devotion, must we now find in ourselves! Doubtless, out of heaven, no object can be so worthy to take up our hearts.

What a clear representation is here, of the great work of our redemption! How is my Saviour, by all my senses, here brought home to my soul! How is His passion lively acted before mine eyes! for lo, my bodily eye doth not more truly see bread and wine, than the eye of my faith sees the body and blood of my Dear Redeemer: thus was His sacred body torn and broken: thus was His precious blood poured out for me. My sins, wretched man that I am! helped thus to crucify my Saviour; and, for the discharge of my sins, would He be thus crucified.

Neither did He only give himself for me upon the Cross; but lo, He both offers and gives Himself to me, in this His blessed Institution.

What had this general gift been, without this application? Now, my hand doth not more sensibly take, nor my mouth more really eat this bread, than my soul doth spiritually receive and feed on the bread of life. O Saviour, Thou art the living bread, that came down from heaven. Thy flesh is meat indeed, and Thy blood is drink indeed. Oh, that I may so eat of this bread, that I may live for ever! He that cometh to Thee, shall never hunger: he that believeth in Thee, shall never thirst. Oh, that I could now so hunger and so thirst for Thee, that my soul could be for ever satisfied with Thee! Thy people, of old, were fed with manna in the wilderness; yet they died: that food of angels could not keep them from perishing: but oh, for the Hidden Manna, which giveth life to the world, even Thy blessed Self! Give me ever of this bread, and my soul shall not die, but live.

Oh, the precious juice of the fruit of the vine, wherewith Thou refreshest my soul! Is this the blood of the grape? Is it not rather Thy blood of the New Testament, that is poured out for me?

Thou speakest, O Saviour, of new wine that Thou wouldest drink with Thy disciples, in Thy Father's kingdom: can there be any more precious and pleasant than this, wherewith Thou cheerest the believing soul? Our palate is now dull and earthly, which shall then be exquisite and celestial: but, surely, no liquor can be of equal price or sovereignty with Thy blood. Oh, how unsavory are all earthly delicacies, to this heavenly draught! O God, let not the sweet taste of this spiritual nectar ever go out of the mouth of my soul. Let the comfortable warmth of this blessed cordial ever work upon my soul; even till and in, the last moment of my dissolution.

Do this in Remembrance of Me.

DOST Thou bid me, O Saviour, do this in remembrance of Thee? oh, how can I forget Thee? how can I enough celebrate Thee, for this Thy unspeakable mercy? Can I see Thee thus crucified before my eyes, and for my sake thus crucified, and not remember Thee? Can I find my sins accessary to this Thy death, and Thy death meritoriously expiating all these my grievous sins, and not remember Thee? Can I hear Thee freely offering Thyself to me, and feel Thee graciously conveying Thyself into my soul, and not remember Thee? I do remember Thee, O Saviour: but oh that I could yet more effectually remember Thee; with all the passionate affections of a soul sick of Thy love; with all zealous desires to glorify Thee; with all fervent longings after Thee and Thy salvation! I remember Thee in Thy sufferings; oh, do Thou remember me in Thy glory.*

THOUGHTS AFTER THE COMMUNION.

OH, what a blessing have I received to-day! no less than my Lord Jesus, with all His merits; and, in and with Him, the assurance of the remission of all sins and everlasting salvation. How happy am I, if I be not wanting to God and myself! How unworthy shall I be, if I do not strive to answer this love of my God and Saviour, in all hearty affection, and in all holy obedience!

And now, after this heavenly repast, how do I feel myself? What strength, what advantage hath my faith gotten? How much am I nearer to heaven than before? How much faster hold have I taken of my blessed Redeemer? How much more firm and sensible is my interest in Him?

---

* It seems to us that under the impression of such devout language James Montgomery must have composed these beautiful lines:—

'Gethsemane can I forget? or there Thy conflict see,
Thine agony and bloody sweat, and not remember Thee?
When to the cross I turn mine eyes, and rest on Calvary,
O Lamb of God, my sacrifice! I must remember Thee!
Remember Thee in all Thy pains, and all Thy love to me;
Yea, while a breath or pulse remains, I will remember Thee!
And when these failing lips grow dumb, and mind and memory flee,
When Thou shalt in Thy kingdom come, Jesus remember me.'

True Penitence.

TRUE penitence is strong and can grapple with the greatest sin; yea, with all the powers of hell. What if your hands be red with blood? behold the blood of your Saviour shall wash away yours. If you can bathe yourself in that, your scarlet soul shall be as white as snow. This course alone shall make your cross the way to the paradise of God. This plaster can heal all the sores of the soul, if never so desperate. Only, take heed that your heart be deep enough pierced, ere you lay it on; else, under a seeming skin of dissimulation, your soul shall fester to death.

Mercy for the Vilest.

'O HAPPY message,' thou sayest, 'were it as sure as it is comfortable! But, alas, my heart finds many and deep grounds of fear and diffidence, which will not easily be removed. That smites me, while you offer to acquit me; and tells me, I am in a worse condition than a looker-on can imagine. My sins are, beyond measure, heinous: such as my thoughts tremble at: such, as I dare not utter to the God that knows them, and against whom only they are committed. There is horror in their very remembrance: what will there then be, in their retribution?'

They are bitter things, that thou urgest against thyself, my son: no adversary could plead worse.

But I admit thy vileness. Be thou as bad as Satan can make thee: it is not either his malice, or thy wickedness, that can shut thee out from mercy.

Be thou as foul as sin can make thee: yet there is *a fountain opened to the house of David*, a bloody fountain in the side of thy Saviour, *for sin and for uncleanness:* Zech. xiii. 1. Be thou as leprous as that Syrian was of old, if thou canst but wash seven times in the waters of this Jordan, thou canst not but be clean: thy flesh shall come again to thee, like to the flesh of a little child: 2 Kings v. 14, thou shalt be, at once, sound and innocent. Be thou stung unto death, with the fiery serpents of this wilderness: yet if thou canst but cast thine eyes to that brazen serpent which is erected there, thou canst not fail of cure.

Wherefore came the Son of God into the world, but *to save sinners?* add, if thou wilt, *whereof I am chief:* thou canst say no worse by thyself, than a better man did before thee; who, in the right of a sinner, claimeth the benefit of a Saviour: 1 Tim. i. 15. Were it not for our sin, what use were there of a Redeemer? Were not our sins heinous, how should it have required such an expiation as the blood of the Eternal Son of God?

Take comfort to thyself, my son: the greatness of thy sin serves but to magnify the mercy of the Forgiver. To remit the debt of some few farthings, it were small thank; but, to strike off the scores of thousands of talents, it is the height of bounty. Thus doth thy God to thee: He hath suffered thee to run on in His books to so deep a sum, that, when thy conscious heart hath proclaimed thee bankrupt, He may infinitely oblige thee and glorify

His own mercy, in crossing the reckoning and acquitting thy soul.

All sums are equally dischargeable to the munificence of our great Creditor in heaven: as it is the act of His justice, to call for the least; so of His mercy, to forgive the greatest. Had we to do with a finite power, we had reason to sink under the burden of our sins: now there is neither more nor less to that, which is infinite: only let thy care be, to lay hold on that infinite mercy which lies open to thee: and, as thou art an object fit for mercy, in that thou art in thyself sinful and miserable enough; so, find thyself, as thou art, a subject meet to receive this mercy, as a penitent believer. Open and enlarge thy bosom, to take in this free grace; and close with thy blessed Saviour; and, in Him possess thyself of remission, peace, salvation.

All are Pilgrims.

THOU art out of thy country:—Who is not so? We are all *Pilgrims* together with Thee: 1 Pet. ii. 11. Heb. xi. 13. *While we are at home in the body, we are absent from the Lord:* 2 Cor. v. 6. Miserable are we, if our true home be not above. That is the *better country* which we seek, *even a heavenly:* Heb. xi. 16; and thither thou mayest equally direct thy course, in whatsoever region. This centre of earth is equidistant from the glorious circumference of heaven: if we may once meet there, what need we make such difference in the way.

Death but a Sleep.

THOU art afraid of death:—When thou art weary of thy day's labor, art thou afraid of rest?

Hear what thy Saviour, who is the Lord of Life, esteems of death; *Our friend Lazarus sleepeth:* John xi. 11: and of Jairus's daughter; *The maid is not dead; but sleepeth:* Matt. ix. 24. Luke viii. 52.

Neither useth the Spirit of God any other language, concerning His servants under the Old Testament: *Now shall I sleep in the dust,* saith holy Job: ch. vii. 21: and of David, *When thy days be fulfilled, and thou shalt sleep with thy fathers:* 2 Sam. vii. 12.

Nor yet under the New: *For this cause, many are weak and sickly among you, and many sleep,* saith the apostle: 1 Cor. xi. 30.

Lo, the philosophers of old were wont to call sleep the brother of death: but God says, death is no other than sleep itself: a sleep, both sure and sweet. When thou liest down at night to thy repose, thou canst not be so certain to awake again in the morning: as, when thou layest thyself down in death, thou art sure to awake in the morning of the resurrection. Out of this bodily sleep, thou mayest be affrightedly startled with some noises of sudden horror: with some fearful dreams; with tumults, or alarms of war; but here, thou shalt rest quietly in the place of silence (Psalm xciv. 17.), free from all inward and outward disturbances: while, in the mean time, thy soul shall see none but visions of joy and blessedness.

But, oh the sweet and heavenly expression of our

last rest, and the issue of our happy resuscitation, which our gracious apostle hath laid forth, for the consolation of his mournful Thessalonians! *For, if we believe,* saith he, *that Jesus died and rose again; even so them also, which sleep in Jesus, will God bring with Him.* Lo, our belief is antidote enough against the worst of death. And why are we troubled with death, when we believe that Jesus died? and what a triumph is this over death, that the same Jesus, who died, rose again! and what a comfort it is, that the same Jesus, who arose, shall both come again, and bring all His with Him in glory! and, lastly what a strong cordial is this to all good hearts, that all those which die well, do sleep in Jesus! Thou thoughtest, perhaps, of sleeping in the bed of the grave; and there, indeed, is rest: but he tells thee of sleeping in the bosom of Jesus; and there is immortality and blessedness. O blessed Jesus, *in Thy presence is the fulness of joy, and at Thy right hand are pleasures for evermore.* Who would desire to walk in the world, when he may sleep with Jesus?

Prayer.

FASHIONABLE suppliants may talk to God: but, be confident, he that can truly pray, can never be truly miserable. Of ourselves we lie open to all evils: our rescue is from above: and what intercourse have we with heaven, but by our prayers? Our prayers are they that can deliver us from dangers, avert judgments, prevent mischiefs, procure blessings; that can obtain pardon for our sins, furnish us with strength against temptations, mitigate the extremity of our sufferings, sustain our infirmities, raise up our dejectedness, increase our graces, abate our corruptions, sanctify all good things to us, sweeten the bitterness of our afflictions, open the windows of heaven, shut up the bars of death, vanquish the power of hell. Pray, and be both safe and happy.

Redemption.

REDEMPTION was the great errand, for which the Son of God came down into the world; and the work which He did, while He was in the world; and that which, in way of application of it, He shall be ever accomplishing, till He shall deliver up His Mediatory kingdom into the hands of His Father. In this He begins, in this He finishes, the great business of our salvation: for those who, in this life, are enlightened by His wisdom, justified by His merits, sanctified by His grace, are yet conflicting with manifold temptations, and struggling with varieties of miseries and dangers; till, upon their happy death and glorious resurrection, they shall be fully freed, by their ever-blessed and victorious Redeemer.

He, therefore, who, by virtue of that heavenly union, is made unto us of God, wisdom, righteousness, sanctification; is also, upon the same ground, made unto us our full redemption.

The Christian in his Devotion.

He is so perpetually resident in heaven, that he is, often in every day, before the throne of grace; and he never comes there, without supplication in his hand: wherein also he loves to be importunate: and he speeds accordingly; for he never departs empty; while other cold suitors, that come thither but in some good fits of DEVOTION, obtain nothing but denials.

He dares not press to God's footstool in his own name: he is conscious enough of his own unworthiness: but he comes in the gracious and powerful name of his righteous Mediator, in whom he knows he cannot but be accepted: and, in an humble boldness, for His only sake craves mercy.

No man is either more awful or more confident.

When he hath put up his petition to the King of heaven, he presumes not to stint the time or manner of God's condescent; but patiently and faithfully waits for the good hour, and leaves himself upon that infinite wisdom and goodness.

He doth not affect length so much as fervor: neither so much minds his tongue, as his heart.

His prayers are suited according to the degrees of the benefits sued for. He, therefore, begs grace absolutely, and temporal blessings with limitation; and is accordingly affected in the grant.

Neither is he more earnest in craving mercies, than he is zealously desirous to be retributory to God when he hath received them; not more heartily suing to be rich in grace, than to improve his graces to the honor and advantage of the bestower.

With an awful and broken heart, doth he make his addresses to that infinite Majesty; from whose presence he returns with comfort and joy.

His soul is constantly fixed there, whither he pours it out. Distraction and distrust are shut out from his closet: and he is so taken up with his devotion, as one that makes it his work to pray. And, when he hath offered up his sacrifices unto God, his faith listens, and looks in at the door of heaven to know how they are taken.

The Christian in his Death.

THE Christian therefore, now laid upon his last bed, when this grim messenger comes to fetch him to heaven, looks not so much at his dreadful visage, as at his happy errand: and is willing not to remember what death is in itself, but what it is to us in Christ; by whom it is made so useful and beneficial, that we could not be happy without it.

Here, then, comes in the last act and employment of faith; for after this brunt passed, there is no more use of faith, but of vision: that heartens the soul in a lively apprehension of that blessed Saviour, who both led him the way of suffering, and is making way for him to everlasting glory: that shews him *Jesus, the Author and Finisher of our faith, who, for the joy that was set before Him, endured the cross, despising the shame, and is set down at the right hand of the throne of God:* that clings close unto him: and lays unremovable hold upon His person, His merits.

His blessedness. Upon the wings of this faith, is the soul ready to mount up toward that heaven, which is open to receive it; and, in that act of evolation, puts itself into the hands of those blessed angels, who are ready to carry it up to the throne of glory.

The Christian's Home.

I AM a stranger here below: my home is above; yet I can think too well of these foreign vanities, and cannot think enough of my home. Surely, that is not so far above my head, as my thoughts; neither doth so far pass me in distance, as in comprehension: and yet, I would not stand so much upon conceiving, if I could admire it enough; but my strait heart is filled with a little wonder, and hath no room for the greatest part of glory that remaineth. O God, what happiness hast Thou prepared for Thy chosen! What a purchase was this, worthy of the blood of such a Saviour. As yet I do but look towards it, afar off; but it is easy to see by the outside, how goodly it is within: although, as Thy house on earth, so that above, hath more glory within, than can be bewrayed by the outward appearance. The outer part of Thy tabernacle here below, is but an earthly and base substance; but within, it is furnished with a living, spiritual, and heavenly guest: so the outer heavens, though they be as gold to all other material creatures; yet they are but dross to Thee. Yet how are even the outmost walls of that house of Thine beautified with glorious lights, whereof every one is a world for bigness, and as a heaven for goodliness! Oh teach me by this to long after, and wonder at the inner part, before Thou lettest me come in to behold it.

Heavenly and Earthly Things.

THE estate of heavenly and earthly things is plainly represented to us, by the two lights of heaven, which are appointed to rule the night and the day. Earthly things are rightly resembled by the moon, which, being nearest to the region of mortality, is ever in changes, and never looks upon us twice with the same face; and, when it is at the full, is blemished with some dark spots, not capable of any illumination. Heavenly things are figured by the sun, whose great and glorious light is both natural to itself, and ever constant. That other fickle and dim star is fit enough for the night of misery, wherein we live here below. And this firm and beautiful light is but good enough for that day of glory, which the saints live in. If it be good living here, where our sorrows are changed with joys: what is it to live above, where our joys change not? I cannot look upon the body of the sun; and yet I cannot see at all without the light of it: I cannot behold the glory of Thy saints, O Lord; yet without the knowledge of it, I am blind. If Thy creature be so glorious to us here below; how glorious shall Thyself be to us, when we are above the sun! This sun shall not shine upward, where Thy glory shineth: the greater light extinguisheth the lesser. O thou

Sun of Righteousness, which shalt only shine to me when I am glorified, do Thou heat, enlighten, comfort me with the beams of Thy presence, till I be glorified. Amen.

Humility.

THE nearer our Saviour drew to His glory, the more humility He expressed. His followers were first His servants, and He their Master; John xiii. 16: then, His disciples, and He their Teacher; John xv. 8: soon after, they were His friends, and He theirs; John xv. 13: straightways after His resurrection and entrance into an immortal condition, they were His brethren. *Go to my brethren, and say unto them, I ascend to my Father and your Father;* John xx. 17: lastly, they are incorporated into Him, and made partakers of His glory, *That they also may be one with us,* saith He, *I in them, and thou in me; that they may be made perfect in one; and the glory which Thou gavest me, I have given them;* John xvii. 21, 22, 23. O Saviour, was this done for the depressing of Thyself, or for the exaltation of us, or rather for both? How couldest Thou more depress Thyself, than thus to match Thyself with us poor wretched creatures? How couldest Thou more exalt us, than to raise us unto this entireness with Thee, the All-Glorious and Eternal Son of God? How should we learn of Thee, to improve our highest advancement to our deepest humility; and so to regard each other, that, when we are greatest, we should be least!

Eternity.

ETERNITY is that only thing, which is worthy to take up the thoughts of a wise man: that being added to evil, makes the evil infinitely more intolerable; and, being added to good, makes the good infinitely more desirable. O Eternity! thou bottomless abyss of misery to the wicked: thou indeterminable pitch of joy to the saints of God: what soul is able to comprehend thee? What strength of understanding is able to conceive of thee? Be thou ever in my thoughts, ever before mine eyes. Be thou the scope of all my actions, of all my endeavors; and, in respect of thee, let all this visible world be to me as nothing: and, since only *the things, which are not seen* by the eye of sense, *are eternal*, Lord, sharpen thou the eyes of my faith, that I may see those things invisible; and may, in that sight, enjoy Thy blessed eternity.

The Celestial City.

THE city that is of God's building is deep and firmly grounded upon the rock of His eternal decree; and hath more foundations than one, and all of them both sure and costly. God's material house, built by Solomon, had the foundation laid with great squared stone: but *the foundations of the walls of this city* of God are *garnished with all manner of precious stones;* Rev. xxi. 19. *Glorious things are spoken of thee, O thou city of God.* Why do I set up my rest in this house of clay, which is every day falling on my head, while I have the assured expectation of so glorious a dwelling above? *For we know, that if our earthly house of this tabernacle were dissolved, we have a building of God, a house not made with hands, but eternal in the heavens;* 2 Cor. v. 1.

The True Christian Happy.

THE true Christian is in a very happy condition; for no man will envy him, and he can envy nobody. None will envy him; for the world cannot know how happy he is: how happy, in the favor of a God; how happy, in the enjoyment of that favor. Those secret delights, that he finds in the presence of his God; those comfortable pledges of love and mutual interchanges of blessed interest, which pass between them; are not for worldly hearts to conceive: and no man will envy an unknown happiness. On the other side, he cannot envy the world's greatest favorite under heaven; for he well knows how fickle and uncertain that man's felicity is: he sees him walking upon ice, and perceives every foot of his sliding, and threatening a fall; and hears that brittle pavement, at every step, crackling under him, and ready to give way to his swallowing up; and, withal, finds if those pleasures of his could be constant and permanent, how poor and unsatisfying they are, and how utterly unable to yield true contentment to the soul. The Christian, therefore, while others look upon him with pity and scorn, laughs secretly to himself in his bosom; as well knowing there is none but he truly happy.

The Saviour's Agony.

WHAT is this that I see? my Saviour in an agony, and an angel strengthening him! Oh the wonderful dispensation of the Almighty! That the Eternal Son of God, who promised to send the Comforter to his followers, should need comfort! That He of whom the voice from heaven said, *This is my beloved Son, in whom I am well pleased*, should be struggling with his Father's wrath even to blood! That the Lord of Life should, in a languishing horror, say, *My soul is exceeding sorrowful, even unto death!* These, these, O Saviour, are the chastisements of our peace; which both Thou wouldest suffer, and Thy Father would inflict. The least touch of one of those pangs would have been no less than a hell to me, the whole brunt thereof Thou enduredst for my soul: what a wretch am I, to grudge a little pain from or for thee, who wert content to undergo such pressure of torment for me, as squeezed from thee a sweat of blood: since my miserable sinfulness deserved more load, than Thou, in Thy merciful compassion, wilt lay upon me; and thy pure nature and perfect innocence merited nothing but love and glory! In this sad case, what service is it, that an angel offers to do unto Thee? Lo, there appears to Thee *an angel from heaven strengthening* Thee; Luke xxii. 43. Still more wonder! Art not Thou the God of Spirits? Is it not Thou, that gavest being, life, motion, power, glory to all the angels of heaven? Shall there be need of one single created spirit, to administer strength and comfort to his Creator?

Were this the errand, why did not all that blessed corps of celestial spirits join their forces together, in so high an employment? Where are the multitudes of that heavenly host, which, at Thy birth, sung, *Glory to God in the highest, and on earth peace?* Luke ii. 13, 14. Where are those angels which ministered to Thee, after Thy combat of temptations in the wilderness? Surely, there was not so much use of their divine cordials in the desert, as in the garden. O my God and Saviour, thus Thou wouldest have it. It is Thy holy will, that is the rule and reason of all Thine actions, and events. Thou, that wouldest make use of the provision of men for Thy maintenance on earth, wouldest employ Thy servants the angels for the supply of Thy consolations; and Thou, that couldest have commanded legions of those celestial spirits, wouldest be served by one: not but that more were present, but that only one appeared: all the host of them ever invisibly attended Thee, as God; but, as man, one only presents himself to Thy bodily eyes: and Thou, who madest Thyself, for our sakes, *a little lower than the angels* (Heb. ii. 9) which Thou madest, wouldest humble Thyself to receive comfort from those hands, to which Thou gavest the capacity to bring it. It is no marvel, if that, which was Thy condescent, be our glory and happiness. I am not worthy, O God, to know what conflicts Thou hast ordained for my weakness: whatever they be, Thou, that hast appointed Thine angels to be *ministering spirits* for the behoof of them *who shall be heirs of salvation*, (Heb. i. 14.) suffer not Thy servant to want the presence of those blessed emissaries of Thine, in any of his extremities: let them stand by his soul, in his last agony; and, after a happy eluctation, convey it to Thy glory.

THE NIGHT OF DEATH.

INDEED, Lord, as Thou sayest, *the night cometh when no man can work*. What can we do, when the light is shut in, but shut our eyes, and sleep? When our senses are tied up, and our limbs laid to rest, what can we do, but yield ourselves to a necessary repose? O my God, I perceive my night hastening on apace: my sun draws low: the shadows lengthen: vapors rise; and the air begins to darken. Let me bestir myself, for the time: let me lose none of my few hours: let me work hard, awhile; because I shall soon rest everlastingly.

HEAVENLY JOYS.

DOUBTLESS, O God, Thou, that hast given to men, even Thine enemies, here upon earth, so excellent means to please their outward senses; such beautiful faces and admirable flowers, to delight the eye; such delicate scents from their garden, to please the smell; such curious confections and delicate sauces, to please the taste; such sweet music from the birds, and artificial devices of ravishing melody from the art of man, to delight the ear; hast much more ordained transcendent pleasures and infinite contentments for Thy glorified saints above. My soul, while it is thus clogged and confined, is too strait to conceive of those incomprehensible ways of spiritual delectation, which Thou hast provided for Thy dear chosen ones, triumphing with Thee in Thy heaven. Oh, teach me to wonder at that which I cannot here attain to know; and to long for that happiness, which I there hope to enjoy with Thee for ever.

Honey from the Rock.

O GOD, Thou didst miraculously refresh Thy murmuring Israel of old with water, out of the rock, in that dry wilderness: and now I hear Thee say, If they had hearkened to Thy voice, and walked in Thy ways, with honey out of the rock Thou wouldest have satisfied them; Pslam lxxxi. 16. Lo, that which Thou wouldest have done to Thine ancient people if they had obeyed Thee, Thou hast abundantly performed to Thine evangelical Israel: with honey, out of the Rock, hast Thou satisfied them: the Rock, that followed them, was Christ my Saviour; 1 Cor. x. 4. Lo, out of this Rock hath flowed that honey, whereby our souls are satisfied. *Out of His side*, saith the evangelist, *came water and blood*. This Rock of our Salvation affordeth both what Israel had, and might have had. Surely, O my God, there can be no honey so sweet, as the effect of the precious blood of my Saviour to the soul of the believer: by that blood, we have *eternal redemption* from death, and *remission of all our sins;* Heb. ix. 12. Eph. i. 7: by that blood, are we *justified* in the sight of our God, and *saved from the wrath to come;*

Rom. v. 9: by that blood, we have our *peace* made in heaven, and are fully *reconciled to our God;* Col. i. 20: by that blood, we are cleansed and *purged* from all our iniquity; Heb. ix. 22: by that blood, we are *sanctified* from our corruptions; Heb. xiii. 12. 1 Pet. i. 2: by that blood, we receive *the promises* and possessions *of an eternal inheritance;* Heb. ix. 15. O the spiritual honey so sweet, that the material honey is but bitterness to it! Jonathan of old did but dip his spear in the honey of the wood ; and, with but one lick of that sweet moisture, had his eyes cleared, and his spirits revived ; 1 Sam. xiv. 29. O God, let me but taste and see how sweet the Lord Jesus is, in all His gracious promises, in all His merciful and real performances; I shall need no more to make me happy. Thy Solomon bids me to eat honey; Prov. xxiv. 13. Lo, this is the honey that I desire to eat of: give me of this honey, and I shall receive both clearness to my eyes, and vigor of my spirits to the foiling of all my spiritual enemies. This is not the honey, whereof I am bidden not to eat too much; Prov. xxv. 16. No, Lord, I can never eat enough of this celestial honey: here I cannot surfeit; or, if I could, this surfeit would be my health. O God, give me still enough of this honey out of the Rock: so shall my soul live, and bless Thee, and be blessed of Thee.

The Heavenly Manna.

VICTORY itself is the great reward of our fight; but what is it, O God, that Thou promisest to give us, as the reward of our victory? even the *Hidden Manna:* surely, were not this gift exceeding precious, Thou wouldest not reserve it, for the remuneration of so glorious a conquest. Behold that material and visible manna, which Thou sentest down from heaven, to stop the mouth of murmuring Israel, perished in their use; and, if it were reserved but to the next day, putrefied; and, instead of nourishing, annoyed them: but the hidden manna, that was laid up in the ark, was incorruptible; as a lasting monument of Thy power and mercy to Thy people. But now, alas, what is become both of that manna, and that ark? Both are vanished, having passed through the devouring jaws of time, into mere forgetfulness. It is the true Spiritual Manna, that came down from the highest heaven, and, ascending thither again, is hidden there, in the glorious ark of eternity, that Thou wilt give to Thy conqueror: that is it, which being participated of here below, nourisheth us to eternal life; and being communicated to us above, is the full consummation of that blessed life and glory. Oh, give me so to fight, that I may overcome; that so overcoming, I may be feasted with this manna. Thou, that art, and hast given me Thyself, the Spiritual Manna, which I have fed on by faith; and the symbolical manna, whereof I have eaten sacramentally; give me of that heavenly manna, whereof I shall partake in glory. It is yet a *hidden manna,* hid from the eyes of the world; yea, in a sort, from our own; hid, in light inaccessible: for, *Our life is hid with Christ in God;* Col. iii. 3. but shall then be fully revealed: for it shall then not only cover the face of the earth round about the tents of Israel, but spread itself over the face of the whole heaven; yea, fill both heaven and earth. I well thought, O my God, that if heaven could afford any thing more precious than other, Thou wouldst lay it up for Thy victor; for it is a hard service, that Thy poor infantry here upon earth are put unto, to conflict with so mighty, so malicious, so indefatigable enemies; and therefore the reward must be so much the greater, as the warfare is more difficult. Oh, do Thou, who art the great Lord of Hosts, give me courage to fight, perseverance in fighting, and power to overcome all my spiritual enemies; that I may receive from Thee this *hidden manna,* that my soul may live forever, and may forever bless Thee.

The Happy Return Home.

EVERY creature naturally affects a return to the original, whence it first came. The pilgrim, though faring well abroad, yet hath a longing homeward: fountains and rivers run back, with what speed they may, to the sea, whence they were derived: all compound bodies return to their first elements: the vapors, rising up from the earth and waters, and condensed into clouds, fall down again to the same earth, whence they were exhaled: this body, that we bear about us, returns at last to that dust, whereof it was framed. And why then, O my soul, dost not thou earnestly desire to return home to the God that made thee? Thou knowest thy original is heavenly: why are not thy affections so? What canst thou find here below, worthy to either withdraw or detain thee from those heavenly mansions? Thou art here, in a region of sin; of misery and death: glory waits for thee above: fly then, O my soul, fly hence to that blessed immortality, not as yet, in thy dissolution; for which thou must wait on the pleasure of thy dear Maker and Redeemer: yet, in thy thoughts, in thy desires and affections, soar thou up thither, and converse there with that blessed God and Father of spirits, with those glorious orders of angels, and with the souls of just men made perfect: and, if the necessity of these bodily affairs must needs draw thee off for a time, let it be not without reluctation and hearty unwillingness, and with an eager appetite of quick return to that celestial society. It will not be long, ere thou shalt be blessed with a free and uninterrupted fruition of that glorious eternity: in the mean time, do thou prepossess it, in thy heavenly dispositions; and, contemning this earth, wherewith thou art clogged, aspire to thy heaven, and be happy.

The Felicity of Heaven.

THERE, there shalt thou, O my soul, enjoy a perfect rest from all thy toils, cares, fears: there shalt thou find a true vital life, free from all the incumbrances of thy miserable pilgrimage; free from the dangers of either sins or temptations: free from all anxiety and distraction; free from all sorrow, pain, perturbation; free from all the possibility of change or death: a life, wherein there is nothing but pure and perfect pleasure; nothing but perpetual melody of angels and saints, singing sweet Hallelujahs to their God: a life, which the most glorious Deity both gives, and is: a life, wherein thou hast the full fruition of the ever-blessed Godhead, the continual society of the celestial spirits, the blissful presence of the glorified humanity of thy Dear Saviour: a life, wherein thou hast ever consort with the glorious company of the apostles, the goodly fellowship of the patriarchs and prophets, the noble army of martyrs and confessors, the celestial synod of all the holy fathers and illuminated doctors of the Church; shortly, the blessed assembly of all the faithful professors of the name of the Lord Jesus, that, having finished their course, sit now shining in their promised glory. See there that unapproachable light, that divine magnificence of the Heavenly King: see that resplendent crown of righteousness, which decks the heads of every one of those saints; and is ready to be set on thine, when thou hast happily overcome those spiritual powers, wherewith thou art still conflicting: see the joyful triumphs of these exulting victors: see the measures of their glory different, yet all full, and the least unmeasureable: lastly, see all this happiness not limited to thousands, nor yet millions of years, but commeasured by no less than eternity.

God Manifest in the Flesh.

O BLESSED Saviour, Thou, the true *God manifested in the flesh*, be Thou pleased to manifest unto the soul of Thy servant the unspeakable riches of Thy love and mercy to mankind, in that great work of our redemption. Vouchsafe to affect my heart, with a lively sense of that infinite goodness of Thine, towards the wretchedest of Thy creatures: that, for our sake, Thou camest down, and clothedst Thyself in our flesh: and clothedst that pure and holy flesh, with all the miseries that are incident to this sinful flesh of ours; and wast content to undergo a bitter, painful, ignominious death from the hands of man; that, by dying, Thou mightest overcome death, and ransom him from that hell, to which he was, without Thee, irrecoverably forfeited; and fetch him forth to life, liberty, and glory. Oh, let me not see only, but feel, this Thy great mystery of Godliness effectually working me to all hearty thankfulness for so inestimable a mercy; to all holy resolutions to glorify Thee, in all my actions, in all my sufferings. Didst Thou, O Saviour, being God Eternal, take flesh for me; and shall not I, when Thou callest, be willing to lay down this sinful flesh for Thee again? Wert Thou content to abridge Thyself, for the time, not only of Thy heavenly magnificence, but of all earthly comforts, for my sake; and shall not I, for Thy dear sake, renounce all the wicked pleasures of sin? Didst Thou wear out the days of Thy flesh in poverty, toil, reproach, and all earthly hardship; and shall I spend my time, in pampering this flesh in wanton dalliance, in the ambitious and covetous pursuit of vain honors and deceivable riches? Blessed Lord, Thou wert manifested in the flesh, not only to be a ransom for our souls, but to be a precedent for our lives: far, far be it from me, thus to imitate the great pattern of holiness. O Jesus, the Author and Finisher of my faith and salvation, teach me to tread in Thy gracious steps; to run, with patience, the race that is set before me; to endure the cross, to despise the shame; to be crucified to the world; to work all righteousness.

THE SAVIOUR RECEIVED UP INTO GLORY.

O BLESSED Saviour, how is my soul ravished with the meditation of Thy glorious reception into Thy heaven! Surely, if the inhabitants of those celestial mansions may be capable of any increase of joy, they then both found and shewed it, when they saw and welcomed Thee, entering, in Thy glorified Humanity, into that Thy eternal palace of blessedness; and, if there could be any higher or sweeter ditty of Hallelujah, it was then sung by the choir of angels and saints. And may Thy poor servants, warfaring and wandering here upon earth, even second them, in those heavenly songs of praises and gratulations: for wherein stands all our safety, hope, comfort, happiness, but in this, that Thou, our Jesus, art *received up into glory;* and having conquered all diverse powers, sittest on the right hand of God the Father, crowned with honor and majesty?

O Jesus, Thou art our Head, we are Thy body: how

can the body but participate of the glory of the Head? As for Thyself therefore, so for us, art Thou possessed of that heavenly glory: as Thou sufferedst for us, so for us Thou also reignest. Let every knee therefore bow unto Thee, *of things in heaven, and things on earth, and things under the earth;* Phil. ii. 10. O blessed be Thy name for ever and ever: *Thine, O Lord, is the greatness, and the power, and the glory, and the victory, and the majesty; for all that is in the heaven, and in the earth is Thine: Thine is the kingdom, O Lord, and Thou art exalted as head over all;* 1 Chr. xxix. 11.

And now, O Saviour, what a superabundant amends is made to Thy glorified Humanity, for all Thy bitter sufferings upon earth! Thine agony was extreme; but Thy glory is infinite: Thy cross was heavy; but Thy crown transcendently glorious: Thy pains were unconceivably grievous, but short; Thy glory everlasting; if Thou wert scorned by men, Thou art now adored by angels: Thou that stoodest before the judgment seat of a Pilate, shalt come, in all heavenly magnificence, to judge both the quick and the dead: shortly, Thou, which wouldest stoop to be a servant upon earth, rulest and reignest forever in heaven, as the King of Eternal Glory.

Heavenly Mindedness.

O THEN, my soul, seeing thy Saviour is *received up into* this infinite *glory*, with what intention and fervor of spirit shouldest thou fix thine eyes upon that heaven, where He lives and reigns. How canst thou be but wholly taken up with the sight and thought of that place of blessedness? How canst thou abide to grovel any longer on this base earth, where is nothing but vanity and vexation; and refrain to mind the things above, where all is felicity and glory? With what longings and holy ambition shouldest thou desire to aspire to that place of eternal rest and beatitude, into which thy Saviour is ascended; and with Him to partake of that glory and happiness, which He hath provided for all that love Him! O Saviour, it is this clog of wretched infidelity and earthliness, that hangs heavy upon my soul; and keeps me from mounting up into Thy presence, and from a comfortable fruition of Thee. Oh, do Thou take off this sinful weight from me, and raise up my affections and conversation unto Thee: enable me constantly to enjoy Thee, by a lively faith, here; till, by Thy mercy, I shall be received into glory.

Heavenly Recognition.

AS then, we shall perfectly love God, and His saints in Him, so shall we know both: and, though it be a sufficient motive of our love in heaven, that we know them to be saints, yet it seems to be no small addition to our happiness, to know that those saints were once ours. And, if it be a just joy to a parent here on earth to see his child gracious, how much more accession shall it be to his joy above, to see the fruit of his loins glorious; when both his love is more pure, and their improvement absolute! Can we make any doubt, that the blessed angels know each other? How senseless were it, to grant that no knowledge is hid from them, but of themselves! Or, can we imagine that those angelical spirits do not take special notice of those souls, which they have guarded here, and conducted to their glory? If they do so, and if the knowledge of our beatified souls shall be like to theirs, why should we abridge our souls more than them, of the comfort of our interknowing? Surely, our dissolution shall abate nothing of our natural faculties; our glory shall advance them, so as what we once knew we shall know better: and, if our souls can then perfectly know themselves, why should they be denied the knowledge of others?

Doubt not then, O my soul, but thou shalt once see, besides the face of thy God whose glory fills heaven and earth, the blessed spirits of the ancient patriarchs and prophets; the holy apostles and evangelists; the glorious martyrs and confessors; those eminent saints, whose holiness thou wert wont to magnify; and amongst them, those in whom nature and grace have especially interested thee: thou shalt see them; and enjoy their joy, and they thine. How oft have I measured a long and foul journey, to see some good friend; and digested the tediousness of the way, with the expectation of a kind entertainment, and the thought of that complacency which I should take in so dear a presence! and yet, perhaps, when I have arrived, I have found the house disordered, one sick, another disquieted, myself indisposed:

with what cheerful resolution should I undertake this my last voyage, where I shall meet with my best friends, and find them perfectly happy, and myself with them!

The Glory of Heaven.

HOW often have I begged of my God, that it would please Him to shew me some little glimpse of the glory of His saints! It is not for me, to wish the sight, as yet, of the face of that Divine Majesty: this was too much for a Moses to sue for: my ambition only is, that I might, if but as it were, through some cranny or key-hole of the gate of heaven, see the happy condition of His glorious servants.

I know what hinders me; my miserable unworthiness, my spiritual blindness. O God, if Thou please to wash off my clay with the waters of Thy Siloam, I shall have eyes: and, if Thou anoint them with Thy precious eye-salve, those eyes shall be clear; and enabled to behold those glories, which shall ravish my soul.

And now, Lord, what pure and resplendent light is this, wherein Thy blessed ones dwell! How justly did Thine ecstatical apostle call it *the inheritance of the saints in light!* Col. i. 12: light inexpressible, light unconceivable, light inaccessible! Lo, Thou, that hast prepared such a light to this inferior world, for the use and comfort of us mortal creatures, as the glorious sun, which can both enlighten and dazzle the eyes of all beholders, has proportionally ordained a light to that higher world, so much more excellent than the sun, as heaven is above earth, immortality above corruption. And, if wise Solomon could say, *Truly the light is sweet; and a pleasant thing it is for the eyes to see the sun;* Eccl. xi. 7: how infinitely delectable is it, in Thy light to see such light, as may make the sun, in comparison thereof, darkness! *In Thy presence is the fulness of joy, and at Thy right hand are pleasures for evermore.* What can be wished more, where there is fulness of joy? and, behold, Thy presence, O Lord, yields it.

The Saviour's Sufferings and Glories.

WHEN I think on my Saviour, in His agony, and on His cross, my soul is so clouded with sorrow, as if it would never be clear again: those bloody drops, and those dreadful ejaculations, methinks, should be past all reach of comfort; but when I see His happy eluctation out of these pangs, and hear Him cheerfully rendering His spirit into the hands of His Father; when I find Him trampling upon His grave, attended with glorious angels, and ascending in the chariot of a cloud to His heaven; I am so elevated with joy, as that I seem to have forgotten there was ever any cause of grief in those sufferings. I could be passionate to think, O Saviour, of Thy bitter and ignominious death; and, most of all, of Thy vehement strugglings with Thy Father's wrath for my sake; but Thy conquest and glory, takes me off, and calls me to Hallelujahs of joy and triumph; *Blessing, honor, glory, and power be unto Him that sitteth upon the throne, and unto the Lamb, for ever and ever;* Rev. v. 13.

Paradise.

O BLESSED Jesus, if from what Thou hast suffered for me, I shall cast mine eyes upon what Thou hast done for my soul, how is my heart divided betwixt the wonders of both! and may as soon tell how great either of them is, as whether of them is the greatest.

And oh, what a heaven is this, that Thou hast laid out for me; how resplendent, how transcendently glorious! Even that lower paradise, which Thou providest for the harbor of innocence and holiness, was full of admirable beauty, pleasure, magnificence; but, if it be compared with this paradise above, which Thou hast prepared for the everlasting entertainment of restored souls, how mean and beggarly it was! O match too unequal, of the best piece of earth with the highest state of the heaven of heavens!

In the earthly paradise, I find Thine angels the cherubim; but it was to keep man off from that garden of delight, and from the Tree of Life in the midst of it: but, in this heavenly one, I find millions of thy cherubim and seraphim rejoicing at man's blessedness, and welcoming the glorified souls to their heaven. There, I find but the shadow of that, whereof the substance is here. There, we were so possessed of life, that yet we might forfeit it: here, is life, without all possibility of death. Temptation could find access thither: here, is nothing but a free and complete fruition of blessedness. There, were delights fit for earthly bodies: here, is glory, more than can be enjoyed of blessed souls. That was watered with four streams, muddy and impetuous: in this, is *the pure river of the water of life, clear as crystal, proceeding out of the throne of God and of the Lamb:* Rev. xxii. 1. There, I find Thee only walking in the cool of the day: here, manifesting Thy Majesty continually. There, I see only a most pleasant orchard*, set with all manner of varieties of flourishing and fruitful plants: here, I find also the city of God, infinitely rich and magnificent; the building of the wall of it of jasper; and the city itself pure gold, like unto clear glass; and the foundations of the wall garnished with all manner of precious stones.

All that I can here attain to see, is the pavement of Thy celestial habitation. And, Lord, how glorious it is! how bespangled with the glittering stars; for number, for magnitude equally admirable! What is the least of them, but a world of light? and what are all of them, but a confluence of so many thousand worlds of beauty and brightness, met in one firmament? And, if this floor of Thy heavenly palace be thus richly set forth, oh, what infinite glory and magnificence must there needs be within! Thy chosen vessel, that had the privilege to be caught up thither, and to see that divine state, whether with

---

* Gardens in general were formerly so called.—CATTERMOLE.

bodily or mental eyes, can express it no otherwise, than that it cannot possibly be expressed. No, Lord, it were not infinite, if it could be uttered. Thoughts go beyond words; yet even these come far short also. He, that saw it, says, *Eye hath not seen, nor ear heard, neither have entered into the heart of man, the things which God hath prepared for them that love Him:* 1 Cor. ii. 9.

Unchangeable Duration.

IN the first minute wherein we live, we enter upon an eternity of being: and, though at the first, through the want of the exercise of reason, we cannot know it; and, afterwards, through our inconsideration and the bewitching businesses of time, we do not seriously lay it to heart, we are in a state of everlastingness. There must, upon the necessity of our mortality, be a change of our condition; but, with a perpetuity of our being: the body must undergo a temporary dissolution, and the soul a remove either to bliss or torment; but both of them, upon their meeting, shall continue in an unchangeable duration for ever and ever. And, if we are wont to slight transitory and vanishing commodities, by reason of their momentary continuance, and to make most account of things durable, what care and great thoughts ought I to bestow upon myself, who shall outlast the present world! and how ought I to frame my life so, as it may fall upon an eternity infinitely happy and glorious! O God, do Thou set off my heart from all these earthly vanities, and fix it above with Thee. As there shall be no end of my being, so let there be no change of my affections. Let them, beforehand, take possession of that heaven of Thine, whereto I am aspiring. Let nothing but this clay of mine be left remaining upon this earth, whereinto it is mouldering. Let my spiritual part be ever with Thee, whence it came, and enter upon that bliss, which knows neither change or end.

Rest in God.

SPEAK, *Lord, for Thy servant heareth:* what is it, which Thou wouldest have me do, that I may find rest to my soul? I am willing to exercise myself in all the acts of piety, which Thou requirest: I am ready to fast, to pray, to read, to hear, to meditate, to communicate, to give alms, to exhort, admonish, reprove, comfort where Thou biddest me; and, if there be any other duty appertaining to devotion or mercy, let me serve Thee in it: but, alas, O my God, howsoever I know these works are, in themselves, well-pleasing unto Thee; yet, as they fall from my wretchedness, they are stained with so many imperfections, that I have more reason to crave pardon for them, than to put confidence in them; and if I could perform them never so exquisitely, yet one sin is more than enough to dash all my obedience. I see, then, O Lord, I will see, there is no act, that I can be capable to do unto Thee, wherein I can find any repose: it must be Thine act to me, which only can effect it. It is Thy gracious word, *Come unto me, all ye that labor, and are heavy laden, and I will give you rest:* Matth. xi. 28. Lo, this rest must be Thy gift; not my earning: and what can be freer, than gift? Thou givest it then, but to those that come to Thee; not to those that come not; to those that come to Thee laden and laboring under the sense of their own wretchedness; not to the proud and careless. O Saviour, Thy sinner is sufficiently laden, with the burden of his iniquities: lade Thou me yet more with true penitent sorrow for my sins; and enable me then to come unto Thee by a lively faith. Take Thou the praise of Thine own work. Give me the grace to come; and give me rest, in coming.

Life a Pilgrimage.

O LORD my God, I am as very a pilgrim as ever walked upon Thy earth: why should I look to be in any better condition than my neighbors, than my forefathers? Even the best of them, that were most fixed upon their inheritance, were no other than strangers at home: it was not in the power of the world to naturalize them; much less, to make them enrol themselves free denizens here below: they knew their country, which they sought was above; so infinitely rich and pleasant, that these earthly regions, which they must pass through, are, in comparison, worthy of nothing but contempt: Heb. xi. 13, 14, 15. My condition is no other than theirs: I wander here, in a strange country; what wonder is it, if I meet with foreigners' fare, hard usage and neglect? Why do I intermeddle with the affairs of a nation, that is not mine? Why do I clog myself, in my way, with the base and heavy lumber of the world? Why are not my affections homeward? Why do I not long to see and enjoy my Father's house? O my God, Thou, that hast put me into the state of a pilgrim, give me a pilgrim's heart: set me off from this wretched world, wherein I am: let me hate to think of dwelling here: let it be my only care, how to pass through this miserable wilderness, to the promised land of a blessed eternity.

On the Length of the Way.

HOW far off is yonder great mountain! My very eye is weary with the foresight of so great a distance; yet time and patience shall overcome it: this night we shall hope to lodge beyond it. Some things are more tedious in their expectation, than in their performance. The comfort is, that every step I take sets me nearer to my end: when I once come there, I shall both forget how long it now seems, and please myself to look back upon the way that I have measured.

It is thus in our passage to heaven. My weak nature is ready to faint, under the very conceit of the length and difficulty of this journey: my eye doth not more guide than discourage me. Many steps of grace and true obedience shall bring me insensibly thither. Only, let me move, and hope; and God's good leisure shall perfect my salvation.

O Lord, give me to possess my soul with patience; and not so much to regard speed, as certainty. When I come to the top of Thy holy hill, all these weary paces and deep sloughs, shall either be forgotten, or contribute to my happiness in their remembrance.

THE DIVINE LOVE.

O GOD, hadst Thou sent down Thy Son to this lower region of earth upon such terms, as that He might have brought down heaven with Him; that He might have come in the port and majesty of a God, clothed with celestial glory, to have dazzled our eyes, and to have drawn all hearts unto Him; this might have seemed, in some measure, to have sorted with His divine magnificence; but Thou wouldest have Him to appear in the wretched condition of our humanity. Yet, even thus, hadst Thou sent Him into the world in the highest estate and pomp of royalty that earth could afford; that all the kings and monarchs of the world should have been commanded to follow His train and to glitter in His court; and that the knees of all the potentates of the earth should have bowed to His Sovereign Majesty, and their lips have kissed His dust; this might have carried some kind of appearance of a state next to divine greatness: but Thou wouldest have Him come in the despised form of a servant.

And Thou, O Blessed Jesus, wast accordingly willing, for our sakes, to submit Thyself to nakedness, hunger, thirst, weariness, temptation, contempt, betraying, agonies, scorn, buffetings, scourgings, distention, crucifixion, death: O love above measure, without example, beyond admiration! *Greater love,* Thou sayest, *hath no man than this, that a man lay down his life for his friends;* but, Oh, what is it then, that Thou, who wert God and Man, shouldest lay down Thy life, more precious than many worlds, for Thine enemies!

Yet, had it been but the laying down of a life in a fair and gentle way, there might have been some mitigation of the sorrow of a dissolution. There is not more difference betwixt life and death, than there may be betwixt some one kind of death and another. Thine, O dear Saviour, was the painful, shameful, cursed death of the Cross; wherein yet all that man could do unto Thee was nothing to that inward torment, which, in our stead, Thou endurest from Thy Father's wrath; when, in the bitterness of Thine anguished soul, Thou criedst out, *My God, my God, why hast Thou forsaken me?* Even thus, thus wast Thou content to be forsaken, that we wretched sinners might be received to mercy: O love, stronger than death, which Thou vanquishedst! more high, than that hell is deep, from which Thou hast rescued us!

I am swallowed up, O God, I am willingly swallowed up, in this bottomless abyss of Thine infinite love; and there let me dwell, in a perpetual ravishment of spirit; till, being freed from this clog of earth, and filled with the fulness of Christ, I shall be admitted to enjoy that, which I cannot now reach to wonder at, Thine incomprehensible bliss and glory which Thou hast laid up in the highest heavens for them that love Thee, in the blessed communion of all Thy saints and angels, Thy cherubim and seraphim, thrones, dominions, and principalities, and powers; in the beatifical presence of Thee, the Ever-Living God, the Eternal Father of Spirits, Father, Son, Holy Ghost, One Infinite Deity in Three, co-essentially, co-eternally, co-equally glorious Persons: To whom be blessing, honor, glory, and power, for ever and ever. Amen. Hallelujah.

RICHARD SIBBES, D. D.
1577–1635.

Grace.

SPARKS by nature fly upwards; so the spirit of grace carrieth the soul heavenward, and setteth before us holy and heavenly aims: as it was kindled from heaven, so it carries us back to heaven. The part followeth the whole: fire mounteth upward, so every spark to its own element. Where the aim and bent of the soul is God-wards, there is grace though opposed. The least measure of it is holy desires springing from faith and love, for we cannot desire anything which we do not believe first to be, and the desire of it issues from love. Hence desires are counted a part of the thing desired in some measure, but then they must be, first, constant; for constancy shows that they are supernaturally natural, and not enforced: secondly, they must be carried to spiritual things, as to believe, to love God, &c., not out of a special exigent, because if now they had grace, they think they might escape some danger, but as a loving heart is carried to the thing loved for some excellency in itself: and thirdly, with desire there is grief when it is hindered, which stirs up to prayer: *Oh that my ways were so directed, that I might keep Thy statutes!* Psalm cxix. 5; *O miserable man that I am, who shall deliver?* &c. Rom. vii. 24: fourthly, desires put us onward still, O that I might serve God with more liberty; O that I were more free from these offensive, unsavory, noisome lusts.

The Holy Spirit our Guide.

THE Holy Spirit of God is our guide: who will displease his guide? A sweet comfortable guide that leads us through the wilderness of this world; as the cloud before the Israelites by day, and the pillar of fire by night: so He conducts us to the heavenly Canaan; if we grieve our guide, we cause Him to leave us to ourselves. The Israelites would not go a step further than God by His angel went before them. It is in vain for us to make toward heaven without our blessed Guide; we cannot do, nor speak, nor think anything that is holy and good without Him: whatsoever is holy, and pious, it grows not in our garden, in our nature, but it is planted by the Spirit.

There is nothing in the world so great and sweet a friend that will do us so much good as the Spirit, if we give Him entertainment. Indeed He must rule, He will have the keys delivered to Him, we must submit to His government. And when He is in the heart, He will subdue by little and little all high thoughts, rebellious risings, and despairing fears. This shall be our happiness in heaven, when we shall be wholly spiritual, that *God shall be all in all;* we shall be perfectly obedient to the Spirit in our understandings, wills, and affections. The Spirit will then dwell largely in us, and will make the room where He dwelleth sweet, and lightsome, and free, subduing whatsoever is contrary; and bring fulness of peace, and joy, and comfort. And in the meantime in what condition soever we are, we shall have suitable help from the Spirit. We are partly flesh, and partly spirit; God is not all in all, the flesh hath a part in us, we are often in afflictions, and under clouds. Let us therefore prize our fellowship with the Spirit. For are we in darkness? He is a Spirit of light; are we in deadness of spirit? He is a Spirit of life; are we in a disconsolate estate? He is a Spirit of consolation; are we in perplexity, and know not what to do? He is a Spirit of wisdom; are we troubled with corruptions? He is a sanctifying, a subduing, a mortifying Spirit: in what condition soever we are, He will never leave us, till He hath raised us from the grave, and taken full possession of body and soul in heaven; He will prove a comforter, when neither friends, nor riches, nor anything in the world can comfort us. How careful should we be to give contentment to this sweet Spirit of God.

No Christian is so happy as the watchful Christian that is careful of his duty, and to preserve his communion with the Holy Spirit of God; for by entertaining Him, he is sure to have communion with the Father and the Son. It is the happiest condition in the world, when the soul is the temple of the Holy Spirit, when the heart is as the Holy of Holies, where there be prayers and praises offered to God. The soul is as it were a holy ark, the memory like the pot of manna, preserving heavenly truths. It is a heavenly condition, a man prospers to heavenward, when the Spirit of God is with him. You know Obed-Edom, when the ark was in his house, all thrived with him: so while the Spirit and His motions are entertained by us, we shall be happy in life, happy in death, happy to eternity.

Beholding of Christ, a Transforming Sight.

THE very beholding of Christ is a transforming sight; the Spirit that makes us new creatures, and stirs us up to behold this Servant, it is a transforming beholding, if we look upon Him with the eye of faith, it will make us like Christ; for the Gospel is a mirror, and such a mirror, that when we look into it, and see ourselves interested in it, *we are changed from glory to glory;* a man cannot look upon the love of God and of Christ in the Gospel, but it will change him to be like God and Christ; for how can we see Christ, and God in Christ, but we shall see how God hates sin, and this will transform us to hate it as God doth, who hated it so that it could not be expiated but with the blood of Christ, God-man; so seeing the holiness of God in it, it will transform us to be holy; when we see the love of God in the Gospel, and the love of Christ giving Himself for us, this will transform us to love God;

when we see the humility and obedience of Christ, when we look on Christ as God's chosen Servant in all this, and as our surety and Head, it transforms us to the like humility and obedience. Those that find not their dispositions in some comfortable measure wrought to this blessed transformation, they have not yet those eyes that the Holy Ghost requireth here, *Behold my Servant whom I have chosen, my Beloved in whom my soul delighteth.*

Comfort in Distress.

SPIRITUAL comfort in distress, such as the world can neither give, nor take away, shows that God looks upon the souls of His with another eye than He beholdeth others. He sends a secret messenger that reports His peculiar love to their hearts. He knows their souls, and feeds them with His hidden manna; the inward peace they feel is not in freedom from trouble, but in freeness with God in the midst of trouble.

Pardoning Mercy.

CONCEIVE of God's mercy as no ordinary mercy, and Christ's obedience as no ordinary obedience. There is something in the very greatness of sin, that may encourage us to go to God, for the greater our sins are, the greater the glory of His powerful mercy, pardoning, and His powerful grace in healing will appear. The great God delights to show His greatness in the greatest things; even men glory, when they are put upon that, which may set forth their worth in any kind. God *delighteth in mercy,* Mic. vii. 18, it pleaseth Him (nothing so well) as being His chief name, which then we take in vain, when we are not moved by it to come unto Him.

That which Satan would use as an argument to drive us from God, we should use as a strong plea with Him. Lord, the greater my sins are, the greater will be the glory of Thy pardoning mercy. David, after his heinous sins, cries not for *mercy,* but for *abundance of mercy, according to the multitude of Thy mercies, do away mine offences:* Psalm li: His mercy is not only above His own works, but above ours too. If we could sin more than He could pardon, then we might have some reason to despair. Despair is a high point of atheism, it takes away God and Christ both at once. Judas, in betraying our Saviour, was an occasion of His death as man, but in despairing he did what lay in him to take away His life as God.

When, therefore, conscience joining with Satan, sets out the sin in its colors, labor thou by faith to set out God in His colors, infinite in mercy and loving kindness.

PRAYER AND PRAISE.

THOUGH in evil times we have cause to praise God, yet so we are, and such are our spirits, for the most part, that affliction straitens our hearts. Therefore the apostle thought it the fittest duty in affliction to pray. *Is any afflicted? let him pray,* saith James; *Is any joyful? let him sing psalms*, James. v. 13; showing that the day of rejoicing is the fittest day of praising God. Every work of a Christian is beautiful in its own time; the graces of Christianity have their several offices at several seasons; in trouble, prayer is in its season; in the evil day call upon me, saith God; in better times praises should appear and show themselves. When God manifests His goodness to His, He gives them grace with it, to manifest their thankfulness to Him. Praising of God is then most comely, though never out of season, when God seems to call for it, by renewing the sense of His mercies in some fresh favor towards us. If a bird will sing in winter, much more in the spring; if the heart be prepared in the winter time of adversity to praise God, how ready will it be when it is warmed with the glorious sunshine of His favor?

Our life is nothing but as it were a web woven with interminglings of wants and favors, crosses and blessings, standings and fallings, combat and victory, therefore there should be a perpetual intercourse of praying and praising in our hearts. There is always a ground of communion with God in one of these kinds, till we come to that condition wherein all wants shall be supplied, where indeed is only matter of praise. Yet praising God in this life hath this prerogative, that here we praise Him *in the midst of His enemies.* In heaven all will be in concert with us. God esteems it an honor in the midst of devils, and wicked men, whose life is nothing but a dishonor of Him, to have those that will make His name as it is in itself so, great in the world.

David comforts himself in this, that he should praise God; which shows he had inured himself well before to this holy exercise, in which he found such comfort, that he could not but joy in the forethoughts of that time, wherein he should have fresh occasion of his former acquaintance with God. Thoughts of this nature enter not into a heart that is strange to God.

PRAISING GOD.

SO soon as we set upon this work, we shall feel our spirits to rise higher and higher as the waters in the sanctuary, as the soul grows more and more heated; see how David riseth by degrees. *Be glad in the Lord*, and then, *rejoice, ye righteous*, and then, *shout for joy, all ye that are upright in heart;* the Spirit of God will delight to carry us along in this duty, until it leaves our spirits in heaven, praising God with the saints and glorious angels there; *To him that hath* and useth *it shall be given;* he that knoweth God aright, will honor Him by trusting of Him; he that honors Him by trusting Him, will honor Him by praying; and he that honors Him by prayer, shall honor Him by praises; he that honors Him by praises here, shall perfect His praises in heaven; and this will quit the labor of setting and keeping the soul in tune; this trading with God is the richest trade in the world; when we return praises to Him, He returns new favors to us, and so an everlasting ever-increasing intercourse betwixt God and the soul is maintained; David here resolved to praise God, because he had assurance of such a deliverance as would yield him a ground of praising Him.

Praising of God may well be called incense, because as it is sweet in itself, and sweet to God, so it sweetens all that comes from us. Love and joy are sweet in themselves, though those whom we love and joy in, should not know of our affection, nor return the like; but we cannot love and joy in God but He will delight in us; when we neglect the praising of God, we lose both the comfort of God's love, and our own too; it is a spiritual judgment to want or lose the sight or sense of God's favors, for it is a sign of want of spiritual life, or at least liveliness; it shows we are not yet in the state of those whom God hath chosen, to set forth the riches of His glory upon.

We ought not only to give thanks, but to be thankful, to meditate and study the praises of God. Our whole life should be nothing else but a continual blessing of His holy name, endeavoring to bring in all we have, and to lay it out for God and His people, to see where He hath any receivers: our goodness is nothing to God; we need bring no water to the fountain, nor light to the sun. Thankfulness is full of invention, it deviseth liberal things, though it be our duty to be good stewards of our talents, yet thankfulness adds a lustre, and a more gracious acceptance, as having more of that which God calls for.

Our praising God should not be as sparks out of a flint, but as water out of a spring, natural, ready, free, as God's love to us is; mercy pleases Him, so should praise please us; it is our happiness when the best part in us is exercised about the best and highest work; it was a good speech of him that said, If God had made me a nightingale, I would have sung as a nightingale, but now God hath made me a man, I will sing forth the *praises of God*, which is the work of a saint only: *all Thy works bless Thee, and Thy saints praise Thee:* all things are either blessings in their nature, or so blessed, as they are made blessings to us by the overruling coming of Him, who maketh all things serviceable to His; even the worst things in this sense are made spiritual to God's people against their own nature; how great is that goodness which makes even the worst things good?

I beseech you therefore labor to be men of praises. If in any duty we may expect assistance, we may in this, that altogether concerns God's glory; the more we praise God, the more we shall please Him. When God by grace enlarges the will, He intends to give the deed. God's children wherein their wills are conformable to God's will, are sure to have them fulfilled. In a fruitful ground, a man will sow his best seed. God intends His own glory in every mercy, and he that *praises Him, glorifies Him.* When our wills therefore carry us to that which God wills above all, we may well expect. He will satisfy our desires. The living God is a living fountain never drawn dry; He hath never done so much for us, but He can and will do more. If there be no end of our praises, there shall be no end of His goodness, no way of thriving like to this. By this means we are sure never to be very miserable; how can he be dejected, that by a sweet communion with God sets himself in heaven? nay, maketh his heart a kind of heaven, *a temple, a holy of holies*, wherein incense is offered unto God? It is the sweetest branch of our priestly office, to offer up these daily sacrifices; it is not only the beginning, but a further entrance of our heaven upon earth, and shall be one day our whole employment for ever.

God our Refuge.

THERE is none of us all but may some time or other fall into such a great extremity, that when we look about us, we shall find none to help us: at which time we shall thoroughly know what it is to have comfort from heaven, and a God to go unto. If there be anything in the world worth laboring for, it is the getting sound evidence to our souls that God is ours. What madness is it to spend all our labor, to possess ourselves of the cistern when the fountain is offered to us. O beloved, the whole world cannot weigh against this one comfort, that God is ours. All things laid in the other balance, would be too light. A moth may corrupt, a thief may take away that we have here, but who can take our God away? though God doth convey some comfort to us by these things, yet when they are gone, He reserves the comfort in Himself still, and can convey that, and more, in a purer and sweeter way, where He plants the grace of faith to fetch it from Him. Why then should we weaken our interest in God, for anything this earth affords? what unworthy wretches are those, that to please a sinful man, or to feed a base lust, or to yield to a wicked custom, will, as much as in them lieth, lose their interest in God? such little consider what an excellent privilege it is to have a sure refuge to fly unto in time of trouble. Labor therefore to bring thy soul to this point with God: *Lord, if Thou seest it fit, take away all from me, so Thou leavest me Thyself: whom have I in heaven but Thee, and there is none on earth that I desire in comparison of Thee?*

Spiritual Desertion.

IN time of desertion put Christ betwixt God and thy soul, and learn to appeal from God out of Christ, to God in Christ. Lord, look upon my Saviour, that is near unto Thee as Thy Son, near to me as my brother, and now intercedes at Thy right hand for me; though I have sinned, yet He hath suffered, and shed His precious blood to make my peace. When we are in any trouble, let us still wait on Him, and lie at His feet, and never let Him go till He casts a gracious look upon us.

God our Portion.

IN the division of things God bequeaths Himself to those that are His, for their portion, as the best portion He can give them. There are many goodly things in the world, but none of these are a Christian's portion; there is in Him to supply all good, and remove all ill, until the time come that we stand in need of no other good. It is our chief wisdom to know Him, our holiness to love Him, our happiness to enjoy Him. There is in Him to be had whatsoever can truly make us happy. We go to our treasure, and our portion in all our wants, we live by it, and value ourselves by it. God is such a portion, that the more we spend on Him, the more we may. *Our strength may fail*, and *our heart may fail*, but *God is our portion forever:* Psalm lxxiii. 26. Every thing else teaches us by the vanity and vexation we find in them, that our happiness is not in them; they send us to God; they may make us worse, but better they cannot. Our nature is above them, and ordained for a greater good; they can go but along with us for a while, and their end swallows up all the comfort of their beginning, as Pharaoh's lean kine swallowed up the fat. If we have no better portion here than these things, we are like to have hell for our portion hereafter. What a shame will it be hereafter when we are stript of all, that it should be said, Lo, this is the man that took not God for his portion. If God be once ours, He goes for ever along with us, and when earth will hold us no longer, heaven shall. Who that hath his senses about him, would perish for want of water, when there is a fountain by him? or for hunger, that is at a feast? God alone is a rich portion; O then let us labor for a large faith, as we have a large object; if we had a thousand times more faith, we should have a thousand times more increase of God's blessings. When the prophet came to the *widow's house*, as many vessels as she had *were filled with oil:* 1 Kings xvii. 14: we are straitened in our own faith, but not straitened in our God. It falls out oft in this world that God's people are like Israel at the Red Sea, environed with dangers on all sides: what course have we then to take but only to look up and wait for the salvation of our God? This is a breast full of consolation; let us teach our hearts to suck, and draw comfort from hence.

Is God our God; and will He suffer anything to befall us for our hurt? Will He lay any more upon us, than He gives us strength to bear? Will he suffer any wind to blow upon us but for good? Doth He not set us before His face? Will a father or mother suffer a child to be wronged in their presence, if they can help it? Will a friend suffer his friend to be injured, if he may redress him? And will God, that hath put these affections into parents and friends, neglect the care of those He hath taken so near unto Himself? No surely, His eyes are open to look upon their condition; His ears are open to their prayers; a *book of remembrance*, Mal. iii. 16, is written of all their good desires, speeches, and actions; He hath bottles for all their tears, their very sighs are not *hid from Him;* He hath written them upon the *palms of His hands,* and cannot but continually look upon them. Oh let us prize the favor of so good a God, who though He dwells on high yet will regard things so low, and not neglect the mean estate of any; nay, especially delights to be called the *Comforter of His elect,* and the God of those that are in misery, and have none to fly unto but Himself.

Comfort in the Hour of Death.

IT is a comfort in the hour of death, that we yield up our souls to Christ, who has gone before to provide a place for us: this was one end of His being taken up to heaven, to provide a place for us. Therefore, when we die, we have not a place to seek, our house is provided beforehand; Christ was taken up to glory, to provide glory for us. Even as paradise was provided for Adam before he was made, so we have a heavenly paradise provided for us; we had a place in heaven before we were born. What a comfort is this at the hour of death, and at the death of our friends, that they are gone to Christ and to glory! We were shut out of the first paradise by the first Adam; our comfort is, that now the heavenly paradise in Christ is open. *This day shalt thou be with me in paradise,* saith Christ to the penitent thief. There was an angel to keep paradise when Adam was shut out; but there is none to keep us out of heaven; nay, the angels are ready to convoy our souls to heaven, as they did Lazarus; and as they accompanied Christ in His ascension to heaven, so they do the souls of His children.

JEREMY TAYLOR, D. D.
1613–1667.

Prayers.   I.

BLESSED and most Holy Jesus, fountain of grace and comfort, treasure of wisdom and spiritual emanations, be pleased to abide with me for ever by the inhabitation of Thy interior assistances and refreshments; give me a corresponding love, acceptable and unstained purity, care and watchfulness over my ways, that I may never, by provoking Thee to anger, cause Thee to remove Thy dwelling, or draw a cloud before thy holy face. But if Thou art pleased, upon a design of charity, or trial, to cover my eyes, that I may not behold the bright rays of Thy favor, nor be refreshed with spiritual comforts, let Thy love support my spirit by ways insensible, and in all my needs give me such a portion as may be instrumental and incentive to performance of my duty; and in all accidents let me continue to seek Thee by prayers, and humiliation, and frequent desires, and the strictness of a holy life; that I may follow Thy example, pursue Thy footsteps, be supported by Thy strength, guided by Thy hand, enlightened by

Thy favor, and may at last, after a persevering holiness and an unwearied industry, dwell with Thee in the regions of light, and eternal glory, where there shall be no fears of parting from the habitations of felicity, and the union and fruition of Thy presence, O blessed and most holy Jesus. Amen.

II.

O ETERNAL Jesus, Thou bright image of Thy Father's glories, whose light did shine to all the world, when Thy heart was inflamed with zeal and love of God and of religion, let a coal from Thine altar, fanned with the wings of the holy dove, kindle in my soul such holy flames, that I may be zealous of Thy honor and glory, forward in religious duties, earnest in their pursuit, prudent in their managing, ingenuous in my purposes, making my religion to serve no end but of Thy glories, and the obtaining of Thy promises: and so sanctify my soul and my body, that I may be a holy temple, fit and prepared for the inhabitation of Thy ever-blessed Spirit; whom grant that I may never grieve by admitting any impure thing to desecrate the place, and unhallow the courts of His abode; but give me a pure soul in a chaste and healthful body, a spirit full of holy simplicity, and designs of great ingenuity, and perfect religion, that I may intend what Thou commandest, and may with proper instruments prosecute what I so intend, and by Thy aids may obtain the end of my labors, the rewards of obedience and holy living, even the society and inheritance of Jesus in the participation of the joys of Thy temple, where Thou dwellest and reignest with the Father and the Holy Ghost, O eternal Jesus. Amen.

III.

O ETERNAL God, who dwellest not in temples made by hands, the heaven of heavens is not able to contain Thee, and yet Thou art pleased to manifest Thy presence amongst the sons of men by special issues of Thy favor and benediction. Make my body and soul to be a temple pure and holy, apt for the entertainments of the Holy Jesus, and for the habitation of the Holy Spirit. Lord, be pleased, with Thy rod of paternal discipline, to cast out all impure lusts, all worldly affections, all covetous desires, from this Thy temple; that it may be a place of prayer and meditation, of holy appetites and chaste thoughts, of pure intentions and zealous desires of pleasing Thee; that I may become also a sacrifice as well as a temple, eaten up with the zeal of Thy glory, and consumed with the fire of love; that not one thought may be entertained by me but such as may be like perfume breathing from the altar of incense, and not a word may pass from me but may have the accent of heaven upon it, and sound pleasantly in Thy ears. O dearest God, fill every faculty of my soul with impresses, dispositions, capacities, and aptnesses of religion: and do Thou hallow my soul, that I may be possessed with zeal and religious affections, loving Thee above all things in the world, worshiping Thee with the humblest adorations and frequent addresses, continually feeding upon the apprehensions of the divine sweetness, and considerations of Thy infinite excellencies, and observations of Thy righteous commandments, and the feast of a holy conscience, as an antepast of eternity, and consignation to the joys of heaven, through Jesus Christ our Lord. Amen.

IV.

O HOLY Jesus, fountain of eternal life, Thou spring of joy and spiritual satisfactions, let the holy stream of blood and water issuing from Thy sacred side cool the thirst, soften the hardness, and refresh the barrenness of my desert soul; that I, thirsting after Thee, as the wearied hart after the cool stream, may despise all the vainer complacencies of this world, refuse all societies but such as are safe, pious, and charitable, mortify all sottish appetites, and may desire nothing but Thee, seek none but Thee, and rest in Thee with entire dereliction of my own caitiff inclinations; that the desires of nature may pass into desires of grace, and my thirst and my hunger may be spiritual, and my hopes placed in Thee, and the expresses of my charity upon Thy relatives, and all the parts of my life may speak my love and obedience to Thy commandments: that Thou possessing my soul and all its faculties during my whole life, I may possess Thy glories in the fruition of a blessed eternity; by the light of Thy gospel here and the streams of Thy grace being guided to Thee, the fountain of life and glory, there to be inebriated with the waters of Paradise, with joy, and love, and contemplation, adoring and admiring the beauties of the Lord for ever and ever. Amen.

V.

O BLESSED Jesus, who art become to us the fountain of peace and sanctity, of righteousness and charity, of life and perpetual benediction, imprint in our spirits these glorious characterisms of Christianity, that we by such excellent dispositions may be consigned to the infinity of blessedness which Thou camest to reveal, and minister, and exhibit to mankind. Give us great humility of spirit; and deny us not, when we beg sorrow of Thee, the mourning and sadness of true penitents, that we may imitate Thy excellencies, and conform to Thy sufferings. Make us meek, patient, indifferent, and resigned in all accidents, changes, and issues of divine Providence. Mortify all inordinate anger in us; all wrath, strife, contention, murmurings, malice, and envy; and interrupt, and then blot out all peevish dispositions and morosities, all disturbances and unevenness of spirit or of habit, that may hinder us in our duty. Oh! teach me so to hunger and thirst after the ways of righteousness, that it may be meat and drink to me to do Thy Father's will. Raise my affections to heaven and heavenly things, fix my heart there, and prepare a treasure for me, which I may receive in the great diffusions and communications of Thy glory. And in this sad interval of infirmity and temptations strengthen my hopes, and fortify my faith, by such emissions of light and grace from Thy Spirit, that I may relish those blessings which Thou preparest for Thy saints with so great appetite, that I may despise the world and all its gilded vanities, and may desire nothing but the crown of righteousness and the paths that lead thither, the graces of Thy kingdom, and the glories of it; that when I have served Thee in holiness and strict obedience, I may reign with Thee in the glories of eternity: for Thou, O holy Jesus, art our hope, and our life and glory, our exceeding great reward. Amen.

VI.

O ETERNAL Jesus, Who art made unto us wisdom, righteousness, sanctification, and redemption, give us of Thy abundant charity, that we may love the eternal benefit of our brother's soul with a true, diligent and affectionate care and tenderness. Give us a fellow-feeling of one another's calamities, a readiness to bear each other's burdens, aptness to forbear, wisdom to advise, counsel to direct, and a spirit of meekness and modesty trembling at our infirmities, fearful in our brother's dangers, and joyful in his restitution and securities. Lord, let all our actions be pious and prudent, ourselves wise as serpents, and innocent as doves, and our whole life exemplary, and just, and charitable; that we may, like lamps shining in Thy temple, serve Thee and enlighten others, and guide them to Thy sanctuary; and that, shining clearly, and burning zealously, when the Bridegroom shall come to bind up His jewels, and beautify His spouse, and gather His saints together, we, and all Thy Christian people knit in holy fellowship, may enter into the joy of our Lord, and partake of the eternal refreshments of the kingdom of light and glory, where Thou, O holy and eternal Jesus, livest and reignest in the excellencies of a kingdom, and the infinite durations of eternity. Amen.

VII.

BLESS me, gracious God, in my calling to such purposes as Thou shalt choose for me, or employ me in: relieve me in all my sadnesses; make my bed in my sickness; give me patience in my sorrows, confidence in Thee, and grace to call upon Thee in all temptations. O be Thou my guide in all my actions; my protector in all dangers; give me a healthful body, and a clear understanding; a sanctified and just, a charitable and humble, a religious and contented spirit; let not my life be miserable and wretched; nor my name stained with sin and shame; nor my condition lifted up to a tempting and dangerous fortune: but let my condition be blessed, my conversation useful to my neighbors, and pleasing to Thee; that when my body shall lie down in its bed of darkness, my soul may pass into the regions of light, and live with Thee for ever, through Jesus Christ. Amen.

VIII.

O ALMIGHTY God, Father and Lord of all the creatures, who hast disposed all things and all chances so as may best glorify Thy wisdom, and serve the ends of Thy justice, and magnify Thy mercy by secret and indiscernible ways, bringing good out of evil, I most humbly beseech Thee to give me wisdom from above, that I may adore Thee and admire Thy ways and footsteps, which are in the great deep and not to be searched out: teach me to submit to Thy providence in all things, to be content in all changes of person and condition, to be temperate in prosperity, and to read my duty in the lines of Thy mercy; and in adversity to be meek, patient, and resigned; and to look through the cloud, that I may wait for the consolation of the Lord and the day of redemption; in the meantime doing my duty with an unwearied diligence, and an undisturbed resolution, having no fondness for the vanities or possessions of this world, but laying up my hopes in heaven and the rewards of holy living, and being strengthened with the spirit of the inner man, through Jesus Christ our Lord. Amen.

Evening Prayers. I.

O ETERNAL God, great Father of men and angels, who hast established the heavens and the earth in a wonderful order, making day and night to succeed each other; I make my humble address to Thy Divine Majesty, begging of Thee mercy and protection this night and ever. O Lord, pardon all my sins, my light and rash words, the vanity and impiety of my thoughts, my unjust and uncharitable actions, and whatsoever I have transgressed against Thee this day, or at any time before. Behold, O God, my soul is troubled in the remembrance of my sins, in the frailty and sinfulness of my flesh, exposed to every temptation, and of itself not able to resist any. Lord God of mercy, I earnestly beg of Thee to give me a great portion of Thy grace, such as may be sufficient and effectual for the mortification of all my sins and vanities and disorders, that as I have formerly served my lust and unworthy desires, so now I may give myself up wholly to Thy service and the studies of a holy life.

II.

INTO Thy hands, most blessed Jesus, I commend my soul and body, for Thou hast redeemed both with Thy precious blood. So bless and sanctify my sleep unto me that it may be temperate, holy, and safe; a refreshment to my wearied body, to enable it so to serve my soul, that both may serve Thee with a never-failing duty. Oh, let me never sleep in sin or death eternal, but give me a watchful and a prudent spirit, that I may omit no opportunity of serving Thee; that whether I sleep or awake, live or die, I may be Thy servant and Thy child; that when the work of my life is done, I may rest in the bosom of my Lord, till by the voice of the archangel, the trump of God, I shall be awakened, and called to sit down and feast in the eternal supper of the Lamb. Grant this, O Lamb of God, for the honor of Thy mercies, and the glory of Thy name, O most merciful Saviour and Redeemer Jesus. Amen.

Prayer for One in Trouble.

O ETERNAL God, Father of mercies, and God of all comfort, with much mercy look upon the sadnesses and sorrows of Thy servant. My sins lie heavy upon me, and press me sore, and there is no health in my bones by reason of Thy displeasure and my sin. The waters are gone over me, and I stick fast in the deep mire, and my miseries are without comfort, because they are punishments of my sin: and I am so evil and unworthy a person, that though I have great desires, yet I have no dispositions or worthiness toward receiving comfort. My sins have caused my sorrow, and my sorrow does not cure my sins; and unless for Thine own sake, and merely because Thou art good, Thou shalt pity me and relieve me, I am as much without remedy as now I am without comfort. Lord, pity me! Lord, let Thy grace refresh my spirit! Let Thy comforts support me, Thy mercy pardon me, and never let my portion be amongst hopeless and accursed spirits; for Thou art good and gracious, and I throw myself upon Thy mercy. Let me never let my hold go, and do Thou with me what seems good in Thine own eyes. I cannot suffer more than I have deserved; and yet I can need no relief so great as Thy mercy is; for Thou art infinitely more merciful than I can be miserable, and Thy mercy, which is above all Thy own works, must needs be far above all my sin and all my misery. Dearest Jesus, let me trust in Thee for ever, and let me never be confounded. Amen.

Prayer for One in Sickness.

O HOLY Jesus, Thou art a merciful High-Priest, and touched with the sense of our infirmities; Thou knowest the sharpness of my sickness and the weakness of my person. The clouds are gathered about me, and Thou hast covered me with Thy storm; my understanding hath not such apprehension of things as formerly. Lord, let Thy mercy support me, Thy Spirit guide me, and lead me through the valley of this death safely; that I may pass it patiently, holily, with perfect resignation; and let me rejoice in the Lord, in the hopes of pardon, in the expectation of glory, in the sense of Thy mercies, in the refreshments of Thy Spirit, in a victory over all temptations.

Thou hast promised to be with us in tribulation. Lord, my soul is troubled, and my body is weak, and my hope is in Thee, and my enemies are busy and mighty; now make good Thy holy promise. Now, O holy Jesus, now let Thy hand of grace be upon me; restrain my ghostly enemies, and give me all sorts of spiritual assistances. Lord, remember Thy servant in the day when Thou bindest up Thy jewels.

O take from me all tediousness of spirit, all impatience and unquietness: let me possess my soul in patience, and resign my soul and body into Thy hands, as into the hands of a faithful Creator and a blessed Redeemer.

O holy Jesus, Thou didst die for us; by Thy sad, pungent, and intolerable pains, which Thou enduredst for me, have pity on me, and ease my pain, or increase my patience. Lay on me no more than Thou shalt enable me to bear. I have deserved it all and more, and infinitely more. Lord, I am weak and ignorant, timorous and inconstant; and I fear lest something should happen that may discompose the state of my soul, that may displease Thee: do what Thou wilt with me, so that Thou dost but preserve me in Thy fear and favor. Thou knowest that it is my great fear, but let Thy Spirit secure that nothing may be able to separate me from the love of God in Jesus Christ: then smite me here that Thou mayest spare me for ever; and yet, O Lord, smite me friendly, for Thou knowest my infirmities. Into Thy hands I commend my spirit; for Thou hast redeemed me, O Lord, Thou God of truth. Come, Holy Spirit, help me in this conflict. Come, Lord Jesus, come quickly.

Prayer before a Journey.

O ALMIGHTY God, who fillest all things with Thy presence, and art a God afar off as well as near at hand; Thou didst send Thy angel to bless Jacob in his journey, and didst lead the children of

Israel through the Red Sea, making it a wall on the right hand and on the left; be pleased to let Thy angel go out before me and guide me in my journey, preserving me from dangers of robbers, from violence of enemies, and sudden and sad accidents, from falls and errors. And prosper my journey to Thy glory, and to all my innocent purposes; and preserve me from all sin, that I may return in peace and holiness, with Thy favor and Thy blessing, and may serve Thee in thankfulness and obedience all the days of my pilgrimage; and at last bring me to Thy country, to the celestial Jerusalem, there to dwell in Thy house, and to sing praises to Thee for ever. Amen.

PRAYERS ON RECEIVING THE SACRAMENT. I.

O MOST gracious and Eternal God, the helper of the helpless, the comforter of the comfortless, the hope of the afflicted, the bread of the hungry, the drink of the thirsty, and the Saviour of all them that wait upon Thee; I bless and glorify Thy name, and adore Thy goodness, and delight in Thy love, that Thou hast once more given me the opportunity of receiving the greatest favor which I can receive in this world, even the body and blood of my dearest Saviour. O take from me all affection to sin or vanity; let not my affections dwell below, but soar upwards to the element of love, to the seat of God, to the regions of glory, and the inheritance of Jesus; that I may hunger and thirst for the bread of life and the wine of elect souls, and may know no loves but the love of God, and the most merciful Jesus. Amen.

II.

O TASTE and see how gracious the Lord is: blessed is the man that trusteth in Him. The beasts do lack and suffer hunger; but they which seek the Lord shall want no manner of thing that is good. Lord, what am I, that my Saviour should become my food; that the Son of God should be the meat of worms, of dust and ashes, of a sinner, of him that was His enemy? But this Thou hast done to me, because Thou art infinitely good and wonderfully gracious, and lovest to bless every one of us, in turning us from the evil of our ways. Enter into me, blessed Jesus: let no root of bitterness spring up in my heart; but be Thou Lord of all my faculties. O let me feed on Thee by faith, and grow up by the increase of God to a perfect man in Christ Jesus. Amen. Lord, I believe: help my unbelief.

Prayers for Pardon of Sins. I.

O JUST and dear God, my sins are innumerable; they are upon my soul in multitudes; they are a burden too heavy for me to bear; they already bring sorrow and sickness, shame and displeasure, guilt and a decaying spirit, a sense of Thy present displeasure, and fear of worse, of infinitely worse. But it is to Thee so essential, so delightful, so usual, so desired by Thee to show mercy, that although my sin be very great, and my fear proportionable, yet Thy mercy is infinitely greater than all the world, and my hope and my comfort rise up in proportions towards it, that I trust the devils shall never be able to reprove it, nor my own weakness discompose it. Lord, Thou hast sent Thy Son to die for the pardon of my sins; Thou hast given me Thy Holy Spirit as a seal of adoption to consign the article of remission of sins; Thou hast, for all my sins, still continued to invite me to conditions of life by Thy ministers the prophets; and Thou hast, with variety of holy acts, softened my spirit and possessed my fancy, and instructed my understanding, and bended and inclined my will, and directed or overruled my passions, in order to repentance and pardon: and why should not Thy servant beg passionately, and humbly hope for, the effects of all these Thy strange and miraculous acts of loving-kindness? Lord, I deserve it not, but I hope Thou will pardon all my sins; and I beg it of Thee, for Jesus Christ's sake, whom Thou hast made the great endearment of Thy promises, and the foundation of our hopes, and the mighty instrument whereby we can obtain of Thee whatsoever we need and can receive.

II.

O MY God, how shall Thy servant be disposed to receive such a favor which is so great that the ever-blessed Jesus did die to purchase it for us; so great that the fallen angels never could hope, and never shall obtain it? Lord, I do from my soul forgive all that have sinned against me; O forgive me my sins, as I forgive them that have sinned against me. Lord, I confess my sins unto Thee daily by the accusations and secret acts of conscience; and if we confess our sins, Thou hast called it a part of justice to forgive us our sins, and to cleanse us from all unrighteousness. Lord, I put my trust in Thee; and Thou art ever gracious to them that put their trust in Thee. I call upon my God for mercy; and Thou art always more ready to hear than we to pray. But all that I can do, and all that I am, and all that I know of myself, is nothing but sin, and infirmity, and misery: therefore I go forth of myself, and throw myself wholly into the arms of Thy mercy through Jesus Christ, and beg of Thee, for His death and passion's sake, by His resurrection and ascension, by all the parts of our redemption, and Thy infinite mercy, in which Thou pleasest Thyself above all the works of the creation, to be pitiful and compassionate to Thy servant in the abolition of all my sins: so shall I praise Thy glories with a tongue not defiled with evil language, and a heart purged by Thy grace, quitted by Thy mercy, and absolved by Thy sentence, from generation to generation. Amen.

On Prayer.

PRAYER is an action of likeness to the Holy Ghost, the spirit of gentleness and dove-like simplicity; an imitation of the holy Jesus, whose spirit is meek, up to the greatness of the biggest example; and a conformity to God, whose anger is always just, and marches slowly, and is without transportation, and often hindered, and never hasty, and is full of mercy: prayer is the peace of our spirit, the stillness of our thoughts, the evenness of recollection, the seat of meditation, the rest of our cares, and the calm of our tempest; prayer is the issue of a quiet mind, of untroubled thoughts; it is the daughter of charity, and the sister of meekness; and he that prays to God with an angry, that is, with a troubled and discomposed spirit, is like him that retires into a battle to meditate, and sets up his closet in the out-quarters of an army, and chooses a frontier-garrison to be wise in. Anger is a perfect alienation of the mind from prayer, and therefore is contrary to that attention which presents our prayers in a right line to God. For so have I seen a lark rising from his bed of grass, and soaring upwards, singing as he rises, and hopes to get to heaven, and climb above the clouds; but the poor bird was beaten back with the loud sighings of an eastern wind, and his motion was made irregular and inconstant, descending more at every breath of the tempest than it could recover by the libration and frequent weighing of his wings, till the little creature was forced to sit down and pant, and stay till the storm was over; and then it made a prosperous flight, and did rise and sing as if it had learned music and motion from an angel, as he passed sometimes through the air about his ministries here below. So is the prayer of a good man, when his affairs have required business, and his business was matter of discipline, and his discipline was to pass upon a sinning person, or had a design of charity, his duties met with the infirmities of a man, and anger was its instrument, and the instrument became stronger than the prime agent, and raised a tempest and overruled the man; and then his prayer was broken and his thoughts were troubled, and his words went up towards a cloud, and his thoughts pulled them back again and made them without intention; and the good man sighs for his infirmity, but must be content to lose the prayer, and he must recover it when his anger is removed and his spirit is becalmed, made even as the brow of Jesus, and smooth like the heart of God; and then it ascends to heaven upon the wings of the holy dove and dwells with God, till it returns, like the useful bee, laden with a blessing and the dew of heaven.

ADVANTAGES OF PRAYER.

PRAYER can obtain everything; it can open the windows of heaven and shut the gates of hell; it can put a holy constraint upon God, and detain an angel till he leave a blessing; it can open the treasures of rain, and soften the iron ribs of rocks till they melt into tears and a flowing river; prayer can unclasp the girdles of the north, saying to a mountain of ice, Be thou removed hence and cast into the bottom of the sea; it can arrest the sun in the midst of his course; and send the swift-winged winds upon our errand, and all those strange things, and secret decrees and unrevealed transactions, which are above the clouds and far beyond the regions of the stars, shall combine in ministry and advantages for the praying man.

The Righteous Safe.

THE righteous is safe; but by intermedial difficulties: and he is safe in the midst of his persecutions; they may disturb his rest and discompose his fancy, but they are like the fiery chariot to Elias; he is encircled with fire, and rare circumstances and strange usages, but is carried up to heaven in a robe of flames. And so was Noah safe when the flood came, and was the great type and instance too of the verification of this proposition; he was put into a strange condition, perpetually wandering, shut up in a prison of wood, living upon faith, having never had the experience of being safe in floods.

And so have I often seen young and unskilful persons sitting in a little boat, when every little wave sporting about the sides of the vessel, and every motion and dancing of the barge seemed a danger and made them cling fast upon their fellows; and yet all the while they were as safe as if they sat under a tree, while a gentle wind shaked the leaves into a refreshment and a cooling shade. And the unskilful, inexperienced Christian shrieks out whenever his vessel shakes, thinking it always a danger that the watery pavement is not stable and resident like a rock; and yet all his danger is in himself, none at all from without; for he is indeed moving upon the waters, but fastened to a rock. Faith is his foundation and hope is his anchor, and death is his harbor, and Christ is his pilot, and heaven is his country; and all the evils of poverty, or affronts of tribunals and evil judges, of fears and sadder apprehensions, are but like the loud wind blowing from the right point: they make a noise and drive faster to the harbor. And if we do not leave the ship and leap into the sea; quit the interests of religion and run to the securities of the world; cut our cables and dissolve our hopes; grow impatient and hug a wave, and die in its embraces, we are as safe at sea, safer in the storm which God sends us, than in a calm when we are befriended with the world.

CONSOLATION.

GOD glories in the appellative that He is the Father of mercies, and the God of all comfort, and therefore to minister in the office is to become like God, and to imitate the charities of heaven; and God hath fitted mankind for it; he most needs it, and he feels his brother's wants by his own experience; and God hath given us speech and the endearments of society, and pleasantness of conversation and powers of seasonable discourse, arguments to allay the sorrow, by abating our apprehensions and taking out the sting, or telling the periods of comfort, or exciting hope, or urging a precept, and reconciling our affections and reciting promises, or telling stories of the divine mercy, or changing it into duty, or making the burden less by comparing it with greater, or by proving it to be less than we deserve, and that it is so intended and may become the instrument of virtue. And certain it is, that as nothing can better do it, so there is nothing greater for which God made our tongues, next to reciting His praises, than to minister comfort to a weary soul. And what greater measure can we have than that we should bring joy to our brother, who with his dreary eyes looks to heaven and round about, and cannot find so much rest as to lay his eyelids close together, than that thy tongue should be tuned with heavenly accents and make the weary soul to listen for light and ease; and when he perceives that there is such a thing in the world, and in the order of things, as comfort and joy, to begin to break out from the prison of his sorrows at the door of sighs and tears, and by little and little melt into showers and refreshment? This is glory to thy voice, and employment fit for the brightest angel.

But so have I seen the sun kiss the frozen earth, which was bound up with the images of death and the colder breath of the north; and then the waters break from their enclosures and melt with joy, and run in useful channels; and the flies do rise again from their little graves in walls, and dance awhile in the air, to tell that there is joy within, and that the great mother of creatures will open the stock of her new refreshment, become useful to mankind, and sing praises to her Redeemer. So is the heart of a sorrowful man under the discourses of a wise comforter; he breaks from the despairs of the grave and the fetters and chains of sorrow, he blesses God, and he blesses thee, and he feels his life returning; for to be miserable is death, but nothing is life but to be comforted; and God is pleased with no music from below so much as in the thanksgiving songs of relieved widows, of supported orphans, of rejoicing and comforted and thankful persons.

This part of communication does the work of God and of our neighbors, and bears us to heaven in streams of joy made by the overflowings of our brother's comfort. It is a fearful thing to see a man despairing. None knows the sorrow and the intolerable anguish but themselves, and they that are damned; and so are all the loads of a wounded spirit, when the staff of a man's broken fortune bows his head to the ground, and sinks like an osier under the violence of a mighty tempest. But therefore in proportion to this I may tell the excellency of the employment and the duty of that charity, which bears the dying and languishing soul from the fringes of hell to the seat of the brightest stars, where God's face shines and reflects comforts forever and ever.

God's Mercy.

HIS mercy is His glory, and His glory is the light of heaven. His mercy is the life of the creation, and it fills all the earth; and His mercy is a sea too, and it fills all the abysses of the deep; it hath given us promises for supply of whatsoever we need, and relieves us in all our fears, and in all the evils that we suffer. His mercies are more than we can tell, and they are more than we can feel. For all the world in the abyss of the divine mercies is like a man diving into the bottom of the sea, over whose head the waters run insensibly and unperceived, and yet the weight is vast and the sum of them is unmeasurable; and the man is not pressed with the burden nor confounded with numbers. And no observation is able to recount, no sense sufficient to perceive, no memory large enough to retain, no understanding great enough to apprehend this infinity; but we must admire and love, and worship and magnify this mercy forever and ever; that we may dwell in what we feel, and be comprehended by that which is equal to God and the parent of all felicity.

The Repenting Sinner.

EVERY sinner that repents causes joy to Christ, and the joy is so great that it runs over and wets the fair brows and beauteous locks of cherubim and seraphim, and all the angels have a part of that banquet; then it is that our blessed Lord feels the fruits of His holy death, the acceptation of His holy sacrifice, the graciousness of His person, the return of His prayers.

ROBERT LEIGHTON, D. D.
1613-1684.

SALVATION.

SALVATION expresses not only that which is negative, but implies likewise positive and perfect happiness; thus forgiveness of sins is put for the whole nature of justification frequently in Scripture. It is more easy to say of this unspeakable happiness, what it is not, than what it is. There is in it a full and final freedom from all annoyance; all tears are wiped away, and their fountain is dried up; all feeling and fear, or danger, of any the least evil, either of sin or punishment, is banished for ever; there are no invasions of enemies, no robbing or destroying in all this holy mountain, no voice of complaining in the streets of the new Jerusalem. Here, it is at the best but interchanges of mornings of joy, with sad evenings of weepings; but there, there shall be no night, no need of sun nor moon, *For the glory of the Lord shall lighten it, and the Lamb shall be the light thereof*, Rev. xxi. 23.

Happy are they who have their eye fixed upon

this salvation, and are longing and waiting for it; who see so much of that brightness and glory, as darkens all the lustre of earthly things to them, and makes them trample upon those things which formerly they admired and doated on with the rest of the foolish world. Those things we account so much of, are but as rotten wood, or glow-worms that shine only in the night of our ignorance and vanity: so soon as the light-beam of this salvation enters into the soul, it cannot much esteem or affect anything below it; and if those glances of it which shine in the word, and in the soul of a Christian, be so bright and powerful, what then shall the full sight and real possession of it be?

Free Grace.

FREE grace being rightly apprehended, is that which stays the heart in all estates, and keeps it from fainting, even in its saddest times. What though there is nothing in myself but matter of sorrow and discomfort, it cannot be otherwise; it is not from myself that I look for comfort at any time, but from my God and His free grace. Here is comfort enough for all times; when I am at the best, I ought not, I dare not, rely upon myself; when I am at the worst, I may, and should rely upon Christ, and His sufficient grace. Though I be the vilest sinner that ever came to Him, yet I know that He is more gracious than I am sinful; yea, the more my sin is, the more glory will it be to His grace to pardon it; it will appear the richer. Doth not David argue thus, Psalm xxv. 11: *For Thy name's sake, O Lord, pardon mine iniquity, for it is very great.*

Redemption the Admiration of Angels.

THE *Word made flesh*, draws the eyes of those glorious spirits, and possesses them with wonder to see the Almighty Godhead joined with the weakness of a man, yea, of an infant. He that stretched forth the heavens bound up in swaddling clothes! and to surpass all the wonders of His life, this is beyond all admiration, that the Lord of Life was subject to death, and that His love to rebellious mankind moved Him both to take on and lay down that life.

It is no wonder the angels admire these things, and delight to look upon them; but it is strange that we do not so. They view them steadfastly, and we neglect them: either we consider them not at all, or give them but a transient look, half an eye. That which was the great business of the prophets and apostles, both for their own times, and to convey them to us, we regard not; and turn our eyes to foolish wandering thoughts, which angels are ashamed at. They are not so concerned in this great mystery as we are; they are but mere beholders, in comparison of us, yea, they seem rather to be losers some way, in that our nature, in itself inferior to theirs, is in Jesus Christ exalted above theirs, Heb. ii. 16. We bow down to the earth, and study, and grovel in it, rake into the very bowels of it, and content ourselves with the outside of the *unsearchable riches of Christ*, and look not within it; but they, having no will nor desire but for the glory of God, being pure flames of fire, burning only in love to Him, are no less delighted than amazed with the bottomless wonders of His wisdom and goodness shining in the work of our redemption.

It is our shame and folly, that we lose ourselves and our thoughts in poor childish things, and trifle away our days we know not how, and let these rich mysteries lie unregarded. They look up upon the Deity in itself with continual admiration; but then they look down to this mystery as another wonder. We give them an ear in public, and in a cold formal way stop conscience's mouth with some religious performances in private, and no more; but to have deep and frequent thoughts and to be ravished in the meditation of our Lord Jesus, once on the cross, and now in glory,—how few of us are acquainted with this!

THE SCRIPTURES.

LET this commend the Scriptures much to our diligence and affection, that their great theme is our Redeemer, and redemption wrought by Him; that they contain the doctrine of His excellences — are the lively picture of His matchless beauty. Were we more in them, we should daily see more of Him in them, and so of necessity love Him more. But we must look within them: the letter is but the case; the spiritual sense is what we should desire to see. We usually huddle them over, and see no further than their outside, and therefore find so little sweetness in them: we read them, but we *search* them not, as He requires. Would we dig into those golden mines, we should find treasures of comfort that cannot be spent, but which would furnish us in the hardest times.

Prayer.

ALL blessings attend this work. It is the richest traffic in the world, for it trades with heaven, and brings home what is most precious there. And as holiness disposes to prayer, so prayer befriends holiness, increases it much. Nothing so refines and purifies the soul as frequent prayer. If the often conversing with wise men doth so teach and advance the soul in wisdom, how much more then will converse with God! This makes the soul despise the things of the world, and in a manner makes it divine; winds up the soul from the earth, acquainting it with delights that are infinitely sweeter.

All the graces of the Spirit are, in prayer, stirred and exercised, and, by exercise, strengthened and increased; faith, in applying the Divine promises, which are the very ground that the soul goes upon to God; Hope looking out to their performance; and Love particularly expressing itself in that sweet converse, and delighting in it, as love doth in the company of the person beloved, thinking all hours too short in speaking with him. Oh, how the soul is refreshed with freedom of speech with its beloved Lord! And as it delights in that, so it is continually advanced and grows by each meeting and conference, beholding the excellency of God, and relishing the pure and sublime pleasures that are to be found in near communion with Him. Looking upon the Father in the face of Christ, and using Him as a mediator in prayer, as still it must, it is drawn to further admiration of that bottomless love which found out that way of agreement, that *new and living way* of our access, when all was shut up, and we must otherwise have been shut out for ever. And then, the affectionate expressions of that reflex love, seeking to find that vent in prayer, do kindle higher, and being as it were fanned and blown up, rise to a greater, and higher, and purer flame, and so tend upward the more strongly. David, as he doth profess his love to God in prayer, in his Psalms, so no doubt it grew in the expressing: *I will love Thee, O Lord my strength*, Psalm xviii. 1. And in Psalm cxvi. 1, he doth raise an incentive of love out of this very consideration of the correspondence of prayer—*I love the Lord because He hath heard;* and he resolves thereafter upon persistence in that course—*therefore will I call upon Him as long as I live*. And as the graces of the Spirit are advanced in prayer by their actings, so for this further reason, because prayer sets the soul particularly near unto God in Jesus Christ. It is then in His presence, and being much with God in this way, it is powerfully assimilated to Him by converse with Him; as we readily contract their habits with whom we have much intercourse, especially if they be such as we singularly love and respect. Thus the soul is moulded further to the likeness of God, is stamped with clearer characters of Him, by being much with Him, becomes more like God, more holy and spiritual, and, like Moses, brings back a bright shining from the mount.

True Rest.

O MY brethren! take heed of sleeping unto death in carnal ease. Resolve to take no rest till you be in the element and place of soul-rest, where solid rest indeed is. Rest not till you be with Christ. Though all the world should offer their best, turn them by with disdain; if they will not be turned by, throw them down, and go over them, and trample upon them. Say, you have no rest to give me, nor will I take any at your hands, nor from any creature. There is no rest for me till I be under His shadow, who endured so much trouble to purchase my rest, and whom having found, I may sit down quiet and satisfied; and when the men of the world make boast of the highest content, I will outvie them all with this one word: *My Beloved is mine, and I am His.*

The Christian Warfare.

THERE is still fighting, and sin will be molesting you; though wounded to death, yet will it struggle for life, and seek to wound its enemy;

it will assault the graces that are in you. Do not think, if it be once struck, and you have given it a stab near to the heart, by the *sword of the Spirit*, that therefore it will stir no more. No, so long as you live in the flesh, in these bowels there will be remainders of the life of this flesh, your natural corruption; therefore you must be armed against it. Sin will not give you rest, so long as there is a drop of blood in its veins, one spark of life in it: and that will be so long as you have life here. This old man is stout, and will fight himself to death; and at the weakest it will rouse up itself, and exert its dying spirits, as men will do sometimes more eagerly than when they were not so weak, nor so near death.

This the children of God often find to their grief, that corruptions which they thought had been cold dead, stir and rise up again, and set upon them. A passion or lust, that after some great stroke lay a long while as dead, stirred not, and therefore they thought to have heard no more of it, though it shall never recover fully again, to be lively as before, yet will revive in such a measure as to molest, and possibly to foil them yet again. Therefore it is continually necessary that they live in arms, and put them not off to their dying day; till they put off the body, and be altogether free of the flesh. You may take the Lord's promise for victory in the end; that shall not fail; but do not promise yourself ease in the way, for that will not hold. If at some times you be undermost, give not all for lost: he hath often won the day, who hath been foiled and wounded in the fight. But likewise take not all for won, so as to have no more conflict, when sometimes you have the better, as in particular battles. Be not desperate when you lose, nor secure when you gain them: when it is worse with you, do not throw away your arms, nor lay them away when you are at best.

Communion with Christ in Suffering.

IT is a sweet, a joyful thing to be a sharer with Christ in anything. All enjoyments wherein He is not, are bitter to a soul that loves Him, and all sufferings with Him are sweet. The worst things of Christ are more truly delightful than the best thing of the world; His afflictions are sweeter than their pleasures, His *reproach* more glorious than their honors, and more rich than their treasures, as Moses accounted them: Heb. xi. 26. Love delights in likeness and communion, not only in things otherwise pleasant, but in the hardest and harshest things, which have not anything in them desirable, but only that likeness. So that this thought is very sweet to a heart possessed with this love: what does the world by its hatred, and persecutions, and revilings for the sake of Christ, but make me more like Him, give me a greater share with Him, in that which He did so willingly undergo for me? *When He was sought for to be made a King*, as St. Bernard remarks, *He escaped; but when He was sought to be brought to the cross, He freely yielded Himself.* And shall I shrink and creep back from what He calls me to suffer for His sake! Yea, even all my other troubles and sufferings, I will desire to have stamped thus, with this conformity to the sufferings of Christ, in the humble, obedient, cheerful endurance of them, and the giving up my will to my Father's.

The following of Christ makes any way pleasant. His faithful followers refuse no march after Him, be it through deserts, and mountains and storms, and hazards, that will affright self-pleasing, easy spirits. Hearts kindled and actuated with the Spirit of Christ, will *follow Him wheresoever He goeth.*

THE BELIEVER'S JOY AT THE REVELATION OF CHRIST.

H*E shall be revealed in His glory*, and ye shall even overflow with joy in the partaking of that glory. Therefore, rejoice now in the midst of all your sufferings. Stand upon the advanced ground of the promises and the covenant of grace, and by faith look beyond this moment, and all that is in it, to that day wherein *everlasting joy shall be upon your heads*, a crown of it, and *sorrow and mourning shall flee away:* Isa. li. 11. Believe in this day, and the victory is won. Oh! that blessed hope, well fixed and exercised, would give other manner of spirits. What zeal for God would it not inspire! What invincible courage against all encounters! How soon will this pageant of the world vanish, that men are gazing on, these pictures and fancies of pleasures and honors, falsely so called, and give place to the real glory of the sons of God, when this blessed Son, who is God, shall be seen appearing in full majesty, and all His brethren in glory with Him, all clothed in their robes! And if you ask, who are they, why, *these are they who came out of great tribulation, and have washed their robes in the blood of the Lamb:* Rev. vii. 14.

Glory of Christ at the last Day.

THE world sees nothing of His glory and beauty, and even His own see not much; they have but a little glimmering of Him, and of their own happiness in Him; know little of their own high condition, and what they are born to. But in that bright day, He shall shine forth in His royal dignity, and *every eye shall see Him*, and be overcome with His splendor. Terrible shall it be to those that formerly despised Him and His saints, but to them it shall be the gladest day that ever arose upon them, a day that shall never set or be benighted; the day they so much longed and looked out for, the full accomplishment of all their hopes and desires. Oh, how dark were all our days without the hope of this day!

Steadfastness in the Faith.

WHEN the soul is surrounded with enemies on all hands, so that there is no way of escape, faith flies above them, and carries up the soul to take refuge in Christ, and is there safe. That is the power of faith; it sets a soul in Christ, and there it looks down upon all temptations as at the bottom of the rock, breaking themselves into foam. When the floods of temptation rise and gather, so great and so many, that the soul is even ready to be swallowed up, then, by faith, it says, Lord Jesus, Thou art my strength, I look to Thee for deliverance; now appear for my help! And thus it overcomes. The guilt of sin is answered by His blood, the power of sin is conquered by His Spirit; and afflictions that arise are nothing to these: His love and gracious presence make them sweet and easy.

Eternal Glory.

OH, that blessed day when the soul shall be full of God, shall be satisfied and ravished with full vision! Should we not admire that such a condition is provided for man, wretched, sinful man? *Lord, what is man, that Thou art mindful of him, and the son of man, that Thou visitest him:* Psalm viii. 3. And is it provided for me, as wretched as any who are left and fallen short of this glory, a base worm taken out of the mire, and washed in the blood of Christ, and within a while set to shine in glory without sin? Oh, the wonder of this! How should it excite us to praise, when we think of such a One there, who will bring us up in the way to this crown! How will this hope sweeten the short sufferings of this life! And death itself, which is otherwise the bitterest in itself, is most of all sweetened by this, as being nearest it, and setting us into it. What though thou art poor, diseased, and despised here? Oh, consider what is there, how worthy the affection, worthy the earnest eye and fixed look of an heir of this glory! What can he either desire or fear, whose heart is thus deeply fixed? Who would refuse this other clause, *to suffer awhile,* a little while, anything outward or inward .which He thinks fit? How soon shall all this be overpast, and then overpaid in the very entry, at the beginning of this glory that shall never end.

MEDITATION ON THE EIGHTH PSALM.

OH, how strong and large that Hand, which without help expands the heavens as a curtain! Look up and see, consider their height and roundness, such a glorious canopy set with such sparkling diamonds: then think how swift their motion, and yet imperceivable to us, no motion here below comparable, and yet they seem not to stir at all. And in all, their great Lord and ours so conspicuous! And yet who looks on them with such an eye as to behold Him, as David here, *When I consider Thy heavens, the work,* &c.! He is admirable in all: the very lowest and smallest creatures have their wonders of Divine wisdom in their frame, more than we are able to think, *Magnus in minimis:* He is great in the least of His works. The smallest flies, how strange the fashioning of the organs of life and use in so little room! The man who is still in search of wisdom will find a school and a lesson in all places, and see everywhere the greatness and goodness of his God! If he walk forth in the evening, when this lower world is clothed with the dark mantle of the night, yet still he can look upward to the pavement of the throne of God, and think how glorious it is on the other side, when the moon and stars make this side, even in the night so beautiful. And this of David's, looks like a night meditation by the view of moon and stars. *Thy heavens*, these Thy works so glorious—Thou, therefore, infinitely more glorious; then can I not but increase in wonder, that, dwelling above these heavens, Thou regardest so poor a worm as man creeping on this earth.

Spiritual Desire of Death.

THERE is a spiritual desire of death, which is very becoming a Christian. For Jesus Christ hath not only opened very clearly the doctrine of eternal life, but He Himself hath passed through death, and lain down in the grave: He hath perfumed that passage, and warmed that bed for us; so that it is sweet and amiable for a Christian to pass through and follow Him, and to be where He is. It is a strange thing, that the souls of Christians have not a continual desire to go to that company which is above (finding so much discord and disagreement among the best of men that are here); to go to *the spirits of just men made perfect*, where there is light, and love, and nothing else; to go *to the company of angels*, a higher rank of blessed spirits; but, most of all to go to *God, and to Jesus the Mediator of the New Testament*. And to say nothing positively of that glory (for the truth is, we can say nothing of it), the very evils that death delivers the true Christian from, may make him long for it; for such a one may say—I shall die, and go to a more excellent country, where I shall be happy for ever: that is, I shall die no more, I shall sorrow no more, I shall be sick no more, and, which is yet more considerable, I shall doubt no more, and shall be tempted no more; and, which is the chiefest of all, I shall sin no more.

Come to the Saviour.

THIS is the great comfort of sinners, this word: *I came to call not the righteous, but sinners.* What can a diffident heart say, that it should not come to Jesus Christ? Art thou a sinner, an eminent sinner? Therefore come to Him, for He came to thee. It is such that He comes to seek— they are the very objects of His grace. He had nothing else to do in the world but to save such; He came on purpose for their sakes. His very name tells it: *He shall be called Jesus, for He shall save His people from their sins.* It is so far from being a just hinderance, that it is the only title to His favorable intentions, that thou art a sinner. Were it not strange if one should say, I am sick, very sick, therefore I will not make an address to the physician? And to say, I am a sinner, and a great one, therefore I dare not go to the Saviour of sinners, would be equally strange. Oh, no; therefore I will go: He came for me; I am sure He is able to heal me—ought to be the language of all such.

Christ the Light of the Christian.

THE Christian that is truly acquainted with Him, enamored with the brightness of His beauty, can generously trample upon the smilings of the world with one foot, and upon her frownings with the other. If he be rich or honorable, or both, yet he glories not in that, but Christ, who *is the glory of the Lord*, is even then his chiefest glory; and the light of Christ obscures that worldly splendor in his estimation. And as the enjoyment of Christ overtops all his other joys, so it overcomes his griefs. As that great light drowns the light of prosperity, so it shines bright in the darkness of affliction: no dungeon so close that it can keep out the rays of Christ's love from his beloved prisoners. The world can no more take away this light, than it can give it.

Happiness of the Life to Come.

WHAT are these things, the false glare and shadows whereof, in this earth, are pursued with such keen and furious impetuosity—riches, honors, pleasures? All these, in their justest, purest, and sublimest sense, are comprehended in this blessed life: it is *a treasure*, that can neither fail nor be carried away by force or fraud: it is *an inheritance* uncorrupted and undefiled, *a crown* that fadeth not away; a never-failing stream of joy and delight: it is a marriage feast, and of all others the most joyous and most sumptuous; one that always satisfies, and never cloys the appetite: it is an eternal spring, and an everlasting light, a day without an evening: it is a paradise, where the lilies are always white and in full bloom, the saffron blooming, the trees sweat out their balsams, and the tree of life in the midst thereof: it is a city, where the houses are built of living pearls, the gates of precious stones, and the streets paved with the purest gold. Yet, all these are nothing but veils of the happiness to be revealed on that most blessed day: nay, the light itself, which we have mentioned among the rest though it be the most beautiful ornament in this visible world, is at best but a shadow of that heavenly glory; and how small soever that portion of this inaccessible brightness may be, which, in the sacred Scriptures, shines upon us through these veils, it certainly very well deserves that we should often turn our eyes toward it, and view it with the closest attention.

Now, the first that necessarily occurs in the constitution of happiness, is a full and complete deliverance from every evil and every grievance; which we may as certainly expect to meet with in that heavenly life, as it is impossible to be attained while we sojourn here below. All tears shall be wiped away from our eyes, and every cause and occasion of tears for ever removed from our sight. There, there are no tumults, no wars, no poverty, no death, nor disease; there, there is neither mourning, nor fear, nor sin, which is the source and fountain of all other evils: there is neither violence within doors nor without, nor any complaint, in the streets of that blessed city. There, no friend goes out, nor enemy comes in.

Full vigor of body and mind, health, beauty, purity, and perfect tranquillity.

The most delightful society of angels, prophets, apostles, martyrs, and all the saints; among whom there are no reproaches, contentions, controversies, nor party-spirit, because there are there none of the sources whence they can spring, nor anything to encourage their growth; for there is there, particularly, no ignorance, no blind self-love, no vain-glory nor envy, which is quite excluded from those divine regions; but, on the contrary, perfect charity, whereby every one, together with his own felicity, enjoys that of his neighbors, and is happy in the one as well as the other: hence there is among them a kind of infinite reflection and multiplication of happiness, like that of a spacious hall adorned with gold and precious stones, dignified with a full assembly of kings and potentates, and having its walls quite covered with the brightest looking-glasses.

But what infinitely exceeds, and quite eclipses all the rest, is that boundless ocean of happiness, which results from the beatific vision of the ever-blessed God, without which, neither the tranquillity they enjoy, nor the society of saints, nor the possession of any particular finite good, nor indeed of all such taken together, can satisfy the soul, or make it completely happy.

Prayers. I.

PRAISE waits for Thee, O Lord, in Zion; and to be employed in paying Thee that tribute is a becoming and pleasant exercise. It is due to Thee from all the works of Thy hands, but particularly proper from Thy saints and celestial spirits. Elevate, O Lord, our minds, that they may not grovel on the earth, and plunge themselves in the mire; but, being carried upward, may taste the pleasures of Thy house, that exalted house of Thine, the inhabitants whereof are continually singing Thy praises. Their praises add nothing to Thee; but they themselves are perfectly happy therein, while they behold Thy boundless goodness without any veil, admire Thy uncreated beauty, and celebrate the praises thereof throughout all ages. Grant us, that we may walk in the paths of holiness, and, according to our measure, exalt Thy name even on this earth, until we also be translated into the glorious assembly of those who serve Thee in Thy higher house.

Remember Thy goodness and Thy covenant to Thy church militant upon this earth, and exposed to dangers amid so many enemies; yet we believe that, notwithstanding all these dangers, it will be safe at last: it may be distressed, and plunged in the waters, but it cannot be quite overwhelmed, or finally perish. We depend upon Thee, O Father, without whose hand we should not have been, and without whose favor we can never be happy. Inspire our hearts with gladness, Thou who alone art the fountain of solid, pure, and permanent joy; and lead us, by the paths of righteousness and grace, to the rest and light of glory, for the sake of Thy Son, our Redeemer, Jesus Christ. Amen.

II.

O INVISIBLE God, who seest all things! Eternal Light, before whom all darkness is light, and in comparison with whom every other light is but darkness! The weak eyes of our understanding cannot bear the open and full rays of Thy inaccessible light; and yet, without some glimpses of that light from heaven, we can never direct our steps, nor proceed toward that country which is the habitation of light. May it therefore please Thee, O Father of Lights, to send forth Thy light and Thy truth, that they may lead us directly to Thy holy mountain. Thou art good, and the Fountain of goodness; give us understanding, that we may keep Thy precepts. That part of our past lives, which we have lost in pursuing shadows, is enough, and, indeed, too much: bring back our souls into the paths of life, and let the wonderful sweetness thereof, which far exceeds all the pleasures of this earth, powerfully, yet pleasantly, preserve us from being drawn aside therefrom by any temptation from sin or the world. Purify, we pray Thee, our souls from all impure imaginations, that Thy most beautiful and holy image may be again renewed within us, and, by contemplating Thy glorious perfections, we may feel daily improved within us that Divine similitude, the perfection whereof we hope will at last make us for ever happy in that full and beatific vision we aspire after. Till this most blessed day break, and the shadows fly away, let Thy Spirit be continually with us, and may we feel the powerful effects of His Divine grace constantly directing and supporting our steps; that all our endeavors, not only in this society, but throughout the whole remaining part of our lives, may serve to promote the honor of Thy blessed name, through Jesus Christ our Lord. Amen.

III.

MOST exalted God, who hast alone created, and dost govern this whole frame, and all the inhabitants thereof, visible and invisible, whose name is alone Wonderful, and to be celebrated with the highest praise, as it is indeed above all praise and admiration. Let the heavens, the earth, and all the elements praise Thee. Let darkness, light, all the returns of days and years, and all the varieties and vicissitudes of things, praise Thee. Let the angels praise Thee, the archangels, and all the blessed court of heaven, whose very happiness it is, that they are constantly employed in celebrating Thy praises. We confess, O Lord, that we are of all creatures the most unworthy to praise Thee, yet, of all others, we are under the greatest obligations to do it: nay, the more unworthy we are, our obligation is so much the greater. From this duty, however unqualified we may be, we can by no means abstain, nor, indeed, ought we. Let our souls bless Thee, and all that is within us praise Thy holy name, who forgivest all our sins, and healest all our diseases: who deliverest our souls from destruction, and crownest them with bounty and tender mercies. Thou searchest the heart, O Lord, and perfectly knowest the most intimate recesses of it: reject not those prayers which Thou perceivest to be the voice and the wishes of the heart. Now, it is the great request of our hearts, unless they always deceive us, that they may be weaned from all earthly and perishing enjoyments; and if there is anything to which they cleave with more than ordinary force, may they be pulled away from it by Thy Almighty hand, that they may be joined to Thee for ever in an inseparable marriage-covenant. And in our own behalf, we have nothing more to ask. We only add, in behalf of Thy church, that it may be protected under the shadow of Thy wings, and everywhere, throughout the world, watered by Thy heavenly dew, that the spirit and heat of worldly hatred against it may be cooled, and its intestine divisions, whereby it is much more grievously scorched, extinguished. Amen.

IV.

ETERNAL God, who art constantly adored by thrones and powers, by seraphim and cherubim, we confess that Thou art most worthy to be praised; but we, of all others, are the most unworthy to be employed in showing forth Thy praise.

How can polluted bodies, and impure souls, which, taken together, are nothing but mere sinks of sin, praise Thee, the pure and holy Majesty of heaven? Yet, how can these bodies which Thou hast wonderfully formed, and these souls which Thou hast inspired, which owe entirely to Thine unmerited favor all that they are, all that they possess, and all they hope for, forbear praising Thee, their wise and bountiful Creator and Father? Let our souls, therefore, and all that is within us, bless Thy holy name: yea, let all our bones say, O Lord, who is like unto Thee, who is like unto Thee? Far be it, most gracious Father, from our hearts, to harbor anything that is displeasing to Thee; let them be, as it were, temples dedicated to Thy service, thoroughly purged from every idol and image, from every object of impure love and earthly affection. Let our most gracious King and Redeemer dwell and reign within us. May He take full possession of us by His Spirit, and govern all our actions. May He extend His peaceable and saving kingdom throughout the whole habitable world, from the rising of the sun to the going down thereof. Amen.

V.

INFINITE and Eternal God, who inhabitest thick darkness and light inaccessible, whom no mortal hath seen, or can see; yet all Thy works evidently declare and proclaim Thy wisdom, Thy power, and Thy infinite goodness: and when we contemplate these Thy perfections, what is it our souls can desire but that they may love Thee, worship Thee, serve Thee, for ever proclaim Thy praise, and celebrate Thy exalted name, which is above all praises and all admiration? Thy throne is constantly surrounded by thousands and ten thousands of glorified spirits, who continually adore Thee and cry out without ceasing, *Holy, holy, holy, Lord God Almighty, who was, who is, and who is to come.* Let others seek what they will, and find and embrace what they can; may we have always this one fixed and settled purpose, that it is good for us to draw near to God. Let the seas roar, the earth be shaken, and all things go to ruin and confusion; yet, the soul that adheres to God will remain safe and quiet, and shall not be moved for ever. O blessed soul that has Thee for its rest, and all its salvation! It shall be like a tree planted by the rivers of water; it shall not fear when heat cometh, nor shall it be uneasy in a year of drought. It is our earnest petition and prayer, O Father, that Thy hands may loosen all our chains, and effectually deliver our souls from all the snares and allurements of the world and the flesh; and that, by that same bountiful and most powerful hand of Thine, they may be for ever united to Thee through Thy only begotten Son, who is our union and our peace. Amen.

VI.

HONOR and praise is due to Thee, O infinite God. This is the universal voice of all the blessed spirits on high, and all the saints on earth:

worthy art Thou, O Lord, to receive glory, and honor, and power, because Thou hast created all things, and for Thy pleasure they are. We, here before Thee, with united hearts and affections offer Thee, as we can, the sacrifice of gratitude, love and praise. How much are we indebted to Thee, for ourselves, and for all that we possess! For in Thee we live, move, and have our being. Thou hast redeemed us from our sins, having given us the Son of Thy love as a sacrifice and ransom for our souls: the chastisement of our peace fell upon Him, and by His stripes we are healed. On this consideration, we acknowledge we are no longer at our own disposal, since we are bought with a price, and so very great a price, that we may glorify Thee, O Father, and Thy Son, in our souls and our bodies, which are so justly Thine. May we devote ourselves to Thee through the whole remaining part of our life, and disdain the impure and ignoble slavery of sin, the world and the flesh, that in all things we may demean ourselves as becomes the sons of God, and the heirs of Thy celestial kingdom, and make daily greater progress in our journey toward the happy possession thereof. Amen.

VII.

ETERNAL Father of mercies and of lights, the only rest of the immortal souls which Thou hast created, and their never-failing consolation. Into what by-paths of error do our souls divert, and to what dangers are they exposed on every hand, when they stray away from Thee! But while they keep within Thy hiding-place, O Most High, they are safe under the shadow of Thy wings. O how happy are they, and how well do they live, who pass their whole lives in that secret abode, where they may continually refresh themselves with the delicious fruits of Thy love, and show forth Thy praise! where they may taste and see that Thou art good, O Lord, and be thoroughly persuaded of the immense riches of Thy bounty, which all our miseries cannot exceed, nor our poverty exhaust; nay, which the constant effusion of them upon the whole universe, and all its parts, cannot in the least diminish. As for us who are before Thee, the most unworthy of all Thy creatures, yet, at the same time, the most excessively loaded with all the instances of Thy goodness, can we avoid crying out with the united voices of our hearts, Let praise be ascribed to the Lord, because He is good, and His mercy endureth for ever. Who shall declare the great and wonderful works of God? Who shall show forth His praise? Who ruleth by His power for ever, and His eyes observe the nations, that the rebellious may not exalt themselves. Who restores our souls to life, and suffers not our feet to be moved. But, on the other hand, alas! how justly may our songs be interrupted with bitter lamentations, that under such strong and constant rays of His bounty, our hearts are so cold toward Him! O how faint and languid is our love to Him! How very little, or near to nothing, is the whole of that flame which we feel within us! And, as that love fails within us, we misplace our affections upon the things around us; and, as we follow vanity, we become vain and miserable at the same time. But may Thy Spirit, O Lord, whom we humbly and earnestly beg of Thee, descending into our hearts, inspire us thoroughly with life, vigor, and celestial purity! Amen.

VIII.

WHATEVER satisfaction we look for without Thee, O heavenly Father, is mere delusion and vanity. Yet, though we have so often experienced this, we have not, to this day, learned to renounce this vain and fruitless labor, that we may depend upon Thee, who alone canst give full and complete satisfaction to the souls of men. We pray, therefore, that, by Thy Almighty hand, Thou wouldst so effectually join and unite our hearts to Thee, that they may never be separated any more. How unhappy are they who forsake Thee, and whose hearts depart from Thy ways! They shall be like shrubs in the desert; they shall not see when good cometh, but dwell in a parched and barren land. Blessed, on the contrary, is he who hath placed his confidence in Thee: he shall be like a tree planted by the rivers of water: he shall not be afraid when heat cometh, nor be uneasy in the time of drought. Take from us, O Lord, whatever earthly enjoyments Thou shalt think proper: there is one thing will abundantly make up all our losses; let Christ dwell in our hearts by faith, and the rays of Thy favor continually refresh us in the face of Thine anointed: in this event, we have nothing to ask, but with grateful minds shall for ever celebrate Thy bounty, and all our bones shall say, 'Who is like unto Thee, O Lord, who is like unto Thee?' Amen.

RICHARD BAXTER.
1615-1691.

Walking with God.

A HAPPY man, that walks with God, though neglected and contemned by all about him! What blessed sights doth he daily see? What ravishing tidings, what pleasant melody, doth he daily hear, unless it be in his swoons or sickness! What delectable food doth he daily taste! He seeth by faith the God, the glory, which the blessed spirits see at hand by nearest intuition! He seeth that in a glass, and darkly, which they behold with open face! He seeth the glorious majesty of his Creator, the eternal King, the cause of causes, the composer, upholder, preserver, and governor of all the worlds! He beholdeth the wonderful methods of His providence; and what he cannot reach to see, he admireth, and waiteth for the time when that also shall be open to his view! He seeth by faith the world of spirits, the hosts that attend the throne of God; their perfect righteousness, their full devotedness to God; their ardent love, their flaming zeal, their ready and cheerful obedience, their dignity and shining glory, in which the lowest of them exceedeth that which the disciples saw on Moses and Elias when they appeared on the holy mount, and talked with Christ! They hear by faith the heavenly concert, the high and harmonious songs of praise, the joyful triumphs of crowned saints, the sweet commemorations of the things which were done and suffered on earth, with the praises of Him that redeemed them by His blood, and made them kings and priests to God: herein he hath sometimes a sweet foretaste of the everlasting pleasures, which though it be but little, as Jonathan's honey on the end of his rod, or as the clusters of grapes which were brought from Canaan into the wilderness, yet are they more excellent than all the delights of sinners. And in the beholding of this celestial glory, some beams do penetrate his breast, and so irradiate his longing soul, that he is changed thereby into the same image, from glory to glory; the Spirit of glory and of God doth rest upon him. And, oh! what an excellent holy frame doth this converse with God possess his soul of! How reverently doth he think of Him! What life is there in every name and attribute of God, which he heareth or thinketh on! The mention of His power, His wisdom, His goodness, His love, His holiness, His truth, how powerful and how pleasant are they to him! when to those that know Him but by the hearing of the ear, all these are but like common names and notions; and even to the weaker sort of Christians, whose walking with God is more uneven, and low, interrupted by their sins, and doubts, and fears, this life and glory of a Christian course is less perceived.*

Prayer in the Hour of Death.

PRAYER in general, and this prayer in particular, that Christ will receive our departing souls, is a most suitable conclusion of all the actions of a Christian's life.

Prayer is the breath of a Christian's life: it is his work and highest converse, and therefore fittest to be the concluding action of his life, that it may reach the end at which he aimed. We have need of prayer all our lives, because we have need of God, and need of His manifold and continued grace. But in our last extremity we have a special need. Though sloth is apt to seize upon us, while prosperity hindereth the sense of our necessities, and health persuadeth us that time is not near its journey's end, yet it is high time to pray with redoubled fervor and importunity when we see that we are near our last. When we find that we have no more time to pray, but must now speak our last for our immortal souls, and must at once say all that we have to say, and shall never have a hearing more. Oh, then, to be unable to pray, or to be faithless and heartless and

* This beautiful passage on walking with God is conceived in the noblest spirit of hallowed eloquence, and is a fine illustration of the intense ardor of Baxter's mind, the vividness of his imagination, and the deep spiritnality of his feelings. It may be specified as one of the sublimest passages in his practical works; and it has been well remarked, that 'it would be difficult to find a nobler passage in the whole compass of devotional writing.'

hopeless in our prayers, would be a calamity beyond expression.

It is not a work that you were never used to, though you have had lamented backwardness and coldness, and omissions. It is not to a God that you were never with before; as you know whom you have believed, so you may know to whom you pray. It is indeed a most important suit to beg for the receiving of a departing soul; but it is put up to Him to whom it properly doth belong, and to Him that hath encouraged you by answering many a former prayer with that mercy which was the earnest of this, and it is to Him that loveth souls much better than any soul can love itself. O live in prayer, and die in prayer, and do not, as the graceless, witless world, despise prayer while they live, and then think, a Lord have mercy on me, shall prove enough to pass them into heaven. O pray, and wait but a little longer, and all your danger will be past, and you are safe forever! Keep up your hands a little longer, till you shall end your conflict with the last enemy, and shall pass from prayer to everlasting praise.

Language and Power of Faith.

IT is faith which overcometh the world and the flesh, which must also overcome the fears of death, and can look with boldness into the loathsome grave, and can triumph over both as victorious through Christ. It is faith which can say, Go forth, O my soul; depart in peace; thy course is finished; thy warfare is accomplished; the day of triumph is now at hand; thy patience hath no longer work; go forth with joy; the morning of thy endless joys is near; and the night of fears and darkness at an end. Thy terrible dreams are ending in eternal pleasures; the glorious light will banish all thy dreadful spectres, and resolve all those doubts which were bred and cherished in the dark. They whose employment is their weariness and toil, do take the night of darkness and cessation for their rest; but this is their weariness: defect of action is thy toil; and thy most grievous labor is to do too little work; and thy incessant vision, love, and praise, will be thy incessant ease and pleasure; and thy endless work will be thy endless rest! Depart, O my soul, with peace and gladness! Thou leavest not a world where wisdom and piety, justice and sobriety, love and peace, and order do prevail; but a world of ignorance and folly, of brutish sensuality and rage, of impiety and malignant enmity to good; a world of injustice and oppression, and of confusion and distracting strifes!

Thou goest not from heaven to earth, from holiness to sin, from the sight of God into an infernal dungeon; but from earth to heaven, from sin and imperfection unto perfect holiness, and from palpable darkness into the vital splendor of the face of God! Thou goest not among enemies, but to dearest friends; not amongst mere strangers, but to many whom thou hast known by sight, and to more whom thou hast known by faith, and must know by the sweetest communion for ever. Thou goest not to unsatisfied justice, nor to a condemning, unreconciled God; but to love itself, to infinite goodness, the fountain of all created and communicated good; to the Maker, Redeemer, and Sanctifier of souls; to Him who prepared heaven for thee, and now hath prepared thee for heaven. Go forth then in triumph, and not with terror, O my soul! The prize is won: possess the things which thou hast so long prayed for, and sought! Make haste and enter into thy Master's joy! Go view the glory which thou hast so long heard of; and take thy place in the heavenly choir; and bear thy part in their celestial melody! Sit down with Abraham, Isaac, and Jacob, in the kingdom of God; and receive that which Christ in His covenant did promise to give thee at the last. Go boldly to that blessed God, with whom thou hast so powerful a Mediator, and to the throne of whose grace thou hast had so oft and sweet access.

Second Coming of Christ.

O BLESSED day, when our blessed Head shall be revealed from heaven with His mighty angels, and shall come to be glorified in His saints and admired in all them that now believe; whose weakness here occasioned His dishonor and their own contempt! When the seed of grace is grown up into glory, and all the world, whether they will or not, shall discern between the righteous and the wicked, between him that serveth God and him that serveth Him not; between the clean and the unclean, and between him that sweareth and him that feareth an oath. And though now 'our life is hid with Christ in God,' and it yet 'appeareth not (to the sight of ourselves or others) what we shall be; yet then when Christ who is our life shall appear, we also shall appear with Him in glory.' 'Away then, my soul, from this dark, deceitful and vexatious world! Love not thy diseases, thy fetters and calamities. Groan daily to thy Lord, and earnestly groan to be clothed upon with thy house that is from heaven: 2 Cor. v. 2, 4: that mortality may be swallowed up of life! Join in the harmonious desires of the creatures, who groan to be delivered from the bondage of corruption, into the glorious liberty of the sons of God: Rom. viii. 20–22. 'Abide in Him and walk in righteousness; that, when He shall appear, thou mayest have confidence and not be ashamed before Him at His coming.'

O watch and pray that thou enter not into temptation! and be patient for the Judge is at the door! Lift up thy head with earnest expectation, O my soul, for thy redemption draweth near! Rejoice in hope before thy Lord, for He cometh; He cometh to judge the world in righteousness and truth. Behold, He cometh quickly, though faith be failing and iniquity abound, and love waxeth cold and scoffers say, Where is the promise of His coming? Make haste, O Thou whom my soul desireth, and come in glory as Thou first camest in humility, and conform them to Thyself in glory whom Thou madest conformable to Thy sufferings and humility! Let the holy city, new Jerusalem, be prepared as a bride adorned for her husband; and let God's tabernacle be with men, that He may dwell with them and be their God, and wipe away their tears; and death and sorrow, and crying and pain may be no more, but former things may pass away! Keep up our faith, our hope, our love, and daily vouchsafe us some beams of Thy directing, consolatory light in this our darkness, and be not as a stranger to Thy scattered flock in this desolate wilderness. But let them hear Thy voice and find Thy presence, and have such conversation with Thee in heaven, in the exercise of faith, and hope, and love, which is agreeable to their low and distant state. Testify to their souls that Thou art their Saviour and Head, and that they abide in Thee, by the Spirit which Thou hast given them, abiding and overcoming in them, and as Thy agent preparing them for eternal life. O let not our darkness nor Thy strangeness feed our odious unbelief! O show Thyself more clearly to Thy redeemed ones! And come and dwell in our hearts by faith! And by holy love let us dwell in God, and God in us, that we grope not after Him, as those that worship an unknown God. O save us from temptation! And if the messenger of Satan be sent to buffet us, let Thy strength be manifest in our weakness, and Thy grace appear sufficient for us. And give us the patience which Thou tellest us we need, that having done Thy will we may inherit the promise. And bring us to the sight and fruition of our Creator, of whom, and through whom, and to whom are all things; to whom be glory forever. Amen.

The Saints' Joy.

JOY is itself a part of the holy qualification of the saints, and of the renewed state that grace hath brought them into. 'For the kingdom of God, as it consisteth in righteousness, so in peace and joy in the Holy Ghost,' Rom. xiv. 17. Believers 'receive not the spirit of bondage again to fear;' that is, they are not under the bondage of the law, nor have the spirit or state of mind which is suited to those legal impositions and terrible comminations: but they 'have received the spirit of adoption by which they cry, Abba, Father;' that is, as they are brought under a more gracious dispensation, and a better covenant and promises, and God is revealed to them in the gospel as a reconciled Father through His Son, so doth He treat them more gently as reconciled children, and the spirit which answereth this gracious covenant, and is given us thereupon, doth qualify us with a child-like disposition, and cause us with boldness, love, and confidence to call God Father, and fly to Him for succor and supply in all our dangers and necessities. And how pleasant it must be to a believing soul, to have this spirit of adoption, this child-like love and confidence and freedom with the Lord, methinks you might conjecture, though it is sensibly known by them only that enjoy it: Gal. v. 22, 'The fruit of the Spirit is love, joy, peace,' &c. When the word is first received by believers, though it may be in much affliction, through the persecutions and cross that attend the gospel, yet is it ordinarily 'in the joy of the Holy Ghost,' 1 Thess. i. 6. The Holy Ghost is the comforter of true believers; and if He have taken it upon Him as His work He will surely do it, in the degree and season fittest for them. And if joy itself be part of the state of grace and holiness, you may see that is the most delightful, pleasant course.

O blessed life! where all that is against us is forbidden, and all that is truly joyous and delightful and necessary to make us happy, is commanded us and made our duty; which is contrary to misery as life to death, and as light to darkness. Come hither, poor deluded sinners that fly from care, and fear and sorrow. If you will but give up yourselves to Christ you shall be exempted from all these, except such as is necessary to your joy. You may do anything, if you will be the servants of the Lord, except that which tendeth to your own and other men's calamity. Come hither, all you that call for pleasure, and love no life but a life of mirth. Let God be your Master and holiness your work, and pleasure then shall be your business and holy mirth shall be your employment. While you serve the flesh your pleasure is small and your trouble great; vexation is your work and unspeakable vexation is your wages. But if you will be the hearty servants of the Lord, rejoicing shall be your work and wages. If you understand not this, peruse your lesson, Psalm xxxiii. 1: 'Rejoice in the Lord, O ye righteous, for praise is comely for the upright.' 'Light is sown for the righteous and gladness for the upright in heart. Rejoice in the Lord, ye righteous; and give thanks at the remembrance of His holiness,' Psalm xcvii. 11, 12. 'Let all those that trust in Thee rejoice: let them ever shout for joy, because Thou defendest them: let them also that love Thy name be joyful in Thee.' Phil. iii. 1; Psalm v. 11. 'Be glad in the Lord and rejoice ye righteous, and shout for joy all ye that are upright in heart,' Psalm xxxii. 11. 'Let Thy priests be clothed with righteousness, and let Thy saints shout for joy,' Psalm cxxxii. 9. 'I will also clothe her priests with salvation; and her saints shall shout aloud for joy,' ver. 16. Such precepts and promises abound in Scripture, which tell you, if you will be saints indeed, that joy and gladness must be your life and work.

The Word of God.

HOW sweet is it to be exercised in the Word of God! in hearing or reading it with serious meditation! for the man that hath been revived by it, renewed, sanctified, saved by it, to hear that powerful, heavenly truth, by which his soul was thus made new! for the soul that is in love with God, to hear or see His blessed name on every leaf! To read His will, and find the expressions of His love, His great, eternal, wondrous love; how sweet this is, experience tells the saints that feel it. If you that feel no sweetness in it, believe not them that say they feel it, at least believe the word of God and the professions of His ancient saints. 'Oh how I love Thy law! it is my meditation all the day. How sweet are Thy words unto my taste! yea, sweeter than the honey and the honeycomb. I have rejoiced in the way of Thy testimonies as in all riches. I will delight myself in Thy statutes: I will not forget Thy word. Thy testimonies are my delight and my counsellors. I will delight myself in Thy commandments which I have loved, and I will meditate in Thy statutes. The law of Thy mouth is better to me than thousands of gold and silver. Unless Thy law had been my delight, I had perished in my affliction. I will never forget Thy precepts, for with them Thou hast quickened me. Thy testimonies have I taken as an heritage for ever: for they are the rejoicing of my heart. I love Thy commandments above gold, yea, above fine gold. I rejoice at Thy word as one that findeth great spoil. Great peace have they that love Thy law, and nothing shall offend them.

Love of God.

THE love of God is so sweet an exercise, that verily, my soul had rather be employed in it with sense and vigor, than to be lord of all the earth. Oh could I but be taken up with the love of God, how easily could I spare the pleasure of the flesh! Might I but see the loveliness of my dear Creator with a clearer view, and see His glory in His noble works; might I but see and feel that saving love which He hath manifested in the Redeemer, till my soul were ravished and filled with His love, how little should I care who had the pleasures of this deceitful world! Had I more of that blessed spirit of adoption, and more of those filial affections to my heavenly Father, which His unutterable love bespeaks; and were I more sensible of His abundant mercy, and did my soul but breathe and long after Him more earnestly, I would pity the miserable tyrants of the world, that are worse than beggars while they domineer, and taste not of that kingdom of love and pleasure that dwelleth in my breast. All the pleasures of the world are the laughing of a madman, or the sports of a child, or the dreams of a sick man, in comparison of the pleasures of the love of God.

Everlasting Joys of Heaven.

WHEN our joys are at the sweetest, this thought must needs be part of that sweetness, that their sweetness shall never have an end. If our foretaste be joy unspeakable and full of glory, what shall we call that joy which flows from the most perfect fruition and perpetuation? 1 Pet. i. 7, 8. We have joy here, but alas, how seldom! alas, how small in comparison of what we may there expect! Some joy we have, but how oft do melancholy, or crosses, or losses in the world, or temptations, or sins, or desertions interrupt it! Our sun is here most commonly under a cloud, and too often in an eclipse; and we have the night as often as the day. Yea, our state is usually a winter; our days are cold and short, and our nights are long. But when the flourishing state of glory comes, we shall have no intermissions nor eclipses. 'The path of the just is as the shining light, that shineth more and more unto the perfect day,' Prov. iv. 18. And the perfect day is a perpetual day, that knows no interruption by the darkness of the night. 'For there shall be no night there, nor need of candle or sun; for the Lord God giveth them light, and they shall reign for ever and ever,' Rev. xxii. 5. This is the life that fears no death, and this is the feast that fears no want or future famine; the pleasure that knows nor fears pain; the health that knows nor fears sickness: this is the treasure that fears no moth, or rust, or thief; the building that fears no storm nor decay; the kingdom that fears no changes by rebellion; the friendship that fears no falling out; the love that fears no hatred or frustration; the glory that fears no envious eye; the possessed inheritance that fears no ejection by fraud, or force, or any failings; the joy that feels or fears no sorrow.

Repose of the Soul.

THE trust and repose of the soul on God, which is another part of the life of grace, is exceeding pleasant and quieting to the soul. To find that we stand upon a Rock, and that under us are the everlasting arms, and that we have so full security for our salvation as the promise and oath of the immutable God, what a stay, what a pleasure is this to the believer! The troubles of the godly are most from the remnants of their unbelief. The more they believe, the more they are comforted and established. The life of faith is a pleasant life. Faith could not conquer so many enemies, and carry us through so much suffering and distress, as you find in that cloud of testimonies, Heb. xi., if it were not a very comfortable work. Even we that see not the salvation ready to be revealed, may yet greatly rejoice, for all the manifold temptations, that for a season make us subject to some heaviness, 1 Pet. i. 5, 6. And we 'that see not Jesus Christ, yet believing can love Him, and rejoice with joy unspeakable and full of glory,' ver. 8. The God of hope doth sometimes 'fill His servants with all joy and peace in believing, and makes them even abound in hope through the power of the Holy Ghost,' Rom. xv. 13.

How to Live a Pleasant Life.

IF you would live a pleasant life draw near to God, and by faith behold Him, and by love adhere to Him, and take a view of His infinite goodness and all His perfections, and behold Him in His wondrous works, and then break forth into His cheerful praises, and you shall taste such pleasures as the earth affordeth not. Launch forth into the boundless ocean of eternity, and let your hearts and tongues expatiate in the praise of the Heavenly Majesty, and use this work, and ply it close, and be not too seldom or customary, or careless in it, and you shall find the difference between the pleasures of faith and of the flesh, of a holy and of a sensual life. 'Ye that stand in the house of the Lord, in the courts of the house of our God, praise the Lord; for the Lord is good: sing praises to His name, for it is pleasant,' Psalm cxxxv. 2, 3. 'Let my mouth be filled with Thy praise and with Thy honor all the day,' Psalm lxxi. 8. 'Sing unto the Lord: bless His name; show forth His salvation from day to day. Honor and majesty are before Him: strength and beauty are in His sanctuary,' Psalm xcvi. 2, 6.

Oh that the Lord will but shine upon my soul with the light of His countenance, and open my heart to the entertainment of His love, and hold a gracious communion with my soul by His Holy Spirit, and keep open these doors to me, and continue this liberty of His house and ordinances which we enjoy this day, that I may join with a faithful, humble people, in holy communion, and in His praise and worship, and that with a heart that is suitable to these works! I shall then say with David, 'The lines are fallen to me in pleasant places; I have a goodly heritage,' Psalm xvi. 6. I will ask for no greater pleasures or honors, or advancement in this world! Let who will surfeit on the pleasures of the flesh; here doth my soul delight to dwell! 'One thing have I desired of the Lord, that will I seek after, that I may dwell in the house of the Lord all the days of my life, to behold the beauty of the Lord, and to inquire in His holy temple. For in the time of trouble He will hide me in His pavilion; and in the secret of His tabernacle shall He hide me; He shall set me up upon a rock. And then shall my head be lifted up above mine enemies round about me: therefore will I offer in His tabernacle sacrifices of joy, I will sing, yea, I will sing praises to the Lord,' Psalm xxvii. 4—6. Till I come to the promised everlasting pleasures, I shall ask of God no greater pleasures. These would be as much as my soul in the prison of flesh could bear. Till I come to the land of promise, may I but have these clusters of its grapes in my present wilderness, I shall not repine: 'My heart here shall be glad, and my glory shall rejoice, and at death my flesh shall rest in hope.' For as the Lord now showeth me the 'path of life,' so in His 'presence is fullness of joy, and at His right hand are pleasures for evermore,' Psalm xvi. 9, 11.

Thanksgiving and Praise.

ANOTHER duty that holiness consisteth in, is thanksgiving and praise to the God of our salvation. He that knows not that this work is pleasant, is unacquainted with it. If there be any thing pleasant in this world, it is the praises of God that flow from a believing, loving soul, that is full of the sense of the mercies and goodness and excellences of the Lord; especially the unanimous conjunction of such souls, in the high praises of God in the holy assemblies. Is it not pleasant even to name the Lord? to mention His attributes? to remember His great and wondrous works? to magnify Him that rideth on the heavens, that dwelleth in the light that cannot be approached, that is clothed with majesty and glory, that infinitely surpasseth the sun in its brightness; that hath His throne in the heavens, and the heaven of heavens cannot contain Him; and yet He delighteth in the humble soul, and hath respect to the contrite; yea, dwells with them that tremble at His word? Is any thing so pleasant as the praises of the Lord? How sweet is it to see and praise Him as the Creator, in the various wonderful creatures which He hath made! How pleasant to observe His works of providence, to them that read them by the light of the sanctuary, and in faith and patience learn the interpretation from Him that only can interpret them! But oh how unspeakably pleasant is it to see the Father in the Son, and the Godhead in the manhood of our Lord, and the riches of grace in the glass of the holy gospel, and the manifold wisdom of God in the Church, where the angels themselves disdain not to behold it! Eph. iii. 10, 11. The praising of God for the incarnation of His Son, was a work that a choir of angels were employed in as the instructors of the church, Luke ii. 13, 14. There is not a promise in the Book of God, nor one passage of the life and miracles of Christ, and the rest of the history of the gospel, nor one of the holy works of the Spirit upon the soul, nor one of those thousand mercies to the Church, or to ourselves or friends, that infinite goodness doth bestow, but contain such matter of praise to God, as might fill believing hearts with pleasure, and find them most delightful work; much more when all these are at once before us, what a feast is there for a gracious soul!

The Redeemed in Glory.

THE true believer hath the small beginnings, and earnests and foretastes of the everlasting blessedness in this life in his approaches to God, and living upon Him by faith and love, and in his believing apprehensions of the favor of God, the grace of Christ, and the happiness which in heaven he shall enjoy for ever.

At death the souls of true believers do go to Christ, and enter upon a state of happiness.

At the last day the body shall be raised and united to the soul, and the Lord Jesus Christ will come in glory to judge the world, where He will openly absolve and justify the righteous, when He condemneth the ungodly, and will be glorified in His saints and admired in all them that do believe; and the saints shall also judge the world, and be themselves adjudged to everlasting glory.

Their everlasting habitation shall be in the heavens, even near unto God, and in the presence of His glory.

Their company will be only blessed spirits, even the holy angels and glorified saints, with whom we shall be one body and constitute the new Jerusalem, and be perfectly one in God for ever.

Their bodies shall be perfected and made immortal, spiritual, incorruptible, and glorious bodies, shining as the stars in the celestial firmament; no more subject to hunger and thirst, or cold or weariness, or shame or pain, nor any of the frailties that now adhere unto them, but be made like the glorified body of Christ.

The souls of the saints united to these bodies shall also be perfected, having far larger capacity to know God and enjoy Him than now we have; being freed from all ignorance, error, unbelief, pride, hard-heartedness, and whatsoever sin doth now accompany us; and perfected in every part of the image of God upon us.

The eyes of the glorified body shall in heaven have a glory to behold, that is suitable to their bodily capacity;—Heaven being not a place where the essence of God is confined, but where a prepared glory will be manifested to make happy the angels and saints with Christ. And whatever other senses the glorified bodies shall then have, (whether formally or eminently, we cannot now conceive what they will be,) they will all be satisfied with suitable delights from God.

The blessed Person of our Redeemer in our nature glorified, will there be the everlasting object of our delightful intuition and fruition: an object suitable to the eye of the glorified body itself. We shall for ever live in the sight of His face, and in the sense of His unspeakable love.

The glorified soul (whether mediately or immediately) shall behold the infinite, most blessed God, and by knowing Him be perfected in knowledge. As we shall see the Person of Jesus Christ, and the glory of God with open face, and not as in a glass as now we do, so we shall know so much of the essence of the Deity as we are capable of, to our felicity.

With the knowledge of God, and the beatifical

vision, will be joined a perfect love unto Him, and closure with His blessed will. So that to love Him will be the everlasting employment of the soul.

This love will be drawn forth into everlasting praise; and it will be our work before the throne of His glory to magnify the Lord forever.

In all this love and praise and glory, and in the full fruition of the eternal God, we shall rejoice with full and perfect joy, and we shall have full content, delight and rest.

In all this blessedness and glory of the saints, the glory of God Himself will shine, and angels shall admire it, and the condemned spirits with anguish shall discern it, that God may be glorified in our glory.

In all this happiness of believers and His own glory, the Lord will be well pleased, and that blessed will which is the beginning and end of all, will be accomplished and will have an eternal complacency, as the saints shall have an endless complacency in God.

Heavenly Recognition.

YOU cannot justly think that the knowledge of the glorified shall be more confused or imperfect than the knowledge of natural men on earth. We shall know much more, but not so much less. Heaven exceedeth earth in knowledge, as much as it doth in joy.

The angels in heaven have now a distinct, particular knowledge of the least believers, rejoicing particularly in their conversion, and being called by

Christ Himself 'their angels.' Therefore, when we shall be equal to the angels, we shall certainly know our nearest friends that there dwell with us, and are employed in the same attendance.

Abraham knew the rich man in hell, and the rich man knew Abraham and Lazarus: therefore we shall have as distinct a knowledge.

The two disciples knew Moses and Elias in the mount, whom they had never seen before; though it is possible Christ told them who they were, yet there is no such thing expressed; and therefore it is as probable that they knew them by the communication of their irradiating glory: much more shall we be then illuminated to a clearer knowledge.

It is said expressly, 1 Cor. xiii. 10–12, that our present knowledge shall be done away only in regard of its imperfection; and not of itself, which shall be perfected: 'When that which is perfect is come, then that which is in part shall be done away;' as we put away childish thoughts and speeches, when we become men: the change will be from 'seeing in a glass' to 'seeing face to face,' and from 'knowing in part' to 'knowing even as we are known.'

And that we shall both know and love and rejoice in creatures, even in heaven, notwithstanding that God is all in all, appeareth further thus:

Christ, in His glorified humanity, is a creature; and yet there is no doubt but all His members will there know and love Him in His glorified humanity, without any derogation from the glory of His Deity.

The body of Christ will continue its union, and every member will be so nearly related, even in heaven, that they cannot choose but know and love each other. Shall we be ignorant of the members of our body? and not be concerned in their felicity with whom we are so nearly one?

The state and felicity of the Church hereafter, is frequently described in Scripture as consisting in society. It is a kingdom, the city of God, the heavenly Jerusalem; and it is mentioned as part of our happiness to be of that society, Heb. xii. 22–24, &c.

It is put into the description of the happiness of the saints, that they shall come from the east, and from the west, and shall sit down with Abraham, Isaac, and Jacob, in the kingdom of God. Therefore they shall know them, and take some comfort in their presence.

Love to Saints in Heaven.

LOVE, even to the saints, as well as unto God, is one of the graces which shall endure for ever, 1 Cor. xiii. It is exercised upon an immortal object, the image and children of the Most High, and therefore must be one of the immortal graces. For grace in the nature of it dieth not; and therefore if the object cease not, how should the grace cease, unless you will call its perfecting a ceasing?

I must profess, from the very experience of my soul, that it is the belief that I shall love my friends in heaven, that principally kindleth my love to them on earth; and if I thought I should never know them after death, and consequently never love them more, when this life is ended, I should in reason number them with temporal things, and love them comparatively but a little; even as I love other transitory things, allowing for the excellency in the nature of grace. But now I converse with some delight with my godly friends, as believing I shall converse with them for ever, and take comfort in the very dead and absent, as believing we shall shortly meet in heaven: and I love them, I hope, with a love that is of a heavenly nature, while I love them as the heirs of heaven, with a love which I expect shall there be perfected, and more fully and for ever exercised.

Loss of Pious Friends.

DO you not seem to forget where you are yourselves, and where you must shortly and for ever live? Where would you have your friends, but where you must be yourselves? Do you mourn that they are taken hence? Why, if they had staid here a thousand years, how little of that time should you have had their company? When you are almost leaving the world yourselves, would you not send your treasure before you to the place where you must abide? How quickly will you pass from hence to God, where you shall find your friends that you lamented as if they had been lost, and there shall dwell with them for ever! O foolish mourners! would you not have your friends at home? at their home and your home, with their Father and your Father, their God and your God? Shall you not there enjoy them long enough? Can you so much miss them for one day, that must live with them to all eternity? and is not eternity long enough to enjoy your friends in?

Live by Faith.

LIVE still by faith; let faith lay heaven and earth as it were together. Look not at God as if He were afar off; set Him always as before you, even as at your right hand, Psalm xvi. 8. Be still with Him when you awake, Psalm cxxxix. 18. In the morning thank Him for your rest; and deliver up yourself to His conduct and service for that day. Go forth as with Him, and to do His work; do every action with the command of God and the promise of heaven before your eyes, and upon your hearts: live as those that have incomparably more to do with God and heaven, than with all this world; that you may say with David, 'Whom have I in heaven but Thee? and there is none on earth that I desire besides Thee:' Psalm lxxiii. 25, 26. And with Paul, 'To me to live is Christ, and to die is gain:' Phil. i. 21. You must shut up the eye of sense, save as subordinate to faith, and live by faith upon a God, a Christ, and a world that is unseen, if you would know by experience what it is to be above the brutish life of sensualists, and to converse with God. O Christian, if thou hadst rightly learned this blessed life, what a high and noble soul-conversation wouldst thou have! How easily wouldst thou spare, and how little wouldst thou miss, the favor of the greatest, the presence of any worldly comfort! City or solitude would be much alike to thee, saving that the place and state would be best to thee, where thou hast the greatest help and freedom to converse with God.

Thus being taken up with God, thou mightest live in prison as at liberty, and in a wilderness as in a city, and in a place of banishment as in thy native land; 'for the earth is the Lord's, and the fulness thereof;' and every where thou mayst find Him, and converse with Him, and lift up pure hands unto Him: in every place thou art within the sight of home; and heaven is in thine eye, and thou art conversing with that God, in whose converse the highest angels do place their highest felicity and delight.

Contemplation of God.

WHEREVER our friends are, God is still at hand to be the most profitable, honorable, and delightful object of our thoughts. There is enough in Him to take up all the faculties of my soul. He that is but in a well-furnished library, may find great and excellent employment for his thoughts many years together; and so may he that liveth in the open world, and hath all the visible works of God to meditate upon: but all this were nothing if God were not the sense of books and creatures, and the matter of all these noble studies. He that is alone, and hath only God Himself to study, hath the matter and sense of all the books and creatures in the world, to employ his thoughts upon. He never need to want matter for his meditation, that hath God to meditate on. He need not want matter of discourse, whether mental or vocal, that hath God to talk of, though he have not the name of any other friend to mention. All our affections may have in Him the highest and most pleasant work. The soul of man cannot have a more sweet and excellent work than to love Him: he wanteth neither work nor pleasure, that in his solitude is taken up in the believing contemplations of Eternal Love, and of all His blessed attributes and works. Oh, then, what happy and delightful converse may a believer have with God alone! He is always present, and always at leisure to be spoken with; and always willing of our access and audience.

Oh, how oft have I been solaced in God, when I found nothing but deceit and darkness in the world! How oft hath He comforted me, when it was past the power of man! How oft hath He relieved and delivered me, when all the help of man was vain! It hath been my stay and rest, to look to Him, when the creature hath been a broken staff, and deceitful friends have been but as a broken tooth, or a foot that is out of joint (as Solomon speaketh of confidence in an unfaithful man in time of trouble, Prov. xxv. 29). Verily, as the world were but a 'horrid dungeon without the sun, so it were a howling wilderness, a place of no considerable employment or delight, were it not that in it we may live to God and do Him service, and sometimes be refreshed with the light of His countenance, and the communications of His love.

Solitude.

THOUGH a wilderness is not heaven, it shall be sweet and welcome, for the sake of heaven, if thence I may but have a clearer prospect of it; and if by retiring from the crowd and noise of folly, I may but be more composed and better disposed to converse above, and to use my faith (alas! my too weak, languid faith) until the beatifical vision and fruition come. If there may be but more of God, or readier access to Him, or more heart-quickening flames of love, or more heart-comforting intimations of His favor, in a wilderness than in a city, in a prison than in a palace, let that wilderness be my city, and let that prison be my palace, while I must abide on earth. If in solitude I may have Enoch's walk with God, I shall in due season have such a translation as shall bring me to the same felicity which he enjoyeth; and in the mean time, as well as after, it is no disadvantage, if by mortal eyes I be seen no more. If the chariot of contemplation will in solitude raise me to more believing, affectionate converse with heaven, than I could expect in tumults and temptations, it shall reconcile me unto solitude, and make it my paradise on earth, till angels, instead of the chariot of Elias, shall convey me to the presence of my glorified Head, in the celestial paradise.

Infinite Goodness of God.

THIS Infinite goodness should be the matter of our daily praises. He that cannot cheerfully magnify this attribute of God, so suitable to the nature of the will, is surely a stranger to the praises of the Lord. The goodness of God should be a daily feast to a gracious soul, and should continually feed our cheerful praises, as the spring or cistern fills the pipes. I know no sweeter work on earth, nay, I am sure there is no sweeter, than for faithful, sanctified souls, rejoicingly to magnify the goodness of the Lord, and join together in His cheerful praises. O Christians, if you would taste the joys of saints, and live like the redeemed of the Lord indeed, be much in the exercise of this heavenly work, and with holy David, make it your employment, and say, 'Oh how great is Thy goodness which Thou hast laid up for them that fear Thee!' Psalm xxxi. 19. 'The earth is full of the goodness of the Lord!' Psalm xxxiii. 5. What then are the heavens? 'Thy congregation hath dwelt therein: Thou, O Lord, hast prepared Thy goodness for the poor.' 'Oh that men would praise the Lord for His goodness, and for His wonderful works to the children of men! for He satisfieth the longing soul, and filleth the hungry soul with goodness:' Psalm cvii. 8, 9. 'The goodness of God endureth continually:' Psalm lii. 1. 'Truly God is good to Israel, even to such as are of a clean heart:' Psalm lxxiii. 1. 'O taste and see that the Lord is good, blessed is the man that trusteth in Him:' Psalm

xxxiv. 8. 'The Lord is good, His mercy is everlasting, His truth endureth from generation to generation:' Psalm c. 5. 'The Lord is good to all, and His tender mercies are over all His works:' Psalm cxlv. 9. Oh praise the Lord, for the Lord is good; sing praises to His name, for it is pleasant:' Psalm cxxxv. 3. Call Him, as David, ' My goodness, and my fortress, my high tower, and my deliverer, and my shield, and He in whom I trust:' Psalm cxliv. 2. ' Let men therefore speak of the glorious honor of His majesty and of His wondrous works: let them abundantly utter the memory of His great goodness, and sing of His righteousness:' Psalm cxlv. 5, 7. If there be a thought that is truly sweet to the soul, it is the thought of the infinite goodness of the Lord. If there be a pleasant word for man to speak, it is the mention of the infinite goodness of the Lord. And if there be a pleasant hour for man on earth to spend, and a delightful work for man to do, it is to meditate on, and with the saints to praise, the infinite goodness of the Lord. What was the glory that God showed unto Moses, and the taste of heaven that He gave him upon earth, but this, ' I will make all my goodness pass before thee, and I will proclaim the name of the Lord before thee; and I will be gracious to whom I will be gracious, and will show mercy on whom I will show mercy!' Exod. xxxiii. 19. And His proclaimed name was, 'The Lord, the Lord God, merciful and gracious, long-suffering, and abundant in goodness and truth:' Exod. xxxiv. 6. These were the holy praises that

Solomon did consecrate the temple with, 'Arise, O Lord God, into Thy resting-place, Thou and the ark of Thy strength: let Thy priests, O Lord God, be clothed with salvation, and let Thy saints rejoice in goodness:' 2 Chron. vi. 41; see Isaiah lxiii. O Christians, if you would have joy indeed, let this be your employment! Draw near to God, and have no low undervaluing thoughts of His infinite goodness; for, 'How great is His goodness and how great is His beauty!' Zech. ix. 17. Why is it that divine consolations are so strange to us, but because divine goodness is so lightly thought upon? As those that think little of God at all, have little of God upon their hearts; so they that think but little of His goodness in particular, have little love, or joy, or praise.

The Saviour's Condescension and Love.

OH wonderful, condescending love! Angels proclaimed it; and angels admire it, and search into it, and in the Church's glass they still behold the manifold wisdom of God: how low, then, should redeemed sinners fall, in the humble admirations of this grace! how high should they rise in the thankful praise of their Redeemer!

He came on earth and conversed with men, to make known to men the invisible God, and the unseen things of the world above. He came as the Light and Saviour of the world, to bring to light immortality and life. He was holy, harmless, and undefiled, separated from sinners, and fulfilling all righteousness, that He might be a meet High Priest and effectual Saviour of sinners. He taught us, by His perfect doctrine and example, to be humble and obedient, and to contemn this world; to deny ourselves, and bear the cross, that we may attain the everlasting crown of glory. He humbled Himself to the false accusations and reproach of sinners, and to the shameful and bitter death of the cross, to make Himself a sacrifice and propitiation for our sins, and a ransom for our guilty souls, that we might be healed by His stripes. Oh matchless love, which even for enemies, did thus lay down His precious life! He hath conquered and sanctified death and the grave to all believers. He, therefore, took part of flesh and blood, that He might by death destroy the devil that had the power of death, and deliver them who, through the fear of death, were all their lifetime subject unto bondage. He hath procured for mankind a covenant of grace, and sealed it as His testament with His blood. And now there is forgiveness with Thee, that Thou mightest be cheerfully feared and obeyed in hope. It was Thine own love to the world, O Father, which gave Thine only begotten Son, that whosoever truly believeth in Him should not perish, but have everlasting life. Thou wast in Christ reconciling the world unto Thyself, and not imputing their sins unto them. Thou hast committed the word of reconciliation to Thy ministers, to beseech sinners, even in Thy name, and in the stead of Christ, to be reconciled to Thee. Thou commandest them to offer Thy mercy unto all, and by importunity to compel them to come in, that Thy house may be filled, and Thy blessed feast may be furnished with guests.

HEAVENLY ASPIRATIONS.

WE foresee, by faith, that happy day. We see, by faith, the new Jerusalem; the innumerable angels; the perfect spirits of the just; their glorious light, their flaming love, their perfect harmony. We hear, by faith, their joyful songs of thanks and praise. Lately they were as low and sad as we; in sins and sorrows, in manifold weaknesses, sufferings, and fears; but by faith and patience they have overcome; and in faith and patience we desire to follow our Lord and them. The time is near; this flesh will quickly turn to dust, and our delivered souls shall come to Thee: our life is short, and our sins and sorrows will be short; then we shall have light: we shall no more groan, and cry out in darkness, Oh that we could know the Lord! then shall we love Thee with pure, unmixed, perfect love; and need no more to groan and cry, Oh that our souls were inflamed with Thy love! then shall we praise Thee with thankful alacrity and joy, which will exceed our present apprehensions and desires.

O blessed streams of light and love, which will flow from Thy opened, glorious face, upon our souls for ever! How far will that everlasting Sabbath, and those perfect praises, excel these poor and dull endeavors, as far as that triumphant city of God excelleth this imperfect, childish, discomposed Church.

Quicken, Lord, our longing for that blessed state and day! O come, Lord Jesus, come quickly, and fulfill Thy word, that we may be with Thee where Thou art, and may behold Thy glory!

Prayer for the Penitent.

O GOD, be merciful to me a sinner! I confess not only my original sin, but the follies and fury of my youth, my manifold sins of ignorance and knowledge, of negligence and wilfulness, of omission and commission, against the law of nature, and against the grace and Gospel of Thy Son. Forgive and save me, O my God, for Thy abundant mercy, and for the sacrifice and merit of Thy Son, and for the promise of forgiveness which Thou hast made through Him; for in these alone is all my trust. Condemn me not, who condemn myself. O Thou that hast opened so precious a fountain for sin and uncleanness, wash me thoroughly from my wickedness, and cleanse me from my sin. Though Thy justice might send me presently to hell, let Thy mercy triumph in my salvation. Thou hast no pleasure in the death of sinners, but rather that they repent and live. If my repentance be not such as Thou requirest, O soften this hardened, flinty heart, and give me repentance unto life. Turn me to Thyself, O God of my salvation, and cause Thy face to shine upon me. Create in me a clean heart, and renew a right spirit within me. Meet not this poor returning prodigal in Thy wrath, but with the embracements of Thy tender mercies. Cast me not away from Thy presence, and sentence me not to depart from Thee with the workers of iniquity: Thou who didst patiently endure me when I despised Thee, refuse me not, now I seek unto Thee, and here in the dust implore Thy mercy. Thou didst convert and pardon a wicked Manasseh, and a persecuting Saul, and there are multitudes in heaven who were once Thine enemies. Glorify also Thy superabounding grace in the forgiveness of my abounding sins. Amen.

Crucified to the World.

WHEN once you are truly crucified to the world, you will have the honor and the comfort of a heavenly life. Your thoughts will be daily steeped in the celestial delights, when other men's are steeped in gall and vinegar. You will be above with God, when your carnal neighbors converse only with the world. Your thoughts will be higher than their thoughts, and your ways than their ways, as the heaven, where your converse is, is higher than the earth. When you take flight from earth in holy devotions, they may look at you, and wonder at you, but cannot follow you; for whither you go they cannot come, till they are such as you.

Now or Never.

HEAVEN is before you! Death is at hand! The eternal God hath sent to call you! Mercy doth yet stretch forth its arms! You have staid too long, and abused patience too much already: stay no longer! O now please God, and comfort us, and save yourselves by resolving that this shall be the day! and faithfully performing of this your resolution. Up and be doing: believe, repent, desire, obey, and do all this with all your might. Love Him that you must love for ever, and love Him with all your soul and might: seek that which is truly worth a seeking, and will pay for all your cost and pains: and seek it first with all your might; remembering still it must be *now* or *never*.

JOHN OWEN, D. D.
1616–1683.

PRAYER TO CHRIST IN SEASONS OF DISTRESS.

TIMES of *great distresses in conscience through temptations and desertions,* are seasons requiring an application unto Christ by especial invocation. Persons in such conditions, when their souls, as the psalmist speaks, are overwhelmed in them, are continually solicitous about compassion and deliverance. Some relief, some refreshment, they often find in pity and compassion from them who either have been in the same condition themselves, or by Scripture light do know the terror of the Lord in these things. When their complaints are despised, and their troubles ascribed unto other causes than what they are really sensible of, and feel within themselves—as is commonly done by physicians of no value—it is an aggravation of their distress and sorrow. And they greatly value every sincere endeavor for relief, either by counsel or prayer. In this state and condition the Lord Christ in the Gospel is proposed as full of tender compassion—as He alone who is able to relieve them. In that Himself hath suffered, being tempted, He is touched with a feeling of our infirmities, and knows how to have compassion on them that are out of the way, Heb. ii. 18, iv. 15, v. 2. So is He also, as He alone who is able to succor, to relieve, and to deliver them. 'He is able to succor them that are tempted,' chap. ii. 18. Hereon are they drawn, constrained, encouraged to make applications unto Him by prayer, that He would deal with them according to His compassion and power. This is a season rendering the discharge of this duty necessary. And hereby have innumerable souls found consolation, refreshment, and deliverance. A time of trouble is a time of the especial exercise of faith in Christ. So Himself gives direction, John xiv. 1, 'Let not your heart be troubled: ye believe in God, believe also in me.' Distinct actings of faith on Christ are the great means of supportment and relief in trouble. And it is by especial invocation, whereby they put forth and exert themselves.

Communion of Believers in Heavenly Worship.

BELIEVERS at present have, by faith, an admission into communion with the Church above, in all its divine worship. For we 'are come unto mount Zion, and unto the city of the living God, the heavenly Jerusalem, and to an innumerable company of angels, to the general assembly and Church of the first-born, which are written in heaven, and to God the Judge of all, and to the spirits of just men made perfect, and to Jesus the Mediator of the new covenant, and to the blood of sprinkling, that speaketh better things than that of Abel,' Heb. xii. 22-24.

In this holy assembly and worship have we communion by faith whilst we are here below, Heb. x. 19-22. O that my soul might abide and abound in this exercise of faith! that I might yet enjoy a clearer prospect of this glory, and inspection into the beauty and order of this blessed assembly! How inconceivable is the representation that God here makes of the glory of His wisdom, love, grace, goodness, and mercy, in Christ! How excellent is the manifestation of the glory and honor of Christ in His person and offices! the glory given Him by the Father! How little a portion do we know, or can have experience in, of the refreshing, satiating communications of divine love and goodness, unto all the members of this assembly; or of that unchangeable delight in beholding the glory of Christ, and of God in Him,—of that ardency of affections wherewith they cleave unto Him, and continual exultation of spirit, whereby they triumph in the praises of God, that are in all the members of it! To enter into this assembly by faith,—to join with it in the assignation of praises unto 'Him that sitteth on the throne, and to the Lamb for evermore,'— to labor after a frame of heart in holy affections and spiritual delight in some correspondency with that which is in the saints above,—is the duty, and ought to be the design, of the Church of believers here below. So much as we are furthered and assisted herein by our present ordinances, so much benefit and advantage have we by them, and no more. A constant view of this glory will cast contempt on all the desirable things of this world, and deliver our minds from any dreadful apprehensions of what is most terrible therein.

Visions of Celestial Glory.

ALL is open unto the saints above. We are in the dust, the blood, the noise of the battle; they are victoriously at peace, and have a perfect view of what they have passed through, and what they have attained unto. They are come to the springs of life and light, and are filled with admiration of the grace of God in themselves and one another. What they see in God and in Jesus Christ, what they have experience of in themselves, what they know and learn from others, are all of them inconceivable and inexpressible. It is well for us, if we have so much experience of these things as to see a real glory in the fulness and perfection of them. The apprehensions by sight, without mixture of unsteadiness or darkness, without the alloy of fears or temptations, with an ineffable sense of the things themselves on their hearts or minds, are the springs or motives of the holy worship which is in heaven.

The Saints' Rest.

THIS, in general, is the first thing that the dismissed saints are at rest from: They sin no more, they wound the Lord Jesus no more, they trouble their own souls no more, they grieve the Spirit no more, they dishonor the gospel no more,— they are troubled no more with Satan's temptations without, no more with their own corruption within; but lie down in a constant enjoyment of one everlasting victory over sin, with all its attendants: saith the Spirit, 'They rest from their labors,' Rev. xiv., those labors which make them faint and weary, their contending with sin to the uttermost. They are no more cold in communion; they have not one thought that wanders off from God to eternity. They lose Him no more, but always lie down in His bosom, without the least possibility of disturbance. Even the very remembrance of sin is sweet unto them, when they see God infinitely exalted and admired in the pardon thereof. They are free from trouble, and that both as to doing and suffering. Few of the saints but are called out, in one kind or another, to both these. Every one is either *doing* for God or *suffering* for God; some both do and suffer great things for Him. In either of them there is pain, weariness, travail, labor, trouble, sorrow, and anxiety of spirit; neither is there any eminent doing or working for God but is carried on with much suffering to the outward man.

The apostle tells us that 'there remaineth a rest for the people of God;' and yet withal, that they who believe are entered into that rest; those who in their labors, in their travails, do take in the sweetness of that promise of rest, do even in their labor make an entrance thereinto.

They rest from all trouble and anxiety that attend them in their pilgrimage, either in doing or suffering for God: Heb. iv. 10. They enter into rest, and cease from their works. God wipes all tears from their eyes. There is no more watching, no more fasting, no more wrestling, no more fighting, no more blood, no more sorrow; the ransomed of the Lord do return with everlasting joy on their heads, and sorrow and sighing flee away. There, tyrants pretend no more title to their kingdom; rebels lie not in wait for their blood; they are no more awakened by the sound of the trumpet, nor the noise of the instruments of death: they fear not for their relations, they weep not for their friends; the Lamb is their temple, and God is all in all unto them. Yet,—

This will not complete their rest; something farther is required thereto,—even something to satisfy, everlastingly content, and fill them in the state and condition wherein they are. Free them in your thoughts from what you please, without this they are not at rest. This, then, you have in the second place, God is the rest of their souls: Psalm cxvi, 'Return to thy rest, O my soul.' Dismissed saints rest in the bosom of God, because in the fruition and enjoyment of Him they are everlastingly satisfied, as having attained the utmost end whereto they were created, all the blessedness whereof they are capable. I could almost beg for liberty a little to expatiate in this meditation of the sweet, gracious, glorious, satisfied condition of a dismissed saint.

The Word of God.

THE entrance of it hath given light to my soul, which was before in darkness, not knowing whither it went. How many glorious mysteries do I see in it! what purity, what spirituality, what holiness! etc.—all which speak the wisdom and power, and goodness and holiness, and truth of the Author of it. What sweetness have I tasted in it! It hath been as the 'honey and honeycomb' to me, Psalm xix. 10. What power, what life, what strange energy have I experienced in it! What a change hath it wrought in me! What lusts hath it discovered and mortified! What duties hath it convinced me of, and engaged me in! What strength hath it furnished me with! How hath it quickened me when I was dead in sin, revived my comforts when they were dying, actuated my graces when they were languishing, roused me up when I was sluggish, awaked me when I was dreaming, refreshed me when I was sorrowful, supported me when I was sinking, answered my doubts, conquered my temptations, scattered my fears, enlarged me with desires, and filled me 'with joy unspeakable and full of glory!' 1 Pet. i. 8. And what word could ever have wrought such effects but that of the eternal, all-wise, all-powerful God? And therefore upon His alone authority I receive it; Him alone I adore in it, whose power I have so often found working by it.

A Hiding Place from the Wind.

CHRIST is a 'hiding-place.' He that was ready to be cast from the top of a rock with a strong wind, would desire nothing more than a hiding-place until the strong blast were over. When fierce winds have driven a vessel at sea from all its anchors, so that it hath nothing to keep it from splitting on the next rock whereunto it is driven, a safe harbor, a hiding-place, is the great desire and expectation of the poor creatures that are in it. Our Saviour tells us what this wind is: Matt. vii. 25. The wind that blows upon and casts down false professors to the ground, is the wind of strong and urging temptations. Is this the condition of the soul? [do] strong temptations beat upon it, which are ready to hurry it down into sin and folly,—that it hath no rest from them, one blast immediately succeeding another,—that the soul begins to faint, to be weary, give over, and say, 'I shall perish; I cannot hold out to the end?' Is this thy condition? See the Lord Christ suited unto it, and the relief that is in Him in this promise,—He is 'a hiding-place.' Saith He, 'These temptations seek thy life; but with me thou shalt be safe.' Fly to His bosom, retreat into His arms, expect relief by faith from Him, and thou shalt be safe.

A Covert from the Tempest.

THERE is a *tempest;* in reference whereunto Christ is here said to be 'a covert.' A tempest, in the Scripture, represents the wrath of God for sin. 'He breaketh me,' saith Job, 'with a tempest,' chap. ix. 17, when he lay under a sense of the displeasure and indignation of God. He threatens to rain upon the wicked 'a horrible tempest,' Psalm xi. 6.

Suppose a poor creature to be under this tempest, full of sad and dreadful thoughts and apprehensions of the wrath of God; behind, before, round about, he can see nothing but hailstones and coals of fire; heaven is dark and dismal over him; he hath not seen sun, moon or stars, in many days,—not one glimpse of light from above or hopes of an end. 'I shall perish; the earth shakes under me; the pit is opening for me. Is there no hope?' Why, see how Christ is suited in this distress also. He is 'a covert' from this tempest; get into Him, and thou shalt be safe. He hath borne all this storm, as far as thou art concerned; abide with Him, and not one hurtful drop shall fall upon thee,—not one hair of thy head shall be singed with this fire. Hast thou fears? hast thou a sense of the wrath of God for sin? Dost thou fear it will one day fall upon thee and be thy portion? Behold a covert, a sure defence, is here provided.

Faith Triumphant in the Hour of Death.

IT is the last victorious act of faith, wherein it hath its final conquest over all its adversaries. Faith is the leading grace in all our spiritual warfare and conflict; but all along while we live, it hath faithful company that adheres to it, and helps it. Love works and hope works, and all other graces,—self-denial, readiness to the cross,—they all work and help faith. But when we come to die, faith is left alone. Now, try what faith will do. The exercise of other graces ceases; only faith comes to a close conflict with its last adversary, wherein the whole is to be tried. And, by this one act of resigning all into the hand of God, faith triumphs over death, and cries, 'O death, where is thy sting? O grave, where is thy victory? Come, give me an inlet into immortality and glory; the everlasting hand of God is ready to receive me!' This is the victory whereby we overcome all our spiritual enemies.

Fullness of Christ.

FOR the *fountain* of grace, the Holy Ghost, He received not Him 'by measure,' John iii. 34; and for the communications of the Spirit, 'it pleased the Father that in Him should all fullness dwell,' Col. i. 19,—'that in all things He might have the pre-eminence.'

This is the *Beloved* of our souls, 'holy, harmless, undefiled;' 'full of grace and truth;' full, to a sufficiency for every end of grace; full, for practice, to be an example to men and angels as to obedience;

full, to a certainty of uninterrupted communion with God; full to a readiness of giving supply to others; full, to suit Him to all the occasions and necessities of the souls of men; full, to a glory not unbecoming a subsistence in the Person of the Son of God; full, to a perfect victory, in trials, over all temptations; full, to an exact correspondency to the whole law, every righteous and holy law of God; full, to the utmost capacity of a limited, created, finite nature; full, to the greatest beauty and glory of a living temple of God; full, to the full pleasure and delight of the soul of His Father; full, to an everlasting monument of the glory of God, in giving such inconceivable excellencies to the Son of man.

Beholding the Glory of Christ.

THE heart of a believer affected with the glory of Christ, is like the needle touched with the loadstone. It can no longer be quiet, no longer be satisfied in a distance from Him. It is put into a continual motion towards Him. This motion, indeed, is weak and tremulous. Pantings, breathings, sighings, groanings in prayer, in meditations, in the secret recesses of our minds, are the life of it. However, it is continually pressing towards Him. But it obtains not its point, it comes not to its centre and rest in this world.

But now above, all things are clear and serene,— all plain and evident in our beholding the glory of Christ; we shall be ever with Him, and see Him as

He is. This is heaven, this is blessedness, this is eternal rest.

The person of Christ in all His glory shall be continually before us; and the eyes of our understandings shall be so gloriously illuminated, as that we shall be able steadily to behold and comprehend that glory.

But, alas! here at present our minds recoil, our meditations fail, our hearts are overcome, our thoughts confused, and our eyes turn aside from the lustre of this glory; nor can we abide in the contemplation of it. But there, an immediate, constant view of it, will bring in everlasting refreshment and joy unto our whole souls.

Saving Grace.

IT is in the nature of this grace to grow and increase unto the end. As rivers, the nearer they come unto the ocean whither they tend, the more they increase their waters and speed their streams; so will grace flow more freely and fully in its near approaches to the ocean of glory.

Flourishing of the Righteous.

THE flourishing of the righteous in grace and holiness is the glory of the office of Christ and of the gospel. Where this is not, there is no glory in the profession of our religion. The glory of kings is in the wealth and peace of their subjects; and the glory of Christ is in the grace and holiness of His subjects.

This flourishing is compared to the palm-tree, and the growth of the cedar. The palm-tree is of the greatest verdure, beauty, and fruitfulness, and the cedar of the greatest and longest growth of any trees. So are the righteous compared to the palm-tree for the beauty of profession and fruitfulness in obedience; and unto the cedar for a continual, constant growth and increase in grace. Thus it is with all that are righteous, unless it be from their own sinful neglect, as it is with many in this day. They are herein rather like the shrubs and heaths in the wilderness, which see not when good cometh, than like the palm-tree or the cedars of Lebanon.

Unless we are planted in the house of the Lord, we cannot flourish in His courts. See Psalm i. 3. Unless we are partakers of the grace administered in the ordinances, we cannot flourish in a fruitful profession. The outward participation of them is common unto hypocrites, that bear some leaves, but neither grow like the cedar nor bear fruit like the palm-tree. So the apostle prays for believers, that Christ may dwell in their hearts by faith, that they may be 'rooted and grounded in love,' Eph. iii. 17, 'rooted, built up and established,' Col. ii. 7. The want hereof is the cause that we have so many fruitless professors; they have entered the courts of God by profession, but were never planted in His house by faith and love. Let us not deceive ourselves herein; we may be entered into the church, and made partakers of the outward privileges of it, and not be so planted in it as to flourish in grace and fruitfulness.

Spiritual Decays in the Christian.

HAVE you, in the way of your profession, had any experience of these spiritual decays? I doubt not but that there are some who have been preserved green and flourishing from their first conversion unto God, who never fell under the power of sloth, neglect, or temptation, at least not for any remarkable season; but they are but few. It was not so with scarce any of those believers under the Old Testament whose lives and walkings are recorded for our instruction; and they must be such as lived in an exact and diligent course of mortification. And some there are who have obtained relief and deliverance from under their decays,—whose backslidings have been healed, and their diseases cured. So it was with David, as he divinely expresseth it, Psalm ciii. 1, 3–5: 'Bless the Lord, O my soul; and all that is within me, bless His holy name. Who forgiveth all thine iniquities; who healeth all thy diseases; who redeemeth thy life from destruction; who crowneth thee with loving-kindness and tender mercies; who satisfieth thy mouth with good things, so that thy youth is renewed like the eagle's.' So doth he celebrate his deliverance from that state whereof he complains, Psalm xxxviii. And there is no grace or mercy that doth more affect the hearts of believers, that gives them a greater transport of joy and thankfulness, than this of deliverance from backslidings. It is a bringing of the soul out of prison, which enlargeth it unto praise: Psalm cxlii. 7. Of this sort I doubt not but that there are many; for God hath given great warnings of the danger of a spiritually-decaying state; and He hath made great promises of recovery from it; and multitudes in the Church are daily exercised herein.

Recovery from Backsliding.

THE work of recovering backsliders or believers from under their spiritual decays, is an act of sovereign grace, wrought in us by virtue of divine promises. Out of this eater cometh meat. Because believers are liable to such declensions, backslidings and decays, God hath provided and given unto us great and precious promises of a recovery, if we duly apply ourselves unto the means of it. One of the places only wherein they are recorded I shall here call over and explain, Hos. xiv. 1–8, 'O Israel, return unto the Lord thy God; for thou hast fallen by thine iniquity. Take with you words, and turn unto the Lord: say unto Him, Take away all iniquity, and receive us graciously: so will we render the calves of our lips,' &c. 'I will heal their backsliding, I will love them freely: for mine anger is turned away from him. I will be as the dew unto Israel: he shall grow as the lily, and cast forth his roots as Lebanon. His branches shall spread, and his beauty shall be as the olive-tree, and his smell as Lebanon. They that dwell under his shadow shall return; they shall revive as the corn, and grow as the vine: the scent thereof shall be as the wine of Lebanon. Ephraim shall say, What have I to do any more with idols? I have heard him, and observed him. I am like a green fir-tree: from me is thy fruit found.'

How to Die Comfortably.

HE, therefore, that would die comfortably, must be able to say within himself and to himself, 'Die, then, thou frail and sinful flesh; 'dust thou art, and unto dust thou shalt return.' I yield thee up unto the righteous doom of the Holy One. Yet therein also I give thee into the hand of the great Refiner, who will hide thee in thy grave, and by thy consumption purify thee from all thy corruption and disposition to evil. And otherwise this will not be. After a long sincere endeavor for the mortification of all sin, I find it will never be absolutely perfect, but by this reduction into the dust. Thou shalt no more be a residence for the least remainder of sin unto eternity, nor any clog unto my soul in its actings on God. Rest therefore in hope; for God, in His appointed season, when He shall have a desire unto the work of His hands, will call unto thee, and thou shalt answer Him out of the dust. Then shall He, by an act of His almighty power, not only restore thee unto thy pristine glory, as at the first creation, when thou wast the pure workmanship of His hands, but enrich and adorn thee with inconceivable privileges and advantages. Be not then afraid; away with all reluctancy. Go into the dust;

rest in hope; 'for thou shalt stand in thy lot at the end of the days.' *

The Departing Soul.

THE soul is now parting with all things here below, and that for ever. None of all the things which it hath seen, heard, or enjoyed, by its outward senses, can be prevailed with to stay with it one hour, or to take one step with it in the voyage wherein it is engaged. It must alone by itself launch into eternity. It is entering an invisible world, which it knows no more of than it hath received by faith. None hath come from the dead to inform us of the state of the other world; yea, God seems on purpose so to conceal it from us, that we should have no evidence of it, at least as unto the manner of things in it, but what is given unto faith by divine revelation.

Wherefore no man can comfortably venture on and into this condition, but in the exercise of that faith which enables him to resign and give up his departing soul into the hand of God, who alone is able to receive it, and to dispose it into a condition of rest and blessedness. So speaks the apostle: 'I am not ashamed; for I know whom I have believed, and am persuaded that He is able to keep that which I have committed unto him against that day.'

Herein, as in all other graces, is our Lord Jesus

---

* The Rev. W. H. Goold, the able editor of Owen's works, has justly remarked, that this passage is wrought up and refined into a high degree of Christian eloquence.

Christ our great example. He resigned His departing spirit into the hands of His Father, to be owned and preserved by Him, in its state of separation: 'Father, into Thy hands I commend my spirit,' Luke xxiii. 46; as did the psalmist, His type, in an alike condition, Psalm xxxi. 5. But the faith of our Lord Jesus Christ herein — the object and exercise of it, what He believed and trusted unto in this resignation of His Spirit into the hand of God — is at large expressed in the 16th Psalm. 'I have,' said he, 'set the Lord always before me: because He is at my right hand, I shall not be moved. Therefore my heart is glad, and my glory rejoiceth; my flesh also shall rest in hope. For Thou wilt not leave my soul in hell; neither wilt Thou suffer Thine Holy One to see corruption. Thou wilt show me the path of life; in Thy presence is fullness of joy, and at Thy right hand there are pleasures for evermore.' He left his soul in the hand of God, in full assurance that it should suffer no evil in its state of separation, but should be brought again with his body into a blessed resurrection and eternal glory. So Stephen resigned his soul, departing under violence, into the hands of Christ Himself. When he died, he said, 'Lord Jesus, receive my spirit.'

This is the last victorious act of faith, wherein its conquest over its last enemy death itself doth consist. Herein the soul says in and unto itself, 'Thou art now taking leave of time unto eternity; all things about thee are departing as shades, and will immediately disappear. The things which thou art entering into are yet invisible; such as 'eye hath not seen, nor ear heard, nor will they enter into the heart of man fully to conceive.' Now, therefore, with quietness and confidence give up thyself unto the sovereign power, grace, truth, and faithfulness of God, and thou shalt find assured rest and peace.'

True Pleasures.

HERE alone—namely, in Christ, and a participation of Him—are true pleasures and durable riches to be obtained; pleasures of the same nature with, and such as, like pleasant streams, flow down into the ocean of eternal pleasures above. A few moments in these joys are to be preferred above the longest continuance in the cursed pleasures of this world. See Prov. iii. 13-18.

WILLIAM BATES, D. D.
1625–1699.

HEAVENLY JOY.

HEAVEN is a state of pure, full, and unfading joy. The joy of the blessed is not mixed with things that may corrupt its excellence. There is an absolute exemption from all evils. 'God shall wipe away all tears from their eyes: and there shall be no more death, neither sorrow, nor crying; neither shall there be any more pain.' The joy is full; it is called 'our Master's joy.' Great God, how ineffable is that joy! It is the richest reward infinite bounty can give to faithful servants. As 'being made like to Christ in glory,' 1 John iii. 2, implies a divine and full perfection: so the 'entering into His joy' implies the most accomplished and incomprehensible felicity. It is a permanent joy that none shall take from the blessed, as our Saviour promises His disciples. Here below, suppose a person encompassed with all the good things of the world, yet this felicity is neither without defects, nor without dependance upon casual things, that he is never completely happy, but only less miserable: and though he lives long in prosperity, and hath a tenor of health to enjoy it; yet, as the clearest evening is presently followed by night, so the most vigorous old age is certainly attended with death, that extinguishes all sensual pleasures. But in the 'presence of God is fullness of joy; at His right hand are pleasures for ever.'

Heavenly Conversation.

LET our conversation be in heaven, whilst we are upon the earth. Every thing in nature hath a tendency to its original and perfection. Rivers that come from the sea, are in a living motion returning thither; if you stop their course, and confine them, though in receptacles of marble, they corrupt and die. The divine nature in the saints hath a strong tendency to heaven, from whence it came, and raiseth the soul by solemn thoughts, and ardent desires, to that blessed place. A philosopher that was asked of what country he was, replied, he was a citizen of the world. The Scripture corrects the language, and teaches us that we are citizens of heaven; we are passing to the Jerusalem above, the 'land of promise, the true land of the living:' and all our aims and endeavors should have a final respect thither. 'Our hearts should be where our treasure is.' How joyful, how advantageous is a heavenly conversation! The serious and believing contemplation of heaven, is a temperate ecstacy, and brings the soul into the divine presence: anticipates the joy of it by a sweet foretaste, by a supernatural elevation of mind: by frequent lively thoughts of our glorious inheritance, we gradually enter into it: the prospect of that causes in the saints a holy contempt of the world, as not worthy our ambition and diligence: it causes such a self-denial from the inviting temptations of sense, that men, whose portion is in this life, are forced to admire their restraint from those objects that ravish carnal hearts.

The Music of Heaven.

WE may judge by the saints here, when they are in a fit disposition to praise God, what fervors they feel in their united praises of Him in heaven. The psalmist in an ecstacy calls to all the parts of the world to join with him: 'The Lord reigns, let the heavens rejoice, and the earth be glad; let the sea roar, let the fields be joyful, and all that dwell therein.' He desires that nature should be elevated above itself, that the dead parts be inspired with life, the insensible feel motions of joy, and those that want a voice, break forth in praises, to adorn the divine triumph. With what life and alacrity will the saints in their blessed communion celebrate the object of their love and praises! The seraphim about the throne 'cried to one another,' to express their zeal and joy, in celebrating His eternal purity and power, and the glory of His goodness. Oh the unspeakable pleasure of this concert! when every soul is harmonious, and contributes his part to the full music of heaven! O could we hear but some echo of those songs wherewith the heaven of heavens resounds, some remains of those voices wherewith the saints above 'triumph in the praises,' in the solemn adoration of the King of spirits, how would it inflame our desires to be joined with them? 'Blessed are those that are in Thy house, they always praise Thee.'

Death and Heaven.

ART thou in the vale of tears, languishing in sorrow, and dying every day? By faith ascend to 'the mountains of spices,' the blessed place above, and thou wilt find the comforts of God to revive and delight thy soul.

Let this reconcile death to us. The pale horse is sent to bring us to our Father's house. The apostle expresses the true Christian temper: 'In this we groan, earnestly desiring to be clothed with our house that is from heaven: and we are willing rather to be absent from the body, and present with the Lord:' 2 Cor. v. 2, 8. . Every saint in the present world is both a prisoner and a captive; and his soul is detained from the glorious liberty of the sons of God, by confinement to his body. Therefore, methinks he should not merely be content to die out of the necessity of nature, when he can live no longer, but desire the happy removal, and say with the Psalmist, 'I rejoiced when they said unto me, let us go into the house of the Lord.' It is true, nature will recoil, and the extinguishing the present life, with all its sensible, pleasant operations, is uneasy to us: but as when the candles are put out, the sun rises in its brightness, so when the natural life ceases, the spiritual life springs forth in its oriency and glory: 'When the earthly tabernacle is dissolved, the naked, separate soul shall be received into a building not made with hands, eternal in the heavens.' Our joyful affections, in leaving the world, and ascending to heaven, should be in some manner suitable to our reception there. What a joyful welcome will entertain us from God Himself! Our Saviour comforted His disciples with a heavenly valediction: 'I go to my Father, and your Father; to my God, and your God.' The gracious relation sweetens the glorious. He that joyfully receives the rebellious but penitent son to grace, will joyfully receive His obedient sons to glory. He that now receives their prayers with the affection of a father, will receive their persons with the dearest expressions of love. His fatherly providence watched over them in the way, and will triumphantly bring them home. Here, many blessed testimonies of God's love are given to the saints, that produce such a spiritual sweetness in their hearts, that they esteem His loving-kindness as better than life, more worth than all the world; but the full revealing of His love is only in heaven.

Death of Pious Friends.

WHAT father is so deserted of reason, as to bear impatiently the parting with his son, that goes over a narrow part of the sea to a rich and pleasant country, and receives the investiture and peaceable possession of a kingdom? Nay, by how much the stronger his love is, so much the more transporting is his joy; especially if he expects shortly to be with him, to see him on the throne, in the state of a king, and to partake of his happiness. If then it be impossible to nature to be grieved at the felicity of one that is loved; according to what principle of nature or faith do believers so uncomfortably lament the death of friends, of whom they have assurance that after their leaving our earth, they enter into an everlasting kingdom, to receive a crown of glory from Christ Himself? Our Saviour tells the disciples, 'If ye loved me, ye would rejoice, because I said, I go to my Father,' to sit down at His right hand in majesty. A pure affection directly terminates in the happiness and exaltation of the person that is loved. I am not speaking against the exercise of tender affections on the loss of our dear friends, and the pensive feeling of God's hand in it, which is a natural and necessary duty. There is a great difference between stupidity and patience: but violent passion, or unremitting sorrow, is most unbecoming the blessed hope assured to us in the Gospel.

Perpetuity of Bliss.

THE blessedness of the saints is without end. This makes heaven to be itself. There is no satiety of the present, no solicitude for the future. Were there a possibility, or the least suspicion of losing that happy state, it would cast an aspersion of bitterness upon all their delights: they could not enjoy one moment's repose; but the more excellent their happiness is, the more stinging would their fear be of parting with it. 'But the inheritance reserved in heaven is immortal, undefiled, and fades not away.' And the tenure of their possession is infinitely firm by the divine power, the true support of their everlasting duration. 'With God is the fountain of life.' They enjoy a better immortality than the tree of life could have preserved in Adam. The revolutions of the heavens, and ages, are under their feet, and cannot in the least alter or determine their happiness. After the passing of millions of years, still an entire eternity remains of their enjoying God. O most desirable state! where blessedness and eternity are inseparably united. O joyful harmony! when the full chorus of heaven shall sing, 'This God is our God for ever and ever.' This adds an infinite weight to their glory. This redoubles their unspeakable joys with infinite sweetness and security. They repose themselves in the complete fruition of their happiness. God reigns in the saints, and they live in Him for ever.

Ever with the Lord.

THE lively hope of this blessedness is powerful to support us under the greatest troubles that can befal us in this our mortal condition. Here we are tossed upon the alternate waves of time, but hereafter we shall arrive at the port, the blessed bosom of our Saviour, and enjoy a peaceful calm; 'and so we shall ever be with the Lord.' Words of infinite sweetness! This is the song of our prosperity, and charm of our adversity: 'We shall ever be with the Lord.' Well might the apostle add immediately after, 'Therefore comfort one another with these words.'

SYMON PATRICK, D.D.
1626–1707.

Prayers. I.

O GOD, who art the full and the filling Good; who satisfieth the desire of every living thing, and therefore will not refuse to answer the desires of immortal spirits, whom Thou hast made to know how good Thou art, and to be satisfied with no less good than Thyself: Thou art ever pouring Thy benefits upon us; and sendest us every day some new token of Thy love, to make our pilgrimage here upon earth the more comfortable to us. But above all, Thou art to be acknowledged in Thy surpassing love and kindness towards us in Christ Jesus, by whom Thou hast made the darkest night of trouble and sorrow not to be without the light of joy and gladness. I thank Thee, O God, for the great satisfaction which Thou hast given to all that is within us, which ought to bless Thy holy name. For Thou hast filled our minds and understandings with the highest knowledge, and our wills with the divinest love, and all our affections with the comforts of hope and joy in Thee our God, sufficient to swallow up all our sadness and grief, and fear and care, and all the troublesome passions that are in our hearts. O my God, how rich art Thou in mercy towards us, who providest that contentment for us, which we seek and labor after in these lower enjoyments, by leading us to Thyself, the fountain of all that good which is in any creature! How excellent is Thy loving-kindness; Who when we desire much in this world, givest us an immortal inheritance in the other; and when our hearts are set upon perishing riches, invitest us to treasures in the heavens, and settest before us eternal honor and glory with our Saviour! Besides all which, Thou dost not deny me the comfort of my friends, lovers and acquaintance; in whom I see likewise how full of love Thou art, and how ready to do us good. Thou wilt never cease Thyself, I believe, to follow me with Thy loving-kindness all my days, to take care of me, help and comfort me; Who hast put such great good will into the hearts of men.

My soul doth magnify Thee, O Lord; and my spirit rejoiceth in Thee, O God my Saviour; particularly for that Thou hast promised me Thy holy Spirit to strengthen and empower me to do my duty faithfully to Thee, and to increase in wisdom, charity, and piety, that I may rejoice in Thee evermore. O that I may feel the effect of these holy thoughts and devout acknowledgments, in the constant stillness and quietness of my soul, whatsoever the condition be into which Thou art pleased to bring me. Dispose my heart to such an humble confidence in Thee, that I may be careful for nothing, but in everything by prayer and supplication make known my request to Thee with thanksgiving. Help me to have my conversation without covetousness, and to be content with such things as I have. Let no solicitude for the future discompose my duty, or disturb my present enjoyment. Root out of my heart all distrust for Thee, all envy, uncharitableness, ambition, murmuring or repining at any of Thy providences, with every thing else that dishonors the gospel of our Lord Jesus, and misbecomes the Christian spirit. In all events, give me grace to acquiesce in Thy wisdom and love; and to study rather how to mend myself, than how to mend my outward estate: that having my soul still more and more furnished with those heavenly goods wherewith Thou hast enriched us by Christ Jesus, I may lead every day a more happy life in this world, and be prepared for that perfect satisfaction of contentment, which we wait for in the world to come. Amen.

II.

O LORD, the fountain of all good, whose blessings are derived in several channels to us, especially to our souls; unto which all things minister, and help to promote their eternal welfare: I see the large and abundant provision which Thou hast made for them in Christ Jesus. Thou hast opened the heavens and let down eternal life unto us. Thou hast set before us the glory of another world, and called us to Thy kingdom, and promised to make us heirs with Thy only-begotten Son, and to give us an everlasting inheritance. I thank Thee that Thou hast brought the word of Thy gospel so nigh me, and put it even into my mouth, and into my heart; and that I have felt Thy Holy Spirit in my soul, so often disposing my mind and affections to seek that blessed immortality. Every good thing in this world bids me love Thee and rejoice in Thee, who art the giver of it: and all the crosses likewise and afflictions of this life tend to make me happy, by teaching me moderation and sobriety, humility and heavenly-mindedness, faith in Thee, and absolute resignation to Thee, with fervent devotion, and passionate desires after a better life.

O God, how excellent is Thy loving-kindness! therefore the children of men put their trust under the shadow of Thy wings. How inexcusable shall I be, if I should starve in the midst of such abundance and perish, when Thou hast sent me such great salvation! How shall I escape, if, after Thou hast done so much without my thought or labor, I should take no pains to attain the end of Thy extraordinary grace towards me? Excite in me, I beseech Thee, a greater sense of Thy love, and endue me with a greater care to improve every thing to the enriching of my soul with spiritual wisdom and all divine virtues; that so I may be the better able to bear all the troubles of this life; and neither the infirmities and pains of this body, nor the poverty and meanness of my outward estate, nor the loss and unkindness of friends, nor any other sad accident, may throw me into discontent and impatience of spirit: but I may still remember, that, as I suffer nothing but what I deserve, so my soul may be a gainer by all my sufferings. Help me, therefore, instead of murmuring and repining at my present condition, to apply myself to make the best use of it, whatsoever it be, to my everlasting advantage. Purify and refine my spirit more perfectly from all unreasonable opinions, and purge out of my heart all inordinate affections. Settle my will in an immovable submission to Thine. And, considering both that I am Thy creature and that I am an offender, enable me always to rest satisfied with Thy proceedings, and acknowledge that I am less than the least of Thy mercies.

Pardon, good Lord, all my ingratitude, and indecent complaints; pity my infirmities; accept my holy desires; confirm all my good purposes; strengthen and empower my endeavors, that I may mortify every bad disposition in me, faithfully discharge my duty, rightly use Thy various blessings, patiently bear the heaviest afflictions, and make for my soul most certain provision; by all the means of grace, by the good counsels of others, the inspirations of the Holy Ghost, Thy many remarkable providences about me, and whatsoever courses Thou takest with me, to bring me safe through this life to a happy eternity. Amen.

III.

O GOD, in whose presence is fullness of joy, and at whose right hand there are pleasures for evermore: we see daily how uncertain and empty all our enjoyments are in this world; and are directed by our constant experience to look up higher, and fix our hearts on Thee, for our true contentment and satisfaction of spirit. Our eye is not satisfied with seeing, nor our ear filled with hearing; but after all that we possess, our spirits are still thirsty and craving more. The very love of ourselves and our own ease, carries us unto Thee; for we are extremely miserable, even in the midst of abundance, if we want Thee. Blessed be Thy goodness that I know Thee, and Thy exceeding great love to mankind in Christ Jesus. Blessed be Thy infinite grace that I understand where my happiness lies, and am not left to wander after the foolish desires of my own heart. O turn away mine eyes from beholding vanity, and quicken me in Thy way. Fasten my mind on that immovable bliss which our Lord hath discovered unto us, and fill me with constant delight and joy in contemplation of it; that so I may not lay out my strength for that which is not bread, and my labor for that which satisfieth not; but earnestly pursue that everlasting life, the very hope of which is so sweet and comfortable in this world.

Thou hast not made me, I know, to be miserable here; for Thou art the Father of mercies, and takest pleasure in enriching others with Thy benefits. It is Thy glory to do good: Thou openest Thy hand and satisfiest the desire of every thing living. The whole creation acknowledges Thy bounty; and therefore I should be the most ungrateful wretch if I should not rejoice in it, which hath made me to want nothing but what I may easily enjoy, and hitherto hath supplied all my needs with a continued care and kindness. Preserve me, O Lord, in a sober and serious sense of the state of my own nature, and of the condition of all things round about me; that I may not stretch my desires greedily after that which I do not need, and which cannot satisfy and fill up the vast emptiness of my soul, if I did enjoy it. Make me so wise as to reflect continually upon the trouble as well as pleasure that I am like to meet withal in every change; that so I may be modest in my desires, and pursue what I desire with an indifferent mind, and enjoy what Thou bestowest on me with a thankful and charitable heart, and with a quiet and undisturbed spirit resign it back into Thy hands, when Thou callest for it. O blessed Jesus, as Thou hast made Thyself my example, so be Thou pleased to be my guide. Inspire me with the same thoughts, inclinations, desires, and resolutions which were in Thy blessed nature. Help me to place my satisfaction there, where Thou livest in perpetual peace, amidst all the troubles and vexations of this life. Raise my spirit to that great and sublime good, which none can touch, much less remove; that, remaining in an unshaken possession of Thy love, and being lifted up in noble hopes of the glory to which Thy love will promote Thy faithful servants, I may not feel myself altered by any of the changes which are in the things that are under my feet. Dispose my mind, O God, to the sweetest and most gentle compliance with Thy providence.

And make me so perfectly in love with Thy will, that all that is great, or glorious, or delightful in this world, I may enjoy in a pure and clear conscience, void of offence towards Thee and towards all men. O the deliciousness of those pleasures! O the divineness of those joys! Bless me daily with a stronger taste of them, and satisfaction in them, till I come to enjoy that reward of well-doing, which exceeds all thoughts and desires, through our Lord and Saviour Christ Jesus. Amen.

IV.

I ADORE and praise, O Lord, Thy greatness, Thy power, wisdom, and goodness, which shine in all Thy works of creation and providence. They all show forth the majesty of Thy glory; and are placed and move in such comely order, that Thou Thyself rejoicest in all Thy works, and art perfectly pleased even in that which gives us grief and trouble. It is our duty, O blessed God, to be pleased too, and to rejoice in this knowledge which Thou hast given us of Thee, who art from everlasting to everlasting, and changest not, but art ever the same immutable love, exercising the most wise and tender providence in every part of this great world; and more especially over mankind, to whom Thou hast shown the highest kindness, and given unquestionable testimonies of Thy singular care of them, and good-will towards them.

O God, what things are those which Thou hast laid up for those that fear Thee; for those that trust in Thee, and depend entirely on Thy goodness, and submit to Thy will and pleasure! In what a kind relation Thou art pleased to stand unto us, that we may be confident Thou dearly lovest us, and wilt take care of us! All ages have experienced this love, that Thou, Lord, hast not forsaken them that seek Thee: therefore Thy face evermore will I seek. I will never doubt of Thy merciful kindness; but always believe that Thou art gracious and full of compassion, just and true in all Thy ways, O Thou King of saints. Confirm and strengthen these holy purposes in me by the assistance of Thy good Spirit, making these thoughts more strong, more lively, and mightily affecting my heart; so that I may be able to say, The Lord is my helper, I will not fear what man can do unto me. He hath not spared His only Son, but delivered Him up for us all: how shall He not with Him give us all things? I will bless the Lord at all times, His praise shall be continually in my mouth; my soul shall make her boast in the Lord, and I will rejoice in His salvation.

O blessed day, when we shall see Jesus again, and feel Him changing this vile body, and making it like His glorious body, by the power whereby He can subdue all things to Himself! O happy day, when all tears shall be wiped away from our eyes, and there shall be no sighing nor sorrow, but present satisfaction and joy for evermore! Amen.

JOHN FLAVEL, B. A.
1627–1691.

EFFICACY OF THE BLOOD OF THE CROSS.

THERE is sufficient efficacy in the blood of the Cross to expiate and wash away the greatest sins. This is manifest, for it is *precious blood*, as it is called, 1 Peter i. 18. 'Ye were not redeemed with corruptible things, as silver and gold; but with the precious blood of the Son of God.' This preciousness of the blood of Christ riseth from the union it hath with that Person, who is over all, God blessed for ever.

Before the efficacy of this blood, guilt vanishes, and shrinks away as the shadow before the glorious sun. Every drop of it hath a voice, and speaks to the soul that sits trembling under its guilt better things than the blood of Abel, Heb. x. 24. It sprinkles us from all evil, i. e. an unquiet and accusing conscience, Heb. x. 22. For having enough in it to satisfy God, it must needs have enough in it to satisfy conscience.

Can God exact satisfaction from the blood and death of His own Son, the surety of believers, and yet still demand it from believers? It cannot be.

'Who (saith the apostle) shall lay any thing to the charge of God's elect? It is God that justifieth. Who shall condemn? It is Christ that died,' Rom. viii. 33, 34. And why are faith and repentance prescribed as the *means* of pardon? Why doth God every where in His Word, call upon sinners to repent, and believe in this blood? encouraging them so to do, by so many precious promises of remission; and declaring the inevitable and eternal ruin of all impenitent and unbelieving ones, who despise and reject this blood? What, I say, doth all this speak, but the possibility of a pardon for the greatest of sinners; and the certainty of a free, full, and final pardon for all believing sinners? O what a joyful sound is this! What ravishing voices of peace, pardon, grace, and acceptance, come to our ears from the blood of the Cross?

The greatest guilt that ever was contracted upon a trembling, shaking conscience, can stand before the efficacy of the blood of Christ no more than the sinner himself can stand before the justice of the Lord, with all that guilt upon him.

Reader, the word assures thee, whatever thou hast been, or art, that sins of as deep a dye as thine, have been washed away in this blood. 'I was a blasphemer, a persecutor, injurious; but I obtained mercy,' saith Paul. 1 Tim. i. 13. But it may be thou wilt object; this was a rare and singular instance, and it is a great question whether any other sinner shall find the like grace that he did. No question of it at all, if you believe in Christ as he did; for he tells us, ver. 16, 'For this cause I obtained mercy, that in me first Jesus Christ might show forth all long-suffering, for a pattern to them which should hereafter believe on Him to life everlasting.' So that upon the same grounds he obtained mercy, you may obtain it also.

Those very men who had a hand in the shedding of Christ's blood, had the benefit of that blood afterwards pardoning them, Acts ii. 36. There is nothing but unbelief and impenitency of heart can bar thy soul from the blessings of this blood.

Fountain of Life.

'BLESSED are they which hunger and thirst after righteousness, for they shall be filled.' They shall then depend no more upon the stream, but drink from the overflowing fountain itself, Psalm xxxvi. 8: 'They shall be abundantly satisfied with the fatness of Thy house, and Thou shalt make them drink of the river of Thy pleasures: for with Thee is the fountain of life, and in Thy light shall we see light.' There they shall drink and praise, and praise and drink for evermore; all their thirsty desires shall be filled with complete satisfaction. O how desirable a state is heaven upon this account! and how should we be restless till we come thither; as the thirsty traveler is until he meet that cool, refreshing spring he wants and seeks for. This present state is a state of thirsting, that to come of refreshment and satisfaction. Some drops indeed come from the fountain by faith, but they quench not the believer's thirst; rather like water sprinkled on the fire, they make it burn the more: but there the thirsty soul hath enough.

The Study of Christ.

THE study of Jesus Christ is the most noble subject that ever a soul spent itself upon; those that rack and torture their brains upon other studies, like children, weary themselves at a low game; the eagle plays at the sun itself. The angels study this doctrine, and stoop down to look into this deep abyss. What are the truths discovered in Christ, but the very secrets that from eternity lay hid in the bosom of God? Eph. iii. 8, 9. God's heart is opened to men in Christ, John i. 18; this makes the Gospel such a glorious dispensation, because Christ is so gloriously revealed therein, 1 Cor. iii. 9, and the studying of Christ in the Gospel stamps such a heavenly glory upon the contemplating soul, ver. 18.

It is the most sweet and comfortable knowledge, to be studying Jesus Christ, what is it but to be digging among all the veins and springs of comfort? and the deeper you dig, the more do these springs flow upon you. How are hearts ravished with the discoveries of Christ in the Gospel. What ecstacies, meltings, transports, do gracious souls meet there.

Vision of God in Glory.

'WHEN I awake I shall be satisfied with Thy likeness.' This sight of God, in glory, called the beatifical vision, must needs yield ineffable satisfaction to the beholding soul, inasmuch as it will be an *intuitive* vision. The intellectual or mental eye shall see God, 1 John iii. 2. The corporeal, glorified eye shall see Christ, Job xix. 26, 27. What a ravishing vision will this be! and how much will it exceed all reports and apprehensions we had here of it! Surely one half was not told us. It will be a *transformative vision*, it will change the beholder into its own image and likeness. 'We shall be like Him, for we shall see Him as He is,' 1 John iii. 2. It will be an *appropriative vision:* 'Whom I shall see for myself,' Job xix. 26, 27. In heaven, interest is clear and undoubted; fear is cast out: no need of marks and signs there; for what a man sees and enjoys, how can he doubt of? It will be a *ravishing vision;* these we have by faith are so, how much more those in glory? How was Paul transported, when he was in a visional way rapt up into the third heaven, and heard the unutterable things, though he was not admitted into the blessed society, but was with them, as the angels are in our assemblies, a stander-by, a looker-on. It will be a *fully satisfying vision;* God will then be all in all. The blessed soul will feel itself blessed, filled, satisfied in every part. Ah, what a happiness is here! to look and love, to drink and sing, and drink again at the fountain head of the highest glory!

Divine Care.

'ALL things shall work together for good.' From what quarter soever the wind bloweth, God will take care that it shall be useful to drive you to your port; the very providences that cast you down, by virtue of this promise, prove as serviceable and beneficial as those that lift you up.

The care of God stands engaged in the promise, for the help and aid of His people in all the extremities and exigencies of their lives, Psalm xlvi. 1. 'God is our refuge and strength, a very present help in trouble.' Never is the care of God more visible and conspicuous than in such times of need.

The care of God is engaged to carry His people safe through all the dangers of the way, and bring them all home to glory at last, John x. 28. 'I give unto them eternal life, and they shall never perish, neither shall any man pluck them out of my hand.' This care of God, thus engaged for you, is your convoy to accompany and secure you, till it set you safe into your harbor of eternal rest.

You have heard how the care of God is engaged for you by promise; now see how it actuates and exerts itself for the people of God in the various methods of providence; and here, O here is the sweetest pleasure of the Christian life, a delight far transcending all the delights of this life. Sit down Christian in this chamber also, and make but such observations upon the care of thy God as follow; and then tell me whether the world, with all its pleasures and delights, can give thee such another entertainment.

Reflect upon the constant, sweet and suitable provisions, that from time to time have been prepared for thee and thine, by this care of thy God; for whensoever thy wants did come, I am sure from hence came thy supplies, it hath enabled thee to return the same answer the disciples did to that question, Luke xxii. 35: 'Lacked ye any thing?' And they said, Nothing.

Reflect with admiration upon the various difficulties of your lives, wherein your thoughts have been entangled, and out of which you have been extricated and delivered by the care of God over you; how oft have your thoughts been like a raveled skein of silk, so entangled and perplexed with the difficulties and fears before you, that you could find no end, but the longer you thought, the more you were puzzled, till you have left thinking and fell to praying; and there you have found the right end to wind up all your thoughts upon the bottom of peace and sweet contentment, according to that direction, Psalm xxxvii. 5: 'Commit thy way unto the Lord, trust also in Him, and He shall bring it to pass.'

Observe with a melting heart, how the care of thy God hath disposed and directed thy way to unforeseen advantages: had He not ordered thy steps when, and as He did, thou hadst not been in possession of those temporal and spiritual mercies that sweeten thy life at this day. Surely the steps of good men are ordered by the Lord: and as for thee, Christian, what reason hast thou, with an heart overflowing with love and thankfulness, to look up and say, *my Father, thou art the guide of my youth?*

It is sweet to live by faith upon Divine care. O what a serene life might we live, careful for nothing, but making known our requests unto God in every thing, Phil. iv. 6, casting all our care on Him that careth for us, 1 Pet. v. 7, perplexing our thoughts about nothing, but rolling every burden upon God by faith!

Faith in God's Unchangeableness.

LIVE by faith upon God's unchangeableness under the greatest changes of your own condition in this world. Providence may make great alterations upon all your outward comforts: it may cast you down, how dear soever you be to God, from riches into poverty, from health into sickness, from honor into reproach, from liberty into bondage. Yet still it is your duty, and will be your great privilege in the midst of all these changes, to act your faith upon the never-changing God, as that holy man did, Hab. iii. 17, 'Although the fig tree shall not blossom, neither fruit be in the vine; the labor of the olive shall fail; and the fields shall yield no meat; the flocks shall be cut off from the fold, and there shall be no herd in the stall; yet will I rejoice in the Lord, I will joy in the God of my salvation.'

Live upon the unchangeableness of God under the greatest and saddest changes of your spiritual condition; God may cloud the light of His countenance over thy soul, He may fill thee with fears and troubles, and the Comforter that should relieve thee may seem to be far off; yet still maintain thy faith in the unchangeableness of His love; trust in the name of the Lord, stay thyself upon thy God, when thou walkest in darkness and hast no light, Isa. 1. 10.

Walking with God.

O SWEET and pleasant walk! all pleasures, all joys are in that walk with God. 'Blessed are the people that hear the joyful sound; they shall walk, O Lord, in the light of Thy countenance,' Psalm lxxxix. 15. The joyful sound there spoken of was the sound of the trumpet, which called the people to the solemn assemblies, where they walked in the light of God's countenance, the sweet manifestations of His favor; and because the world is so apt to suspect the reality and certainty of this doctrine, the apostle again asserts it, Phil. iii. 20, 'Truly our conversation is in heaven.' We breathe below, but we live above; we walk on earth, but our conversation is in heaven.

Rest in God.

WHEN we attain perfect communion with God in heaven, we attain to perfect rest, and all the rest the spirit of man finds on earth, is found in communion with God. Take a sanctified person, who hath intermitted for some time his communion with the Lord, and ask him, Is your soul at rest and ease? He will tell you, no! The motions of his soul are like those of a member out of joint, neither comely nor easy. Let that man recover his spiritual frame again, and, with it, he recovers his rest and comfort. Christians, you meet with variety of troubles in this world; many a sweet comfort is cut off, many a hopeful project dashed by the hand of providence; and what think you is the meaning of those blasting, disappointing providences? Surely this is their design and errand, to disturb your false rest in the bosom of the creature; to pluck away those pillows you were laying your heads upon, that thereby you might be reduced unto God, and recover your lost communion with Him; and say, with David, 'Return unto thy rest, O my soul.' Sometimes we are settling ourselves to rest in an estate, in a child, or the like; at this time it is usual for God to say, go, losses, smite and blast such a man's estate; go, death, and take away the desire of his eyes with a stroke, that my child may find rest no where but in me. God is the ark; the soul, like the dove Noah sent forth, let it fly where it will, it shall find no rest till it come back to God.

Communion with God.

IT is the *desire* of all gracious souls throughout the world. Wherever there is a gracious soul, the desires of that soul are working after communion with God. As Christ was called, *The desire of all nations,* so communion with Him is *the desire of all nations:* and this speaks the excellency of it, Psalm xxvii. 4: 'One thing have I desired of the Lord, that will I seek after; that I might dwell in the house of the Lord all the days of my life, to see the beauty of the Lord, and to enquire in His temple;' i. e. to enjoy communion with Him in the public duties of His worship. *One thing have I desired*, that is, one thing above all other things; such a one, as, if God shall give me, I can comfortably bear the want of all other things. Let Him deny me what He will, if so be He will not deny me this one thing; this one thing shall richly recompense the want of all other things. Hence the desires of the saints are so intense and fervent after this one thing; Psalm xlii. 1: 'My soul panteth after Thee, O God;' and Psalm cxix. 81: 'My soul fainteth for Thy salvation.' Psalm ci. 2: 'When wilt Thou come unto me?' No duties can satisfy without it; the soul cannot bear the delays, much less the denials of it. They reckon their lives worth nothing without it. Ministers may come, ordinances and Sabbaths may come; but there is no satisfaction to the desires of a gracious heart, till God comes too; *O when wilt Thou come unto me?*

CHRIST'S LOVE MANIFESTED FROM THE CROSS.

THE transcendent love of Christ shines out in its full strength upon the souls of sinners from the Cross; and there is nothing like love to draw love. When Christ was lifted up upon the Cross, He gave such a glorious demonstration of the strength of His love to sinners, as one would think should draw love from the hardest heart that ever lodged in a sinner's breast. 'Herein is love,' saith the apostle, ' not that we loved God, but that He loved us, and sent His Son to be a propitiation for our sins,' 1 John iv. 10 q. d. Here is the triumph, the riches and glory of Divine love; never was such love manifested in the world. There is much of God's love in temporal providences, but all is nothing to this; this is love in its highest elevation; love in its meridian glory; before it was none like it, and after it shall none appear like unto it.

Free Grace.

THE willingness of Christ to receive the willing soul, how many and great soever its sins and unworthiness be, appears from the *actual grants* of pardon and mercy, even to the vilest sinners that ever were upon the earth, when they thus came unto Him. Here you see how the waters of free-grace rise higher and higher. An invitation is much; a promise of welcome is more: but the actual grant of mercy is most satisfying of all. Come on, poor trembling soul, do not be discouraged, stretch out the small, weak arms of thy faith to that great and gracious Redeemer; open thy heart wide to receive Him; He will not refuse to come in. He hath sealed thousands of pardons to as vile wretches as thyself; He never yet shut the door of mercy upon a willing, hungering soul.

Grace of God.

IT is superabounding grace. Waters do not so abound in the ocean, nor light in the sun, as grace and compassion do in the bowels of God towards broken-hearted and hungry sinners, Isa. lv. 6: 'Let him return unto the Lord, and He will have mercy upon him; and to our God, for He will abundantly pardon.' The compassions of our God inserted that word on purpose to relieve poor souls, fainting under the sense of their abounding iniquities. Here is abundant pardon for abounding guilt; and yet, lest a desponding sinner should not find enough here to quiet his fears, the Lord goes yet farther in the expression of His grace, Rom. v. 20: 'Where sin abounded, grace did much more abound.' It overflowed all the bounds, it rose quite above the high-water mark of sin and guilt: but these overflowings of grace run only through that channel of all grace, Jesus Christ, to broken-hearted and obedient sinners.

Pardon for the most Heinous Sins.

THERE is a sacrifice laid out and appointed for these sins. O bless God for that! they are no where excepted from the possibility of forgiveness. Nothing but the impenitency of thy heart, and obstinacy of thy will, can bar thee from a full and final pardon. Jesus Christ can save thee to the uttermost. Say not within thyself, can the virtue of His blood extend itself to the remission of this or that sin? He can save to the uttermost. Look round about thee to the uttermost horizon of all thy guilt, and Christ can save thee to the uttermost that the eye of thy conscience can discern, yea, and beyond it too; but then thou must come unto Him. You speak of the greatness of sin, and you have cause to have sad thoughts about it; but, in the mean time, you consider not, that your unbelief, by which you stand off from Christ, your only remedy, is certainly the greatest of all the sins that ever you stood guilty of against the Lord. This is the sin that binds the guilt of all your other sins upon you.

Peace to the Soul.

FAITH is not only the messenger that brings you a pardon from heaven; but it is, as I may say, that heavenly *herald* that publishes peace in the soul of a sinner. O *peace*, how sweet a word art thou! how welcome to a poor condemned sinner! 'Beautiful upon the mountains are the feet of them that publish peace.' Now it is faith that brings this blessed news and publishes it in the soul, without which all the publishers of peace without us, can administer but little support, Rom. v. 1. Faith brings the soul out of the storms and tempests with which it was tossed, into a sweet rest and calm, Heb. iv. 3: 'We which have believed do enter into rest.' Is the quiet harbor welcome to poor weather-beaten seamen, after they have past furious storms and many fears upon the raging sea? O how welcome then must peace be to that soul that hath been tossed upon the tempestuous ocean of its own fears and terrors, blown up and incensed by the terrible blasts of the law and conscience? It was a comfortable sight to Noah and his family, to see an *olive-leaf* in the mouth of the dove, by which they knew the waters were abated. But, oh! what is it to hear such a voice as this from the mouth of faith, *Fury is not in me*, saith the Lord; His anger is turned away, and He comforteth thee? Fear not thou poor tempest-tossed soul, the God of peace is thy God.

Joy in the Holy Ghost.

THIS is somewhat beyond peace; it is the very quintessence and spirit of all consolation. The kingdom of God is said to consist in it, Rom. xiv. 17; it is somewhat near to the joy of the glorified, 1 Pet. i. 8; it is heaven upon earth. All believers do not immediately attain it, but one time or other God usually gives them a taste of it; and when He doth, it is as it were a short salvation. O, who can tell what that is which the apostle calls, 'The shedding abroad of the love of God in the heart, by the Holy Ghost, which is given to us!' Rom. v. 5. It is a joy that wants an epithet to express the sweetness of it, 1 Pet. i. 8. 'Joy unspeakable and full of glory.' It hath the very scent and taste of heaven in it, and there is but a gradual difference betwixt it and the joy of heaven. This joy of the Holy Ghost is a spiritual cheerfulness streaming through the soul of a believer upon the Spirit's testimony, which clears his interest in Christ and glory. No sooner doth the Spirit shed forth the love of God into the believer's heart, but it streams and overflows with joy. Joy is no more under that soul's command. And this will evidently appear, if you consider the matter of it; it arises from the light of God's countenance, Psalm iv. 6, 7, the heavenly glory, 1 Pet. i. 8. 'Whom having not seen we love,' &c. The soul is transported with joy, ravished with the glory and excellency of Christ. Didst thou ever see this Christ whom thy soul is so ravished with? No, I have not seen Him; yet my soul is transported with so much love to Him, *whom having not seen we love.* But if thou never sawest Him, how comes thy soul to be so delighted and ravished with Him? why, though I never saw Him by the eye of sense, yet I do see Him by the eye of faith; and by that sight my soul is flooded with spiritual joy. *Believing we rejoice.* But what manner of joy is that which you taste? why, no tongue can express that, *for it is joy unspeakable.* But how are Christ and heaven turned into such ravishing joys to the soul? why, the Spirit of the Lord gives the believing soul not only a sight to discern the transcendent excellency of these spiritual objects, but a sight of his interest in them also. This is my Christ, and this the glory prepared for me. Without interest, heaven itself cannot be turned unto joy, 'My soul rejoices in God my Saviour,' Luke i. 47.

This joy of the Lord shall be your strength, Neh. viii. 10. Let God but give a person a little of this joy into his heart, and he shall presently feel himself strengthened by it, either to do or to suffer the will of God. Now he can pray with enlargement, hear with comfort, meditate with delight: and if God call him to suffer, this joy shall strengthen him to bear it. This was it that made the martyrs go singing to the stake. This therefore transcends all the joys of this lower world.

Foretastes of Heaven.

BELIEVERS have a double pledge, or earnest for heaven, one in the person of Christ, who is entered into that glory for them, John xiv. 2, 3, the other in the joys and comforts of the Spirit, which they feel, and taste in themselves. These are two great securities, and the designs of God in giving us these earnests and foretastes of heaven, are not only to settle our minds but to whet our industry, that we may long the more earnestly, and labor the more diligently for the full possession. The Lord sees how apt we are to flag in the pursuit of heavenly glory, and therefore gives His people a taste, an earnest of it, to excite their diligence in the pursuits of it.

As the visions of God are begun on earth, so the heavenly delights are begun here also. Some drops of that delight, are let fall here, Psalm xciv. 19. 'In the multitude of the thoughts I had within me, Thy comforts delight my soul.' David's heart, it is likely, had been full of sorrow and trouble; a sea of gall and wormwood had overflowed his soul: God lets fall but a drop or two of heavenly delight, and all is turned into sweetness and comfort. Is there not something here of that transformation of the soul into the image of God, which is complete in heaven, and a special part of the glory thereof? It is said in 1 John iii. 2: 'We shall be like Him, for we shall see Him as he is.' This is heaven, this is glory, to have the soul moulded into full conformity with God: something thereof is experienced in this world: O that we had more! 2 Cor. iii. 18: 'But we all with open face, beholding as in a glass the glory of the Lord, are changed into the same image, from glory to glory, as by the Spirit of the Lord.' Is there not something felt here of the ravishing sweetness of God's presence in ordinances and duties, which is a faint shadow, at least, of the joys of His glorious presence in heaven? There is certainly a felt presence of God, a sensible nearness unto God at sometimes and in some duties of religion, wherein His name is as ointment poured forth, Cant. i. 3, something that is felt beyond and above all the comforts of this world. In a word, the joys of heaven are unspeakable joys, no words can make known to others what they are. When Paul was caught up into *paradise* he heard unspeakable words, 2 Cor. xii. 4, and are there not times, even in this life, wherein the saints do feel that which no words can express? 1 Pet. i. 8, Rev. ii. 17.

If a relish, a taste of heaven, in the earnest thereof, be so transporting and ravishing, what then is the full fruition of God! If these be unutterable, what must that be! Give me leave to say, whatever the comforts and joys of any believer in this world may be, yet heaven will be a surprise to him when he comes thither.

The Longing Soul's Reflection.

I HAVE waited for Thy salvation, O God! Having received Thy first fruits, my soul longs to fill its bosom with the full ripe sheaves of glory: 'As the hart panteth for the water brooks, so panteth my soul for Thee, O God! O when shall I come and appear before God!' I desire to be dissolved and to be with Christ! When shall I see that most lovely face? When shall I hear His soul-transporting voice! Some need patience to die: I need it as much to live. Thy sights, O God, by faith, have made this world a burden, this body a burden, and this soul to cry, like thirsty David, 'O that one would give me of the waters of Bethlehem to drink!' The husbandman longs for his harvest, because it is the reward of all his toil and labor. But what is his harvest to mine? What is a little corn to the enjoyment of God? What is the joy of harvest to the joy of heaven? What are the shoutings of men in the fields to the acclamations of glorified spirits in the kingdom of God? Lord, I have gone forth bearing more precious seed than they; when shall I return rejoicing, bringing my sheaves with me? Their harvest comes when they receive their corn; mine comes when I leave it. O much desired! O day of gladness of my heart! How long, Lord! how long! Here I wait as the poor man at Bethesda's pool, looking when my turn will come, but every one steps into heaven before me; yet Lord, I am content to wait till my time is fully come: I would be content to stay for my *glorification* till I have finished the work of my *generation;* and when I have done the will of God, then to receive the promise. If Thou have any work on earth to use me in, I am content to abide: behold, the husbandman waiteth, and so will I; for Thou art a God of judgment; and blessed are all they that wait for Thee.

Reflection of a Growing Christian.

CHEER thyself, O my soul! with the heart-strengthening bread of this Divine meditation. Let faith turn every drop of this truth into a soul-reviving cordial. God hath sown the precious seed of grace upon my soul; and though my heart hath been an unkindly soil, which hath kept it back, and much hindered its growth, yet, blessed be the Lord, it still grows on, though by slow degrees; and from the springing of the seed, and shooting forth of those gracious habits, I may conclude an approaching harvest: Now is my salvation nearer than when I believed; every day I come nearer to my salvation, Rom. xiii. 11. O that every day I were more active for the God of my salvation! Grow on, my soul, and add to thy faith virtue, to thy virtue knowledge, &c. Grow on from faith to faith; keep thyself under the ripening influences of heavenly ordinances: The faster thou growest in grace, the sooner thou shalt be reaped down in mercy, and bound up in the bundle of life, 1 Sam. xv. 29. I have not yet attained the measure and proportion of grace assigned to me, neither am I already perfect, but am reaching forth to the things before me, and pressing towards the mark for the prize of my heavenly calling, Phil. iii. 12, 13.

Lost and Found.

O MY soul! for ever bless and admire the love of Jesus Christ, who came from heaven to seek and save such a lost soul as I was. Lord, how marvelous! how matchless is Thy love! I was lost, and am found: I am found, and did not seek; nay, I am found by Him from whom I fled. Thy love, O my Saviour, was a preventing love, a wonderful love; Thou lovedst me much more than I loved myself; I was cruel to my own soul, but Thou wast kind; Thou soughtest for me a lost sinner, and not for lost angels; Thy hand of grace caught hold of me, and hath let go thousands and ten thousands as good as myself by nature; like another David, Thou didst rescue my poor lost soul out of the mouth of the destroyer; yea, more than so, Thou didst lose Thine own life to find mine: and now, dear Jesus, since I am thus marvelously recovered, shall I ever straggle again from Thee? O let it forever be a warning to me, how I turn aside into the by-paths of sin any more.

The Ocean of Divine Mercy.

IN the vastness of the ocean, we have also a lively emblem of eternity. Who can comprehend or measure the ocean, but God? And who can comprehend eternity but He that is said *to inhabit it?* Isa. lvii. 5. Though shallow rivers may be drained and dried up, yet the ocean cannot. And though these transitory days, months, and years will at last expire; yet eternity shall not. O! it is a long word! and amazing matter! what is eternity but a constant permanency of persons and things, in one and the same state and condition forever; putting them beyond all possibility of change?

And is the mercy of God like the great deep, an ocean that none can fathom? What unspeakable comfort is this to me? may the pardoned soul say. Did Israel sing a song when the Lord had overwhelmed their corporeal enemies in the seas? And shall not I break forth into His praises, who hath drowned all my sins in the depth of mercy? O my soul, bless thou the Lord, and let His high praises ever be in thy mouth. Mayest thou not say, that He hath gone to as high an extent and degree of mercy in pardoning thee as ever He did in any? O my God, who is like unto Thee! that pardoneth iniquity, transgression and sin. What mercy, but the mercy of a God, could cover such abomination as mine?

Joy of the Redeemed.

O WHAT a transcendent joy, yea, ravishing, will over-run the hearts of saints, when, after so many conflicts, temptations, and afflictions, they arrive in glory and are harbored in heaven, where they shall rest for ever! 2 Thess. i. 7. The Scripture saith, 'They shall sing the song of Moses and of the

Lamb,' Rev. xv. 3. The song of Moses was a triumphant song composed for the celebration of that glorious deliverance at the Red sea. The saints are now fluctuating upon a troublesome and tempestuous sea; their hearts sometimes ready to sink, and die within them at the apprehension of so many and great dangers and difficulties. Many a hard storm they ride out, and many straits and troubles they here encounter with, but at last they arrive at their desired and long-expected haven, and then heaven rings and resounds with their joyful acclamations. And how can it be otherwise, when as soon as ever they set foot upon that glorious shore, Christ Himself meets and receives them with a 'Come, ye blessed of my Father,' Matth. xxv. 34.

ASSURANCE.

IT is the very riches of faith, the most pleasant fruit which grows upon the top branches of faith. The Scripture tells us of an assurance of understanding, hope and faith. All these graces are precious in themselves; but the assurance of each of them is the most sweet and pleasant part. Knowledge above knowledge, is the full assurance of knowledge: hope above hope, is the full assurance of hope: and faith above faith, is the full assurance of faith. The least and lowest act of saving faith is precious, and above all value; what then must the highest and most excellent acts of faith be? Certainly there is a sweetness in the assurance of faith, that few men have the privilege to taste: and they that do, can find no words able to express it to another's understanding. The weakest Christian is exalted above all other men; but the assured Christian hath a preference before all other Christians.

It is heart's ease; the very sabbath and sweet repose of the soul. Thousands of poor Christians would part with all they possess in this world to enjoy it; but it flies from them. The life that most of them live, is a life betwixt hopes and fears; their interest in Christ is very doubtful to them. Sometimes they are encouraged, from sensible workings of grace; then all is dashed again by the contrary stirrings and workings of their own corruptions. Now the sun shines out clear, by and by the heavens are overcast and clouded again: but the assured Christian is at rest. He can take Christ into the arms of faith, and say, 'My Beloved is mine, and I am His. Return to thy rest, O my soul, for the Lord hath dealt bountifully with thee!'

It is the pleasure of life; yea, the most rational, pure, and transporting pleasure. What is life without pleasure? And what pleasure is there in the world, comparable to this pleasure?

Constancy of Christ's Love.

THE constancy of Christ's love to His people passeth knowledge: No length of time, no distance of place, no change of condition, either with Him or us, can possibly make any alteration of His affections towards us: 'He is the same yesterday, to-day, and for ever,' Heb. xiii. 8. It is noted also by the evangelist, John xiii. 1: 'That having loved His own which were in the world, He loved them to the end.' It is true His condition is altered; He is no more in this world conversing with His people, as He did once in the *days of His flesh:* He is now at the right-hand of God, in the highest glory; but yet His heart is the same that ever it was, for love and tenderness to His people. Our conditions also are often altered in this world; but His love suffers no alteration. Yea, which is much more admirable, we do many things daily that grieve Him and offend Him; yet He takes not away His loving-kindness from us, nor suffers His faithfulness to fail. We pour out so much cold water of unkindness and provocation, as is enough to cool and quench any love in the world, except His love; but notwithstanding all, He continues unchangeable in love to us.

Maturity of Grace.

WHEN the corn is near ripe, it bows the head and stoops lower than when it was green. When the people of God are near ripe for heaven, they grow more humble and self-denying than in the days of their first profession. The longer a saint grows in this world, the better he is still acquainted with his own heart and his obligations to God; both which are very humbling things. Paul had one foot in heaven when he called himself the chiefest of sinners, and least of saints, 1 Tim. i. 15; Eph. iii. 8. A Christian, in the progress of his knowledge and grace, is like a vessel cast into the sea; the more it fills the deeper it sinks.

End of the Christian's Trials.

THE time is coming, when thy heart shall be as thou wouldst have it; when thou shalt be discharged of all these cares, fears, and sorrows, and never cry out, O my hard, my proud, my vain, my earthly heart, any more! When all darkness shall be vanished from thine understanding; and thou shalt clearly discover all truths in God, that crystal ocean of truth: When all vanity shall be purged perfectly out of thy thoughts, and they be everlastingly, ravishingly and delightfully entertained and exercised upon that supreme goodness, and infinite excellency of God, from whom they shall never start any more like a broken bow. And as for thy pride, passion, earthliness, and all other matters of thy complaint and trouble, it shall be said of them, as of the Egyptians to Israel, 'Stand still, and see the salvation of God.' These corruptions thou seest to day, henceforth thou shalt see them no more for ever! when thou shalt lay down thy weapons of prayers, tears and groans, and put on the armor of light, not to fight but triumph in.

Lord! when shall this blessed day come? How long! how long! Holy and True? My soul waiteth for Thee! Come, my Beloved! and be Thou like a roe or a young hart upon the mountains of Bether. Amen.

STEPHEN CHARNOCK, B. D.
1628-1680.

MEDITATION ON THE GLORY OF CHRIST.

MEDITATE upon the glory of Christ: without a due and frequent reflection upon it, we can never have a spirit of thankfulness for our great redemption; because we cannot else have sound impressions of the magnificent grace of God in Christ. It is the least we can do, to give Him a room in our thoughts, who hath been a forerunner in glory, to make room for us in a happy world. As the ancient Israelites linked their devotion to the temple and ark at Jerusalem, the visible sign God had given them of His presence, ought we not also to fix our eyes and hearts on the holy place which contains our ark, the body of the Lord Jesus? The meditation on this glory will keep us in acts of faith on Him, obedience to Him, a lively hope of enjoying blessedness by Him, 1 Peter i. 21. If we did believe Him dignified with power at the right hand of His Father, it would be the strongest motive to encourage and quicken our obedience and fill us with hopes of being with Him, since He is gone up in triumph as our Head: it would make us highly bless God for the glory of Christ, since it is the day of our triumph, and the assurance of our liberty.

It would alienate our affections from the world, and fix them upon heaven. The thoughts of His glory would put our low and sordid souls to the blush, and shame our base and unworthy affections, so unsuitable to the glory of our Head. If we looked upon Christ in heaven, 'our conversation would be more there,' Phil. iii. 20, 21: our hearts would seek more 'the things which are above,' Col. iii. 1; we should loathe every thing, where we do not find Him; and think on that heaven, where only we can fully enjoy Him. It would make us have heavenly pantings after the glory of another world, and disjoin our affections from the mud and dirt of this. This would elevate our hearts from the cross to the throne, from the grave to His glory, from His winding-sheet to His robes. If we think on Him mounted to heaven, why should we have affections groveling upon the earth? It is not fit our hearts should be where Christ would not vouchsafe to reside Himself after His work was done. If He would have had our souls tied to the earth, He would have made earth His habitation; but going up to the higher world, He taught us that we should follow Him in heart, till He fetched our souls and bodies thither, to be with Him in person.

It would quicken our desires to be with Christ. How did the apostle long to be a stranger to the body, that he might be in the arms of his triumphant Lord! Phil. i. 23. How did Jacob ardently desire to see Joseph, when he heard he was not only living, but in honor in Egypt! And should not we upon the meditation of this glory be inflamed with a longing to behold it, since we have the prayer of Christ Himself to encourage our belief that it shall be so? What spouse would not desire to be with her husband in that glory she hears he is in? What loving member hath not an appetite to be joined to the head?

It would encourage those at a distance from Him to come to Him, and believe in Him. What need we fear, since He is entered into glory, and set down upon a throne of grace? If our sins are great, shall we despair, if we do believe in Him, and endeavor to obey Him? This is not only to set light by His blood, but to think Him unworthy of the glory He is possessed of, in imagining any guilt so great that it cannot be expiated, or any stain so deep that it cannot be purified by Him. A nation should run to Him because He is glorified, Isaiah lv. 5. The most condescending affections that ever He discovered, the most gracious invitations that ever He made, were at those times when He had a sense of this glory in a particular manner, to show His intention in His possessing it. When He spake of all things delivered to Him by His Father, an invitation of men to come unto Him is the use He makes of it, Matt. xi. 27, 28. If this be the use He makes of His glory to invite us, it should be the use we should make of the thoughts of it, to accept His proffer. Well then, let us be frequent in the believing reviews of it. When Elisha fixed his eyes upon his master Elijah ascending into heaven, he had a double portion of his spirit. If we would exercise our understandings by faith on the ascension and glory of the Redeemer, and our hearts accompany Him in His sitting down upon the throne of His Father, we might receive from Him fuller showers, be revived with more fresh and vigorous communications of the Spirit; for thus He bestows grace and gifts upon men.

Christ our Advocate.

'If any man sin, we have an Advocate with the Father, Jesus Christ the righteous!' 1 John ii. 1. Believers, while in the world, are liable to acts of sin. 'If any man;' he supposeth that grace may be so weak, temptation so strong, that a believer may fall into a grievous sin. While men are in the flesh, there are indwelling sins, and invading temptations; there is a body of death within them, and snares about them. The apostle excludes not himself, for, putting himself by the term 'we' into the number of those that want the remedy, he supposes himself liable to the disease: 'We have an Advocate with the Father.'

Though believers do, through the strength of the flesh, subtlety of the tempter, power of a temptation, and weakness of grace, fall into sin, yet they should not despair of succor and pardon. 'If any man sin, we have an Advocate.' Such a total despondency would utterly ruin them; despair would bind their sins upon them. Be not only cast down under the consideration of the curses and threatenings of the law, but be erected by the promises of the Gospel, and the standing office of Christ in heaven.

Faith in Christ must be exercised as often as we sin. 'If any man sin, we have an Advocate.' What is it to us that there is an Advocate, unless we will put our cause into His hand; though we have a faithful attorney in our worldly affairs, yet upon any emergency we must entertain him, let him know our cause, if we expect relief. Though Christ, being omniscient, knows and compassionates our case, yet He will be solicited; as, though God knows our wants, He will be supplicated to for the supplies of our necessities; though He understands our case, He would have us understand it too, that we may value His office. Faith ought therefore to be exercised, because, by reason of our daily sins, we stand in need of a daily intercession. 'If any man sin;' it implies that every man ought to make reflections on his conscience, lament his condition, turn his eye to his great Advocate, acquaint Him with his state, and entertain Him afresh in his cause. Though He lives for ever to make intercession, it is only for those who come to God by Him, as their Agent and Solicitor; for those who come to the Judge, but first come to Him as their Attorney.

The proper intention of this office of Christ, is

for sins after a state of faith. He was a Priest in His propitiation, to bring God and man together; He is a Priest in His intercession, to keep God and man together; His propitiation is the foundation of His intercession, but His intercession is an act distinct from the other; that was done by His death, this is managed in His life; His death was for our reconciliation, but His life is for the perpetuating that reconciliation: Rom. v. 10. 'If any man sin, we have an Advocate.' If any man sin that hath entered into a state of communion with God, let him know that this office was erected in heaven to keep him right in the favor of the Judge of all the world. We should quickly mar all, and be as miserable the next minute after regeneration and justification as before, if provision were not in this way made for us. In the first acts, faith eyes the propitiation of Christ, and pitches upon His death: Christ, as dying, is the great support of a soul newly come out of the gulf of misery, and terrors of conscience: in after acts, it eyes the life of Christ as well as the death, taking in both His propitiation and intercession together.

How divine is the Gospel! 'Sin not,' — 'if any man sin.' It gives us comfort against the demerit of sin, without encouraging the acts of sin; it teaches us an exact conformity to God in holiness, and provides, for our full security, in Christ a powerful Advocate. No religion is so pure for the honor of God, nor any so cordial for the refreshment of the creature.

Christ presenting the Memorials of His Death.

IT is by the displaying the whole merit of His passion, that He doth solicit for us. Intercession is not properly a sarcedotal act without respect to the sacrifice. It was with the blood of the sacrifice that the high priest was to enter into the holy of holies, and sprinkle it there. The same blood that had been shed without on the day of expiation, was to be carried within the veil. What was done typically, Christ doth really; first give Himself a sacrifice, and then present Himself as the sacrifice for us. The apostle shows us the manner of it, Heb. xii. 24; the blood of Christ is a speaking blood, as well as the blood of Abel. It speaks in the same manner as Abel's blood did, though not for the same end. As the blood of Abel, presenting itself before the eyes of God, was as powerful to draw down the vengeance of God, as if it had uttered a cry so loud as to reach to heaven; so the blood of Christ, being presented before the throne of God, powerfully excites the favor of God by the loudness of its cry. He speaks by His blood, and His blood speaks by its merit. The petitions of His lips had done us no good without the voice of His blood. He stands as a Lamb slain, when He presents the prayers of the saints, Rev. v. 6, 8; with His bleeding wounds open as so many mouths full of pleas for us, and every one of them is the memorial and mark of the things which He suffered, and for what end He suffered them; as the wounds of a soldier, received in the defence and for the honor of his country, displayed to persons sensible of them, are the loudest and best pleas for the grant of his request. If the party-colored rainbow being looked upon by God, reminds Him of His covenant not to destroy the world again by a deluge, Gen. ix. 14-16, much more are the wounds which Christ bears both in His hands, feet, and side, remembrancers to Him of the covenant of grace made with repenting and believing sinners. The look of God upon these wounds whereby so great an oblation is remembered, doth as efficaciously move Him to look kindly upon us, as the look upon the rainbow disposeth Him to the continuance of the world. If our Saviour had not a mouth to speak, He hath blood to plead, and His blood cries louder in heaven for us, than His voice did in any of the prayers He uttered upon earth; for by this His performance of the articles on His part is manifested, and the performance of the promises on God's part solicited; when He sees what the Redeemer hath done, He reflects upon what He Himself is to do; the blood of Christ speaks the tenor of the covenant of redemption made with Christ on the behalf of sinners.

It is a presenting our persons to God together with His blood in an affectionate manner. As the high priest, when he went into the holy of holies, was to bear the names of the children of Israel in the breast-plate of judgment upon his heart, Exod. xxviii. 29, to which the Church alludes in her desire that she might be 'set as a seal upon the heart of her Beloved,' Cant. viii. 6; and perhaps there may be also an allusion in Rev. iii. 5, confessing the names of the victorious sufferers before His Father, bearing their names visibly before Him. The persons of believers are His jewels locked up in the cabinet of His own breast, and showed to His Father in the exercise of His priestly office.

Perpetuity of Christ's Intercession.

THE first evidence is in the text: 'We have an Advocate.' We have, at this present moment; we have an Advocate actually remembering us in His thoughts, and presenting us to His Father; we in this age, we in all ages, till the dissolution of the world; without any faintness in the degrees of His intercession, without any interruption in time; He never ceases the exercise of this office, so far as it is agreeable to that high and elevated state wherein He is. As there are continual sins of believers in all ages of the world, so there are constant pleas of the Advocate.

Christ is an Intercessor for us in the whole course of our pilgrimage, all the time that we have any need of Him; His voice is the same still: 'I will that they behold my glory which Thou hast given me,' till they are wafted from hence to a full vision of it. This is the true end of His heavenly life, and His living for ever there: 'Seeing He ever liveth to make intercession for them,' Heb. vi. 25; He lives solely to this purpose, to discharge this part of His priesthood for us. His advocacy is like His life, without end: as He died once, to merit our redemption, so He lives always, to make application of redemption. He would not answer the end of His life, if He did not exercise the office of His priesthood. It would not be a love like that of a God, if He did not bear His people continually upon His heart. He was the Author of our faith, by enduring the cross; and the Finisher of our faith, by 'sitting down at the right hand of God,' Heb. xii. 2. He will be exercised in it as long as there is any faith to be finished and completed in the world. His oblation was a transient act, but His appearance in heaven for us is a permanent act and continues for ever. His mediatorial glory is not consummate, though His personal be. He hath yet a mystical self to be perfected, a fullness to be enriched with: He cannot be intent upon this without minding the concerns of, and putting up pleas for His people; for they are one with Him, 'the fullness of Him that filleth all in all,' Eph. i. 23. There can be no cessation of His work, till His enemies be conquered, and His whole mystical body wrapt up in glory.

He is always in the presence of His Father in the dignity of His Person, and fullness of His merit, continually spreading every part of His meritorious sacrifice in the view of God. The high priest entered into the holy of holies but once a year, but this High Priest sits forever in the court in a perpetual exercise of His function, both as a priest and a sacrifice. And since His own sacrifice for sins offered on earth was sufficient, He hath nothing to do perpetually in heaven, but to sprinkle the blood of that sacrifice upon the mercy-seat. He is never out of the presence of God, and the infiniteness of His compassions may hinder us from imagining a silence in Him, when any accusations are brought in against us. The accusations might succeed well, were He out of the way; but being always present, He is always active in His solicitations; no clamor can come against us, but He hears it, as being on the right hand of His Father, and appears as our Attorney there in the presence of God, to answer it, as the high-priest appeared in the holy of holies for all the people.

Efficacy of Christ's Intercession.

HE is an Advocate to the Father; not only to Him at a distance, but with Him: the constant presence of a favorite with a king, of a princely son with a royal father, is a means to make his intercessions of force with him: He is an Advocate, and He is constantly with the Father in that capacity. A letter from a friend is not so successful as a personal appearance, for gaining a suit. If His death were meritorious, His prayer must be so too, as being put up in the virtue of His meritorious blood; and though we are reconciled by His death, yet we are saved by His life, with a 'much more,' Rom. v. 10; not formally in regard of merit, for that was the effect of His death, but in regard of application of that merit, the end for which He lives, to render it efficacious to us, as it had been in His passion valuable for us. If He separated Himself to death to procure it, He will employ the authority and dignity of His life to finish and apply it. As none offered so noble a sacrifice, so none lives a more powerful life. As when He was on earth, never man spake as He spake; so now He is in heaven, never did man or angel plead as He pleads. 'If whatsoever we ask in His name,' we shall receive, John xvi. 23, surely whatsoever He asks in His own name, will not be refused.

Love to Christ as our Advocate.

LET our affections be in heaven with our Advocate. Though the people of Israel were barred from entering into the holy of holies with the high priest, when he went to sprinkle the blood on the mercy-seat, yet they attended him with their hearts, continued their wishes for his success, and expected his return with the notice of his acceptation. Since Christ is entered into the holy place, and acts our business in the midst of His glory, we should raise our hearts to Him where He is, and link our spirits with Him; and rejoice in the assured success of His negotiation. Though a man be not personally present with his advocate in the court, yet his heart and soul is with him; the heart is where the chief business is. Let us not keep our hearts from Him who employs Himself in so great a concern for us.

Glorify and love this Advocate. If Christ presents our persons and prayers in heaven, it is reason we should live to His glory upon earth. If He carries our names on His breast near His heart, as a signal of His affection to us, we should carry His name upon our hearts in a way of ingenuous return. We should empty ourselves of all unworthy affections, be inflamed with an ardent love to Him, and behave ourselves towards Him as the most amiable object. This is but due to Him as He is our Advocate.

The Glorified Redeemer.

IF the righteous are to shine 'as the sun in the kingdom of their Father,' Matt. xiii. 43, the Head of the righteous shines with a splendor above that of the sun, for He hath a glory upon His body, not only from the glory of His soul, as the saints shall have, but from the glory of His Divinity, in conjunction with it. The glory of His Divinity redounds upon His humanity, like a beam of the sun that conveys a dazzling brightness to a piece of crystal. There was an interruption of this glory while He was in this world, though the human nature then was united with the divine; but this interruption was necessary for those acts which He was to perform in our stead, for the satisfaction of God, and the discharge of His office. Had the glory of the divinity broke out upon His body, He had not been capable of suffering. What mortal could have stood before Him, much less laid hands on Him? What mortal durst have accounted Him a blasphemer, an imposter, and have exercised any violence against Him, had His divinity so fashioned His humanity?

But now it is, as it was in His transfiguration, Matt xvii. 2; the glory He had then wrought an alteration not only in His body, but in His garments, which could not be of the most splendid, as not suiting His present state of humiliation, yet 'they became shining, exceeding white as snow, so as no fuller on earth can white them,' Mark ix. 3; much more must that firm and perpetual glory in heaven have the same influence upon His refined body, that hath cast off those corruptible qualities which hung upon it on earth, and doth more excel in glory that body He had on earth, than the glory of the sun surpasseth that of a glow-worm. It is such a glory as would dazzle mortals to behold it; for if His glory upon Mount Tabor cast Peter into an ecstacy, what effect would His glory upon His throne work upon a mortal nature? Whence it follows, that there must be a mighty change of the bodies of the glorified saints, to capacitate them for the beholding this glory of Christ, the intent views whereof are part of their happiness, John xvii. 24.

The Substance of the Gospel.

THE doctrine of the death of Christ is the substance of the Gospel; though there be many doctrines in it beside that, there is no comfort from any of them, without the consideration of the Cross of Christ; for though God be merciful in His own nature, yet since sin hath made a separation between God and His creature, it is impossible to renew any communion with Him without a propitiation for the offence. We see then Christ is the only meritorious cause of our justification; nothing that we can do can justify us before God; we must be wholly off from ourselves and our own righteousness, as to any dependence on it, and act faith in the death of the Son of God, if we would be secure here in our consciences, or happy hereafter.

Love of God.

THIS love is perpetual. He was in Christ reconciling the world; He will to the end of the world beseech men to be reconciled to Him. Love was the motive, the glory of His grace was the end; what was so from eternity, will be so to eternity. His love is as strong as it was, for infinite receives no diminution; His glory is as dear as it was, for to deny His glory is to deny himself. How great will be the joy of those that accept it! how dismal the torment and sorrow of those that refuse it!

Our Access to God.

SINCE God was in Christ reconciling the world, we go to Him upon the account of an immutable righteousness, a righteousness He settled as an act of grace to us, and security to His own glory; whereas Adam could approach to Him but upon the account of a mutable righteousness, which might be as the grass standing this day, and withered to-morrow. Our access to God is with a joy in the 'hope of the glory of God,' Rom. v. 2. And when we take hold of His covenant, this covenant of peace, we have His word that He will make us 'joyful in the house of prayer,' Isa. lvi. 6, 7; actively joyful, full of delight in His service, solacing ourselves in a sweet consideration of the infinite grace of a reconciling God, whereby a transcendent delight is raised in the soul, which is a direct delight in God as the object of faith, discovered in Christ, and apprehended by spiritual reason and sense: passively joyful, by receiving in His service more of the refreshing waters of life, and being fed with the 'hidden manna,' which God communicates in and by Christ to His friends. And beside, though our services are imperfect, God expects not a perfect obedience from us, but from His Son Christ; it is a full assurance of faith He expects from us, and a true heart, not a perfect obedience; His promise gives us joy, though the sense of our imperfections creates a sorrow. Though we cannot delight in ourselves, we may in God, in His promise, in His gracious condescension, in the compensation He hath from His Son for us, in His acceptation of it, and application of it to our souls.

The Covenant of Redemption.

FLY to this covenant of redemption, as well as to the covenant of grace, since that is the foundation of this. All other considerations of Christ's death, merit, and every thing stored up in Christ, can give us little hope, unless we consider this covenant, which supports all the other stones of the building. Fly to it when your souls are in heaviness; though there may be sometimes clouds upon the face of God, yet consider those compassions in His heart when He struck this covenant with Christ: He covenanted to bruise His own Son by His wrath, while He promised to support Him by His strength, and the sounding of His bowels always kept pace with the blows of His hand. The consideration of this will encourage our faintness, silence our fears, nonplus our scruples, and settle our staggering faith. Is a believer in a storm; here is an anchor to hold him: is he sinking? here is a bough to catch at: is he pursued by spiritual enemies? here is a refuge to fly to. Sin cannot so much oblige God's justice to punish as His oath to Christ obligeth Him to save a repenting and believing sinner. These two covenants, that of redemption and the other of grace, are as a Hur and Aaron to hold up the hands of a feeble faith. His love cannot die as long as His faithfulness remains, nor His peace with the soul perish as long as the covenant with His Son endures. This covenant of redemption is to be pleaded by us, as well as the merit of Christ's death, because the merit of His death is founded upon this compact.

Christ Filled with the Spirit.

HE is filled with His Spirit by the Father, *i. e.* with all the gifts and graces of the Spirit. That precious ointment composed of so many sweet and excellent ingredients, wherewith the Levitical high priest was anointed, Exod. xxx. was a type of those excellent graces of the great High Priest, whereby He was qualified for the exercise of His offices. As the Spirit espoused the human nature to the divine, so He espoused all His gifts and graces to the human. As the body was conceived by the power of the Holy Ghost, so His soul was beautified and adorned by the grace of the Holy Ghost, whereby He became 'fairer than the children of men, and grace was poured into His lips.' Psalm xlv. 2. 'His going forth is prepared as the morning,' Hos. vi. 3, furnished with all things necessary to work out redemption and free the world from the wrath of God, as the sun is with light to deliver the world from the darkness of the night.

'He had the Spirit not by measure,' John iii. 34, not as light in a room, but as light in the sun: not as water in a vessel where the bounds are visible, but like water in the ocean, where the depths and limits are unknown. In Him there was nothing but Spirit and fullness, without limits for quantity; without imperfection for quality; all the treasures; the fountain, not the rivers. There are varieties of gifts as there are of stars, and the qualities of them in heaven; and of flowers, and the beauties of them upon earth; what were various in others were entire in Him.

Infinite Compassion of God.

O MARVELOUS grace! that Christ should be endued with the richest grace by His Father, to relieve our poverty; with the highest might to help our weakness; with a powerful assistance to conquer our enemies; with an overflowing fullness to fill up our emptiness; and abundant grace poured into His lips to comfort our dejectedness. God cannot show greater love than to send His Son to make the peace and unlock His cabinet wherewith to furnish Him. An old frame of thankfulness will not fit an evangelical discovery of love. Isa. xlii. 9, 10. When God tells them of 'His servant in whom His soul delights,' and upon whom He had put His Spirit for the redemption of man, then He makes this use of exhortation of it, 'Sing unto the Lord a new song.' New love calls for new praise. God might have destroyed us with less cost than He hath reconciled us; for our destruction there was no need of His counsel nor of fitting out His Son, nor opening His treasures; a word would have done it, whereas our reconciliation stood Him in much charge. It was performed at the expense of His grace and Spirit, to furnish His eternal Son to be a sacrifice for our atonement. An inexpressible wonder that the Father should prepare His Son a mortal body that our souls might be prepared for an incorruptible glory.

The Saviour's Agony.

HOW was His soul begirt with the wrath of God before His agony in the garden! What an excess of sorrow do those words signify, 'sore amazed, sorrowful, very heavy;' Matt. xxvi. 37, Mark xiv. 33; an inward quaking, an inexpressible amazement! What a deluge fell from heaven upon our Ark, of which that of Noah was a type! How was His soul ground to powder in His agony! How did His soul boil under the fire of wrath, and His blood leak through every pore of the vessel by the extremity of the flame! Must it not be more than a finite breath that thus melted His soul in the garden? Must it not be a stronger than a finite stroke that wrung out those bitter cries? Was there any visible person to afflict Him? Yet His agonies there are thought to have more of hell-fire in them than His sufferings on the cross; clots of blood dropped from Him when there was no visible hand to strike Him: inconceivable must be the afflictions of His soul that could make such dismal commotions in His body, and put the whole instrument out of tune; that should make a dissolution of the parts, and make His heart like melted wax 'in the midst of His bowels.' Psalm xxii. 14. His spotless conscience could not flash such lightnings, as to melt the sword when nothing touched the scabbard; His Father was then charging Him with our sins, actuating His knowledge and sense of them. He had all His lifetime a knowledge of the ingratitude and rebellion of sin; He knew how it had offended and injured God; how it had deformed and ruined the creature: now was His knowledge actuated, and the charging upon Him the punishment of them made His knowledge sensible and experimental. This cup discovers more bitter ingredients than any creature could wring out into it.

Christ's Love as Manifested in His Death.

CHRIST was now upon the highest manifestation of His compassions to mankind. His death was the emphasis of His love; His love was stronger and purer than the love of any creature, not only in regard of the excellency of His person, but the greatness of His sufferings. Had He endured only a death of the body, and not such a death that could have been inflicted only by an infinite hand, His love had lost much of its lustre. His love is principally laid upon the score of His death: 'Who loved me and gave Himself for me.' Gal. ii. 20.

God Spared not His Son.

HOW great is this love that valued our salvation above the life of an only Son, and shed a blood more valuable than the whole creation to preserve ours, which could not be equivalent to the price of it; and put Him into the posture of an enemy to His Son to make us His friends! If the thunders of the law had been shot upon us, what strength had we to bear them? What merit to remove them? How great is the love of the Redeemer, to be willing not to be spared for a time, rather than millions of men and women should fail of being spared forever! 'It was for our transgressions He was wounded, for our iniquities He was bruised, and the chastisement of our peace was upon Him.' Isa. liii. 5. In every wound God gave Him He minded the full punishment of our sin, in the person of our Saviour, that those whom He represented might go free. He spared Him not, abated not a mite of what justice might demand, that so His people might have a full redemption. 'He spared not His own Son, but delivered Him up for us all.' Rom. vii. 32. He did not spare Him in regard of the strength of justice, wherewith He punished Him. What could more enhance the love of God than the terrors inflicted on Christ? And what could more enhance the love of Christ than that He endured not only a bodily death, but a wrathful death in His soul for us?

Let, then, this love engage every man to come to God through Christ. How should it ravish us into an humble compliance with Him and subjection to Him! If He hath bruised Him for us, He will not bruise us if we come to Him. The blood shed by the order of God is able to expiate a world of sins. God hath spent His wrath upon Him, and hath none for those that accept of Him. God hath discovered a propensity to be reconciled, though we lie open to the stroke of His justice and have no strength to withstand Him; a higher evidence He cannot give.

Our Acceptance in Christ.

THE acceptation of our persons and services redounds to us from the Father's acceptance of Christ. His love to Christ as Mediator, is the ground of our acceptation: 'To the praise of the glory of His grace, wherein He hath made us accepted in the beloved.' Eph. i. 6. He chose Him first as the head, and His members in Him; He accepts Him as the first beloved, and believers in Him. Had not Christ been accepted first, none could have pretended a holiness worthy of the notice of God. The grace of God is the cause, His love to Christ the ground, acceptation of us in Him the effect of both. In ourselves, we are the objects of His anger; in Christ, the marks of His choice affection.

His death is so valuable as to procure the casting our sins into the depths of the sea, and the advancing our persons to the heights of glory, to stand before God in His kingdom.

Since this acceptance how doth justice itself smile! The rod of God's fury falls out of His hand upon the sweetness of His Son's offering, and gives way to a sceptre of grace: nothing was omitted which was necessary for the pleasure of God's piercing eye. This may well calm the fears in our hearts, because it smooths the frowns in God's face. If no charge can be brought against Christ, since the acknowledgment of the sufficiency of His offering, no charge can be brought against believers. For whom was it performed but for them? For whom was it accepted but for them? The acceptation must be for the same ends for which His sufferings were endured: shall not then the influence of it upon them, answer the intention of it for them? If it should not, the first acceptation would be in vain: Christ must then return to offer another sacrifice, which shall never be. In the acceptation of Christ for you, He hath accepted you in Him. He stood in no need of it, but in relation to you; He was the eternal Son of God, acceptable to the Father; but by this He is established an eternal Saviour. An obedient faith on our part, will entitle us to salvation on His part: 'And being made perfect, He became the Author of eternal salvation unto all them that obey Him.' Heb. v. 9. Since God hath accepted Him for you, God will appear full of omniscience to understand your wants, full of compassion to pity you, full of power to relieve you, full of wisdom to guide you, full of grace to pardon you, full of glory to bless you forever. Every believer will be accepted by God, because by his faith he owns that which gives God a rest, and as the grace of God assists him, so he contributes to God's contentment. Oh then remember your offences against God, to be humbled; and God's acceptation of the blessed offering to be comforted. The odor of this sacrifice was so agreeable to God, that not content to discharge us from the condemnation we had merited, He would also that we should partake of the life and enjoy the kingdom of His Son, judging it not equity to make any separation between the Head and the members, the Redeemer and the redeemed; and a disparagement to the greatness of the offer and offering, to shut heaven against them; hereby is not only condemnation removed, but eternal glory assured. It is not only a 'not perishing' but an 'eternal life' upon faith. John iii. 16.

The Gospel.

THE gospel is the dove bringing an olive-branch of peace, put into its mouth by God; it brings us news of the allay of His wrath, which was due to our sins, and that His sword is blunted by Himself in the bowels of His Son, that it might not be sheathed in ours. It shows us a shelter for storms, a light in God's countenance even in the shadow of darkness. Here God draws near to man, that man may have access to Him. He makes His Son like to man, that man might be rendered capable of approaching to God. Two natures are joined in one person, that there may be an amiable conjunction of two different parties; He exposeth His beloved Son to the strokes of His justice for a time, that He might reassume His life with honor for ever.

God in the gospel presents us with a Mediator of His own choosing, of His own fitting, of His own ordering; One that He will not refuse, whose intercessions He is pleased with: that He might keep off the darts of divine justice from us, that we might draw near through the veil of His flesh, Heb. x. 20, that we may look upon God in Christ, without being dazzled by His glory or scorched by His wrath. Now, may devouring fire and combustible stubble meet together; fire without scorching, stubble without consuming. Here misery may approach to glory, because glory condescends to misery. Hereby guilt is removed, which makes us incapable of access to God; and wrath is removed, which hinders our actual access. Here may all that will believe in God through Christ and conform to His laws, walk in the midst of the furnace of God's justice without having a hair of their heads touched, without feeling the smart of that which will be quick in consuming unregenerate men. Since nothing else discovers any peace with God, no doctrine else can make any peace in the conscience. It is the old way gives rest to the soul, Jer. vi. 16, the way as old as the first promise of a Reconciler. All other ways, if rightly considered, rather promote than allay suspicions of God. Conscience hath no ground to make any comfortable reflection without some plain declaration of God's reconcilableness and reconciliation. Conscience can show us our guilt, but nothing in the world evidenceth the way of our peace but the gospel; no other religion discovers God in treaty about reconciliation.

Comfort against Death.

IF God be the author of reconciliation by Christ, then death, which was the fruit of that sin which is now removed, can be no dreadful apparition. God was in Christ and is still, conquering His enemies, and this is one enemy which must fall under His sword and be made His footstool. As God was in Christ reconciling you, He is in death calling for you to enjoy the full-blown felicities of that peace. It is no more than a departure in peace, when God is a God of peace: old Simeon thought so, Luke ii. 29. He speaks, says Gurnal, like a merchant that had got all His goods on shipboard, and now desires the master of the ship to hoist sail and begone homeward. Death was before a servant of divine justice; since justice is satisfied, it is the messenger of divine mercy. It was a jailer to inclose us in the prison of the grave; it is now a conductor to the glories of heaven. The reconciled soul is beyond the fears of it. It hath lost its sting, which was God's justice; Christ satisfying the one hath disarmed the other of what is hurtful.

God to be Praised in Reconciliation.

SINCE God sends out such a blessing to us, we should send out loud prayers to Him. Heaven smiles upon earth, and earth should bless heaven. Glorify God as the Father of our Lord Jesus Christ; though we have all immediately from Christ, yet Christ hath all from the Father. He is the propitiation for our sins, but He was appointed by the Father. He came to redeem, but He was sent by God upon that errand. He paid our debts as a surety, but He was accepted by God. He was a Mediator to bring us to God, but He was commissioned by God to that end.

Such free and full compassion deserves our thankfulness, though we could not merit His grace. It is not a contracted, half-made, or oppressive peace; it is an extensive, tender, and abundant 'peace, like a river and a flowing stream;' a peace whereby we are borne in His bosom. Isa. lxvi. 12. How should we adore the depth of that wisdom which found a refuge for us when heaven and earth were at war with us!

God is only praised in and through Christ; God and Christ are joined together in the saints' praise: 'Blessing, honor, glory and power be unto Him that sits upon the throne, and to the Lamb for ever and ever;' Rev. v. 13; and so they should in ours. How beautiful will this whole work appear, when the whole methods of it come to be read in heaven in the original copy! when they shall be seen in the face, in the bosom of God in fair and plainer characters! To conclude, if all the sparks that ever leaped out of any fire since the creation, and all the drops of rain that have fallen upon the world were so many angelical tongues, their praise would come short of the excess of this love. Let the praise of God for this be not the business of a day, but the work of our lives, since eternity is too short to admire it.

JOHN BUNYAN.
1628–1688.

On Prayer.

PRAYER is a sincere, sensible, and an AFFECTIONATE pouring out of the soul to God. O the heat, strength, life, vigor, and *affection*, that is in right prayer! 'As the hart panteth after the water-brooks, so panteth my soul after Thee, O God,' Psalm xlii. 1. 'I have longed after Thy precepts,' Psalm cxix. 40. 'I have longed for Thy salvation,' Psalm xvii. 4. 'My soul longeth, yea, even fainteth, for the courts of the Lord; my heart and my flesh crieth out for the living God,' Psalm lxxxiv. 2. 'My soul breaketh for the longing that it hath unto Thy judgments at all times,' Psalm cxix. 20. Mark ye here, 'My soul longeth,' it longeth, it longeth, &c. O what affection is here discovered in prayer! The like you have in Daniel. 'O Lord, hear; O Lord, forgive; O Lord, hearken and do; defer not, for Thine own sake, O my God,' Daniel ix. 19. Every syllable carrieth a mighty vehemency in it. This is called the fervent, or the working prayer, by James. And so again, 'And being in an agony, He prayed more earnestly;' Luke

xxii. 44; or had His affections more and more drawn after God for His helping hand. O how wide are the most of men with their prayers from this prayer, that is, PRAYER in God's account! Alas! the greatest part of men make no conscience at all of the duty; and as for them that do, it is to be feared that many of them are very great strangers to a sincere, sensible, and affectionate pouring out their hearts or souls to God; but even content themselves with a little lip-labor and bodily exercise, mumbling over a few imaginary prayers. When the affections are indeed engaged in prayer, then, then the whole man is engaged, and that in such sort, that the soul will spend itself to nothing, as it were, rather than it will go without that good desired, even communion and solace with Christ. And hence it is that the saints have spent their strengths, and lost their lives, rather than go without the blessing, Psalm lxix. 3; xxxviii. 9, 10; Gen. xxxii. 24, 26.

Grace of Christ.

THOU Son of the Blessed, what grace was manifest in Thy condescension! Grace brought Thee down from heaven, grace stripped Thee of Thy glory, grace made Thee poor and despicable, grace made Thee bear such burdens of sin, such burdens of sorrow, such burdens of God's curse as are unspeakable. O Son of God! grace was in all Thy tears, grace came bubbling out of Thy side with Thy blood, grace came forth with every word of Thy sweet mouth, Psalm xlv. 2; Luke iv. 22. Grace came out where the whip smote Thee, where the thorns pricked Thee, where the nails and spear pierced Thee. O blessed Son of God! Here is grace indeed! Unsearchable riches of grace! Unthought-of riches of grace! Grace to make angels wonder, grace to make sinners happy, grace to astonish devils. And what will become of them that trample under foot this Son of God?

Christ made Sin for us.

IS this indeed the truth of God, that Christ was made to be sin for me? was made the curse of God for me? Hath He indeed borne all my sins, and spilt His blood for my redemption! O blessed tidings! O welcome grace! 'Bless the Lord, O my soul, and all that is within me, bless His holy name.' Now is peace come; now the face of heaven is altered; 'Behold, all things are become new.' Now the sinner can abide God's presence, yea, sees unutterable glory and beauty in Him.

'God was in Christ, reconciling the world unto Himself, not imputing their trespasses unto them.' O what work will such a word make upon a wounded conscience, especially when the next words follow: 'For He hath made Him to be sin for us, who knew no sin, that we might be made the righteousness of God in Him!'

Coming to God by Christ.

WHAT a joy will it be to the truly godly to think, now that they are come to God by Christ! It was their mercy to begin to come, it was their happiness that they continued coming; but it is their glory that they are come, that they are come to God by Christ. To God! why, He is all! all that is good, essentially good, and eternally good. To God! the infinite ocean of good. To God, in friendly-wise, by the means of reconciliation; for the other now will be come to Him to receive His anger, because they come not to Him by Jesus Christ. Oh! that I could imagine; oh! that I could think, that I might write more effectually to Thee of the happy estate of them that come to God by Christ.

Christ's Intercession.

HIS intercession is for those for whom He died with full intention to save them; wherefore it must be grounded upon the validity of His sufferings. And, indeed, His intercession is nothing else, that I know of, but a presenting of what He did in the world for us unto God, and pressing the value of it for our salvation. The blood of sprinkling is that which speaketh meritoriously, Heb. xii. 24; it is by the value of that that God measureth out and giveth unto us grace and life eternal; wherefore Christ's intercessions also must be ordered and governed by merit: 'By His own blood He entered into the holy place, having (before by it) obtained eternal redemption for us,' for our souls, Heb. ix. 12.

Now, if by blood He entered in thither, by blood He must also make intercession there. His blood made way for His entrance thither, His blood must make way for our entrance thither. Though here, again, we must beware; for His blood did make way for Him as Priest to intercede; His blood makes way for us, as for those redeemed by it, that we might be saved. This, then, shows sufficiently the worth of the blood of Christ, even His ever living to make intercession for us; for the merit of His blood lasts all the while that He doth, and for all them for whom He ever liveth to make intercession. Oh, precious blood! oh, lasting merit!

Giving Glory to Christ.

CHRIST *ought to bear and wear the glory of our salvation forever.* He has done it, He has wrought it out. 'Give unto the Lord, O ye kindreds of the people, give unto the Lord glory and strength.' Do not sacrifice to your own inventions, do not give glory to the work of your own hands. Your reformations, your works, your good deeds, and all the glory of your doing, cast them at the feet of this High Priest, and confess that glory belongs unto Him: 'Worthy is the Lamb that was slain, to receive power, and riches, and wisdom, and strength, and honor, and glory, and blessing, Rev. v. 12. 'And they shall hang upon Him all the glory of His Father's house, the offspring and the issue, all vessels of small quantity, from the vessels of cups, even to all the vessels of flagons,' Isaiah

xxii. 24. Oh! the work of our redemption by Christ is such as wanteth not provocation to us to bless, and praise, and glorify Jesus Christ. Saints, set to the work and glorify Him in your body and in your souls; Him who has bought us with a price; and glorify God and the Father by Him, 1 Cor. vi. 20.

Church Fellowship.

THE doctrine of the Gospel is like the dew and the small rain that distilleth upon the tender grass, wherewith it doth flourish, and is kept green, Deut. xxxii. 2. Christians are like the several flowers in a garden, that have upon each of them the dew of heaven, which being shaken with the wind, they let fall their dew at each other's roots, whereby they are jointly nourished, and become nourishers of one another. For Christians to commune savourly of God's matters one with another, it is as if they opened to each other's nostrils boxes of perfume.* Saith Paul to the church at Rome, 'I long to see you, that I may impart unto you some spiritual gift, to the end ye may be established; that is, that I may be comforted together with you, by the mutual faith both of you and me,' Rom. i, 11, 12. Christians should be often affirming the doctrine of grace, and justification by it, one to another.

* This is a most beautiful passage.—Offor.

Grace.

O GRACE, O happy Church of God! all things that happen to thee are, for Christ's sake, turned into grace. They talk of the philosopher's stone, and how, if one had it, it would turn all things into gold. O! but can it turn all things into grace? can it make all things work together for good? No, no, this quality, virtue, excellency, what shall I call it, nothing has in it, but the grace that reigns on the throne of grace, the river that proceeds from the throne of God. This, this turns majesty, authority, the highest authority, glory, wisdom, faithfulness, justice, and all into grace. Here is a throne! God let us see it. John had the honor to see it, and to see the streams proceeding from it. O sweet sight! O heart-ravishing sight! 'He showed me a pure river of water of life proceeding out of the throne of God.'

The Pilgrims Entering the Celestial City.

NOW, when they were come up to the gate, there was written over it in letters of gold, 'Blessed *are* they that do His commandments, that they may have right to the tree of life, and may enter in through the gates into the city.' Rev. xxii. 14.

Then I saw in my dream, that the Shining Men bid them call at the gate; the which, when they did, some looked from above over the gate, to wit, Enoch, Moses, and Elijah, &c., to whom it was said, These pilgrims are come from the City of Destruction, for the love that they bear to the King of this place; and then the pilgrims gave in unto them each man his certificate, which they had received in the beginning; those, therefore, were carried in to the King, who, when He had read them, said, Where are the men? To whom it was answered, They are standing without the gate. The King then commanded to open the gate, 'That the righteous nation,' said He, 'which keepeth the truth, may enter in,' Is. xxvi. 2.

Now I saw in my dream that these two men went in at the gate; and lo, as they entered, they were transfigured, and they had raiment put on that shone like gold. There were also that met them with harps and crowns, and gave them to them — the harps to praise withal, and the crowns in token of honor. Then I heard in my dream that all the bells in the city rang again for joy, and that it was said unto them, 'ENTER YE INTO THE JOY OF YOUR LORD.' I also heard the men themselves, that they sang with a loud voice. saying, 'BLESSING, AND HONOR, AND GLORY, AND POWER, BE UNTO HIM THAT SITTETH UPON THE THRONE AND UNTO THE LAMB, FOR EVER AND EVER,' Rev. v. 13.

Now just as the gates were opened to let in the men, I looked in after them, and, behold, the City shone like the sun; the streets also were paved with gold, and in them walked many men, with crowns on their heads, palms in their hands, and golden harps to sing praises withal.

There were also of them that had wings, and they

answered one another without intermission, saying, 'Holy, holy, holy, is the Lord,' Rev. iv. 8. And after that, they shut up the gates; which, when I had seen, I wished myself among them.*

Last Words of Mr. Stand-fast.

WHEN Mr. Stand-fast had thus set things in order, and the time being come for him to haste him away, he also went down to the river. Now there was a great calm at that time in the river; wherefore Mr. Stand-fast, when he was about halfway in, stood a while and talked to his companions that had waited upon him thither; and he said, This river has been a terror to many; yea, the thoughts of it also have often frightened me. Now, methinks, I stand easy, my foot is fixed upon that upon which the feet of the priests that bare the ark of the covenant stood, while Israel went over this Jordan, Jos. iii. 17. The waters, indeed, are to the palate bitter, and to the stomach cold; yet the thoughts of what I am going to, and of the conduct that waits for me on the other side, doth lie as a glowing coal at my heart.

I see myself now at the end of my journey, my toilsome days are ended. I am going now to see that Head that was crowned with thorns, and that Face that was spit upon for me.

I have formerly lived by hearsay and faith; but

---

* James Montgomery has justly characterized this last paragraph of the first part of the *Pilgrim's Progress* as ' a crown of glory to the whole work.'

now I go where I shall live by sight, and shall be with Him in whose company I delight myself.

I have loved to hear my Lord spoken of; and wherever I have seen the print of His shoe in the earth, there I have coveted to set my foot too.

His name has been to me as a civet-box; yea, sweeter than all perfumes. His voice to me has been most sweet; and His countenance I have more desired than they that have most desired the light of the sun. His word I did use to gather for my food, and for antidotes against my faintings. 'He has held me, and hath kept me from mine iniquities; yea, my steps hath He strengthened in His way.'*

Comfort in Christ's Intercession.

SINCE Christ is an Intercessor, I infer that believers should not rest at the Cross for comfort; justification they should look for there; but, being justified by His blood, they should ascend up after Him to the throne. At the Cross you will see Him in His sorrows and humiliations, in His tears and blood; but follow Him to where He is now, and then you shall see Him in His robes, in His priestly robes, and with His golden girdle about His paps. Then you shall see Him wearing the breastplate of judgment, and with all your names written upon His heart. Then you shall perceive that the whole family in heaven and earth is named by Him, and how He prevaileth with God the Father of mercies,

---

* 'This speech has been justly admired as one of the most striking passages in the *whole work*' Pilgrim's Progress].—Rev. Thos. Scott.

for you. Stand still awhile and listen; yea, enter
with boldness into the holiest, and see your Jesus
as He now appears in the presence of God for you;
what work He makes against the devil and sin, and
death and hell, for you. Heb. x. 9. Ah! it is brave
following of Jesus Christ to the holiest, the veil is
rent, you may see with open face as in a glass, the
glory of the Lord. This, then, is our High-Priest,
this His intercession, these the benefits of it! It
lieth on our part to improve it; and wisdom to do
that also comes from the mercy-seat, or throne of
grace, where He, even our High Priest, ever liveth
to make intercession for us: to whom be glory for
ever and ever.

The New Song in Glory.

NOTHING will so edge the spirit of a Christian
as, 'Thou wast slain, and hast redeemed us to
God by Thy blood.' This makes the heavens themselves ring with joy and shouting. Mark the words,
'Thou wast slain, and hast redeemed us to God by
Thy blood, out of every kindred, and tongue, and
people, and nation; and hast made us unto our God
kings and priests: and we shall reign on the earth.'
What follows now? 'And I beheld, and I heard
the voice of many angels round about the throne, and
the beasts and the elders: and the number of them
was ten thousand times ten thousand, and thousands
of thousands; saying with a loud voice, Worthy is
the Lamb that was slain, to receive power, and riches, and wisdom, and strength, and honor,' and glory,

and blessing. And every creature which is in heaven, and on the earth, and under the earth, and such as are in the sea, and all that are in them, heard I saying, Blessing, and honor,' and glory, and power, be unto Him that sitteth upon the throne, and unto the Lamb, for ever and ever.' Rev. v. 9–14.

Thus also is the song, that new song that is said to be sung by the hundred forty and four thousand which stand with the Lamb upon Mount Sion, with His Father's name written in their foreheads. These are also called harpers, harping with their harps: 'And they sung as it were a new song before the throne, and before the four beasts, and the elders: and no man could learn that song but the hundred and forty and four thousand, which were redeemed from the earth.' Rev. xiv. 1–3.

But why could they not learn that song? Because they were not redeemed: none can sing of this song but the redeemed; they can give glory to the Lamb, the Lamb that was slain, and that redeemed them to God by His blood. It is faith in His blood on earth that will make us sing this song in heaven. These shoutings and heavenly songs must needs come from love put into a flame by the sufferings of Christ.

JOHN TILLOTSON, D. D.
1630–1694.

Eternal Happiness.

THIS happiness shall be eternal; and though this be but a circumstance and do not enter into the nature of our happiness, yet it is so material a one that all the felicities which heaven affords would be imperfect without it. It would strangely damp and allay all our joys to think that they should some time have an end; and the greater our happiness were, the greater trouble it would be to us to consider that it must have a period. It would make a man sorrowful indeed to think of leaving such vast possessions. Indeed, if the happiness of heaven were such as the joys of this world are, it were fit they should be as short, for after a little enjoyment, it would cloy us and we should soon grow weary of it; but being so excellent, it would scarce be a happiness if it were not eternal. It would embitter the pleasures of heaven, as great as they are, to see to an end of them, though it were at never so great a distance; to consider that all this vast treasure of happiness would one day be exhausted, and that after so many years were past, we should be as poor and miserable again as we were once in this world. God hath so ordered things, that the vain and empty delights of this world should be temporary and transient, but that the great and substantial pleasures of the other world should be as lasting as they are excellent; for heaven, as it is an exceeding, so it is an eternal weight of glory. And this is that which crowns the joys of heaven, and banishes all fear and trouble from the minds of the blessed; and thus to be secured in the possession of our happiness is an unspeakable addition to it. For that which is eternal, as it shall never determine, so it can never be diminished; for to be diminished and to decay is to draw nearer to an end, but that which shall never have an end can never come nearer to it.

O vast eternity! how dost thou swallow up our thoughts and entertain us at once with delight and amazement. This is the very top and highest pitch of our happiness, upon which we may stand secure and look down with scorn upon all things here below; and how small and inconsiderable do they appear to us, compared with the vast and endless enjoyments of our future state. But oh, vain and foolish souls, that are so little concerned for eternity, that for the trifles of time, and 'the pleasures of sin which are but for a season,' can find in our hearts to forfeit an everlasting felicity! Blessed God! why hast Thou prepared such a happiness for those who neither consider it, nor seek after it? 'Why is such a price put into the hands of fools, who have no heart to make use of it;' who fondly choose to gratify their lusts, rather than to save their souls, and sottishly prefer the temporary enjoyments of sin before a blessed immortality?

Glorified Bodies of the Righteous.

THE consideration of the glorious change of our bodies at the resurrection of the just, cannot but be a great comfort to us, under all bodily pain and sufferings.

For *these vile bodies shall be changed, and fashioned like to the glorious body of the Son of God.* When our bodies shall be raised to a new life, they shall become incorruptible; *for this corruptible must put on incorruption, and this mortal must put on immortality; and then shall come to pass the saying that is written, death is swallowed up in victory.* When this last enemy is conquered, there shall be no *fleshly lusts*, nor brutish passions, *to fight against the soul; no law in our members, to war against the law of our mind;* no disease to torment us, no danger of death to amaze and terrify us. Then all the passions and appetites of our outward man shall be subject to the reason of our minds, and our bodies shall partake of the immortality of our souls. It is but a very little while, that our spirits shall be crushed, and clogged with these heavy and sluggish bodies; at the resurrection they shall be refined from all dregs of corruption, and become spiritual, and incorruptible, and glorious, and every way suited to the activity and perfection of a glorified soul, and *the spirits of just men made perfect.*

Earthly and Heavenly Joys.

IN our pursuit of the things of this world, we usually prevent enjoyment, by expectation; we anticipate our own happiness, and eat out the heart and sweetness of worldly pleasures, by delightful forethoughts of them; so that when we come to possess them they do not answer the expectation, nor satisfy the desires which were raised about them, and they vanish into nothing: but the things which are above, are so great, so solid, so durable, so glorious, that we cannot raise our thoughts to an equal height with them; we cannot enlarge our desires beyond a possibility of satisfaction. Our hearts are greater than the world; but God is greater than our hearts; and the happiness which He hath laid up for us, is, like Himself, incomprehensibly great and glorious. Let the thoughts of this raise us above this world, and inspire us with greater thoughts and designs, than the care and concernments of this present life.

We all profess most firmly to believe, that after a few days we shall leave this world, and all the enjoyments of it, and go to the place from whence we shall not return; that we shall enter upon an unchangeable state of happiness or misery, according as we have demeaned ourselves in this present life; that great care and diligence is necessary *to work out our own salvation;* that there must be a great preparation of ourselves, by unspotted purity of heart and life, to make ourselves *meet for an inheritance with them that are sanctified;* that we must *labor, and strive, and run, and fight, and give all diligence to make our calling and election sure;* that we had need to watch and pray always, that we may be accounted worthy to escape the judgment of the great day, and to stand before the Son of Man. Such thoughts as these should continually possess our souls, and heaven should be always in our eye, as if, with Stephen, *we saw the heavens opened, and Jesus standing at the right hand of God,* to see how we behave ourselves here below, and when *we have fought a good fight, and finished our course, and kept the faith, to receive us to Himself, that where He is, there we may be also.*

Resurrection of Christ.

THE resurrection of Christ is a demonstration of a future state after this life, and a pledge of a blessed immortality in another world. For our Lord, by his resurrection from the dead, hath conquered death, and *abolished it, and brought life and immortality to light.* He is *the first fruits of them that slept,* and His resurrection is an earnest and assurance of ours; and from thence the apostle makes this inference, *Therefore, my beloved brethren, be ye steadfast and unmoveable, always abounding in the work of the Lord; forasmuch as ye know that your labor shall not be in vain in the Lord.* The belief of a future state after this life should put us upon the most earnest and vigorous endeavors to secure this happy condition to ourselves; *if by any means,* as the apostle expresseth it, *we may attain the resurrection of the dead.* It should raise us above the world and the lusts of it, above all the terrors and temptations of it.

Excellency of Heavenly Things.

THE transcendent and incomparable excellency of heavenly things above things on the earth, the apostle intimates by the opposition, *set your affections on things above; not on things on the earth.* Earthly things are perishing and transitory, gross and unsatisfactory, and cannot be the felicity of an immortal soul, being neither suited to the spiritual nature, nor to the immortal duration of our souls; they can neither satisfy us while we live, nor preserve us from death, nor comfort us in it, nor accompany us into the other world, nor contribute any thing to our happiness there; and if they can do nothing toward our happiness, why should we set our hearts upon them? They that seek for happiness in earthly things, are like the women sitting over our Saviour's sepulchre with their faces bowed down to the earth; they *seek the living among the dead;* our happiness *is not here, it is risen,* it is above. Let our hearts ascend thither, where our happiness and our treasure is. Why should we bestow our affections upon those low and mean things, when there are incomparably better objects to fix them upon?

The inference from all this shall be to engage and persuade us by all these arguments and considerations, *to seek and mind the things which are above, where Christ sitteth at the right hand of God; and to have our conversation there, where our Saviour is, and from whence also we look for Him again: to change these vile bodies, that they may be made like unto His glorious body, according to the working of that mighty power, whereby He is able to subdue all things to Himself.* Let all our actions have relation to another world, and our conversation declare, that we are *mindful of another country, that is, a heavenly.* Is Christ our Head risen and ascended into heaven? Let us in our hearts and affections follow Him thither, and patiently wait till He receive our souls, and raise our bodies, and take us wholly to Himself, that we may be *for ever with the Lord.*

ISAAC BARROW, D. D.
1630–1705.

Duty of Thanksgiving.

THIS is a most sweet and delightful duty. *Praise the Lord*, saith the most experienced psalmist, *for the Lord is good; sing praises to his name, for it is pleasant:* and otherwhere, *Praise the Lord, for it is good to sing praises to our God; for it is pleasant, and praise is comely*, Psalm cxxxv. 3; cxlvii. 1; ix. 1. The performance of this duty, as it especially proceeds from good humor, and a cheerful disposition of mind; so it feeds and foments them; both root and fruit thereof are hugely sweet and sapid. Whence St. James: *If any man be afflicted, let him pray; is any merry, let him sing psalms*, James v. 13. *Psalms*, the proper matter of which is praise and thanksgiving.

Other duties of devotion have something laborious in them, something disgustful to our sense. Prayer minds us of our wants and imperfections; confession induces a sad remembrance of our misdeeds and bad deserts: but thanksgiving includes nothing uneasy or unpleasant; nothing but the memory and sense of exceeding goodness.

All love is sweet; but that especially which arises, not from a bare apprehension only of the object's worth and dignity, but from a feeling of its singular beneficence and usefulness unto us. And what thought can enter into the heart of man more comfortable and delicious than this, that the great Master of all things, the most wise and mighty King of heaven and earth, hath entertained a gracious regard, hath expressed a real kindness towards us? that we are in capacity to honor, to please, to present an acceptable sacrifice to Him who can render us perfectly happy? that we are admitted to the practice of that wherein the supreme joy of paradise, and the perfection of angelical bliss, consists? For praise and thanksgiving are the most delectable business of heaven; and God grant they may be our greatest delight, our most frequent employment upon earth!

Now the blessed Fountain of all goodness and mercy inspire our hearts with His heavenly grace, and thereby enable us rightly to apprehend, diligently to consider, faithfully to remember, worthily to esteem, to be heartily affected with, to render all due acknowledgment, praise, love, and thankful obedience for all His (infinitely great and innumerably many) favors, mercies, and benefits freely conferred upon us: and let us say with David, 'Blessed be the Lord God of Israel, who only doth wondrous things: and blessed be His glorious name forever;

and let the whole earth be filled with His glory. Blessed be the Lord God of Israel from everlasting to everlasting: and let all the people say, Amen. Psalm lxxii. 18, 19; cvi. 48.

Imitation of Christ.

IF any earnest desire of happiness, any high esteem of virtue, any true affection to genuine sanctity, do lodge in our breasts, we should apply this most excellent means of attaining them; the study and endeavor of imitating the life of our Lord. If we have in us any truth and sincerity, and do not vainly prevaricate in our profession of being Christ's disciples and votaries of that most holy institution, let us manifest it by a real conformity to the practice of Him who is our Master and Author of our faith. If we have in us any wisdom or sober consideration of things, let us employ it in following the steps of that infallible Guide, designed by heaven to lead us in the straight, even and pleasant ways of righteousness, unto the possession of everlasting bliss. If we do verily like and approve the practice of Christ, and are affected with the innocent, sweet and lovely comeliness thereof, let us declare such our mind by a sedulous care to resemble it. If we bear any honor and reverence, any love and affection to Christ; if we are at all sensible of our relations, our manifold obligations, our duties to our great Lord, our best Friend, our most gracious Redeemer; let us testify it by a zealous care to become like to Him: let a lively image of His most righteous and innocent, most holy and pious, most pure and spotless life be ever present to our fancies; so as to inform our judgments, to excite our affections, to quicken our endeavors, to regulate our purposes, to correct our mistakes, to direct, amend and sanctify our whole lives. Let us, with incessant diligence of study, meditate upon the best of histories, wherein the tenor of His divine practice is represented to us; revolving frequently in our thoughts all the most considerable passages thereof, entertaining them with devout passions, impressing them in our memories, and striving to express them in our conversations: let us endeavor continually to walk in the steps of our Lord, and *to follow the Lamb withersoever He goeth;* which that we may be able to do, do Thou, O blessed Redeemer, draw us; draw us by the cords of Thy love; draw us by the sense of Thy goodness; draw us by the incomparable worth and excellency of Thy person; draw us by the unspotted purity and beauty of Thy example; draw us by the merit of Thy precious death, and by the power of Thy Holy Spirit; *draw us,* good Lord, *and we shall run after Thee.* Amen.

Almighty God, who hast given Thine only Son to be unto us both a sacrifice for sin and also an ensample of godly life; give us grace, that we may always most thankfully receive that His inestimable benefit; and also daily endeavor ourselves to follow the blessed steps of His most holy life, through the same Jesus Christ our Lord. Amen.

Consolation in Affliction.

AS it may debase and imbitter all the prosperity in the world, to consider that it is very fading and short-lived; that its splendour is but a blaze, its pleasure but a flash, its joy but as the *cracking of thorns;* so it should abate and sweeten any adversity, to remember that it is passing away, and suddenly will be gone. Put, I say, the worst case that can be: that it were certainly determined, and we did as certainly know it, that those things which cause our displeasure should continue through our whole life; yet since our life itself will soon be spun out, and with it all our worldly evils will vanish, why are we troubled? What is said of ourselves, must in consequence be truly applied to them: *They flee like a shadow and continue not;* they are *winds passing and coming not again;* they are *vapors appearing for a little time and then vanishing away;* they *wither like grass and fade away as a leaf;* they may die before us, they cannot outlive us; our life is but *a handbreadth:* and can then our evils have any vast bulk? *Our age is as nothing,* and can any crosses therein be then any great matter? How can anything so very short be very intolerable?

We have but a very narrow strait of time to pass over, but we shall land on the firm and vast continent of eternity; when we shall be freed from all the troublesome agitations, from all the perilous storms, from all the nauseous qualms of this navigation; death (which may be very near, which cannot be far off) is a sure haven from all the tempests of life, a safe refuge from all the persecutions of the world, an infallible medicine of all the diseases of our mind and of our state: it will enlarge us from all restraints, it will discharge all our debts, it will ease us from all our toils, it will stifle all our cares, it will veil all our disgraces; it will still all our complaints and bury all our disquiets; it will wipe all tears from our eyes and banish all sorrow from our hearts: it perfectly will level all conditions, setting the high and low, the rich and poor, the wise and ignorant altogether upon even ground; smothering all the pomp and glories, swallowing all the wealth and treasures of the world.

It is therefore but holding out a while, and all our molestation, of its own accord, will expire: time certainly will cure us, but it is better that we should owe that benefit to reason, and let it presently comfort us: it is better, by rational consideration, to work content in ourselves, using the brevity and frailty of our life as an argument to sustain us in our adversity, than only to find the end thereof as a natural and necessary means of evasion from it.

Our Life.

THE Scripture aptly resembles our life to a wayfaring, a condition of travel and pilgrimage: now he that hath a long journey to make, and but a little time of day to pass it in, must in reason strive to set out soon and then to make good speed; must proceed on directly, making no stops or deflections (not calling in at every sign that invites him, not standing to gaze at every object seeming new or strange to him; not staying to talk with every passenger that meets him; but rather avoiding all occasions of diversion and delay), lest he be surprised by the night, be left to wander in the dark, be excluded finally from the place whither he tends: so must we, in our course toward heaven and happiness, take care that we set out soon (procrastinating no time, but beginning instantly to insist in the ways of piety and virtue), then proceed on speedily and persist constantly; nowhere staying or loitering, shunning all impediments and avocations from our progress, lest we never arrive near or come too late unto the gate of heaven. St. Peter tells us that the end of all things doth approach, and thereupon advises us *to be sober and to watch unto prayer;* for that the less our time is, the more intent and industrious it concerns us to be. And St. Paul enjoins us to *redeem the time because the days are evil;* that is, since we can enjoy no true quiet or comfort here, we should improve our time to the best advantage for the future: he might have also adjoined, with the patriarch Jacob, the paucity of the days to their badness; because *the days of our life are few and evil,* let us redeem the time; *man that is born of a woman is of few days and full of trouble:* so few indeed they are that it is fit we should lose none of them, but use them all in preparation toward that great change we are to make: that fatal passage out of this strait time into that boundless eternity. So, it seems, we have Job's example of doing: *All the days* (says he) *of my appointed time will I wait, till my change come.* I end this point with that so comprehensive warning of our Saviour: *Take heed to yourselves, lest at any time your hearts be overcharged with surfeiting and drunkenness and cares of this life, and so that day come upon you unawares. Watch ye therefore and pray, that ye may be counted worthy to escape—and to stand before the Son of man.*

Incarnation of Christ.

THE power of God doth brightly shine in the creation, the wisdom of God may clearly be discerned in the government of things: but the incarnation of God is that work, is that dispensation of grace, wherein the divine goodness doth most conspicuously display itself. How indeed possibly could God have demonstrated a greater excess of kindness toward us, than by thus, for our sake and good, sending His dearest Son out of His bosom into this sordid and servile state, subjecting Him to all the infirmities of our frail nature, exposing Him to the worst inconveniences of our low condition? What expressions can signify, what comparisons can set out, the stupendous vastness of this kindness? Psalm xxxvi. 6; cviii. 4. If we should imagine, that a great prince should put his only son (a son most lovely, and worthily most beloved) into rags, should dismiss him from his court, should yield him up into the hardest slavery, merely to the intent that he thereby might redeem from captivity the meanest and basest of his subjects, how faint a resemblance would this be of that immense goodness, of that incomparable mercy, which in this instance the King of all the world hath declared toward us His poor vassals, His indeed unworthy rebels!

The Great Physician.

IS an overture of health acceptable to sick and languishing persons? Luke x. 33; Matt. ix. 12. Behold, the great Physician, endued with admirable skill, and furnished with infallible remedies, is come to cure us of our maladies, and ease us of our pains, 1 Pet. ii. 24; to bind up our wounds, and to pour in balm (the most sovereign balm of His own blood) into them; to free us, not only from all mortiferous diseases, but from mortality itself: He who was *sent to bind up and heal the broken hearted;* He who *Himself took our infirmities, and bear our sickness,* Isa. lxi. 1; Luke iv. 18; Isa. liii. 4; Matt. viii. 17; He of whom the prophet (in relation to corporal, and much more to spiritual infirmities) did foretell; *God will come and save you: then the eyes of the blind shall be opened, and the ears of the deaf shall be unstopped; then shall the lame man leap as an hart, and the tongue of the dumb shall sing,* Isaiah xxxv. 4, 5, 6; Matt. xi. 5; Luke v. 17. He, whose art no disease can resist, who is able to cure our most desperate, our most inveterate distempers; to heal the corruption and impotency of our nature, to void the ignorances and errors of our understanding, to correct the stupidity of our hearts, the perverseness of our wills, the disorder of our affections, to mitigate our anguish of conscience, and cleanse our sores of guilt, Ezek. xxxvi. 26; Eph. ii. 10; by various efficacious medicines, by the wholesome instructions of His doctrine, by the powerful inspirations of His grace, by the refreshing comforts of His Spirit, by the salutary virtue of His merits and sufferings.

RESURRECTION OF CHRIST.

THE contemplation of this point should elevate our thoughts and affections unto heaven and heavenly things, above the sordid pleasures, the fading glories, and the unstable possessions of this world; for *Him we should follow whithersoever He goeth;* rising with Him not only from all sinful desires, but from all inferior concernments, soaring after Him in the contemplations of our mind and affections of our heart; that *although we are absent from the Lord in the body,* we may be *present with Him in spirit,* having our *conversation in heaven,* and *our heart there, where our treasure is,* Rev. xiv. 4; Eph. ii. 6; 2 Cor. v. 6; Phil. i. 23; iii. 20; Matt. vi. 21; for if our souls do still grovel on the earth, if they be closely affixed to worldly interests, deeply immersed in sensual delights, utterly enslaved to corruption, we do not partake of our Lord's resurrection, being quite severed from His living body, and continuing in vast distance from Him: I shall therefore conclude, recommending that admonition of St. Paul: *If ye then be risen with Christ, seek those things which are above, where Christ sitteth on the right hand of God: set your affections on things above, not on things on the earth: for you are dead, and your life is hid with Christ in God; that when Christ, who is our life, shall appear, then ye may also appear with Him in glory.* Amen. 2 Pet. ii. 19; Rom. viii. 21; Gal. vi. 8; Rev. iii. 1; 1 Tim. v. 6; Col. iii. 1–4.

Our Saviour's Ascension and Glorification.

THE consideration of these points should elevate our thoughts and affections from these inferior things here (the vain and base things of this world) unto heavenly things; according to that of St. Paul, *If ye be risen with Christ, seek the things above, where Christ is sitting at the right hand of God,* Col. iii. 1. To the Head of our body we should be joined; continually deriving sense and motion, direction and activity from Him; where the Master of our family is, there should our minds be, constantly attentive to His pleasure, and ready to serve Him; where the city is, whose denizens we are, and where our final rest must be, there should our thoughts be, careful to observe the laws and orders, that we may enjoy the immunities and privileges thereof; in that country where only we have any good estate, or valuable concernment, there our mind should be, studying to secure and improve our interest therein, Heb. xi. 16; our resolution should be conformable to that of the holy psalmist, *I will lift up mine eyes to the hills, from whence cometh my help. Christ is our life,* saith St. Paul; and shall our souls be parted from our life? *Christ,* saith he again, *is our hope;* and shall our mind and hope be asunder? Psalm cxxi. 1; Col. iii. 4; Gal. ii. 20; 1 Tim. i. 1; Col. i. 27. Christ is the principal object of our love, of our trust, of our joy, of all our best affections; and shall our affections be severed from their best objects? By His being in heaven, all our treasure becometh there; *and where our treasure is, there* (if we apprehend, and believe rightly, there naturally) *our hearts will be also:* if they be not, it is a sign we take Him not for our best treasure. *We do in our bodies sojourn from the Lord,* as St. Paul saith; but in our spirits we may and should be ever present, ever conversant with Him, 2 Cor. v. 6; contemplating Him with an eye of faith, fastening our love upon Him, reposing our confidence in Him, directing our prayers and thanksgivings to Him; meditating upon His good laws, His gracious promises, His holy life, and His merciful performances for us. We should not, by fixing our hearts and desires upon earthly things (upon the vain delights, the sordid interests, the fallacious and empty glories, the sinful enjoyments here), nor by a dull and careless neglect of heavenly things, avert, estrange, or separate ourselves wholly from Him. No: let us, unloosing our hearts from these things, and with them soaring upward, follow and adhere to our Lord; so shall we anticipate that blessed future state, so shall we assure to ourselves the possession of heaven, so here enjoying our Lord in affection, we shall hereafter obtain a perfect fruition of His glorious and blissful presence: the which, God of His mercy by His grace vouchsafe us, through the same our ever blessed Saviour, to whom be for ever all glory and praise. Amen.

O God, the King of glory, who hast exalted Thine own Son Jesus Christ, with great triumph unto Thy kingdom in heaven, we beseech Thee leave us not comfortless, but send Thine Holy Ghost to comfort us, and exalt us to the same place, whither our Saviour Christ is gone before; who liveth and reigneth with Thee and the Holy Ghost, one God, world without end. Amen.

The Life Everlasting.

WHAT is the state of life? it is a state of highest dignity and glory; of sweetest comfort and joy; of joy full in measure, pure in quality, perpetual in duration, in all respects perfect in the utmost capacity of our nature; wherein all our parts and faculties shall be raised to the highest pitch of perfection, our bodies shall become free from all corruptibility and decay, all weakness and disease, all grossness and unwieldiness, all deformity and defilement: for they shall, as St. Paul teaches us, be rendered incorruptible, strong, healthful, glorious, and spiritual: our souls also shall in their faculties be advanced, in their inclinations rectified, in their appetites satisfied; the understanding becoming full of light, clear and distinct in knowledge of truth, free from ignorance, doubt, and error; the will being steadily inclined to good, ready to comply with God's will, free from all weakness and all perverseness; our affections being set in right order and frame, with a constant regularity tending unto that which is really best, and taking a full delight therein: wherein we shall enjoy the blissful sight of God, smiling in love and favor upon us; the presence of our gracious Redeemer, embracing us with most tender affection; the society of the holy angels, and of the just made perfect; whose company and conversation, how unconceivably sweet and delightful must it be! wherein nothing adverse or troublesome can befall us; no unpleasant or offensive object shall present itself to us; no want, or need of anything shall appear; no care, or fear, or suspicion; no labor or toil, no sorrow or pain, no distaste or regret, no stir or contention, no listlessness or satiety, shall be felt, or shall come near us; where God (as it is in the Apocalypse) will wipe every tear from the eyes (of them who shall come there), and death shall be no more, Rev. xxi. 4; nor sorrow, nor clamor, nor pain any more: it is, in fine, a state in excellency surpassing all words to express it, all thoughts to conceive it: of which the brightest splendors and the choicest pleasures here are but obscure shadows and faint resemblances; comparable to which no eye hath seen, nor ear hath heard any thing; nor hath it entered into any heart of man to conceive the like, 1 Cor. ii. 9; as St. Paul, out of the prophet Isaiah, telleth us.

JOHN HOWE, M. A.
1630–1705.

ANTICIPATION OF THE JOYS OF HEAVEN.

RECKON much upon an eternal abode in that presence where is fulness of joy and pleasures for evermore. Enjoy by a serious, believing foresight the delights of heaven; labor to rejoice in hope of the glory of God. Look beyond this your present state. Confine not your eye and delight to what is now to be enjoyed, but think of what shall be. Set before your eyes the glorious prospect of the blessed God communicating Himself to that vast assembly of angels and the spirits of just men made perfect, in clearest discoveries of His glory, and richest effusions of His goodness. The best appearance of things in this world, makes but a dull scene in comparison of this. If you look towards God according to what now appears of His glory in the frame of the universe, and the course of His administrations and government over His creatures, He hath not, 'tis true, left Himself without witness. And you may behold much that would be to you the matter of delightful admiration; if your eye be clear, and can pierce through clouds and darkness and a manifold veil. He hath made this world, and is every where in it, but it knows Him not. His light shines in darkness, that doth not comprehend it. Beams of His glory do every where break forth, through every creature, providence, law, and ordinance of His. But much of His glory that shines in the creation is hid by a train of second causes, through which few look to the first. His laws men judge of according to their interests and inclinations, while the holy, glorious majesty that enacted them is out of sight. His work in the world is carried on in a mystery. His interest lives, but is depressed. They who are most devoted to Him are supported indeed by His invisible hand, but are, in the meantime, low, for the most part, and afflicted. If you now limit and confine your apprehensions of Him to His present appearances, the matter of your delight is real, but much diminished. But conceive of Him (as your faith can behold Him at a distance) in that posture wherein having settled the eternal state of things He will finally show Himself. Conceive Him as having now gathered home all that have been recovered to Him out of the apostasy, and joined them to those numberless legions of innocent and pure spirits about His throne that never offended. Conceive Him as dispensing rewards, pouring out blessings, upon the loyal heads and hearts of them that expressed fidelity and duty to Him in the time and state of trial and temptation; letting His glory shine out with bright and direct beams, to so many beholding and admiring eyes; giving forth the full and satisfying communications of His love, and making rivers of pleasure flow perpetually to the replenishing the vast, enlarged capacities of so innumerable a multitude of grateful, adoring spirits, to whom it is now sensibly to be perceived how His fulness filleth all in all. Take this view of Him; and let your faith and hope thus enter into that which is within the veil. And remember there is only a little time between you and that blessed state; that then you are to enter into the joy of your Lord; so that the very element and region wherein you are to live for ever, shall be nothing else but delight and joy.

Humility.

CHERISH the great grace of humility; and be ever mean and low in your own eyes. That temper carries in it even a natural disposition to delight in God. How sweet complacency will such a soul take in Him! His light and glory shine with great lustre in the eyes of such a one while there is not a nearer imagined lustre to vie therewith. Stars are seen at noon by them that descend low into a deep pit. They will admire God but little that admire themselves much; and take little pleasure in Him, who are too much pleased with themselves. And how sweet a relish have His love and grace to an humble, lowly soul, that esteems itself less than the least of His mercies! With what ravishing delight will Divine mercy be entertained, when it is so unexpectedly vouchsafed; when this shall be the sense of the soul now caught into the embraces of God's love, What I, vile creature! impure worm! what, beloved of God! Expectation, grounded especially upon an opinion of merit, would unspeakably lessen a favor, if it were afforded, as also expected evils seem the less when they come. But the lowly soul, that apprehends desert of nothing but hell, is surprised and overcome with wonder and delight, when the great God expresses kindness towards it. Besides that He more freely communicates Himself to such, To this man will I look, even to him that is poor and of a contrite spirit, &c., Isa. lxvi. 1, 2. And He looks to such with a design of habitation; heaven and earth are not to Him so pleasant a dwelling. Down then into the dust; there you are in the fittest place and posture for delightful converse with God.

THE RIGHTEOUS WILLING TO DIE.

O HAPPY souls! that finding the key is turning, and opening the door for them, are willing to go forth upon such terms, as 'knowing whom they have believed,' &c. And that neither 'principalities, or powers, life or death, &c., can ever separate them from the love of God in Christ Jesus their Lord.' Life, they find, hath not separated—whereof was the greater danger; and death is so far from making this separation, that it shall complete their union with the blessed God in Christ, and lay them infolded in the everlasting embraces of Divine love! Happy they, that can hereupon welcome death, and say, 'Now, Lord, lettest Thou Thy servant depart in peace!' that before only desired leave to die, and have now obtained it; that are, with certainty of the issue, at the point of becoming complete victors over the last enemy, and are ready to enter upon their triumph, and take up their triumphal song, 'Death is swallowed up in victory. Thanks be to God, who giveth us the victory through Jesus Christ our Lord.' Happy soul! here will be a speedy end of all thy griefs and sorrows; they will be presently swallowed up in an absolute plentitude and fulness of joy. There is already an end put to thy tormenting cares and fears; for what object can remain to thee of a rational fear, when once, upon grounds such as shake not under thee, thou art reconciled to death! This is the most glorious sort of victory, *viz.* by *reconciliation.* For so thou hast conquered, not the enemy only, but the enmity itself, by which he was so. Death is become thy friend, and so no longer to be feared; nor is there any thing else, from whence thou art to fear hurt; for death was thy last enemy, even this bodily death. The whole region beyond it, is to one in thy case, clear and serene, when to others is reserved the blackness of darkness for ever.

O the transports of joy that do now most rationally result from this state of the case, when there is nothing left lying between the dislodging soul, and the glorious, unseen world, but only the dark passage of death, and that so little formidable, considering who hath the keys of the one, and the other! How reasonable is it upon the account of somewhat common herein to the Redeemer and the redeemed, although every thing be not, to take up the following words, that so plainly belong to this very case: 'Therefore my heart is glad, and my glory rejoiceth; my flesh also shall rest in hope. For Thou wilt not leave my soul in *sheol*, or *hades;* Thou wilt not forsake or abandon it in that wide world, neither wilt Thou suffer thine Holy One to see corruption. Thou wilt show me the path of life; the path that leads unto that presence of Thine, where is fulness of joy, and to those pleasures which are at Thy right hand, or in Thy power, and which are for evermore; and shall never admit either of end or diminution,' Psalm xvi. 9-11.

Christian Hope.

THOUGH you admit a just and very solicitous fear, be sure that you exclude not hope; though you apprehend your case to be dangerous, look not upon it as desperate. Your hope must not be in yourself, but in Him that raises the dead, and calleth things that are not, as though they were; yea, makes them exist and be. But if you cast away all hope, you yield yourself to perish. This stops your breath; so that even all strugglings for life, and the very graspings of your fainting heart, must immediately cease and end in perfect death. The danger of your case, as bad as it is, calls not for this; nor will the exigency of it comport with it. When once the soul says there is no hope, Jer. ii. 25, it immediately proceeds to say, I have loved strangers, and after them will I go. Your hope is as necessary to your safety as your fear; we are saved by hope, Rom. viii. 24, *i. e.* of the end itself, which therefore animates to all the encounters and difficulties of our way, as well from within as from without. Great distempers appear in you and often return; yea, such as are of a threatening aspect and tendency. You should yet consider you are under cure; the prescribed means and method whereof are before you. There is balm in Gilead, and a Physician there: One in whose hands none that trusted Him ever miscarried. 'Tis well if you find yourself sick. The whole need Him not, and will not therefore commit themselves to His care. He hath relieved many such as you, that, apprehending their case, have been restored to Him: let them despair that know no such way of help. Say within yourself, though I am fallen and low, I shall rise and stand, renewed by Thee, O my God. Was there never such a time with you before, when in the like case you cried to the Lord and He answered you, and strengthened you with strength in your soul? Psalm cxxxviii. Say within yourself, 'Why art thou cast down, O my soul, hope thou in God; for I shall yet praise Him, who is the health of my countenance (where health shows itself in lively, sprightly, pleasant looks) and my God.' Psalm xlii. And this very hope, as it preserves life, so it doth the delight and pleasure of life from being quite extinct. The joy of hope is not to go for nothing, when it can only be said, not, it is well, but it shall be. It is pleasant to consider that the state wherein saints on earth are, is a state of recovery; that though it be not a state of perfect health, yet it is not (also) a state of death; but wherein they are tending to life in the perfection of it. And their frequent (and very faulty) relapses shall be found but to magnify the more the skill and patience of their great Physician. Therefore, however you are not hence to be secure, or imposing upon Him; yet let not your hearts sink into an abject despair and sullen discontent, that you find a distempered frame sometimes returning. Let there be tender relentings after God. Your heart ought often to smite you, that you have been no more careful and watchful; but not admit a thought that you will therefore cast off all: that it's in vain ever to strive more, or seek to recover that good frame that you have often found is so soon gone.

Meditating on Heavenly Things.

Do not think that Christ came into the world and died to procure the pardon of your sins, and so translate you to heaven, while your hearts should still remain cleaving to the earth. He came and returned to prepare a way for you; and then call, not drag you thither: that by His precepts, and promises, and example, and Spirit, He might form and fashion your souls to that glorious state; and make you willing to abandon all things for it. And lo! now the God of all grace is calling you by Jesus Christ unto His eternal glory. Direct then your eyes and hearts to that mark, the prize of the high calling of God in Christ Jesus. 'Tis ignominious, by the common suffrage of the civilized world, not to intend the proper business of our calling. 'Tis your calling to forsake this world and mind the other; make haste then to quit yourselves of your entanglements, of all earthly dispositions and affections. Learn to live in this world as those that are not of it, that expect every day, and wish to leave it, whose hearts are gone already.

O get then the lovely image of the future glory into your minds. Keep it ever before your eyes. Make it familiar to your thoughts. Imprint daily there these words: I shall behold Thy face; I shall be satisfied with Thy likeness. And see that your souls be enriched with that righteousness, have inwrought into them that holy rectitude, that may dispose them to that blessed state. Then will you die with your own consent, and go away, not driven, but allured and drawn. You will go, as the redeemed of the Lord, with everlasting joy upon their heads; as those that know whither you go, even to a state infinitely worthy of your desires and choice, and where 'tis best for you to be. You will part with your souls, not by a forcible separation, but by a joyful surrender and resignation. They will dislodge from this earthly tabernacle, rather as putting it off than having it rent and torn away. Loosen yourselves from this body by degrees, as we do any thing we would remove from a place where it sticks fast. Gather up your spirits into themselves. Teach

them to look upon themselves as a distinct thing.
Inure them to the thoughts of a dissolution. Be
continually as taking leave. Cross and disprove the
common maxim, and let your hearts, which they use
to say are wont to die last, die first. Prevent death,
and be mortified towards every earthly thing beforehand, that death may have nothing to kill but your
body; and that you may not die a double death in
one hour, and suffer the death of your body and of
your love to it both at once. Much less that this
should survive to your greater, and even incurable,
misery. Shake off your bands and fetters, the ter-
rene affections that so closely confine you to the
house of your bondage. And lift up your heads in
expectation of the approaching jubilee, the day of
your redemption; when you are to go out free, and
enter into the glorious liberty of the sons of God;
when you shall serve, and groan, and complain no
longer. Let it be your continual song, and the
matter of your daily praise, that the time of your
happy deliverance is hastening on; that ere long you
shall be absent from the body, and present with the
Lord.

The Saints' Delight in God.

IN what transports have holy souls been upon the
view and contemplation of His sovereign power
and dominion; His wise and righteous government;
His large and flowing goodness, that extends in common to all the works of His hands! Labor to imitate
the ingenuous and loyal affection of this kind, where-

of you find many expressions in the sacred Volume. For what hath been matter of delight to saints of old, ought surely still as much to be accounted so. To give instances:

You sometimes find them in a most complacential adoration of His wonderful wisdom and counsels. O the depth of the riches both of the wisdom and knowledge of God! How unsearchable are His judgments, and His ways past finding out! Rom. xi. 33. And again, To God only wise be glory, through Jesus Christ, for ever. Amen. Chap. xvi. 27. To the King eternal, immortal, invisible, the only wise God, be honor and glory for ever, 1 Tim. i. 17, &c. To the only wise God our Saviour, be glory and majesty, dominion and power, now and ever, Jude 25, &c. Elsewhere we have them in transports admiring His holiness. Who is like unto Thee, O Lord, among the gods! Who is like Thee glorious in holiness, Exod. xv. 11. There is none holy as the Lord; for there is none besides Thee, neither is there any rock like our God, 1 Sam. ii. 2. And this is recommended and enjoined to His holy ones as the special matter of their joy and praise: Rejoice in the Lord, ye righteous, and give thanks at the remembrance of His holiness, Psalm xcvii. 12. At other times we have their magnificent celebrations of His glorious power, and that by way of triumph over the paganish gods: Our God is in the heavens, He hath done whatsoever He pleased, Psalm cxv. Their idols are silver and gold, &c. Be Thou exalted, O God, in Thine own strength, Psalm xxi. 13. We will sing and praise Thy power. Forsake me not until I have showed Thy strength unto this generation, and Thy power to every one that is to come, Psalm lxxi. 18, &c. This is given out as the song of Moses and the Lamb: Who shall not fear Thee, O Lord, and glorify Thy name?' Great and marvelous are Thy works, Lord God Almighty, &c. And how do they magnify His mercy and goodness, both towards His own people and His creatures in general, Psalm xxxi. 19. O how great is Thy goodness which Thou hast laid up for them that fear Thee, that Thou hast wrought for them that trust in Thee before the children of men! Rejoice in the Lord, O ye righteous, for praise is comely for the upright; praise the Lord with harp; sing unto Him with the psaltery, Psalm xxxiii. 1, &c. The earth is full of the goodness of the Lord. I will extol Thee, my God, O King, I will bless Thy name for ever and ever, Psalm cxlv. 1, &c. Men shall speak of the might of Thy terrible acts, they shall abundantly utter the memory of Thy great goodness, and shall sing of Thy righteousness. The Lord is gracious and full of compassion, slow to anger, and of great mercy. The Lord is good to all, and His tender mercies are over all His works. To insert all that might be mentioned to this purpose, were to transcribe a great part of the Bible. And in what raptures do we often find them, in the contemplation of His faithfulness and truth, His justice and righteousness, His eternity, the boundlessness of His presence, the greatness of His works, the extensiveness of His dominion, the perpetuity of His kingdom, the exactness of His government: Who is a strong God like unto Thee, and to Thy faithfulness, round about Thee, Psalm lxix. Thy mercy, O Lord, is in the heavens, and Thy faithfulness reaches unto the clouds, Psalm xxxvi. Before the mountains were brought forth, or ever Thou hadst formed the earth or the world, from everlasting to everlasting Thou art God, Psalm xc. 2. But will God indeed dwell on the earth? Behold, the heaven and heaven of heavens cannot contain Thee, 1 Kings viii. The works of the Lord are great, sought out of them that have pleasure therein. His work is honorable and glorious, Psalm cxi, &c. All Thy works shall praise Thee, O Lord, and Thy saints shall bless Thee; they shall speak of the glory of Thy kingdom, and talk of Thy power, to make known to the sons of men His mighty acts, and the glorious majesty of His kingdom, Psalm cxlv. Thy kingdom is an everlasting kingdom, and Thy dominion endureth throughout all generations.

And His glory in the general, (which results from His several excellencies in conjunction,) how loftily is it often celebrated with the expression of the most loyal desires, that it may be every where renowned, and of greatest complacency, in as far it is apprehended so to be. The glory of the Lord shall endure for ever. They shall sing in the ways of the Lord, for great is the glory of the Lord. Be Thou exalted above the heavens, let Thy glory be above all the earth, Psalm civ. 31, cxxxviii. 5, lvii. 7, 11. Let them praise the name of the Lord, for His name alone is excellent, His glory is above the earth and the heavens, Psalm cxlviii. 13. When you read such passages as these, (whether they be elogies or commendations of Him, or doxologies and direct attributions of glory to Him,) you are to bethink yourselves, with what temper of heart these things were uttered! with how raised and exalted a spirit! what high delight and pleasure was conceived in glorifying God, or in beholding Him glorious! How large and unbounded a heart, and how full of His praise, doth still every where discover itself in such strains; when all nations, when all creatures, when every thing that hath breath, when heaven and earth are invited together, to join in the concert, and bear a part in His praises! And now eye Him under the same notions under which you have seen Him so magnified, that in the same way you may have your own heart wrought up to the same pitch and temper towards Him. Should it not provoke an emulation, and make you covet to be amidst the throng of loyal and devoted souls, when you see them ascending as if they were all incense! when you behold them dissolving and melting away in delight and love, and ready to expire, even fainting that they can do no more; designing their very last breath shall go forth in the close of a song! I will sing unto the Lord as long as I live, I will sing praise to my God while I have my being, Psalm civ. 33. How becoming is it to resolve, 'This shall be my aim and ambition, to fly the same, and if it were possible, a greater, height.' Read over such psalms as are more especially designed for the magnifying of God; Psalms viii. xlviii. xcv. xcvi. xcvii. xcviii. xcix. &c.; and when you see what were the things that were most taking to so spiritual and pious hearts; thence receive instruction, and aim to have your hearts alike affected and transported with the same things. Frame the supposition, that you are meant, that the invitation is directed to you, 'O come let us sing unto the Lord, let us come before His presence with thanksgiving, and make a joyful noise to Him with psalms; for the Lord is a great God, and a great King above all gods, &c. And think with yourselves, Is He not as great as He was? Is He not as much our Maker as He was theirs? Is it not now as true, that 'The Lord reigneth, and is high above all the earth, and exalted far above all gods.' Now since these were the considerations upon which so great complacency was taken in Him, set the same before your own eyes. And since these were proposed as the matter of so common a joy, and the creation seems designed for a musical instrument of as many strings as there are creatures in heaven and earth; awake, and make haste to get your heart fixed; lest 'the heavens rejoice, and the earth be glad, the world and all that dwell therein; lest the sea roar, and the fulness thereof, the floods clap their hands, the fields and the hills be joyful together, and all the trees of the wood rejoice before the Lord,' while you only are silent and unconcerned.*

* This passage is expressed in an exalted strain of sacred eloquence; and no more fervid or soul-stirring one can be found in the writings of Howe.

Live With Eternity in View.

MORE particularly labor to have your apprehensions of the future state of the unseen world, and eternal things, made more lively and efficacious daily, and that your faith of them may be such as may truly admit to be called the very substance and evidence of those things. Shall that glorious everlasting state of things be always as a dark shadow with us, or as the images we have of things in a dream, ineffectual and vanishing, only because we have not seen with our eyes, where God Himself hath by His express word made the representations of them to us, who never deceived us, as our own eyes and treacherous senses have done? Why do we not live as just now entering into the eternal state, and as if we now beheld the glorious appearing of the great God our Saviour, when we are as much assured of them as if we beheld them? Why do we not oftener view the representation of the heavens vanishing, the elements melting, the earth flaming, the angels every where dispersed to gather the elect, and them ascending, caught up to meet the Redeemer in the air, ever to be with the Lord? What a trifle will the world be to us then!

EZEKIEL HOPKINS, D. D.
1633-1690.

The Christian's Joy.

A HEAVENLY Christian feels sometimes a ponderous and weighty joy; a joy springing up in his soul, almost intolerable, and altogether unutterable; a joy, that melts him into ecstasy and rapture. How infinitely doth he then disdain, that any soul should be so wretchedly sottish, as to prefer the world before, or equalize it with God! He thinks the happiness he then enjoys so great, that, although he believes it is, yet he cannot conceive how it should be more or greater in heaven itself. Then the soul claps its wing: it would fain take its flight, and be gone; it breathes, it pants, it reaches, after God, and falls into an agony of joy and desire inconceivably mixed together. Can the world give us any such overpowering joy as this? It may afford us corn and wine; the weak recruits of a frail life: but, when it hath emptied all its store and abundance into our bosoms, it is not worthy to be mentioned with the love and favor of God, which is *better than life itself*, Psalm lxiii. 3. And therefore, the psalmist makes it his prayer, Psalm iv. 6, 7.

Lord, lift Thou up the light of Thy countenance upon us. Thou hast put gladness in my heart, more than in the time that their corn and wine increased.

Inconstancy of Earthly Enjoyments.

WHEN the sun shines bright and warm, all the flowers of the field open and display their leaves, to receive him into their bosoms; but, when night comes, they fold together, and shut up all their glories: and, though they were like so many little suns shining here below, able, one would think, to force a day for themselves; yet, when the sun withdraws his beams, they droop, and hang the head, and stand neglected, dull and obscure things. So hath it fared with us: while God hath shone upon us with warm and cherishing influences, we opened, and spread, and flourished into a great pomp and glory; but He only hides His face, draws in His beams, and all our beautiful leaves shut up, or fall to the ground, and leave us a bare stalk, poor and contemptible.

Pardon of Sin.

PARDON of sin is, in Scripture, set forth by very sweet and full expressions. It is called, a blotting out of transgression: a metaphor taken from a creditor's crossing the debt-book, signifying thereby a discharge of the debt. And, lest we might possibly fear God will implead us for them without book, the prophet adds forgetting unto blotting out: Is. xliii. 25. *I, even I, am he, that blotteth out thy transgressions for my name's sake; and I will not remem-*

ber thy sins. It is called, a covering of our sins: Psalm xxxii. 1. *Blessed is* the man, *whose transgression is forgiven, and whose sin is covered.* Yea, we have a farther ground of comfort, for it is not only a covering of our sins, but it is a covering of God's face from them, Psalm li. 9. *Hide Thy face from my sins, and blot out all mine iniquities.* It is a casting of them behind God's back, as a thing that He will never more regard: Is. xxxviii. 17. *Thou hast cast all my sins behind Thy back.* And, lest we should suspect He should turn again to behold them, it is called, a casting of them into the bottom of the sea: Mic. vii. 19, as we do with things we would have irrecoverably lost and gone. It is a scattering them *as a thick cloud:* Is. xliv. 22, when the vapors of it are so dissipated, that there shall not remain the least spot, to obstruct the shining of God's face and favor upon our souls. Yea, and so perfect an abolition shall be made of all our iniquities, that, though Divine justice should enter into a strict search and scrutiny after them, they shall not be found against us: so the prophet Jeremiah tells us, Jer. l. 20. *In those days, shall the iniquity of Israel be sought for; and there shall be none: and the sins of Judah; and they shall not be found.* How hath God heaped up expressions of his grace and mercy one upon another! and studied words, as it were, to assure us of the validity of our pardon; giving to us abounding consolations, as our sins have been abounding!

Grace Opposing Sin.

GRACE is an immortal seed, that will certainly sprout up and flourish into glory: it is a living fountain, that will certainly spring up unto eternal life; a ray of heavenly light, that will wax brighter and brighter to a heavenly day. It is immortal, in its seed; victorious, in a spark; triumphant, in its dawn: yea, take it when it is weakest, when this dawn is clouded, when this spark twinkles, when this seed is unspirited; yet, even then, is it mighty through God, and is still an over-match for sin.

Heavenly Rest.

THAT rest, that is there to be expected and enjoyed, is operative working rest: it is both rest and exercise, at once; and, therefore, it is a true paradox. Though the saints in heaven rest from their working, continually are they blessing and praising God; ascribing glory, and honor, and power to Him that sits upon the throne, and to the Lamb for evermore: always are they beholding, admiring and adoring God, and burning in love to each other, and mutually rejoicing in God and in one another. And this is the work of that eternal rest; a work never to be intermitted nor to cease.

Heavenly Hope.

HOPE is called, the *anchor of the soul*—that *entereth into that within the veil:* Heb. vi. 19, that is, into heaven: it lays hold on all that glory, that is there laid up and kept in reversion for us.

Hope is, in itself, a solid and substantial possession; for it stirs up the same affections, it excites the same joy, delight and complacency, as fruition itself doth. It is the taster of all our comforts: and, if they be but temporal, it not only tastes them, but sometimes, quite devours them; and leaves us in suspense whether it be not better to be expectants than enjoyers. Heavenly hope gives the same real contentment and satisfaction: it antedates our glory; and puts us into the possession of our inheritance, whilst we are yet in our nonage: only it doth not spend and devour its object, beforehand, as earthly hope doth.

The Work of Grace and Sanctification.

GRACE is glory in the seed, and glory is but grace in the flower. Thus the apostle, 2 Cor. iii. 18, We *are changed into the same image from glory to glory:* that is, the image of God is still perfecting in us by His Spirit, carrying on His work from one measure and degree of grace unto another. For the whole life of a Christian here on earth, is but as it were one continued sitting under the hand and pencil of the Holy Ghost; till those first lines and obscurer shadows, which were laid in His new birth, receive more life, sweetness and beauty from His progressive sanctification. And this is a being *changed from glory to glory.* And when this is come to that perfection as to need only the last hand, and the completing touch, then, God glorifies us by the full consummation of our holiness and happiness in heaven. Thus Christ prays, John xvii. 1, *The hour is come: glorify Thy Son:* and so, v. 5, *Glorify Thou me with Thine own self with the glory which I had with Thee before the world was.* And so, when our hour is likewise come, when we have attained to the full measure of our stature in Christ Jesus, God will then glorify us with Himself; in that glory, which He hath prepared for us before the world was.

Comfort in the Death of Pious Friends.

IS it your own loss which you lament; because they are taken from you, with whom, nay for whom, you would willingly have died, and given up yourselves to the death? even this is but the effect of self-love, and shows that you are more concerned in your own contentment than in their glory; and, that you might enjoy them yourselves, you would keep them from their near and intimate enjoyment of God. Can you not, for a while, dispense with their absence, for their advantage; and make up the comfort which you want in their presence, by the comfort which you have in the assurance of their happiness? What our Saviour saith to his disciples, John xiv. 28, that may I say to you: If you love them, you will rejoice, because they are gone to their Father. And this separation, by this absence of theirs, is but for a short time: do you but tread the paths of their example and follow their track, and, as their works went before them to heaven, so yours shall follow you; where you shall rest from all your sorrows and troubles; where no affliction nor discontentment shall overcast your perfect joy; where, without fear of another separation, you shall be satisfied in the enjoyment of one another, and all in the enjoyment of God.

THOMAS KEN, D. D.
1637-1711.

A Prayer for Spiritualized Affections.

O LORD, enlighten my understanding, that I may know Thee; sanctify my affections, that I may love Thee; and put Thy fear into my heart, that I may dread to offend Thee.

Wean my affections, O Lord, from the things of this world, and whatever my state and condition may be here, give me grace therewith to be content.

O my God! let the consideration of the emptiness of pleasure, the troubles and miseries of riches, and the shortness and vanity of all things in the world, inspire me with due contempt of all enjoyments here below; and make me ever shun these hindrances to a life of holiness and virtue, that I may with the greater freedom enjoy Thee, O my God! in meditating on Thy perfections and Thy glories. Let me, dearest Jesus, have those influences of Thy blessed Spirit in my retirements, that I may at last grow wholly weary of the world, and then fix my thoughts upon that heavenly kingdom, where true pleasures, fulness of riches, and lasting honors are only to be met withal ; whither let Thy mercy speedily bring me, that I may be satisfied with the fulness of Thy presence, and meditate for ever on Thy great perfections, joining with all the glorious attendants on Thy throne in endless songs of Thy eternal praises. Amen.

On Communion with God.

RETIRE, O my soul! from the busy world, and employ thyself about that for which thou wert created:—The contemplation of thy God. I will hasten to my closet, or yonder solitary walk, and there sequestered from a vexatious world, I will not suffer a single thought of it to approach me, unless by way of pity and contempt.

How delightful is it, O my soul ! for thee to enjoy this sweet communion with thy God, and thus to dwell upon divine objects. Here am I safe, and at rest in this dear place of quiet; and earnestly pity all the men of business and hurry, whose heads are full of perplexing contrivances, to procure a little happiness in a world where there is no such thing.

O blessed freedom ! O charming solitude ! I will grasp you, and I will hold you fast—the delight of silence and retreat ! Here I can unburthen my soul, and pour it out before my God. Here I can wrestle with the powers of heaven, and not let them go till I have obtained a blessing. Here I can confess my sins, and with hopes of comfort lay open my troubled breast before the merciful Hearer of my prayers.

On The Love of The Saviour.

O GOD, my Saviour and my Lord, grant, I beseech Thee, that the contemplations of Thy dear love may ever inspire my inflamed heart with the zealous return of love to Thee, my God, and with the most fervent charity to all the members of Thy holy Church, whether they are my friends or my causeless enemies. O let me never, by the coldness of my affections for my neighbors and fellow-Christians, make myself unworthy of that love of Thine which has now employed my meditations; and since without charity, no other virtue or religious duty is acceptable in Thy sight, let it be my daily exercise to attain it, that at length I may be a perfect proficient in the school of love, and my humble soul may breathe out nothing else; that no provocation or affronts of the most wilful malice may ever stir up in me the spirit of revenge, or abate my charity; but let this celestial fire of heavenly love ever burn in my fervent breast upon earth, till it is perfected at last in the blessed regions of eternal love.

On The Joys of Heaven.

HAIL, the despised followers of the poverty of Jesus! He had no estates,—He had no purchase on earth, not 'a hole wherein to lay His sacred head.' In this you were like your suffering Lord; for your treasures were in heaven, where you now enjoy them with an assurance of an everlasting possession; you are now no longer heirs but actual inheritors of that kingdom of inexpressible wealth.

from which He has utterly debarred all that are encumbered with riches here below, and place their security and reliance on them. What divine melody is this, O my soul, which thus charms my ravished thoughts? What vigorous echoes of joy inexpressible are these I hear? These can be none other than the voices of angels. Oh, the fervor of this joy! as if their heavenly breasts were unable to contain the flaming zeal within. Lo! how they break forth into the most ardent expressions, and pathetic hallelujahs to your Creator's glory! Hark! what heavenly song is this I hear? 'Holy, holy, holy, Lord God Almighty! which was, and is, and is to come. Blessing, honor, power, and glory, be unto Him that sitteth upon the throne, and to the Lamb, for ever and ever!'

A Prayer for one in Affliction.

'I KNOW, Lord, that Thy judgments are right, and that Thou of very faithfulness hast caused me to be troubled;' Psalm cxix. 75; for 'before I was afflicted I went astray: but now have I kept Thy word.' Psalm cxix. 6. Blessed be Thy goodness for afflicting me.

I humbly beg of Thee, O merciful Father, that this affliction may strengthen my faith, which Thou sawest was growing weak; fix my hope, which was staggering; quicken my devotion, which was languishing; re-kindle my charity, which was cooling; revive my zeal, which was dying; confirm my obedience, which was wavering; recover my patience, which was fainting; mortify my pride, which was presuming; and perfect my repentance, which was daily decaying: for all these and the like infirmities, to which my soul is exposed, O make Thy affliction my cure!

Grant, O my God, that this affliction Thou hast in mercy laid on me, may wean all my affections from the world, which I was apt to grow too fond of; rescue me from those occasions of evil of which I was in danger; secure me from those temptations which were ready to assault me; restrain me from those sins to which my nature was strongly inclined; preserve me from all those abuses of health I am apt to incur; and purify my soul from all that dross, and from all those vicious propensions which either my repentance has left behind, or which I have since contracted.

O my God, let Thy affliction produce my amendment, and all the happy effects in me, which it is wont to do in Thy children, and which Thou in mercy dost design it should, and then continue Thy affliction, if it seem good in Thy sight: behold, Lord, 'happy is the man whom Thou thus correctest.' Job v. 7.

What is best for me, O my God, I know not: my flesh desires a deliverance from this distemper, and if it be Thy pleasure, O Lord, deliver me: my spirit desires that Thou only wouldst choose for me. Do Thou then, O Heavenly Father, choose for me, because Thou art my Father, and out of Thy fatherly tenderness wilt be sure to choose what is best for me. I resign my own will entirely to Thine. Let me be enabled to say, after my gracious Saviour's example, 'Father, if Thou be willing, remove this cup from me: nevertheless, not my will, but Thine, be done.' St. Luke xxii. 42.

Hear, Lord, and have compassion on me, for the merits and sufferings of Jesus Christ, whose perfect resignation may I always imitate. Amen.

The Righteous Eternally Secure.

THIS world is founded upon the seas, and established on the floods; the very foundation of it is laid in mutability. But he that loves God, and trusts in His Beloved, is like Mount Sion, that cannot be removed, but stands fast for ever; he is built on the rock of ages, he stands firm on a height that has no precipice—is above all assaults—and is in eternal security.

THOMAS COMBER, D. D.
1644-1699.

MEDITATIONS ON THE LORD'S SUPPER. I.

MOST merciful Jesus, although Thou reservest the full manifestation of Thy love to my soul till the glorious resurrection, yet, as if Thou wert impatient of so great a delay, Thou here givest me a pledge of Thy love, and an earnest of my title to a never fading bliss. Thou hast dearly bought it for me, and Thou hast freely given it to me; wherefore I will vigorously seek it, patiently wait for it, and earnestly expect it. Ah! my gracious Redeemer, here I am vexed with crosses, oppressed with enemies, troubled with corruptions, and tossed on the waves of a thousand sins and miseries. But it is my comfort, amid all these sorrows, to receive this assurance that I shall, ere long, be translated into a blissful state, never to know sin or feel pain; to be in danger of enemies or fear of evil any more. O how welcome shall be that blessed hour that summons me to enter into the joys of my Lord! While I continue here, let me behave myself, O my Saviour, as the heir of Thy kingdom, crucifying those sins that crucified Thee, and would exclude me from those felicities which Thou hast offered me. Lord, I would hate everything that keeps me from heaven, and love nothing but what may further me in my way thither. O give me Thy grace to live as one that is above all the trifling pleasures and sorrows of this lower world, and to conduct myself as becomes an heir of glory, as one designed to be a companion of angels, and to partake of Thy bliss for ever and ever.

II.

I WILL go to Thy table with joy and tell of Thy works with gladness, O most mighty Saviour, who hast not only died for my sins, but risen again for my justification. Indeed, what comfort would I have found in this memorial of Thy death, if it had not been for Thy resurrection. This sacrament then would only have represented Thy sufferings, and renewed my sorrow: to think that so excellent a Person had failed of my deliverance! but now it is become a feast of joy, because it is an assurance of Thy resurrection, as well as a commemoration of Thy passion. Since Thou livest, glorified Jesus, we live also. Thy resurrection gives life to our hopes, makes our sorrows light, our lives cheerful, and our death the gate of immortality. Our fears are dispelled, and our troubled hearts are quieted with this,—*The Lord* is risen; yea, *The Lord is risen indeed.*

III.

BLESSED Jesus, the Author and Finisher of our faith, who art *the same yesterday, to-day, and for ever;* Thou hast given spiritual *meat to them that fear Thee,* and *wilt ever be mindful of Thy covenant:* but my goodness is as a morning cloud which soon passes, and my devotion *flies like a shadow and never continues in one stay.* O do Thou *establish me with Thy free Spirit,* that I may not so easily forfeit my comfort, forget my duty, and break my vows, as I have formerly done. How unwearied art Thou, gracious Saviour, in doing well unto me! How constant is Thy love! How amiable and attractive are Thy endless mercies and Thy varied graces! And shall I be so ungrateful to Thee, and so cruel to myself, as to forsake Thee and my own happiness! Alas! I justly suspect my own weakness; I fear the power and policy of my enemies; and I do with shame and sorrow call to mind my former returns to folly. Therefore, O blessed Redeemer! I do most earnestly entreat Thee never to leave me to myself. I beseech Thee to give me constant and continual supplies of Thy grace, that I may be able to perform whatsoever I have promised. O let not forgetfulness or indevotion seize on me hereafter. Let me hold fast that which I have, and daily strive to gain more; and finally make me faithful unto death; and so shall I receive from Thee the crown of life, when I appear before Thee at the last day.

BENJAMIN JENKS.
1646–1724.

A Morning Prayer.

O LORD God Almighty, Thou art the sovereign Majesty of heaven and earth, against whom all our sins have been committed, and by whom alone they can be pardoned! there is none but Thee, by whom our iniquities can be subdued, our souls be sanctified or our necessities supplied. But Thou art able, and also ready to hear and help, to bless and save Thy people that call upon Thee; Thou delightest to show mercy, and lovest the occasions of glorifying Thy compassion. We come to Thee therefore, O Lord, begging that mercy, which Thou knowest we extremely want, and grace to help us in this time of our need. We beg the same for the sake of Thine infinitely beloved Son who alone is worthy, and in whose precious blood is all our trust.

We are unclean, Lord, we are unclean; and Thou mayest well abhor our guilty souls: but O look upon us in the Son of Thy love; and prepare us for the mercies which Thou hast treasured up for us in Him. Make us to feel the burden and the bitterness of our sins; nor let us ever attempt to cover and conceal them, lest they find us out at the last, and overwhelm us with shame and misery. Holy Father! carry on with power Thy great work, even the work of faith and the sanctification of our souls. Quicken us, O Lord our God, and stir us up to Thy work; and assist us in the performance of all our duties, which of ourselves Thou knowest we are unable to perform. Work in us to will and to do of Thy good pleasure; establish the things, O God, which Thou hast already wrought for us; and go on to work mightily upon our hearts by Thy grace, till our souls are fitted for the enjoyment of Thy glory.

Gracious Lord, Thy mercies are fresh and new to us every morning. We have laid us down and slept, and awaked again; for Thou hast sustained us: Thou hast kept us from the terrors of the night and from all evil accidents; so that we are once more risen in peace and safety. Glory be to Thee, O God of our salvation, who art still so mindful of us, so merciful unto us. Go on, we pray Thee, to be good to us this day, and teach us how to demean ourselves aright, and to order our affairs to Thy glory. O direct our undertakings and prosper our endeavors. Rule our hearts in Thy fear and love, and keep us living to Thy praise and honor. Behold, we commit ourselves to Thee, and shelter ourselves under the shadow of Thy wings: O keep us from evil, and help us to do that which is good and pleasing to our God, through Jesus Christ. Give us, Lord, all that we have asked as we should; forgive us all that we have asked amiss; and bestow on us all things needful, which we should have asked; and which we continue to ask, in the comprehensive words of Thy dear Son—*Our Father*, &c.

An Evening Prayer.

OUR ever blessed and most gracious God! Thou art the Lord and giver of our lives, and of all the blessings we enjoy. To Thee we owe ourselves, and all that we are capable of rendering unto Thee. For by Thee, O Lord, we were created; and through Thy good Providence it is that we have been spared and provided for unto this present time. From Thee, our God, comes all our help; and in Thee is reposed all our hope. Thou art the bountiful giver of all the good that our souls desire, and the merciful withholder of all the evil that our sins deserve. We acknowledge Thy great and daily goodness to us, and our own exceeding unworthiness of the least of all Thy mercies. We take shame and confusion to ourselves, that we have so little improved and so greatly abused all Thy patience with us, and all the various instances of Thy bounty to us. We confess it to be a heinous aggravation of our offences, that we have done so much against Thee, after all the great things Thou hast done for us. But we desire, O Lord, to be humbled for our offences; and we entreat Thy gracious favor, in Christ Jesus, for the pardon of them. Forgive us, we pray Thee, for His sake, all the sins that ever we have committed against Thee, and absolve us from all the evil whereof we now stand guilty before Thee. And, being justified by faith, let us have peace with God, through our Lord Jesus Christ.

And seeing Thou art pleased yet to hold our souls in life, and to make us find and feel, by every day's experience, how abundantly gracious and merciful Thou art, O give us hearts more sensible of Thy love, more affected with Thy mercy, and more thankful for those continued favors, which Thou art pleased to multiply unto us. And help us to show forth Thy praise, not only by speaking good of Thy name, but by ordering our conversation aright, and by adorning the gospel of God our Saviour in all things.

And now, most merciful Father, we humbly recommend ourselves, and all that we have, to Thy care and protection; beseeching Thee, for Thy dear Son's sake, to preserve and defend, to bless and keep us, both in soul and body. We know that by reason of our weakness and wickedness we are exposed to many and great dangers; but we commit ourselves to Thee, trusting that Thou wilt sustain us. O be with us through the night season and grant us comfortable repose; that our frail nature being refreshed, and our decayed strength renewed, we may rise again better fitted for the duties of the following day, if Thou shalt be pleased to add another day to our lives. And as Thou daily multipliest Thy mercies to us, be pleased also to increase our repentance, and to renew us daily after Thine image: that every day may not only bring us nearer to Thy kingdom, but make us fitter for the enjoyment of that glory which Thou hast prepared for them that love Thee.

Accept these our prayers, most gracious and merciful Lord God: and for all the good things we have received, or at present enjoy, or hope for in future from Thy bountiful hands, enable us to render our grateful thanks: and let it be our employment now, as we hope it shall be hereafter, abundantly to utter the memory of Thy great goodness, and to sing of Thy praise without ceasing. *Amen* and *Amen*.

A Prayer on Going Abroad.

O LORD! Thou art the same God in all places: and nowhere can I go but Thou art there. Both at home and abroad, on my way and at the end, Thou art ever with me, by Thine universal presence. O let me also experience the presence of Thy grace, and of Thy good Spirit with me; to conduct and guide me continually, to protect and save me from all dangers and mischiefs, and to make my way prosperous and all my affairs successful. Let the blessing of the Lord follow me and rest upon me: and do Thou preserve my going out and my coming in; and never leave me nor forsake me, O Lord, but be my God and guide this day, in all this journey and all my life long. And make me to feel that my whole life is but a pilgrimage and passage through this world; in which I am continually hastening home to the end of all my travels, and to the place where I must take up my everlasting abode.

O merciful God! make me continually mindful of

that progress, and of that journey's end: and keep me from either wandering from Thy way or falling into sin of any kind; which would be the greatest evil that could come upon me. Take care of me, I beseech Thee, and lead me, and keep me: and after all my journeyings here, O bring me safe at last to Thy holy hill, and to Thy heavenly rest; even to that blessed end of my faith, the everlasting salvation of my soul. I humbly ask this through the greatness of Thy mercy to me in Thy dear Son, my gracious Lord and only Saviour, Jesus Christ. *Amen.*

A Prayer for Faith and Trust in God.

WITHOUT faith, it is impossible to please Thee, O God: and therefore I come to beg of Thee that faith which is Thy gift. Lord, help my unbelief; and increase my faith. Whatever Thou hast revealed, let me take it upon the credit of Thy word: and where I have Thy promise, let me not stagger through unbelief, but fully persuade myself that it shall be as Thou hast said. O bless and enrich my soul with such a holy, lively and unfeigned faith, as may enlighten my mind and purify my heart, and influence my whole life; such a faith as may enable me to receive Jesus Christ for my Saviour, and heartily to give up myself to Him as my Lord: that, being ruled and sanctified by Him in this life, I may be for ever saved and glorified by Him in the life that is to come. O help me so to assent unto the truths, that I may also consent to the terms of the gospel. And give me that effectual faith which shall work by love; that faith which shall enable me to overcome the world, and to fix my attention on those great and glorious things which are unseen and eternal.

In my greatest darkness and distress, O let me trust in the name of the Lord and stay myself upon my God; committing my ways unto Thee, and casting my burthen upon Thee, and putting my trust in Thee, though Thou slay me. Let me trust in Thine almighty power to help and save; in Thy tender inclinations to pity and relieve; and in the sure promises which Thy love hath made (and which Thy faithfulness will certainly make good) unto all that wait and call upon Thee. And though I am not presently answered in the wishes of my heart, O let me tarry and wait patiently for the salvation of the Lord; and have my eyes upon the Lord my God, till Thou have mercy upon me. Yea, make me so sound and strong in the faith, that my faith may never fail: but that it may be found to praise and honor and glory in every time of trial; and at the great appearing of our Lord and Saviour Jesus Christ. Amen.

A Prayer for Increase of Grace.

BLESSED Saviour! who camest into the world that we might have life, and have it more abundantly, let me receive out of Thy fulness grace sufficient for me; that I may be strong in the Lord, and ready to every good work. My Life, my Strength and my Redeemer! leave me not under the curse of barrenness, to halt or decline in my spiritual estate:

but, as Thou hast wrought all my works in me, stablish, I beseech Thee, that which Thou hast wrought for me; and strengthen the things which remain, that are ready to die. Let the seeds of grace which Thou hast sown in my heart be watered by Thy good Spirit; that my soul may prosper and increase with the increase of God, even as a watered garden or as a spring whose waters fail not. Make me to grow in knowledge and in grace; and to abound in all those fruits of righteousness, which are by Jesus Christ, to the glory and praise of God; so that I may have the witness in myself, that I am Thy servant. O my Lord, carry on with power the work of faith and holiness in my soul; that my sinful corruption may grow weaker and weaker; and Thy grace in me may grow stronger and stronger; till, from groaning under the body of sin and death, I come to triumph over all the enemies of my soul. And as Thou art pleased to afford me the means of grace, O grant me the increase of Thy grace that they may not be lost upon me; but that in the use of them I may be made still wiser and holier and better, and fitter for Thy blessed acceptance in Jesus Christ my only Saviour. Amen.

A PRAYER FOR GOD'S GRACIOUS PRESENCE.

MY Lord and my God! whom have I in heaven but Thee? and there is none upon earth that I desire besides Thee. O be not as a stranger to the soul in which Thou hast planted an inclination to serve Thee: but bless and honor me with that divine fellowship of which Thou hast made me capable, and which my soul panteth after. O give me the satisfaction to find that Thou hast given me a heart to seek. Yea, give me grace, O my Lord, to go on seeking till I find Thee, whom my soul desires above all to love. Let me endure any thing rather than Thine absence and displeasure; and desire nothing so much as Thy presence and favor.

And be not Thou far from me, O my God; but let me experience Thy gracious presence with me, and behold Thy goodness passing before me. Lord Jesus, Thou hast promised to be with Thy people even to the end of Thy world: O come, be with my spirit and dwell in my heart by faith. Be with me, O my Saviour, every where and at all times, in health and in sickness, in prosperity and trouble, in all estates and in all events and circumstances of my life; let Thy presence sanctify and sweeten to me whatever befalls me. Never leave nor forsake me in my present pilgrimage, but abide with me till Thou hast brought me safe through all trials and dangers to Thy heavenly kingdom; that I may there dwell in Thy sight and enjoy Thy love, and inherit Thy glory for evermore. Amen.

A Prayer on Preparation for Death.

LORD, what is our life but a vapor, that appears for a little time and then vanisheth away! Even at the longest, how short! and at the strongest, how frail! and when we think ourselves most secure, yet we know not what a day may bring forth, nor how soon Thou mayest come to call us to our last account. Quickly shall we be as water spilt on the ground, that cannot be gathered up again; quickly snatched away from hence, and our place here shall know us no more for ever. Our days, one after another, are spent apace: and we know not how near to us is our last day, when our bodies shall be laid in the grave, and our souls be called to appear at the tribunal of God, to receive their eternal doom. Yet how have I lived in this world, as if I should never leave it; how unmindful of my latter end! how improvident of my time! how careless of my soul! how negligent in my preparation for my everlasting condition! so that Thou mayest justly bring my last hour as a snare upon me, to surprise me in my sins, and to cut me off in my iniquities. But, O Father of mercies, remember not my sins against me; but remember Thy own tender mercies and Thy loving kindnesses, which have been ever of old. O remember how short my time is; and spare me, that I may recover strength before I go hence and be no more seen. Make me so wise as to consider my latter end: and teach me so to number my days that I may apply my heart to true wisdom. Lord, what have I to do in this world but to make ready for the world to come! O that I may be mindful of it, and be careful to finish my work before I finish my course!

In the days of my health and prosperity, O that I may remember and provide for the time of trouble, and sickness and death, when the world's enjoyments will shrink away from me, and prove utterly unable to support and comfort me. Let me never allow myself in any course of living wherein I would be loath or afraid to die. But let me see my corruptions mortified and subdued, that they may never rise up in judgment against me. Enable me so to die unto sin daily that I may not die for sin eternally. Instruct me, good Lord, and assist me in my preparation for a dying hour: that I may not then be fearfully surprised; but may meet it with comfort and composure. Quicken me to a serious concern about that great work; and help me to perform it acceptably and with good success. O that I may be fitted for heaven ere I leave this earth, and may have peace with God through Jesus Christ, before I depart hence into that state in which I must abide for ever! O my Lord, make me so ready to meet Thee at Thy coming, that Thine appearance may be the matter of my hopes and desires, and joyful expectations: that I may look and long for that blessed time when Thou wilt put an everlasting period to all my troubles and temptations, and exchange my present state of infirmity and sin for a state of endless happiness and glory. O Thou who art my life and my strength, help me so to live as, at the hour of death, I shall wish I had lived; and so to make ready for death all my days that, at my last day, I may have nothing to do but to die, and cheerfully to resign my spirit into Thy gracious hands. O my Father, hear and answer my humble petitions; and let me find a merciful admission to Thy favor and Thy kingdom, for the sake of Jesus Christ. Amen.

MATTHEW HENRY.

1662–1714.

PLEASURES OF COMMUNION WITH GOD.

A DAY in God's courts, and an hour at His table in communion with Him, is very pleasant, better than a thousand days, than ten thousand hours, in any of the enjoyments of sense; but this very much increaseth the pleasantness of it, that it is the pledge of a blessed eternity, which we hope to spend within the veil, in the vision and fruition of God. Sabbaths are sweet, as they are earnests of the everlasting sabbatism, or keeping of a Sabbath, (as the apostle calls it, Heb. iv. 9,) which remains for the people of God. Gospel feasts are therefore sweet, because earnests of the everlasting feast, to which we shall sit down with Abraham, and Isaac, and Jacob. The joys of the Holy Ghost are sweet, as they are earnests of that joy of our Lord, into which all Christ's good and faithful servants shall enter. Praising God is sweet, as it is an earnest of that blessed state, in which we shall not rest day or night from praising God. The communion of saints is sweet, as it is an earnest of the pleasure we hope to have in the 'general assembly, and church of the first-born,' Heb. xii. 23.

They that travel wisdom's ways, though sometimes they find themselves walking in the low and darksome valley of the shadow of death, where they can see but a little way before them, yet at other times they are led with Moses to the top of Mount Pisgah, and thence have a pleasant prospect of the land of promise, and the glories of that good land, not with such a damp upon the pleasure of it as Moses had, Deut. xxxiv. 4, 'Thou shalt see it with thine eyes, but thou shalt not go over thither;' but such an addition to the pleasure of it as Abraham had, when God said to him, Gen. xiii. 14, 15, 'All the land which thou seest, to thee will I give it.' Take the pleasure of the prospect, as a pledge of the possession shortly.

Exercise of Holy Joy and Praise.

LET us be much in the exercise of holy joy, and employ ourselves much in praise. Joy is in the heart of praise, as praise is the language of joy; let us engage ourselves to these, and quicken ourselves in these. God has made these our duty, by these to make all the other parts of our duty pleasant to us; and for that end we should abound much in them, and attend upon God with joy and praise. Let us not crowd our spiritual joys into a corner of our hearts, nor our thankful praises into a corner of our prayers, but give both scope and vent to both. Let us live a life of delight in God, and love to think of

Him as we do of one whom we love and value. Let the flowing in of every stream of comfort lead us to the fountain; and in every thing that is grateful to us, let us 'taste that the Lord is gracious.' Let the drying up of every stream of comfort drive us to the fountain; and let us rejoice the more in God for our being deprived of that which we used to rejoice in. Let us be frequent and large in our thanksgiving; it will be pleasant to us to recount the favors of God, and thus to make some returns for them, though poor and mean, yet such as God will graciously accept. We should have more pleasure in our religion, if we had but learned 'in every thing to give thanks,' 1 Thess. v. 18, for that takes out more than half the bitterness of our afflictions, that we can see cause even to be thankful for them; and it infuseth more than a double sweetness into our enjoyments, that they furnish us with matter for that excellent heavenly work of praise; 'sing praises unto His name, for it is pleasant,' comfortable, as well as comely, Psalm cxxxv. 3.

Meditation on the Heavenly Rest.

LET us converse much with the glory that is to be revealed. They that by faith send their hearts and best affections before them to heaven, while they are here on this earth, may in return fetch thence some of those joys and pleasures that are at God's right hand. That which goes up in vapors of holy desire, though insensible, in 'groanings which cannot be uttered,' will come down again in dews of heavenly consolations, that will make the soul as a watered garden. Let us look much to the end of our way, how glorious it will be, and that will help to make our way pleasant. This abundantly satisfies the saints, and is the fatness of God's house on earth, Psalm xxxvi. 8, 9. This makes them now to drink of the river of God's pleasures, that with Him is the fountain of life, whence all these streams come, and in His light they hope to see light,—everlasting light. By frequent meditations on that rest which remains for the people of God, Heb. iv. 3, we now enter into that rest, and partake of the comfort of it. Our hopes of that happiness through grace would be very much strengthened, and our evidences for it cleared up insensibly, if we did but converse more with it, and the discoveries made of it in the Scripture. We may have foretastes of heavenly delights, while we are here on earth,— clusters from Canaan, while we are yet in this wilderness,—and no pleasures are comparable to that which these afford. That is the sweetest joy within us, which is borrowed from the joy set before us; and we deprive ourselves very much of the comfort of our religion, in not having our eye more to that joy. We rejoice most triumphantly, and with the greatest degrees of holy glorying, when we 'rejoice in hope of the glory of God,' Rom. v. 2. In this our heart is glad, and our glory rejoiceth, Psalm xvi. 9.

The Bible.

LET us value the Bible as the best book, because it is a book for the soul; it discovers our souls to us as a glass, and is a 'discerner of the thoughts and intents of the heart.' It discovers to our souls the way that leads to their present and future happiness. In the Scriptures we think we have eternal life,—life for the soul. It is the excellency of the word of God, that it 'converteth the soul, it enlightens the mind, it rejoiceth the heart;' and for this we should value it, because it makes the soul wise to salvation, and furnisheth it for every thing that is good.

Pious Ejaculations.

BE frequent and serious in pious ejaculations. In waiting upon God we must often speak to Him,—must take all occasions to speak to Him,—and when we have not opportunity for a solemn address to Him, He will accept of a sudden address, if it come from an honest heart. In these David waited on God all day, as appears by Psalm xxv. 1, 'Unto Thee, O Lord, do I lift up my soul,' to Thee do I dart it, and all its gracious breathings after Thee. We should in a holy ejaculation ask pardon for this sin, strength against this corruption, victory over this temptation, and it shall not be in vain. This is to pray always, and without ceasing. It is not the length or language of the prayer that God looks at, but the sincerity of the heart in it; and that shall be accepted, though the prayer be very short, and the groanings such as cannot be uttered.

A Life of Communion With God.

IF there be a heaven upon earth, certainly this is it, by faith to set the Lord always before us, having an eye to Him with suitable affections, as the first cause and last end of all things that concern us. And so, having communion with Him in providences as well as ordinances, when we receive the common comforts of every day from His hand with love and thankfulness, and bear the common crosses and disappointments of every day, as ordered by His will, with patience and submission; when we commit every day's care to Him, and manage every day's business and converse for Him; having a constant habitual regard to God in the settled principles of the divine life, and frequent actual outgoings of soul towards Him in pious ejaculations, the genuine expressions of devout affections; then we live a life of communion with God. Did we know by experience what it is to live such a life as this, we would not exchange the pleasures of it for the peculiar treasures of kings and provinces.

The Soul's Triumph Over Death.

LEARN then, my soul, learn thou to triumph over death and the grave: 'O Death! where is thy sting? O Grave! where is thy victory?' Having laid up thy treasure within the veil, and remitted thy best effects and best affections thither, and having received the earnest of the purchased possession, be still looking, still longing, for that blessed hope. Fear not death, for it cannot hurt thee, but desire it rather, for it will greatly befriend thee. When the 'earthly house of this tabernacle shall be dissolved,' thou shalt remove to the house not made with hands, eternal in the heavens. Wish then, wish daily, for the coming of Thy Lord, for He shall appear to thy joy. 'The vision is for an appointed time, and at the end it shall speak, and shall not lie.' Look through the windows of this house of clay, like the mother of Sisera, when she waited for her son's triumphs, and cry through the lattice, 'Why is His chariot so long in coming, why tarry the wheels of His chariot?' Come, Lord Jesus, come quickly.

Divine Knowledge.

THERE is no pleasure in any learning like that of learning Christ, and the things that belong to our everlasting peace; for that which is known is not small and trivial, is not doubtful and uncertain, is not foreign to us, and which we are not concerned in; which are things that may much diminish the pleasure of any knowledge; but it is great and sure, and of the last importance to us, and the knowledge of it gives us satisfaction: here we may rest our souls. To know the perfections of the divine nature, the unsearchable riches of divine grace, to be led into the mystery of our redemption and reconciliation by Christ, this is food; such knowledge as this is a feast to the soul; it is meat indeed, and drink indeed; it is the knowledge of that which the angels desire to look into, 1 Peter i. 12. If the knowledge of the law of God was so sweet to David, 'sweeter than honey to his taste,' Psalm xix. 10, and cxix. 103, how much more so should the knowledge of the gospel of Christ be to us? When God gives this wisdom and knowledge, with it He gives joy to him that is good in His sight, Eccl. iii. 26.

A Sacramental Petition.

LORD, meet me with a blessing, a Father's blessing, at Thy table: grace Thine own institutions with Thy presence; and fulfil in me all the good pleasure of Thy goodness, and the work of faith with power, for the sake of Jesus Christ my blessed Saviour and Redeemer. To Him, with the Father, and the Eternal Spirit, be everlasting praise. Amen.

THOMAS WILSON, D. D.
1663-1755.

AFFLICTIONS.

AFFLICTIONS are no marks of God's displeasure. *Jesus loved Mary and Lazarus*, yet they were both afflicted.

Punishment is due to sin. We must be punished here or hereafter; it is the cause of all afflictions, and designed by our gracious God to bring us to repentance.

Prosperity is a most dangerous state; we fancy it is owing to our merit, and it is followed with pride, neglect of duty, fearlessness.

It is happy for us when God counts us worthy to suffer for His name's sake; to contend with Satan, as Job did, and be able, through God's grace, to overcome so powerful a spirit.

Afflictions, undergone with resignation, are the great test of our love of God; when we love Him, when He chastens us. May God sanctify all our afflictions to us all.

May I receive every thing from Thy hand with patience and with joy!

Remember me, O God, in the day of trouble.

Secure me, by Thy grace, from all excess of *fear*, *concern*, and *sadness*.

Let the afflictions I meet with be in some measure serviceable towards the appeasing of Thy wrath. Let them prove the happy occasion of forwarding my conversion and salvation.

The Saviour's Patience.

WHAT sorrows did He undergo, and with what patience did He suffer them! Patient when Judas unworthily betrayed Him with a kiss; patient when Caiaphas despitefully used Him; patient when hurried from one place to another; patient when Herod with his men of war set Him at naught; patient when Pilate so unrighteously condemned Him; patient when scourged and crowned with thorns; patient when His cross was laid upon Him, when He was reviled, reproached, scoffed at, and every way abused. Lord Jesus, grant me patience, after this example to bear Thy holy will in all things.

A Prayer for Submission of Spirit.

FORTIFY my soul, blessed Jesus, with the same spirit of submission with which Thou underwentest the death of the Cross, that I may receive all events with resignation to the will of God; that I may receive troubles, afflictions, disappointments, sickness, and death itself, without amazement; these being the appointment of Thy justice for the punishment of sin, and of Thy mercy for the salvation of sinners.

Let this be the constant practice of my life, to be pleased with all Thy choices, that when sickness and death approach, I may be prepared to submit my will to the will of my Maker.

And O that, in the mean time, my heart may always go along with my lips in this petition,—*Thy will be done.* Amen.

A Morning Prayer.

BLESSED be the Lord for His mercies renewed unto me every morning; for my *preservation* and *refreshment*, and for all the blessings of the night past;—for which all thanks and glory be to Thee, my God and Father!

Gracious God, continue to me these, and all other Thy blessings, so long, and in such a measure, as shall be most for Thy glory and my salvation.

Possess my soul, I beseech Thee, with a true and saving faith, and with such a sense of Thy goodness to me, and of my dependance upon Thee, that it may be my delight, as it is my interest and duty, to serve and obey Thee.

But that I may serve Thee with a quiet mind, forgive me all my sins, I beseech Thee, for Thy dear Son's sake, and withhold the judgments of which my conscience is afraid.

Keep it ever in the heart of Thy servant, that it is an evil thing and bitter to *forsake and offend the Lord.* And above all things, *keep me from wilful and deliberate sins,* that I may never grieve Thy Holy Spirit, nor provoke Thee to leave me to myself.

Let Thy restraining grace preserve me from the temptations of the *world,* the *flesh,* and the *devil;* that I may fall into no sin, nor run into any kind of danger; but that all my doings may be ordered by Thee, that I may do always that which is righteous in Thy sight: and that I may live and act as having Thee, O God, the constant witness of all my *thoughts, designs, words,* and *actions.*

May I never render myself, by new sins, unworthy of Thy guidance and protection!

Suffer me not to go astray, or bring me back by such ways as to Thee shall seem meet.

May I love Thee with all my heart, and all mankind for Thy sake! And may I ever have this sure proof of Thy love abiding in me, that I study to please Thee, and to keep Thy commandments! And that I may forgive, and love, and do good to my neighbors, as becomes a disciple of Jesus Christ!

Assist me by Thy grace, faithfully to perform all the duties of my calling; and thankfully to receive, and patiently to bear, whatever Thy providence shall order for me.

Preserve me from an *idle* and *useless* life; ever remembering, *that the night cometh when no man can work;* and that *now* is the time in which to provide for eternity.

And grant, O Lord, that no worldly pleasure, no worldly business, may ever make me *lose the sight of death.*

And may the thoughts of death oblige me to be truly and sincerely good; to mortify all *pride,* and *vanity, covetousness, hatred, envy,* and *malice;* to be *serious, sober,* and *watchful,* while I continue in this state of trial.

Hear me, O Heavenly Father, not according to my imperfect petitions, but according to the full meaning of that holy prayer, which Thy beloved Son hath taught us, in compassion to our infirmities:

Our Father, which art in heaven, &c.
The Grace of our Lord Jesus Christ, &c.

An Evening Prayer.

THAT it hath pleased Thee, O God, to add another day to the years of my life, and to keep me from the dangers of an evil world: For these, and for all Thy mercies from day to day bestowed upon me, I bless Thy good and gracious providence, most earnestly beseeching Thee to pardon my offences of the day past, and to grant that they may never rise up in judgment against me.

Lord, the frailty of man, without Thee, cannot but fall: in all temptations, therefore, I beseech Thee to succor me, that no sin may ever get the dominion over me.

Give me a salutary dread of the corruption of my own heart: Make me truly sensible of the end of sin, and mindful of my own infirmities and backslidings.

Vouchsafe unto all sinners a true sense of their unhappy state, a fear of Thy judgments, and grace and strength to break their bonds.

Enlighten my soul with saving truth. Correct me

in mercy, and reduce me when I go astray. Make me ever mindful of my latter end, and fix in my heart a lively sense of the happiness and misery of the world to come.

May the thoughts of death mortify in me all pride and covetousness, and a love for this world; and may my firm belief of a judgment to come make me ever careful to please Thee, my Lord and Judge, that I may find mercy at that day!

Grant that I may lie down to sleep with the same charitable and forgiving temper, in which I desire and hope to die.

And may the Almighty God take me, and all that belong to me, under His gracious and powerful protection! May He give His angels charge concerning us, and keep us in perpetual peace and safety, through Jesus Christ our Lord.

St. John, xvi. 23. *Verily, I say unto you, Whatsoever ye shall ask the Father in my name, He will give it you.*

In Thy name, O Jesus, and in the full meaning of the words which Thou hast taught us, I pray God, for Thy sake, to hear me, and to give me what is most convenient for me:

Our Father, which art in heaven, &c.

The Grace of our Lord Jesus Christ, &c.

ISAAC WATTS, D. D.
1674–1748.

Holy Breathings.

O HAPPY day and happy hour indeed, that shall finish the long absence of my Beloved, and place me within sight of my adored Jesus! When shall I see that lovely, that illustrious Friend, who laid down His own life to rescue mine, His own valuable life to ransom a worm, a rebel that deserved to die? He suffered, He groaned, He died; but He rose again, the blessed Saviour arose, He lives, He reigns exalted over all the creation. Faith beholds Him risen, and reigning, but it is through a glass, it is at a distance, and but darkly. I wait, I hope for a more divine pleasure; it is a delight worth dying for, to behold Him face to face, to see Him as He is, to converse with His wondrous person, and to survey His glories. Alas! my soul is too patient of this long distance and separation. O for the wings of love, to bear my spirit upward in holy breathings! Methinks I would long to be near Him, to be with Him, to give Him my highest praises and thanks for my share in His dying love. I would rise to join with the blessed acclamations, the holy songs of the saints on high, while they behold their exalted Saviour. How sweet their songs! How loud their acclamations! This is the man, the God-man who died for me! This is the Son of God, who was buffetted, who was crowned with thorns, who endured exquisite anguish, and unknown sorrows for me, who was scourged, and wounded, and crucified for me! This is the glorious Person, the Lamb of God, who washed me from my sins in His own blood. Blessing, honor, and salvation to His holy name for ever. Amen.

>I shall behold His glories there,
>And pay Him my eternal share
>Of praise, and gratitude, and love
>Among ten thousand saints above.

Holy Fortitude.

GIVE me, O my God, give me the spirit of prayer, and let me keep ever near to the throne of grace, that my soul may not come thither as a stranger, but that in every surprise I may address Thee as a God near at hand, and that in the name of my great High Priest, Jesus the Son of God, I may find grace ready to help me in the time of need.

Wean me, O Lord, from all the delights and hopes of flesh and sense! Mortify me to all the honors and the joys of a perishing life, and a vain world. Arm my soul all over with a religious hardiness, that I may venture into the field of battle, and may scarce feel the wounds which I receive in Thy cause. Give me the happy skill of diverting my fears, when I cannot at once subdue them, and lead me into proper employments of my heart and hand for this purpose.

I would live as under the eye of God. I would take notice of His hand in all the affairs of life, and all the dangers that attend me. I would learn of Moses to endure the fight of afflictions, as seeing Him who is invisible. Let me hear Thy voice, O Jesus, my Saviour, let me hear Thy voice walking upon the waters; when I am tossed about upon the waves of distress and difficulty, speak to my soul and say, *It is I, be not afraid.*

I would be bravely prepared for the worst of sufferings to which my circumstances in this life may expose me. I would be ready to meet contempt and scandal, poverty, sickness, and death itself. Jesus can support me in the heaviest distresses, though all the sorrows I fear should come upon me. He can bear me on the wings of faith and hope, high above all the turmoils and disquietudes of life: He can carry me through the shadow of the dark valley, and scatter all the terrors of it. Give me, O Lord, these wings of faith and hope, and bear me upon them through all the remains of my short journey in the wilderness: Make me active and zealous in Thy cause while I live, and convey me safely above the reach of fear, through the valley of death, to the inheritance prepared for me in the land of light. Then my fears shall cease for ever, for enemies and dangers are not known in that land. There all our conflicts shall be changed into everlasting triumphs, while songs of honor and salvation ascend in a full choir to the grace that has made us overcomers. Amen.

Fly to the Mercy-seat.

FLY daily to the mercy-seat for divine aid: Commit thy soul and body to the keeping of Christ; He is exalted and authorized to take care of sinners, who make Him their refuge; He is also compassionate, and ready to succor the tempted. There is cleansing virtue in the blood of Christ to wash away the foulest guilt, and to sprinkle the conscience of the humble penitent with peace and pardon; and there is all-sufficient power and grace with Him to subdue the most raging vices. Make haste to Him by humble faith, and most importunate prayer; Continue instant at the throne: Never rest till He hath by His providence and His grace delivered you from the dangerous temptation, or made you conqueror over the sin that easily besets you. There are a thousand souls in heaven, who were once conflicting here with the same impure temptations, but they gained the victory by the blood and Spirit of Christ, *and are made more than conquerors through Him who hath loved them.*

Uncertainty of Life.

WE are all borderers upon the river of death, which conveys us into the eternal world, and we should be ever waiting the call of our Lord, that we may launch away with joy to the regions of immortality: But thoughtless creatures that we are, we are perpetually wandering far up into the fields of sense and time, we are gathering the gay and fading flowers that grow there, and filling our laps with them as a fair treasure, or making garlands for ambition to crown our brows, till one and another of us is called off on a sudden and hurried away from this mortal coast: Those of us who survive are surprised a little, we stand gazing, we follow our departing friends with a weeping eye for a minute or two, and then we fall to our amusements again and grow busy, as before, in gathering the flowers of time and sense. O how fond we are to enrich ourselves with these perishing trifles, and adorn our heads with honors and withering vanities, never thinking which of us may receive the next summons to leave all behind us and stand before God! but each presumes 'it will not be sent to me.' We trifle with God and things eternal, or utterly forget them, while our hands and our hearts are thus deeply engaged in the pursuit of our earthly delights: All our powers of thought and action are intensely busied amongst the dreams of this life, while we are asleep to God, because we vainly imagine He will not call us yet.

Awake to God.

WHEN we are awake, we are not only fitter for the coming of our Lord to call us away by death, and fitter for His appearance to the great judgment, but we are better prepared also to attend Him in every call to present duty, and more ready to meet His appearance in every providence. It is the Christian soldier who is ever awake and on his guard, that is only fit for every sudden appointment to new stations and services; He is more prepared for any post of danger and hazardous enterprise, and better furnished to sustain the roughest assaults. We shall be less shocked at sudden afflictions here on earth, if our souls keep heaven in view and are ready winged for immortality. When we are fit to die, we are fit to live also and to do better service for God, in whichsoever of His worlds He shall please to appoint our station. 'My business, O Father, and my joy is to do Thy will among the sons of mortality, or among the spirits of the blessed on high.'

'Let us remember we have slept too long already in days past, and it is but a little while that we are called to watch.' We have worn away too much of our life in sloth and drowsiness. *The night is far spent* with many of us, *the day is at hand; it is now high time to awake out of sleep, for now is our salvation nearer than when we first believed*, Rom. xiii. 11, 22. Another hour or two, and the night will be at an end with us; Jesus, the Morning Star, is just appearing: *What, can we not watch one hour?* Matt. xxvi. 40. O happy souls, that keep themselves awake to God in the midst of this dreaming world! Happy indeed when our Lord shall call us out of these dusky regions, and we shall answer His call with holy joy and spring upward to the inheritance of the saints in light! Then all the seasons of darkness and slumbering will be finished for ever; there is no need of laborious watchfulness in that world, where there is no flesh and blood to hang heavy upon the spirit; but the sanctified powers of the soul are all life and immortal vigor. There is no want of the sunbeams to make their daylight, or to irradiate that city; *the glory of God enlightens it* with divine splendors, *and the Lamb is the light thereof*, Rev. xxi. 23. No inhabitant can sleep under such a united blaze of grace and glory: No faintings of nature, no languor or weariness are found in all that vital climate; every citizen is for ever awake and busy under the beams of that glorious day; zeal and love, and joy, are the springs of their eternal activity, and *there is no night there*, Rev. xxii. 5.

Heavenly Rest.

THE grace of God works us up to a preparation for heaven, 'by carrying us through those trials and sufferings, those labors and conflicts here in this life, which will not only make heaven the sweeter to us, but will make it more honorable for God Himself to bestow this heaven upon us.' When the spirits of a creature are almost worn out with the toilsome labors of the day, what an additional sweetness does he find in rest and repose! What an inward relish and satisfaction to the soul, that has been fatigued under a long and tedious war with sins and temptations, to be transported to such a place where sin cannot follow them, and temptation can never reach them! How will it enhance all the felicities of the heavenly world when we enter into it, to feel ourselves released from all the trials and distresses, and sufferings which we have sustained in our travels thitherwards! The review of the waves and the storms wherein we had been tossed for a long season, and had been almost shipwrecked there, will make the peaceful haven of eternity, to which we shall arrive, much more agreeable to every one of the sufferers, 2 Cor. iv. 17, *Our light afflictions, which are but for a moment, are* in this way *working for us a far more exceeding and eternal weight of glory*, and preparing us for the possession of it.

> There shall I bathe my weary soul
> In seas of heavenly rest,
> And not a wave of trouble roll
> Across my peaceful breast.

No Sorrow in Heaven.

IN that world there is no sorrow, for there is no sin; *the inhabitants* of that city, of the heavenly Jerusalem, *shall never say I am sick; for the people that dwell therein shall be forgiven their iniquity*, Isaiah xxxiii. 24. When the righteous are dismissed from this flesh *they enter into peace*, their bodies *rest in their beds* of earth, and their spirits *walk* in heaven, *each one in his* own *uprightness*, Isaiah lvii. 2. And as there is no sin within them to render them uneasy, so there is no troublesome guest, no evil attendant without them, that can give them fear or pain; no sinners to vex them, no tempter to deceive them, no spirit of hell to devour or destroy, Isaiah xxxv. 9. 10, *No lion shall be there, nor any ravenous beast shall go up thereon, it shall not be found there; but the redeemed shall walk there. And the ransomed of the Lord shall return and come to Zion with songs, and everlasting joy upon their heads; they shall obtain joy and gladness, and sorrow and sighing shall flee away.*

Our Pious Departed Friends.

WHEN we think of our pious friends departed, our foolish imagination is too ready to indulge and improve our sorrow. We sit solitary in the parlor and the chamber, we miss them there, and we cry, 'They are lost.' We retire melancholy to the closet, and bewail a lost father, or lost mother, or perhaps a nearer and dearer relative. We miss them in our daily conversation, we miss them in all their friendly offices, and their endearing sensible characters, and we are ready to say again, 'Alas! they are lost.' This is the language of flesh and blood, of sense and fancy. Come, let our faith teach us to think and speak of them under a more cheerful and a juster representation: They are not utterly lost, for they are present with Christ and with God. They are departed our world, where all things are imperfect, to those upper regions where light and perfection dwell. They have left their offices and stations here among us, but they are employed in a far diviner manner, and have new stations and nobler offices on high. Their places on earth indeed know them no more, but their places in heaven know them well, even those glorious mansions that were prepared for them from the foundation of the world. Their place is empty in the earthly sanctuary, and in the days of solemn assembly, but they appear above in the heavenly Jerusalem as fair *pillars* and ornaments *in the temple of God* on high, and shall for ever dwell with Him there.

Are the spirits of the just, who are departed from earth, *made perfect* in heaven? then they are not the proper subjects for our perpetual sorrows and endless complaints. Let us moderate our grief, therefore, for that very providence that has fixed them in perfect holiness and joy.

We lament their absence, and our loss indeed is great; but the spirit of Christian friendship should teach us to rejoice in their exaltation. Is it no pleasure to think of them as released from all the bonds of infirm nature, from pains of mortality, and the disquietudes of a sinful world? Is it not better to lift our eyes upward, and view a parent or beloved friend adorned with perfect grace and complete in glory, exulting in the fulness of joy near the throne of God, than to behold him laboring under the tiresome disorders of old age, groaning under the anguish and torment of acute distempers, and striving with the troublesome attendants of this sinful and painful state? Do we profess fondness and affection for those that are gone, and shall we not please ourselves a little in their happiness, or at least abate our mourning? Doth not St. Paul tell the Corinthians, this is what *we wish, even your perfection?* 2 Cor. xiii. 9; and should not saints in the lower world take some satisfaction when a fellow-saint is arrived at the sum of his own wishes, even perfect holiness and joy on high?

THE LORD'S SUPPER.

HOW happily is the *Lord's supper* contrived by divine wisdom to represent the death and love of our blessed Saviour, and the benefits that we derive from His sufferings? Jesus Christ crucified is *evidently set forth before our eyes*, Gal. iii. 1. He is represented even in His bleeding and dying love, while the bread is broken, and the wine poured out before us. O how should we loose the springs of pious passion at such a season! How should our love to our Redeemer kindle and rise high at the sight of the sufferings of the Son of God, who took our flesh and blood, that He might be capable of dying; that His flesh might be torn, and cut and bruised, that His blood might be spilled for our sakes, that He might bear such agonies as belonged to sinful creatures, with a gracious design to deliver us from misery and everlasting death. For ever blessed be the name of Jesus, who has suffered such pangs and sorrows in our stead, and blessed be His wisdom and grace who has appointed the continual repetition of such an ordinance, and such a lively memorial of His dying love, to touch all the springs of religious affection within us.

The End of Time.

IT is finished, said our blessed Lord on the Cross: It is finished, may every one of His followers say at the hour of death, and at the end of time: My sins and follies, my distresses and my sufferings, are finished for ever, and the mighty angel swears to it, that the time of these evils is no longer; they are vanished, and shall never return. O happy souls, who have been so wise as to count the short and uncertain number of your days on earth, as to make an early provision for a removal to heaven! Blessed are you above all the powers of thought and language. Days, and months, and years, and all these short and painful periods of time, shall be swallowed up in a long and blissful eternity; the stream of time which has run between the banks of this mortal life, and borne you along amidst many dangerous rocks of temptation, fear, and sorrow, shall launch you out into the ocean of pleasures which have no period: those felicities must be everlasting, for duration has no limits there; time with all its measures *shall be no more.*

No Pain Among the Blessed.

O GLORIOUS and happy state! where millions of creatures who have dwelt in bodies of sin and pain, and have been guilty of innumerable follies and offences against their Maker, yet they are all forgiven, their robes are washed and made white in the blood of Jesus, their iniquities are canceled for ever, and there shall not be one stroke more from the hand of God to chasten them, nor one more sensation of pain to punish them. Divine and illustrious privilege indeed, and a glorious world, where complete sanctification of all the powers of nature shall for ever secure us from new sins, and where the springs and causes of pain shall for ever cease, both within us and without us! Our glorified bodies shall have no avenue for pain to enter; the gates of heaven shall admit no enemy to afflict or hurt us; God is our everlasting friend, and our souls shall be satisfied with the *rivers of pleasure which flow for ever at the right hand of God,* Psalm xvi. 11.

No Night in Heaven.

'UNDER our darkest nights, our most inactive and heavy hours, our most uncomfortable seasons here on earth, let us remember we are traveling to a world of light and joy.' If we happen to lie awake, in midnight darkness, and count the tedious hours one after another in a mournful succession, under any of the maladies of nature, or the sorrows of this life, let us comfort ourselves that we are not shut up in eternal night and darkness without hope, but we are still making our way towards that country where there is no night, where there is neither sin nor pain, malady nor sorrow.

What if the blessed God is pleased to try us by the withholding of light from our eyes for a season? What if we are called to seek our duty in dark providences, or are perplexed in deep and difficult controversies, wherein we cannot find the light of truth?

What if we 'sit in darkness and mourning, and see no light, and the beams of divine consolation are cut off, let us *still trust in the name of the Lord, and stay ourselves upon our God*, especially as He manifests Himself in the Lamb that was slain, the blessed medium of His mercy:' Isaiah 1. 10. Let us learn to say with the prophet Micah, in the spirit of faith, Micah vii. 8, 9: *When I sit in darkness, the Lord will be a light unto me;—He will bring me forth to the light and I shall behold His righteousness.*

Blessed be God, that the night of ignorance, grief, or affliction, which attends us in this world, is not everlasting night. Heaven and glory are at hand; wait and watch for the morning Star, for Jesus and the resurrection. Roll on apace in your appointed course, ye suns and moons, and all ye twinkling enlighteners of the sky; carry on the changing seasons of light and darkness in this lower world with your utmost speed, till you have finished all my appointed months of continuance here. The light of faith shows me the dawning of that glorious day, which shall finish all my nights and darknesses for ever. Make haste, O delightful morning, and delay not my hopes. Let me hasten, let me arrive at that blessed inheritance, those mansions of paradise, where night is never known, but one eternal day shall make our knowledge, our holiness, and our joy eternal.

Joy at the Resurrection.

AWAKE, O my soul, and bless the Lord with all thy powers, and give thanks with holy joy for the gospel of His Son Jesus. It is Jesus, by His rising from the dead, has left a divine light upon the gates of the grave, and scattered much of the darkness that surrounded it. It is the gospel of Christ which casts a glory even upon the bed of death, and spreads a brightness upon the graves of the saints in the lively views of a great rising-day. O blessed and surprising prospect of faith! O illustrious scenes of future vision and transport! When the Son of God shall bring forth to public view all His redeemed ones, who had been long hidden in night and dust, and shall present them all to God the Father in His own image, bright, and holy, and unblemished, in the midst of all the splendors of the resurrection! O blessed and joyful voice, when He shall say with divine pleasure, *Here am I, and the children which Thou hast given me:* Isaiah viii. 18; Heb. ii. 13. We have both passed through the grave, and I have made them all conquerors of death, and vested them with immortality, according to Thy divine commission! *Thine they were, O Father, and Thou hast given them into my hands*, and behold I have brought them all safe to Thy appointed mansions, and I present them before Thee *without spot or blemish*, John xvii. 6.

And many a parent of a pious household in that day, when they shall see their sons and their daughters around them, all arrayed with the beams of the

Sun of righteousness, shall echo with holy joy to the voice of the blessed Jesus, *Lord, here am I, and the children which Thou hast given me*, Heb. ii. 13. I was afraid, as Job once might be when his friends suggested this fear; I was afraid that my *children had sinned against God, and He had cast them away for their transgression*, Job viii. 4. But I am now convinced, when He seized them from my sight, He only took them out of the way of temptation and danger, and concealed them for a season in His safe hiding-place: I mourned in the daytime for a lost son or a lost daughter, and in the night my couch was bedewed with my tears: I was scared with midnight dreams on their account, and the visions of the grave terrified me, because my children were there: I gave up myself to sorrow, for fear of the displeasure of my God both against them and against me: But how unreasonable were these sorrows! How groundless were my fears! How gloriously am I disappointed this blessed morning! I see my dear offspring called out of that long retreat where God had concealed them, and they arise to meet the divine call. I hear them answering with joy to the happy summons. My eyes behold them risen in the image of my God and their God; they are near me, they stand with me at the right hand of the Judge; now shall we rejoice together in the sentence of eternal blessedness from the lips of my Lord, my Redeemer, and their Redeemer.

Death of Pious Youth.

OUR blessed Jesus *walks among the* roses and *lilies* in the garden of His church, and when He sees a wintry storm coming upon some tender *plants of righteousness,* He hides them in the earth to preserve life in them, that they may bloom with new glories when they shall be raised from that bed. The blessed God acts like a tender Father, and consults the safety and the honor of His children, when the hand of His mercy snatches them away before that powerful temptation comes, which He foresees would have defiled and distressed, and almost destroyed them. They are not lost, but they are gone to rest a little sooner than we are. Peace be to that bed of dust where they are hidden, by the hand of their God, from unknown dangers! Blessed be our Lord Jesus, who has the keys of the grave, and never opens it for His favorites but in the wisest season.

Death of Christian Relatives.

IF our departed relative were a Christian indeed, and gave us comfortable hope in his death, then it leads our thoughts naturally to heaven, and most powerfully touches the springs of our heavenly hopes. It raises our pious wishes to the upper world, and we say, as Thomas did at the death of Lazarus, *Let us go, that we may die with him,* John xi. 16. Let us go to our God and our holy kindred, and enjoy their better presence there. Let us not *sorrow for the dead as those that mourn without hope,* 1 Thess. iv. 13, but look upward to things unseen and forward to the great rising-day, and rejoice in the promised and future glories that are beyond life and time.

Every dear relative that dies and leaves us, gives us one motive more to be willing to die: Their death furnishes us with one new allurement toward heaven, and breaks off one of the fetters and bonds that tied us down to this earth. Alas! we are tied too fast to these earthly tabernacles, these prisons of flesh and blood. We are attached too much to flesh and blood still, though we find them such painful and such sinful companions. We love to tarry in this world too well, though we meet with so many weaning strokes to divide our hearts from it. O it is good to live more loose from earth, that we may be ready for the parting hour: Let us not be angry with the sovereign hand of God that breaks one bond after another; though the strokes be painful, yet they loosen our spirits from this cottage of clay; they teach us to practice a flight heavenward in holy meditations and devout breathings; and we learn to say, *How long, O Lord, how long?*

The recollection.— Have any of us lately felt such parting strokes as these? Have we lost any of our beloved kindred? God calls upon us now, and enquires, 'What have you learned of these divine lessons?' I would ask myself this day, Have I seen the emptiness and the insufficiency of creatures, and recalled my hope and confidence from every thing beneath and beside God? Have I passed through this solemn hour of trial well, and shown my supreme love to God, and my most entire submission to His sovereignty, by resigning so dear a comfort at His demand? Have I been taught by the inward pain which I felt at parting, and by the smart which still remains, how dangerous a thing it is to love a creature too well? Have I duly considered my past conduct toward my relations deceased, and does it approve itself to my conscience at the review? Or have I found matter for self-condemnation and repentance? Have I treasured up the memory of their virtues in my heart, and set them before me as the copy of my life? Have my thoughts followed the soul of my dear departed friend, and traced it with pleasure to the world of blessed spirits; and does my own soul seem to fix its hope and joy there, and to dwell there above? Are my thoughts become more spiritual and heavenly? Do I live more as a borderer on the other world, since a piece of me is gone thither? And am I ready for the summons, if it should come before to-morrow?

Happy Christian, who has been taught by the spirit of grace to improve the death of the dearest relative to so divine an advantage. The words of my text are then fulfilled experimentally in you: *Death is yours:* Death itself is made a part of your treasures. The parting stroke is painful indeed, but it carries a blessing in it too; for it has promoted your heavenly and eternal interest.

The Believer's Possessions.

'REMEMBER, O my soul, *death is thine:* There is nothing in that dark valley shall hurt thee. Lift up thy head, arise, and shake thyself out of the dust. Let thy faith take a sweet prospect over the little hills of time, and beyond the vale of death: Look far into the invisible world, and banish all thy fears under the strong allurement of the joys that are prepared for thee; wait with pleasure for the hour of thy departure, and rejoice and triumph when the divine message shall come. While thou continuest here, *life is thine.* When thou goest hence, *death is thine; things present and things to come are thine;* and the invisible world to which thou art hastening, has everlasting joys in reserve for thee: Heaven itself is thine: Heaven is the inheritance of all the saints: The glories laid up there are waiting for thy possession: The dissolution of thy earthly tabernacle shall convey thee into the midst of them.

'Awake, arise, and meet the happy moment, when thou shalt be undressed of this sinful flesh and blood: O let these defiled garments ever sit loose about thee, that they may be cast off without pain and regret: Go, my soul, at the summons of thy God and Father, and when thy symptoms of dying nature shall say, *Hark, He calleth thee,* let thy faith and thy love, and thy joy answer, *Lord, I come.* Go, my soul, at the invitation of thy Redeemer, at the voice of thy Beloved: Behold, He appears, He comes! Go forth and meet Him. Drop this fleshy clothing with holy delight; arise, *put on thy beautiful garments,* and shine, for the *glory of the Lord is rising upon thee:* Go shine among *the spirits of the just made perfect,* thyself a spirit released from earth, and divested of all imperfection. O happy farewell to life and time! O glorious entrance into immortality!'

The Christian's Hidden Life in Heaven.

HOW little is death to be dreaded by a believer, since it will bring the soul to the full possession of its hidden life in heaven! It is a dark valley that divides between this world and the next; but it is all a region of light and blessedness beyond it. We are now borderers on the eternal world, and we know but little of that invisible country. Approaching death opens the gates to us, and begins to give our holy curiosity some secret satisfaction; and yet how we shrink backward when that glorious unknown city is opening upon us! and are ready to beg and pray that the gates might be closed again: 'O! for a little more time, a little longer continuance in this lower visible world!' This is the language of the fearful believer; but it is better to have our Christian courage wrought up to a divine height, and to say, '*Open, ye everlasting gates, and be ye lift up, O ye immortal doors,* that we may enter into the place where *the King of glory is.*' There shall we see God, the great unknown, and rejoice in His overflowing love. We shall see Him not as we do on earth, darkly, through the glass of ordinances; but inferior spirits shall converse with the supreme Spirit, as bodies do with bodies; that is, face to face, 1 Cor. xiii. 12.

There shall we behold Christ our Lord in the dignity of His character as Mediator, in the glory of His kingdom, and the all-sufficiency of His Godhead; and we shall be for ever with Him. There shall we see millions of blessed spirits, who have lived the same hidden life as we do, and passed through this vale of tears, with the same attending difficulties and sorrows, and by the same divine assistances. They were unknown, and covered with dust as we are, while they dwelt in flesh, but they appear all-glorious and well-known in the world of spirits, and exult in open and immortal light; we shall see them, and we shall triumph with them in that day; we shall learn their language, and taste their joys; we shall be partakers of the same glory, which Christ our life diffuses all around Him, on the blessed inhabitants of that intellectual world.

> There shall we see His face
> And never, never sin;
> And from the rivers of His grace
> Drink endless pleasures in.

All-sufficiency of God.

THE Godhead is an infinite ocean of life and blessedness, and finite vessels may be for ever swelling, and for ever filling in that sea of all-sufficiency. There must be no tiresome satiety in that everlasting entertainment. God shall create the joys of His saints ever fresh: He shall throw open His endless stores of blessing, unknown even to the first rank of angels: and feast the sons and daughters of men with pleasures akin to those which were prepared for the Son of God. For verily He took not upon Him the nature of angels, but the likeness of sinful flesh: and when He shall appear the second time without sin to our salvation, we shall then be made like Him, for we shall see Him as He is.

THOMAS ADAM.
1701–1784.

The Man of Prayer.

NO words can describe the blessedness of a soul which lives in communion with God; asking and receiving, seeking and finding, knocking and having the door opened. For what is happiness but this? Or how can we describe it better, than by saying that a man wishes for the very thing he ought, and is sure to have it? And such is the man of prayer, the Christian. He chooses the Fountain of all happiness for his portion, and cannot be disappointed of his desire. He is happy in the very act of prayer, knowing it to be the right frame of his mind, the proof of his renewed state, and his capacity for receiving blessing from God. And he is happy in the returns of it; increasing in knowledge, faith and holiness, and passing through the world with a hope full of immortality. O blessed Jesus, teach us all to pray: for the desire is from Thee, and Thou givest Thyself with it, and we cannot receive Thee till we do pray.

Prayers. I.

O LORD, we pray Thee send down Thy Spirit to kindle the holy fire of love in our hearts. Let the sense of Thy excellencies and perfections, various gifts and blessings, be always present to our minds, and the continual subject of our meditations, that we may adore and bless and imitate Thee. The heavens declare Thy glory, the earth is filled with Thy bounties, and wherever we turn our eyes we see Thee in the riches of Thy goodness. But Thou hast more especially manifested Thy love to mankind, and magnified Thy name and Thy glory, by giving Thy only begotten Son to die for us. Give us, we beseech Thee, such a knowledge of Thee, as the God and Father of our Lord Jesus Christ, and such an assured faith in Thy great mercy to us in Him that we may love Thee, for the great love wherewith Thou hast loved us, and all mankind for Thy sake; do all our works on this ground; and be accepted of Thee for the sake, and through the alone merits of Jesus Christ. Amen.

II.

HOLY Father, open our eyes, we beseech Thee, to see the danger and misery of our condition in sin. Let Thy Son be our Master to teach us the strictness and purity of Thy law; let Thy Spirit go with us into the depth of our hearts, to convince us of our transgressions of it; that we may fly to the mercy of the gospel, be revived with a sense of forgiveness, live unto Him that died for us, and do all our works from a holy principle of faith and love to Thee. Deliver us from all guile and hypocrisy, from all blindness and hardness of heart; and as we know the Lord Jesus Christ to be the way, the truth, and the life, grant that we may humbly and thankfully receive Him in the grace and power of all His offices. Oh! grant, for Thy mercy's sake, that as He is the only rest of our guilty consciences, the reliever of all our burdens, and has opened the kingdom of heaven to all believers, we may rejoice in His salvation, be faithful to His truth, commit our souls to Him to be guided in the way which leadeth to everlasting life, and be received into Thy kingdom of glory, through Him, our blessed Saviour and Redeemer. Amen.

III.

O LORD, who hast sent Thy blessed Son a light into the world, and givest Thy Spirit to guide us into all truth; grant us grace thankfully to receive and obediently to follow, the doctrine He has delivered to us in Thy name. Let the study of Thy Word be our constant employment and the delight of our souls, that we may know Thee the only true God, and Jesus Christ whom Thou hast sent. From all blindness and hardness of heart, from all guile and insincerity, good Lord, deliver us. Help us to discover and remove all the impediments to Thy coming and gracious presence in our souls. Open our eyes, turn us from darkness to light, confirm us in the faith of Thy mercy, and make us fruitful in all good works. Grant that, by Thy holy inspiration, we may think those things that be good, and, by Thy merciful guiding, may perform the same, through our Lord Jesus Christ. Amen.

IV.

O LORD our God, pour upon us the spirit of grace and supplications, to receive the instructions and follow the doctrine of the great Teacher, Thy Son Jesus Christ our Lord, with all humility and thankfulness. As Thou hast taught us what is acceptable unto Thee, and delivered to us the rule of holy living; we beseech Thee, turn the desire of our hearts to it, and all our hearts to Thee, in prayer for a blessing upon what we learn from Thy holy Word. Convince us of our blindness, corruption and weakness, that we may come to Christ for help, rejoice in His salvation, and in the power of the Holy Ghost be enabled to do whatever Thou requirest of us. Make us Thy own people, make our souls and bodies Thy living temples; that, consecrating ourselves to Thee in faith and purity, and reverencing Thee in our hearts, we may gladly embrace all occasions of presenting ourselves before Thee in Thy house, as the house of prayer, worship Thee in spirit and in truth whilst we live here upon earth; and sing praises to Thee for ever in heaven, with all those whom Thou hast redeemed to Thyself by the blood of Jesus Christ, our blessed Lord and Saviour. Amen.

PHILIP DODDRIDGE, D. D.
1702–1751.

Praising the Lord.

PRAISE the Lord, all ye His saints; be thankful unto Him, and bless His name! Praise Him, who graciously purposed your salvation, and predestinated you to the adoption of children by Jesus Christ unto Himself! Praise Him, who rendered this purpose effectual, and wrought it out by a high hand and outstretched arm! Praise Him, who gave His own Son to be a sacrifice for you, and to bring in everlasting righteousness! Praise Him, who sent His Spirit, as the great agent in His Son's kingdom, to bring the hearts of sinners to a subjection to the gospel, and gently to captivate them to the obedience of faith! Praise Him, who has revealed this glorious gospel to you, at so great a distance of time and place! Praise Him, who has impressed your hearts with a disposition to regard it! Praise Him, who has subdued your prejudices against it! Praise Him, who, having implanted faith in your souls, continues even to this day to animate and support it! Let all ranks and ages join in this cheerful song! Praise ye the Lord, ye that are rich in temporal possessions, if you have been enabled to renounce the world as your portion, and to triumph over it by this divine principle! Praise Him, you that are poor in this world, if you are rich in faith, and heirs of the kingdom which God has promised to them that love Him! Praise Him, you that are cheerful and vigorous, and capable of rendering Him that active service which may speak the gratitude of your hearts towards Him! Praise Him, you that are weak and languishing, since His strength is made perfect in your weakness, and your infirmities illustrate the force of that faith which He has wrought in you! Praise Him, ye youths who, with this guide and companion of your way, are setting forth in the journey of life with courage, and lifting up your feet in His paths! Praise Him, ye aged saints, who stand on the borders of eternity, and live in a daily expectation, that you shall receive the end of your faith in the salvation of your souls! Begin that work now, in which you are all so soon to join! Break forth into one joyful anthem, and sing: 'Not unto us, O Lord, not unto us, but to Thy name be all the praise of that salvation, which Thou hast already begun in our souls, and which Thy faithfulness has engaged to complete.'

The Water of Life.

THE waters which followed Israel through the wilderness, failed when they came into an inhabited land. But this river of life will never forsake the believer; it will flow with him sweetly through the dark valley of the shadow of death, till it spreads itself into wider and deeper streams, in the lovely regions of the heavenly Canaan. Thus we are told, that in the New Jerusalem the river of the water of life proceedeth from the throne of God and of the Lamb. And thus our Lord assures the woman of Samaria, Whosoever drinketh of the water that I shall give him, shall never thirst; but it shall be in him as a well of water springing up into everlasting life. What then remains, but that we each of us cry out, as she did, Lord, give us of this living water, that we may thirst no more, nor come, as now, to these ordinances to draw!

> Clear spring of life! flow on, and roll
> With growing swell from pole to pole,
> 'Till flowers and fruits of paradise
> Round all thy winding current rise!
>
> Still near thy stream may I be found,
> Long as I tread this earthly ground!
> Cheer with thy wave death's gloomy shade;
> Then through the fields of Canaan spread!

A Devout Meditation.

O MY God, what shall I say? what, but that I love Thee above all in the power of language to express. While I feel Thy sacred Spirit breathing upon my heart, and exciting these fervors of love to Thee, I cannot doubt of its influence, any more than I can doubt of the truth of this animal life while I exert the acts of it. Surely, if ever I knew the appetite of hunger, my soul hungers after righteousness, and longs for a greater conformity to Thy blessed nature and will. If ever my palate felt thirst, my soul thirsts for God, even the living God! and for a more abundant communication of His favor. If ever my weary body knew what it was to wish for the refreshment of my bed, and longed for rest, even so my soul, with sweet acquiescence, rests upon Thy gracious bosom, O my Heavenly Father, and returns to its repose in the embraces of its God, who has dealt so bountifully with it. And if ever I saw the face of a beloved friend or child with complacency and joy, so I rejoice in beholding Thy mercy, O Lord, and in calling Thee my Father in Christ. Such Thou art, and such Thou wilt be for time, and for eternity. What have I more to do but to commit myself to Thee for both, and leave Thee to choose my inheritance, and order my affairs for me, while all my business is to serve Thee, and all my delight to praise Thee. My soul follows hard after my God, because His right hand supports me. Let it still bear me up, and I shall still press forward.

Our Great Intercessor.

HOW admirable and how amiable does the blessed Jesus appear, when considered as the great Intercessor of His people!

How admirable is He in this view! What an honor is done Him in the heavenly world! How dear to the Father does He appear to be, when God will not accept the services of the greatest and best of mankind, unless presented by Him; and for His sake will graciously regard the meanest and vilest sinner! And how great does this Intercessor appear in Himself! 'Blessed Jesus,' may the Christian say, 'who is like unto Thee, who canst at once sustain so many different relations, and canst fill them all with their proper offices, of duty to Thy Father, and of love to Thy people! who canst thus bear, without encumbering Thyself, without interfering with each other, the priestly censer and the royal sceptre! How wise are Thy counsels! How extensive Thy views! How capacious Thy thoughts! and yet, at the same time, how compassionate Thy gracious heart! That amidst all the exaltations of heaven, all the splendors of Thy Father's right hand, Thou shouldst still thus graciously remember Thine humble followers! That Thine eye should be always watchful over them, Thine ear be always open to their prayers, Thy mouth be ever ready to plead for them, and Thine arm to save them! As if it were not love enough to descend and die, unless Thou didst forever live and reign for them, and even glory in being made Head over all for Thy church.'

'But especially,' may the Christian say, 'when I think of Thee, blessed Jesus, not only as the Intercessor of Thy people in general, but as my Intercessor; when I think that Thou hast espoused my character and my cause, vile and obnoxious as it is; and that Thou art recommending my poor broken services, which I daily blush to present before Thee; and art using Thine interest and Thine authority in the world above, to complete my salvation, which

Thou hast begun; what shall Thy poor servant say unto Thee? All these astonishing and kind regards to me, who am unworthy to wash the feet of the least of Thy followers! Shall not the wonders of such condescending grace engage my gratitude to all eternity? My praises now are so exceeding feeble, and so low, I am almost ashamed to offer them. O when shall those nobler praises begin, which I hope ere long to offer in that world of perfection to which Thy gracious intercession is bringing me?'

A Prayer for Gospel Blessings.

BLESSED Jesus, Thou that knowest all things, knowest that I thirst after the blessings of Thy gospel. Thou seest that I most ardently long for the pardon of sin, the favor of God, the influences of Thy Spirit, and the glories of Thine heavenly kingdom. I am fully persuaded, that with regard to all these Thou art able to do for me abundantly above all I can ask or think. And wilt Thou not relieve me? Wilt Thou not give me to drink? Wherefore, then, are Thine invitations published in the gospel? Why does Thy Spirit even now work upon my heart, and raise there this fervency of desire? Wherefore didst Thou weep? Wherefore didst Thou bleed? Wherefore didst Thou die, if Thou hadst no compassion for perishing sinners? But Thou hast compassion; Thou hast already extended it to thousands on earth and millions in heaven. Lord, I believe; help Thou my unbelief! I throw myself at Thy feet; nor can I fear I shall perish there, unless infinite power be weakened, and infinite love be exhausted.

My Father's House.

IF it be so pleasant to me now and then, to cast a longing look towards my Father's house, and to read, as it were, this letter which His goodness sends to me, and to receive in the wilderness the tokens of His care, what will it be to come and dwell with Him, and with all my brethren in the Lord? O earth! all thy charms are not worth a moment's stay. It would be better, much better for me to be dissolved. How would my heart leap to see His chariot appearing! How welcome would the messenger be by which He should call me to His house, and to His bosom!

Heaven Our Home.

SEEING heaven is our country, let us take care to live like those who belong to such a country. This is what the apostle recommends to us by his own example. *Our conversation,* saith he, *is in heaven;* or we behave ourselves like citizens of heaven. Let us remember, that whilst we are in this world, we sojourn in a strange land, and are at a distance from our home; and, therefore, do not let us be inordinately affected with anything in it. Let us not be too much transported with the entertainments, nor too much dejected with the disappointments which we meet with in this land of our pilgrimage; but, let us be carrying on a constant, regular design of a happy abode in this glorious country; and let all the actions of our life have a tendency towards it; and to animate us to prosecute our journey with the greatest vigor and cheerfulness, let us be endeavoring to form an acquaintance with it. In the Scripture, God has given us a map of this heavenly Canaan. Let us take our notions of it from thence, and make this description of it very familiar to us. Let us keep up a constant correspondence with it, by frequent and earnest addresses to the throne of the King of heaven, and by meditating and discoursing upon the happiness of it. Let us be zealous for the interests of this heavenly country, and do our utmost to increase the number of the inhabitants of it. Let us endeavor to reflect an honor upon it, by imitating the manners of those who live there, and showing the same zeal for the honor of God, and the same affectionate regard to the good of our fellow creatures, that they do. Especially, let us maintain a peculiar affection for our fellow-citizens, and endeavor to help them forward on their journey thither. And, in the last place, let us be ready to leave this world, whenever it shall please God to give us a dismission from it; that so we may go into this country where we shall be no more strangers and foreigners, but *fellow-citizens with* the glorified *saints, and of the* highest *household of God*.

Death to the Believer.

ART thou, oh believer! unwilling to think of death? Methinks the remembrance of it should be thy daily refuge, and thy daily joy. For terrible as it is to him who goes on still in his trespasses, to thee it must have an angel's face. Dost thou not know that it is a friendly messenger sent to thee from heaven to tell thee that an habitation there is ready to receive thee? that the days of thy warfare are fully accomplished, so that the crown of victory is immediately to be set on thine head; and the triumphant palm to be borne? Dost thou not know, oh Christian! that when conquered, it was also reconciled by a Redeemer, and added to the treasures and possessions of His people. It is now become a gentle slumber, in which thou shalt lose thy fatigues and thy cares, thy sorrows and thy fears; and from which thou shalt awake to transporting joy and incorruptible glory. How canst thou forget so kind a friend, from whom thou hast such grand and such certain expectations? How canst thou forget that important day which shall be the period of calamity and of sin, and the commencement of complete holiness, of eternal felicity?

A Prayer on Committing the Soul to Jesus.

BLESSED Jesus! I have heard of Thy power and Thy love; and I believe what I have heard of them. Conscious that I have in my breast an immortal spirit, and trembling in a survey of its infinite importance, I humbly beg leave to consign it to Thy faithful care. *Lord Jesus, receive my spirit!* I would now call upon Thee with all the earnestness of a dying creature. From this hour, from this moment, receive it! Oh! take it under Thy care; wash it in Thy blood; adorn it with Thy righteousness; form it, O Lord! by Thy Spirit, to every branch of the Christian character; to every lineament of Thy blessed image; to a full conformity to that employment and happiness for which the spirits of Thy people are intended. And oh! watch over it, while I travel through this dangerous wilderness; and when it breaks loose from the flesh, fold it in Thine embrace. Remember, O Lord! if I should not be able to repeat it, remember the humble petition which I have now uttered. *Remember Thy word unto Thy servant, on which Thou hast caused me to hope;* and be surety unto me for good against all the terrors of death and hell; against all the frailties of this degenerate nature, in the meantime yet more to be feared.

Safe in Jesus.

BLESSED Jesus, I rejoice in Thee as my hope. and the louder the storm rages around me, the more violently the enemies of my soul are invading me, the closer will I adhere to Thee, and the more will I rejoice in Thy care.

Advice to the Afflicted.

O THOU afflicted, thou who art tossed with the tempest, and not comforted! look unto Jesus. Let thy conflicts and dangers drive thee to Him;

though Satan would thereby attempt to drive thee from Him. Accustom not thyself to think of Christ as dreadful and severe. Terrify not thyself with the thought of the iron rod of vengeance, whilst thou feelest thyself disposed to submit to the golden sceptre of His grace, to the pastoral rod by which He guides His sheep. And when thou findest thy doubts arising, flee to the representations and assurances of His Word, and pray, that the influences of His Spirit may strengthen thy faith in them.

MUTUAL JOY OF CHRIST AND BELIEVERS IN HEAVEN.
THERE they shall be no longer exposed to necessities and alarms; but all the purposes of His love shall be completed in their everlasting security and joy. And surely the gracious Redeemer must be inconceivably delighted, when He there sees of the travail of His soul. When He has with a gentle and gracious hand conducted His sheep through the dark valley of the shadow of death, with what joy will He open to them those better pastures! with what congratulations will He receive them to a state of inseparable nearness to Him, and administer unto them an abundant entrance into the everlasting kingdom of their Lord and Saviour! Therefore it is beautifully represented in the book of the Revelation, as the business and joy of Christ, even on the throne of His glory, to lead on His saints to the various scenes of divine pleasure and enjoyment, which are provided for them there. The Lamb which is in the

midst of the throne shall feed them, and shall lead them unto fountains of living waters.

And, O gracious Redeemer, what will the joy of Thy flock then be, when thus fed and conducted by Thee! If it be so delightful at this humble distance, to believe ourselves the objects of Thy care and favor, and to taste of these little streams which Thou art causing to flow in upon us here in the wilderness, what will that river of life be? If it be now the joy of our hearts, awhile to forget our cares and our fears, when we are perhaps at Thy table, and to lean our weary heads for a few moments on Thy dear breast; what will it be, forever to dwell in Thine embrace, and to say once for all, Return unto thy rest, O my soul, for the Lord hath dealt bountifully with thee! Bountifully indeed! when they who were brought out with weeping, and led on with supplication, shall, as the redeemed of the Lord, come to Zion with songs, and everlasting joy upon their heads, and sorrow and sighing shall flee away.

In the meantime, we rejoice in hope of this blessed scene, and would raise such feeble praises, as earth will admit, to this great Shepherd, whose arm is so strong to guard us; whose bosom is so soft to cherish us; and whose heart is so compassionate, notwithstanding all our unworthiness, as to exert that arm for our protection, and to open that bosom for our repose.

A Model of Devotion for the Evening.

O MY God, Thou art ever merciful and gracious. Thou causest the outgoing of the morning, and the return of the evening to rejoice with me. I now offer Thee my repeated tribute of praise. May my prayer come before Thee as incense, and the lifting up of my hands as an evening sacrifice.

I heartily thank Thee, that my forfeited life hath been lengthened out another day; and that every period and every moment of it, has been crowned with the instances of Thy care and Thy bounty. I thank Thee for my food and raiment. I thank Thee for my health, for the enjoyment of my friends, for the success of my studies; and, above all, for opportunities of conversing with Thee and of offering Thee my humble services, though I acknowledge them infinitely beneath Thy regard.

I earnestly entreat Thy gracious forgiveness with regard to all the sins which I have this day been chargeable with. Innumerable evils compass me about. And in the most innocent and most faithful days of my life, I see abundant need, to forfeit Thy favor and to awaken Thy displeasure. May the blood of Christ Jesus be sprinkled upon my soul, to cleanse me from this new guilt which I have contracted, as well as from all I have formerly contracted. For His sake continue Thy gracious protection this night. Deliver me from all dangers and temptations. Give me speedy, sound and refreshing sleep; and awake me in due time, fitted and determined for the duties of the day. And never leave me nor forsake me till

Thou hast brought me to that happy world, where these revolutions of nature shall be known no more; but where there shall be one everlasting day of glory and of joy, through Jesus Christ. Amen.

SALVATION NEAR.

YOU have salvation, complete salvation, in view; and it approaches; it *is nearer than when you believed;* it comes daily nearer and nearer. We may look upon every true Christian and say to him, and especially to one advanced in the journey of life, *Thou art not far from the kingdom of God.* A few days, or at most a few years more, will bring Thee to its glories and joys. Thou shalt be there, even in the kingdom, beholding the King in His glory, eating bread and drinking wine there, living and reigning with Him. Bear it daily in Thy mind, and endeavor to form thy soul more and more to that song in which, I hope, through Divine grace, so many of us shall join: *Salvation be to Him that sitteth upon the throne, and to the Lamb, who has redeemed us to God by His blood, and made us kings and priests;* that we might reign and worship for ever. To Him be glory, world without end. Amen.

>Awake, ye saints, and raise your eyes
> And raise your voices high;
>Awake, and praise that sovereign love,
> That shows salvation nigh.
>
>On all the wings of time it flies,
> Each moment brings it near;
>Then welcome each declining day!
> Welcome each closing year!

Not many years their rounds shall run,
  Nor many mornings rise,
Ere all its glories stand revealed
  To our admiring eyes.

Ye wheels of nature, speed your course;
  Ye mortal powers, decay;
Fast as ye bring the night of death,
  Ye bring eternal day.

JONATHAN EDWARDS, A. M.
1703-1758.

ON RELIGIOUS AFFECTIONS.

HOW insensible and unmoved are most men about the great things of another world! how dull are their affections! how heavy and hard their hearts in these matters! here their love is cold, their desires languid, their zeal low, and their gratitude small. How they can sit and hear of the infinite height and depth, and length and breadth of the love of God in Christ Jesus; of His giving His infinitely dear Son to be offered up a sacrifice for the sins of men, and of the unparalleled love of the innocent, holy Lamb of God manifested in His dying agonies, His bloody sweat, His loud and bitter cries and bleeding heart; and all this for enemies, to redeem them from deserved, eternal burnings, and to bring to unspeakable and everlasting joy and glory; and yet be cold, heavy, insensible and regardless! Where are the exercises of our affections proper, if not here? what is it that more requires them? and what can be a fit occasion of their lively and vigorous exercise, if not such as this? Can any thing be set in our view greater and more important? any thing more wonderful and surprising? or that more nearly concerns our interest! Can we suppose that the wise Creator implanted such principles in our nature as the affections, to lie still on such an occasion as this? Can any Christian, who believes the truth of these things, entertain such thoughts?

The Saint's Love to God.

THE love of God in the most eminent saints in this world, is truly very little in comparison of what it ought to be. Because the highest love that ever any attain to in this life is poor, cold, exceeding low, and not worthy to be named in comparison of what our obligations appear to be, from the joint consideration of these two things: viz. 1. The reason God has given us to love Him, in the manifestations He has made of His infinite glory, in His Word and works; and particularly in the gospel of His Son, and what He has done for sinful man by Him. And, 2. The capacity there is in the soul of man, by those intellectual faculties which God has given it, of seeing and understanding these reasons, which God has given us to love Him. How small indeed is the love of the most eminent saint on earth, in comparison of what these things jointly considered do require! And of this, grace tends to convince men; and especially eminent grace: for grace is of the nature of light and brings truth to view. And therefore he that has much grace, apprehends much more than others that great height to which his love ought to ascend; and he sees better than others how little a way he has risen towards that height. And therefore, estimating his love by the whole height of his duty, hence it appears astonishingly little and low in his eyes.

Christ's Invitations.

HOW much Christ appears as the Lamb of God in His invitations to you to come to Him and trust in Him! With what sweet grace and kindness does He, from time to time, call and invite you; as Prov. viii. 4: 'Unto you, O men, I call, and my voice is to the sons of men.' And Isaiah lv. 1, 2, 3: 'Ho, every one that thirsteth, come ye to the waters, and he that hath no money, come ye, buy and eat; yea, come, buy wine and milk without money, and without price.' How gracious is He here in inviting every one that thirsts, and in so repeating His invitation over and over, 'Come ye to the waters; come, buy and eat; yea, come!' Mark the excellency of that entertainment which He invites you to accept of, 'Come, buy wine and milk!' your poverty, having nothing to pay for it, shall be no objection,—'Come, he that hath no money, come without money, and without price!' What gracious arguments and expostulations He uses with you! 'Wherefore do ye spend money for that which is not bread? and your labor for that which satisfieth not? Hearken diligently unto me, and eat ye that which is good, and let your soul delight itself in fatness.' As much as to say, It is altogether needless for you to continue laboring and toiling for that which can never serve your turn, seeking rest in the world and in your own righteousness: I have made abundant provision for you of that which is really good, and will fully satisfy your desires and answer your end, and stand ready to accept of you: you need not be afraid; if you will come to me, I will engage to see all your wants supplied and you made a happy creature. As He promises in the third verse, 'Incline your ear, and come unto me: Hear, and your soul shall live, and I will make an everlasting covenant with you, even the sure mercies of David.' And so, Prov. ix. at the beginning. How gracious and sweet is the invitation there: 'Whoso is simple, let him turn in hither;' let you be never so poor, ignorant and blind a creature, you shall be welcome. And in the following words, Christ sets forth the provision that He has made for you, 'Come, eat of my bread and drink of the wine which I have mingled.' You are in a poor famishing state, and have nothing wherewith to feed your perishing soul; you have been seeking something, but yet remain destitute. Hearken how Christ calls you to eat of His bread and to drink of the wine that He hath mingled! And how much like a lamb does Christ appear in Matt. xi. 28–30: 'Come unto me, all ye that labor and are heavy laden, and I will give you rest. Take my yoke upon you and learn of me, for I am meek and lowly in heart; and ye shall find rest to your souls. For my yoke is easy and my burden is light.' O thou poor distressed soul! whoever thou art, consider that Christ mentions thy very case, when He

calls to them who labor and are heavy laden! How
He repeatedly promises you rest if you come to Him!
In the 28th verse he says, 'I will give you rest.'
And in the 29th verse, 'Ye shall find rest to your
souls.' This is what you want. This is the thing
you have been so long in vain seeking after. O how
sweet would rest be to you if you could but obtain
it! Come to Christ, and you shall obtain it. And
hear how Christ, to encourage you, represents Himself as a lamb! He tells you that He is meek and
lowly in heart; and are you afraid to come to such
a One? And again, Rev. iii. 20: 'Behold, I stand at
the door and knock: if any man hear my voice and
open the door, I will come in to him, and I will sup
with him and he with me.' Christ condescends not
only to call you to Him, but He comes to you; He
comes to your door and there knocks. He might
send an officer and seize you as a rebel and vile male-
factor; but instead of that He comes and knocks at
your door, and seeks that you would receive Him
into your house as your friend and Saviour. And
He not only knocks at your door, but He stands there
waiting while you are backward and unwilling. And
not only so, but He makes promises what He will do
for you if you will admit Him, what privileges He
will admit you to; He will sup with you, and you
with Him. And again, Rev. xxii. 16, 17: 'I am the
root and the offspring of David, and the bright and
morning star. And the Spirit and the bride say,
Come. And let him that heareth say, Come. And
let him that is athirst come. And whosoever will,

let him take of the water of life freely.' How does Christ here graciously set before you His own winning attractive excellency! And how does He condescend to declare to you not only His own invitation, but the invitation of the Spirit and the bride, if by any means He might encourage you to come! And how does He invite every one that will, that they may 'take of the water of life freely,' that they may take it as a free gift, however precious it be, and though it be the water of life!

Spiritual Light.

THIS is the most excellent and divine wisdom that any creature is capable of. It is more excellent than any human learning; it is far more excellent than all the knowledge of the greatest philosophers or statesmen. Yea, the least glimpse of the glory of God in the face of Christ, doth more exalt and ennoble the soul than all the knowledge of those that have the greatest speculative understanding in divinity without grace. This knowledge has the most noble object that can be, *viz.* the divine glory and excellency of God and Christ. The knowledge of these objects is that wherein consists the most excellent knowledge of the angels, yea, of God Himself.

This knowledge is that which is above all others sweet and joyful. Men have a great deal of pleasure in human knowledge, in studies of natural things; but this is nothing to that joy which arises from this divine light shining into the soul. This light gives a view of those things that are immensely the most exquisitely beautiful, and capable of delighting the eye of the understanding. This spiritual light is the dawning of the light of glory in the heart. There is nothing so powerful as this to support persons in affliction, and to give the mind peace and brightness in this stormy and dark world.

This light is such as effectually influences the inclination and changes the nature of the soul. It assimilates our nature to the divine nature, and changes the soul into an image of the same glory that is beheld. 2 Cor. iii. 18: 'But we all with open face, beholding as in a glass the glory of the Lord, are changed into the same image, from glory to glory, even as by the Spirit of the Lord.' This knowledge will wean from the world and raise the inclination to heavenly things. It will turn the heart to God as the fountain of good, and to choose Him for the only portion. This light, and this only, will bring the soul to a saving close with Christ. It conforms the heart to the gospel, mortifies its enmity and opposition against the scheme of salvation therein revealed: it causes the heart to embrace the joyful tidings, and entirely to adhere to, and acquiesce in, the revelation of Christ as our Saviour: it causes the whole soul to accord and symphonize with it, admitting it with entire credit and respect, cleaving to it with full inclination and affection; and it effectually disposes the soul to give up itself entirely to Christ.

Pardon for the Greatest Sinners.

CHRIST *will not refuse* to save the greatest sinners, who in a right manner come to God for mercy; for this is His work. It is His business to be a Saviour of sinners; it is the work upon which He came into the world; and therefore He will not object to it. He did not come to call the righteous, but sinners to repentance, Matt. ix. 13. Sin is the very evil which He came into the world to remedy: therefore He will not object to any man that he is very sinful. The more sinful he is, the more need of Christ. The sinfulness of man was the reason of Christ's coming into the world; this is the very misery from which He came to deliver men. The more they have of it, the more need they have of being delivered: 'They that are whole need not a physician, but they that are sick,' Matt. ix. 12. The physician will not make it an objection against healing a man who applies to him, that he stands in great need of his help. If a physician of compassion comes among the sick and wounded, surely he will not refuse to heal those that stand in most need of healing, if he be able to heal them.

Herein doth the *glory of grace* by the redemption of Christ much consist, *viz.* in its sufficiency for the pardon of the greatest sinners. The whole contrivance of the way of salvation is for this end, to glorify the free grace of God. God had it on His heart from all eternity to glorify this attribute; and therefore it is that the device of saving sinners by Christ was conceived. The greatness of divine grace appears very much in this, that God by Christ saves the greatest offenders. The greater the guilt of any sinner is, the more glorious and wonderful is the grace manifested in his pardon: Rom. v. 20. 'Where sin abounded, grace did much more abound.' The apostle, when telling how great a sinner he had been, takes notice of the abounding of grace in his pardon, of which his great guilt was the occasion: 1 Tim. i. 13. 'Who was before a blasphemer and a persecutor, and injurious. But I obtained mercy; and the grace of our Lord was exceeding abundant, with faith and love which is in Christ Jesus.' The Redeemer is glorified, in that He proves sufficient to redeem those who are exceeding sinful, in that His blood proves sufficient to wash away the greatest guilt, in that He is able to save men to the uttermost and in that He redeems even from the greatest misery. It is the honor of Christ to save the greatest sinners when they come to Him, as it is the honor of a physician that he cures the most desperate diseases or wounds. Therefore, no doubt, Christ will be willing to save the greatest sinners if they come to Him; for He will not be backward to glorify Himself and to commend the value and virtue of His own blood. Seeing He hath so laid out Himself to redeem sinners, He will not be unwilling to show that He is able to redeem to the uttermost.

Pardon is as much *offered and promised* to the greatest sinners as any, if they will come aright to God for mercy. The invitations of the gospel are always in universal terms: as, Ho, every one that thirsteth; Come unto me, all ye that labor and are heavy laden; and, Whosoever will, let him come. And the voice of wisdom is to men in general: Prov. viii. 4. 'Unto you, O men, I call, and my voice is to the sons of men.' Not to moral men, or religious men, but *to you, O men*. So Christ promises, John vi. 37: 'Him that cometh to me, I will in no wise cast out.' This is the direction of Christ to His apostles, after His resurrection, Mark xvi. 15, 16: 'Go ye into all the world and preach the gospel to every creature: he that believeth and is baptized, shall be saved.' Which is agreeable to what the apostle saith, that 'the gospel was preached to every creature which is under heaven,' Col. i. 23.

Attractions in the Saviour.

THE wisdom of God hath contrived that there should be in the *person* of the Saviour all manner of attractives to draw us to Him. He has in Him all possible excellency. He is possessed of all the beauty and glory of the God-head. So that there can be no manner of excellency, nor degree of excellency that we can devise, but what is in the person of the Saviour. But yet so redundant has the wisdom of God been, in providing attractives in order that we should come to Christ, it hath so ordered that there should also be all human excellencies in Him. If there be any thing attractive in this consideration, that Christ is one in our own nature, one of us; this is true of Christ. He is not only in the divine, but in the human nature. He is truly a man, and has all possible human excellencies. He was of a most excellent spirit; wise and holy, condescending and meek, and of a lowly, benign and benevolent disposition.

Again: The wisdom of God hath chosen a person of great love to sinners, and who should show that love in the most endearing manner possible. What more *condescending* love can there be, than the love of a divine person to such worms of the dust? What *freer* love can there be than love to enemies? What *greater* love can there be than dying love? And what more endearing *expression* of love, than dying for the beloved? And the wisdom of God hath so contrived that Christ shall sustain that office which should most tend to endear Him to us, and draw us to Him: the office of a Redeemer, a Redeemer from eternal misery, and the purchaser of all happiness.

And if all this be not enough to draw us, the wisdom of God hath ordered more; it hath provided us a Saviour that should offer Himself to us in the most endearing relation. He offers to receive us as friends. To receive us to a union with Himself, to become our spiritual husband and portion forever. And the wisdom of God has provided us a Saviour that woos in a manner that has the greatest tendency to win our hearts. His word is most attractive. He stands at our door and knocks. He does not merely command us to receive Him: but He condescends to apply Himself to us in a more endearing manner. He entreats and beseeches us in His Word and by His messengers.

The wisdom of God hath contrived that there should be all manner of attractives in the *benefits* that Christ offers you. There are not only the excellencies of the person of Christ to draw you to Him, but the desirable benefits He offers. Here is what is most suitable to the cravings of the human nature. Men when distressed and burdened, long for ease and *rest:* here it is offered to us in Christ. 'Come unto me,' says He, 'all ye that labor and are heavy laden, and I will give you rest.' Men when in fear of danger, long for *safety;* here it is provided for us in Christ. God promises that He will become a shield and buckler, a strong rock and high tower to those that trust in Him. Those that mourn need *comfort:* Christ tells us that 'He came to comfort those that mourn,' Isa. lxi. 2. The blind need to have their eyes opened. The light is sweet to men: Christ offers to anoint our eyes with eye-salve that we may see glorious light. He will be our sun, and the light of God's countenance. What is more dear to men than *life?* Christ hath purchased for men that they should live for ever, Psalm xxi. 4. 'He asked life of Thee, and Thou gavest it Him, even length of days for ever and ever.' How greatly is a crown prized and admired by the children of men! And Christ offers this; not a corruptible crown, but an incorruptible and far more glorious crown than any worn by earthly kings: a crown of glory, the lustre of which shall never fade, nor decay; with an everlasting kingdom. Do men love *pleasures?* Here are pleasures for ever more. What could there be more to draw our hearts to Jesus Christ, and to make us willing to accept of Him for our Saviour, with all His unspeakable benefits?

Our Journey towards Heaven.

LABOR to be much acquainted with heaven. If you are not acquainted with it, you will not be likely to spend your life as a journey thither. You will not be sensible of its worth, nor will you long for it. Unless you are much conversant in your mind with a better good, it will be exceeding difficult to you to have your hearts loose from these things, and to use them only in subordination to something else, and be ready to part with them for the sake of that better good. Labor therefore to obtain a realizing sense of a heavenly world, to get a firm belief of its reality, and to be very much conversant with it in your thoughts.

Seek heaven only by Jesus Christ. Christ tells us that He is the way, and the truth, and the life, John xiv. 6. He tells us that He is the door of the sheep. 'I am the door, by me if any man enter in he shall be saved; and go in and out and find pasture,' John x. 9. If we therefore would improve our lives as a journey towards heaven, we must seek it by Him, and not by our own righteousness; as expecting to obtain it only for His sake, looking to Him, having our dependence on Him, who has procured it for us by His merit. And expect strength to walk in holiness, the way that leads to heaven, only from Him.

Let Christians help one another in going this journey. There are many ways whereby Christians might greatly forward one another in their way to heaven, as by religious conference, &c. Therefore let them be exhorted to go this journey as it were in company, conversing together, and assisting one another. Company is very desirable in a journey, but in none so much as this. Let them go united, and not fall out by the way, which would be to hinder one another; but use all means they can to help each other up the hill. This would insure a more successful traveling, and a more joyful meeting at their Father's house in glory.

JOHN WESLEY, A. M.
1703-1791.

Religion in the Heart.

LET thy religion be the religion of the heart. Let it lie deep in thy inmost soul. Be thou little, and base, and mean, and vile (beyond what words can express) in thy own eyes; amazed and humbled to the dust, by the love of God which is in Christ Jesus. Be serious. Let the whole stream of thy thoughts, words and actions, flow from the deepest conviction that thou standest on the edge of the great gulf, thou and all the children of men, just ready to drop in, either into everlasting glory or everlasting burnings! Let thy soul be filled with mildness, gentleness, patience, long-suffering towards all men;—at the same time that all which is in thee is athirst for God, the living God; longing to awake up after His likeness, and to be satisfied with it! Be thou a lover of God, and of all mankind! In this spirit, do and suffer all things! Thus show thy faith by thy works; thus 'do the will of thy Father which is in heaven!' And, as sure as thou now walkest with God on earth, thou shalt also reign with Him in glory!

Walking by Faith.

THEY that *live* by faith, *walk by faith*. But what is implied in this? They regulate all their judgments concerning good and evil, not with reference to visible and temporal things, but to things invisible and eternal. They think visible things to be of small value, because they pass away like a dream; but, on the contrary, they account invisible things to be of high value, because they will never pass away. Whatever is invisible is eternal: the things that are not seen, do not perish. So the apostle: 'The things that are seen are temporal; but the things that are not seen are eternal.' Therefore, they that walk 'by faith' do not desire the 'things which are seen;' neither are they the object of their pursuit. They 'set their affection on things above, not on things on the earth.' They seek only the things which are 'where Jesus sitteth at the right hand of God.' Because they know 'the things that are seen are temporal;' passing away like a shadow; therefore, they 'look not at them:' they desire them not; they account them as nothing: but 'they look at the things which are not seen; that are eternal;' that never pass away. By these they form their judgments of all things. They judge them to be good or evil, as they promote or hinder their welfare, not in time, but in eternity. They weigh whatever occurs in this balance: what influence has it on my eternal state? They regulate all their tempers and passions, all their desires, joys and fears, by this standard. They regulate all their thoughts and designs, all their words and actions, so as to prepare them for that invisible and eternal world, to which they are shortly going. They do not *dwell*, but only *sojourn* here; not looking upon earth as their home, but only

> 'Traveling through Immanuel's ground,
> To fairer worlds on high.'

Our Redemption Near.

THE time of our eternal redemption draweth nigh. Let us hold out a little longer, and all tears shall be wiped from our eyes, and we shall never sigh nor sorrow any more. And how soon shall we forget all we endured in this earthly tabernacle, when once we are clothed with that house which is from above? We are now but on our journey towards home, and so must expect to struggle with many difficulties; but it will not be long ere we come to our journey's end, and that will make amends for all. We shall then be in a quiet and safe harbor, out of the reach of all storms and dangers. We shall then be at home in our Father's house, no longer exposed to the inconveniences, which, so long as we abide abroad in these tents, we are subject to. And let us not forfeit all this happiness for want of a little more patience. Only let us hold out to the end, and we shall receive an abundant recompense for all the trouble and uneasiness of our passage, which shall be endless rest and peace.

Second Coming of Christ.

SEE! see! He cometh! He maketh the clouds His chariot! He rideth upon the wings of the wind! A devouring fire goeth before Him, and after Him a flame burneth! See! He sitteth upon His throne, clothed with light as with a garment, arrayed with majesty and honor! Behold, His eyes are as a flame of fire, His voice as the sound of many waters!

How will ye escape? Will ye call to the mountains to fall on you, the rocks to cover you? Alas, the mountains themselves, the rocks, the earth, the heavens, are just ready to flee away! Can ye prevent the sentence? Wherewith? With all the substance of thy house, with thousands of gold and silver? Blind wretch! Thou camest naked from thy mother's womb, and more naked into eternity. Hear the Lord, the Judge! 'Come ye blessed of my Father! inherit the kingdom prepared for you from the foundation of the world.' Joyful sound! How widely different from that voice which echoes through the expanse of heaven, 'Depart, ye cursed, into everlasting fire, prepared for the devil and his angels!' And who is he that can prevent or retard the full execution of either sentence? Vain hope! Lo, hell is moved from beneath to receive those who are ripe for destruction! And the everlasting doors lift up their heads, that the heirs of glory may come in.

Felicity of Heaven.

OH when shall we arrive at that happy land where no complaints were ever heard, where we shall all enjoy uninterrupted health both of body and mind, and never more be exposed to any of those inconveniences that disturb our present pilgrimage? When we shall have once passed from death unto life, we shall be eased of all the troublesome care of our bodies, which now takes up so much of our time and thoughts. We shall be set free from all those mean and tiresome labors which we must now undergo to support our lives. You robes of light, with which we shall be clothed at the resurrection of the just, will not stand in need of those careful provisions which it is so troublesome to us here either to procure, or to be without. But then, as our Lord tells us, 'Those who shall be accounted worthy to obtain that world, neither marry nor are given in marriage, neither can they die any more, but they are equal to the angels.' Their bodies are neither subject to disease, nor want that daily sustenance, which these mortal bodies cannot be without. 'Meats for the belly, and the belly for meats; but God will destroy both it and them.' This is that perfect happiness which all good men shall enjoy in the other world. A mind free from all trouble and guilt, in a body free from all pains and diseases. Thus our mortal bodies shall be raised immortal. They shall not only be always preserved from death (for so these might be if God pleased), but the nature of them shall be wholly changed, so that they shall not retain the same seeds of mortality: they cannot die any more.

The Poor in Spirit.

'THEIRS is the kingdom of heaven.' Whosoever thou art, to whom God hath given to be 'poor in spirit,' to feel thyself lost, thou hast a right thereto, through the gracious promise of Him who cannot lie. It is purchased for thee by the blood of the Lamb. It is very nigh: thou art on the brink of heaven! Another step, and thou enterest into the kingdom of righteousness, and peace, and joy! Art thou all sin? 'Behold the Lamb of God, who taketh away the sin of the world!'—All unholy? See thy 'Advocate with the Father, Jesus Christ, the righteous!'—Art thou unable to atone for the least of thy sins? 'He is the propitiation for [all thy] sins.' Now believe on the Lord Jesus Christ, and all thy sins are blotted out!—Art thou totally unclean in soul and body? Here is the 'fountain for sin and uncleanness!' 'Arise, and wash away thy sins!' Stagger no more at the promise through unbelief! Give glory to God! Dare to believe! Now cry out from the ground of thy heart,

'Yes, I yield, I yield at last,
   Listen to Thy speaking blood;
Me, with all my sins, I cast
   On my atoning God!'

WILLIAM ROMAINE, A. M.
1714-1795.

Privileges of Prayer.

THOU goest, O my soul, to meet thy God in it—to converse with thy Father—to call on Him for the fulfilling of His promises made in Jesus—to wait on Him for His answers—and to give Him His glory. Oh what blessed seasons hast thou enjoyed in this communion with thy God! How has He manifested His nearness to thee, and bounty towards thee! Hast thou not found His heart open, His ears open, and His hands open, to grant thee the request of thy lips? And when thou hast not found such sweet fellowship with thy God in prayer, yet thy dependence on His faithful word has been exercised and improved. Thou hast left thy petitions with thy Friend and Advocate, trusting to that most glorious description of Him in Rev. viii. 3, 4; 'And another angel came and stood at the altar, having a golden censer; and there was given unto him much incense, that he should offer it with the prayers of all saints upon the golden altar, which was before the throne. And the smoke of the incense, which came with the prayers of the saints, ascended up before God out of the angel's hand.' O Thou great Angel of the covenant, thus present my prayers! They are nothing worth, but as perfumed with Thy divine odors. Let them ever ascend before God out of Thy hand with the smoke of the incense of Thy sacrifice and intercession. Blessed Spirit of prayer, increase my faith, that I may trust more to a prayer-hearing God and Father, who is always ready to grant every good thing promised to His children in Christ Jesus. Amen.

Prayers.   I.

LO, I come before Thee, Holy Father! to plead the blood-shedding and the righteousness of Thy dear Son; and I hope my plea will be admitted, through the intercession of the High Priest of the house of God. Oh, look, Thou God of peace, upon the face of Thy Beloved! See me in Him. I desire to be found in Him. And for His sake let the faithful witness for Thy love in Jesus abide with me, that, in hearing and reading Thy word, in prayer and meditation, He may increase my faith in Thee and love to Thee.

O God the Holy Ghost! I beseech Thee to make practical upon my heart what Thou hast revealed in Scripture of the Father's love. Deliver me from guilt and condemnation by the sprinkling of the blood of Jesus. Apply it effectually. Apply it continually. Help me to believe with more comfort in my conscience, and with more steadfastness in my walk, that His blood cleanseth from all sin. O blessed Spirit! carry on Thy work in my soul. Lead me from faith to faith, that I may at all times have freedom to enter within the veil to a reconciled God and Father, and may be able to maintain peace with Him against doubts and fears, against corruptions and enemies. Oh, teach me to draw near to Him with a true heart, steadfastly persuaded of His love, and in full assurance of faith. This is Thy gracious office: Oh, fulfil it in me, that my heart may be sprinkled from an evil conscience, and my body washed with pure water. Let me find grace sufficient for me, for Jesus' sake; to whom, with Thee, O Father, and the eternal Spirit, three persons in one Jehovah, be equal honor and glory for ever and ever. Amen.

II.

O FATHER of mercies, hear me for Jesus' sake! I acknowledge my sinfulness and unworthiness, even in my closest walk with Thee. I am less than the least of Thy mercies; yea, deserving the heaviest of Thy vengeance. It is of the Lord's mercy, that it has not fallen upon me long ago; and I trust in His word, that it will never fall upon me. Who is a God like unto Thee, that pardoneth iniquity, and passeth by the transgression of the remnant of Thine heritage? Thou retainest not Thine anger against them for ever; because Thou delightest in mercy. Glory be to Thee for Thine unspeakable mercies: for Thou hast given me faith in the atonement of Jesus, by whom I have peace with Thee, my reconciled God, and by whom I have experienced Thy great love to me. On Thee, O my God, is still my hope. I look up to Thee, the giver of those graces, for strength to maintain them in my daily walk. I do believe in the sacrifice and righteousness of Immanuel; Lord, help mine unbelief! I find it hard to preserve in my practice, what I believe to be true in doctrine; and therefore on Thy present help I must continually depend. Lord, strengthen me mightily by Thy Spirit in the inner man against temptations. I am daily and hourly called upon to exercise my faith; and when Thy grace does not hold me up, I fall. The fiery darts of Satan easily inflame me, when they are thrown at my legal hopes, false dependencies, or self righteous tempers. My shield, which should quench them, is ready to drop out of mine hand. I should fall a prey to the enemy and the fire would consume me, if Thy mercy was not over me for good. O my God and Father, strengthen my faith against the wiles and assaults of Satan, and against the workings of mine own unbelief. When these trials come, keep me sensible of my weakness, and dependent on Thy promised strength, that I may meet them strong in the Lord and in the power of Thy might. Oh let every trial teach me more of Thy peace in my conscience, and more of Thy love in my heart, that I may keep on in a steady course, walking humbly with my God. This is the work of Thy good Spirit. I cannot preserve, nor improve His graces, unless He be every moment present with me. He is the giver, the continuer, the increaser of them all. O God the Holy Ghost, I therefore beseech Thee to water Thy graces every moment. Lest any hurt them, keep them, keep them night and day. Never leave me, nor forsake me; but what thou hast graciously begun, that mightily carry on, in my soul. Temptations are strong, and I am weak; stand by me in the hour of need. And if my faith be tried with fiery temptations, let it come out of them like gold out of the fire. O Thou almighty Spirit, confirm by trials, improve by experience, my trust in Thy promised help. Let me go on from faith to faith. Keep up the confidence of my rejoicing in my reconciled God and loving Father, that I may walk humbly with Him in sweet communion and holy fellowship in the way everlasting. Grant me these mercies, gracious Father, for Thy dear Son's sake, by the influence of the Eternal Spirit, three persons in one Jehovah, to whom be equal praise for ever and ever. Amen.

Praise and Prayer.

PRAISE and prayer go together. The prayer of faith will afford continual matter for praise. The one is a dependence on God for every promised blessing; the other is the acknowledgment of His having bestowed it. Innocent man had his heart in this sweet work. It was his happiness. Every breath in paradise was praise. The redeemed man has more reason. His obligations are far greater than Adam was under to his God—raised from his fall—saved from the guilt and misery of it—chosen and called to this salvation by mere grace—through faith a partaker of it—an heir of God, and a joint-heir with Christ. Oh what motives are these, to continual thankfulness! And these motives are effectual when the Holy Spirit discovers the things that are freely given to us of God. He makes us sensible of them and thankful for them; for He preserves in the soul a blessed poverty of spirit, an humble, abiding sense of wants and unworthiness; and thus He lays a sure foundation for thankfulness.

Institution and Benefits of the Lord's Supper.

LOOK well to the end of the institution. It was not only to remind thee of, but also to convey to thee, all the blessings of that one offering, which perfects for ever. It was to teach thee that thy spiritual life, and every grace and comfort of it, are as dependent upon Christ crucified as the life of thy body is upon the meat and drink of this world. Thy life comes from His death. Thy life is nourished by feeding upon Christ thy passover, who was sacrificed for thee. He intended by the bread to point out unto thee His body, and by the wine, His blood—by eating and drinking them, thy taking and living upon Him—by thy bodily support received from them, the nourishment of thy soul by eating His flesh and drinking His blood. He would have thee to look through the signs to the things signified. Thou art not to rest in the outward act, but to rest in the promise in the Word of God. Thy faith is not to be exercised about the Lord's Supper as a duty: but it is to be exercised upon His Word; and what He has therein promised to make it, that thou art to expect in taking it. He appointed it to be the means of communicating with Him, and of thy enjoying fellowship with Him in His sufferings. It is a spiritual believing act, in which thou art invited to partake of the paschal lamb. It is the Lord's passover, and will certainly answer every purpose for which He instituted it. He appointed it to be the means of safety from the destroyer, of deliverance from bondage, of free and full forgiveness of all sins, of a happy passage through the Red Sea, and of the everlasting possession of the promised inheritance.

THE FULL VISION AND ENJOYMENT OF CHRIST.

MAKE haste, my Beloved, and take me to Thyself: let me see Thee face to face, and enjoy Thee, Thou dearest Jesus, whom my soul longeth after. It is good to live upon Thee by faith, but to live with Thee is best of all. I have found one day in Thy courts, conversing sweetly with Thee, better than a thousand; but this has only whetted my appetite: the more communion I have with Thee, I hunger and thirst still for more. My soul panteth for nearer, still nearer communion with Thee. When shall I come to appear before the presence of God? O Thou Light of my life, Thou Joy of my heart, Thou knowest how I wish for the end of my faith, when I shall no longer see through a glass darkly, but with open face behold the glory of my Lord. Thou hast so endeared Thyself to me, Thou precious Immanuel! by ten thousand thousand kindnesses, that I cannot be entirely satisfied, until I have the full vision and complete enjoyment of Thyself. The day of our espousals has been a blessed time. Oh, for the marriage of the Lamb, when I shall be presented as a chaste virgin to my heavenly Bridegroom! How can I but long earnestly for this full enjoyment of Thy everlasting love! Come, Lord Jesus; let me see Thee as Thou art. Come and make me like unto Thee. I do love Thee; I am now happy in Thy love; but not so as I hope to be. I am often interrupted here, and never love Thee so much as I desire; but these blessed spirits standing now round Thy throne are perfected in love. Oh! that I was once admitted to see, as they do, the glory of God in the face of Jesus Christ! Is not that the voice of my Beloved, which I hear answering, *Surely I come quickly!* Amen, say I, even so come, Lord Jesus. Make haste, my Beloved, and be Thou like to a roe, or to a young hart, upon the mountains of spices.

ROBERT WALKER.
1716–1783.

On Prayer.

PRAYER keeps the communication open between the Head and the members; it is the messenger that goes from earth to heaven, and returns with all necessary blessings from thence. Beware, then, of neglecting this necessary duty. Pray in faith, pray in the name of Christ, pray without ceasing; and beg of Christ to teach you to pray aright, that you may ask and receive, and then your joy shall be full.

The Believing Soul's Address to Christ.

O BLESSED Jesus! saith the soul that comes to Him, Thou true and living way to the Father! I adore Thy condescending grace in becoming a sacrifice and sin-offering for me: and now, encouraged by Thy kind invitation, I flee to Thee as my only city of refuge; I come to Thee 'wretched, and miserable, and poor, and blind, and naked'—I have no price to offer Thee, no goodness at all to recommend me to Thy favor: 'laboring, and heavy laden,'

I cast myself at Thy feet, and look to Thy free mercy alone for the removal of this burden, which, without Thy interposition, must sink me down to the lowest hell. Abhorring myself in every view I can take, I embrace Thee for my righteousness; sprinkled with Thy atoning blood, I shall not fear the destroying angel—justice hath already had its triumph on Thy Cross, and therefore I take Thy Cross for my sanctuary. This is my rest; and here will I stay, for I like it well.

Nor is this my only errand to Thee, O Thou complete Saviour! I bring to Thee a dark benighted mind to be illuminated with saving knowledge. 'Thou hast the words of eternal life;' 'in Thee are hid all the treasures of wisdom:' I therefore resign my understanding to Thy teaching: for 'No man knoweth the Father but the Son, and those to whom the Son shall reveal Him.'

I likewise choose Thee for my Lord and my King; for 'Thou art altogether lovely,' and in every character necessary to my soul. Here are enemies whom none can vanquish but Thyself; here are corruptions, which nothing less than all-conquering grace can subdue: I therefore implore Thine almighty aid. Do Thou possess Thy throne in my heart, and cast out of it whatever opposeth or offendeth Thee. It is Thine already by purchase; O make it Thine also by conquest! and perform the whole work of a Saviour upon it.

The Heavy Laden Invited to Christ.

OUR Lord Himself hath declared in the most solemn manner, that none shall be rejected who come to Him for salvation. These are His words: 'Him that cometh to me I will in no wise cast out.' I will receive him with outstretched arms; I will tenderly embrace and cherish him, and so unite him to myself, that the combined force of earth and hell shall never be able to dissolve the union, or to separate His soul from my unchangeable love.

Lift up thy head, then, O 'laboring and heavy laden' sinner! Doth the Father *command* you to believe on His Son? Doth the Lord Jesus invite, nay, entreat you to come to Him, and at the same time assure you that 'He will in no wise cast you out?' And shall not this multiplied security remove all your doubts, and bring you to Him with an humble, but steadfast hope of obtaining that *rest* which He offers unto you? Say not henceforth, My burden is so heavy, and my guilt so great, that I dare not go to Him; but rather say, my burden is so heavy that I *must* go to Him; for no other arm can remove it but His own. He offers you His help, because you are miserable; He invites you to come to Him, not because you deserve, but because you need His aid. Arise then, O sinners! and obey His call: cast your burden upon Him who is mighty to save; yield yourselves, without reserve, to this faithful Redeemer, to be justified by His blood and sanctified by His Spirit; 'take His yoke upon you, and learn of Him;' and then you shall find *rest* to your soul.

Grace.

GRACE, though a small rivulet in appearance, is fed with an everlasting spring. Where the Lord Jesus begins a good work, He will carry it on to perfection, and never leave the objects of His love till He hath made them like Himself, all glorious both within and without, and presented them to His Father without spot and blemish.

Resignation to the Divine Will.

RESIGNATION to the will of God frees the mind from a grievous bondage, the bondage of earthly pursuits and expectations. Whatever God wills, is pleasing to the resigned soul; and when a Christian hath, by prayer and supplication, made known his requests to God, then the peace of God which passeth all understanding, keeps his heart and mind through Jesus Christ. Then only is life truly enjoyed, when we relish its comforts, at the same time that we are prepared to part with them. The anxieties of the worldly man torment him with the pangs of a thousand deaths. His soul dies within him as often as he conceives the apprehension of losing those good things which he would wish always to enjoy. Whereas he who hath resigned his will to the will of God, 'eats his bread with joy, and drinks his wine with a merry heart.' Even the thought of his dying hour throws no damp on the joys of his mind. From the contemplation of God's goodness to him in life, he can pass without terror or amazement to the thought of His protection in the dark valley and shadow of death. Even in that gloomy passage he fears no evil; but commits himself to the Lord his Shepherd, who will make goodness and mercy to follow him all the days of his life, and at last will bring him to dwell in His house above for ever.

Christ's Presence with Believers at Death.

WHEN they walk through the valley of the shadow of death, His rod and His staff comfort and sustain them. He fortifies and cheers their departing spirits; and when the evening shadows gather thick around them, the Holy Ghost, the Comforter, is sent to say to them, that death as well as life is theirs. Nay, the Good Shepherd Himself, who gave His life for the sheep,' will say to them in this awful hour, ' Fear not, I am He that liveth and was dead; and behold, I am alive for evermore, and have the keys of hell and death:—I am the resurrection and the life: he that believeth on me, though he were dead, yet shall he live.' What a multitude of saints, who now inherit the promises, have in their last moments experienced the effect of these gracious and joyful assurances! In how many instances hath a lively and unexpected view of the promises of God, and of the great redemption, sustained and even elevated a dying saint, who from the infirmities of the body, or other causes, was, through fear of death, subject to bondage all his life! The sensible presence of the good Shepherd, in these awful moments, will support the most fearful, and the feeblest of the flock. It will enable him that hath no might, to triumph over death, and him that hath the power of death; and, even in the presence of the king of terrors, it will teach him this song of victory, 'My flesh and my heart faileth; but God is the strength of my heart, and my portion forever.' —'Thanks be unto God, which hath given me the victory, through Jesus Christ my Lord.'—'For I am persuaded that neither death, nor life, nor angels, nor principalities, nor powers, nor things present, nor things to come, nor height, nor depth, nor any other creature, shall be able to separate me from the love of God, which is in Christ Jesus, my Lord.'

SAMUEL DAVIES, A. M.
1724–1761.

Excellency of the Divine Being.

CONSIDER the excellency of the Divine Being, the sum total, the great original of all perfections. How infinitely worthy is He of the adoration of all His creatures! how deserving of their most intense thoughts and most ardent affections! If majesty and glory can strike us with awe and veneration, does not Jehovah demand them, who is clothed with majesty and glory as with a garment, and before whom all the inhabitants of the earth are as grasshoppers, as nothing, as less than nothing, and vanity? If wisdom excites our pleasing wonder, here is an unfathomable depth. O the depth of the riches of the wisdom and knowledge of God! If goodness, grace, and mercy attract our love and gratitude, here these amiable perfections shine in their most alluring glories. If justice strikes a damp to the guilty, here is justice in all its tremendous majesty. If veracity, if candor, if any or all of the moral virtues engage our esteem, here they all centre in their highest perfection. If the presence of a king strikes a reverence; if the eye of his judge awes the criminal, and restrains him from offending, certainly we should fear before the Lord all the day, for we are surrounded with His omnipresence, and He is the inspector and judge of all our thoughts and actions. If riches excite desire, here are unsearchable riches: if happiness has charms that draw all the world after it, here is an unbounded ocean of happiness; here is the only complete portion for an immortal mind. Men are affected with these things in one another, though found in a very imperfect degree. Power awes and commands; virtue and goodness please; beauty charms; justice strikes with solemnity and terror; a bright genius is admired; a benevolent, merciful temper is loved: thus men are affected with created excellences. Whence is it, then, they are so stupidly unaffected with the supreme excellences of Jehovah?

LOVE OF GOD IN THE GIFT OF HIS SON.

NEVER was there such a display of love in heaven or on earth. You can no more find love equal to this among creatures, than you can find among them the infinite power that formed the universe out of nothing. This will stand upon record to all eternity, as the unprecedented, unparalleled, inimitable love of God. And it appears the more illustrious when we consider that this unspeakable gift was given to sinners, to rebels, to enemies, that were so far from deserving it, that, on the other hand, it is a miracle of mercy that they are not all groaning for ever under the tremendous weight of

His justice. O! that I could say something becoming this love; something that might do honor to it! but, alas! the language of mortals was formed for lower subjects. This love passes all description and all knowledge.

The Saints' Happiness at the Judgment Day.

SEE the bright and triumphant army marching up to their eternal home, under the conduct of the Captain of their salvation, where they *shall ever be with the Lord*, 1 Thess. iv. 17, as happy as their nature in its highest improvement is capable of being made. With what shouts of joy and triumph do they ascend! with what sublime hallelujahs do they crown their Deliverer! with what wonder and joy, with what pleasing horror, like one that has narrowly escaped some tremendous precipice, do they look back upon what they once were! once mean, guilty, depraved, condemned sinners! afterward imperfect, broken-hearted, sighing, weeping saints! but now innocent, holy, happy, glorious immortals!

> ' Are these the forms that mouldered in the dust?
> O the transcendent glories of the just!'—Young.

Now with what pleasure and rapture do they look forward through the long, long prospect of immortality, and call it their own! the duration not only of their existence, but of their happiness and glory! O shall any of us share in this immensely valuable privilege? how immensely transporting the thought?

'Shall we, who some few years ago were less
Than worm, or mite, or shadow can express;
Were nothing; shall we live, when every fire
Of every star shall languish or expire?
When earth's no more, shall we survive above,
And through the shining ranks of angels move?
Or, as before the throne of God we stand,
See new worlds rolling from His mighty hand?—
All that has being in full concert join,
And celebrate the depths of love divine!'—YOUNG.

THE PRECIOUSNESS OF CHRIST.

HE is precious in Himself, as possessing all the fulness of the Godhead bodily, the sum total of all divine excellencies, and as clothed with all the virtues of a perfect man. In short, all moral excellency, divine and human, created and uncreated, centre in Him, and render Him infinitely precious and valuable. He is precious to His Father; His *beloved Son, in whom He is well pleased;* His elect, in whom His soul delighteth. He is precious to angels; *Worthy is the Lamb that was slain,* is their eternal song. He is dear to all good men in all ages. *To you therefore that believe He is precious,* says St. Peter, 1 Peter ii. 7. How precious are His atoning blood and meritorious righteousness to the guilty, self-condemned soul! how precious is His sanctifying grace to the soul heavy-laden with sin, and groaning under that body of death! how precious the assistance of His almighty arm to His poor soldiers in the spiritual warfare! how precious the light of His instructions to the benighted, wandering mind; how sweet the words of His mouth; sweeter than honey from the honey-comb. How precious the light of His smiling countenance, and the sensations of His love to the desponding, sinking soul! how precious that eternal salvation which He imparts! and how precious the price He paid for it! *Not corruptible things, such as silver and gold,* says St. Peter, *but His own precious blood,* 1 Peter i. 18, 19. In short, He is altogether lovely, altogether precious.

Christ the Only Foundation.

IF you have already made Him so, then be assured you are safe and immoveable for ever. Let storms of private or public calamity rise and beat upon you; let your fears and doubts rise to ever so high a deluge; let temptations make ever so severe attacks upon you, still the foundation on which you stand abides firm and unshaken. Nay, let all nature go to wreck, and seas and land, and heaven and earth be blended together, still this foundation stands firm, and the living temple built upon it will remain immoveable for ever. You that believe need not make haste, you need not be struck with consternation upon the appearance of danger, nor fly to unlawful means of deliverance: your all is safe, and therefore you may be serene and calm. Is the burden of guilt intolerable, and are you ready to sink under it? Or are you sinking under a load of sorrow? Whatever be the burden, cast it upon the Lord, and He will sustain you. This foundation is able to bear you up, however great the pressure. Come, ye that are weary and heavy-laden, come, and build your hopes, and place your rest here. O! what joyful tidings are these! I hope they will prove a word in season to some soul that is weary.

The Saviour in His Exaltation.

LIFT up your eyes to seats above: there you may behold Him who tasted of death, crowned with glory and honor. His head, that was once crowned with thorns, is now adorned with a crown of glory: His face, that was once bruised with blows, and disgraced with spitting, shines brighter than the sun in his meridian glory: His hands, that were once nailed to the cross, now sway the sceptre of the universe: and His feet, that were cruelly pierced, now walk the crystal pavement of heaven. He that was insulted by Jews and Gentiles, He at whom they wagged their heads, is now adored by all the heavenly hosts, who congratulate His exaltation, and cry with united voice, 'Worthy is the Lamb that was slain to receive power, and riches, and wisdom, and strength, and honor, and glory, and blessing,' Rev. v. 11, 12. This is the voice of ten thousand times ten thousand, and thousands of thousands in that world where Jesus is best known. And shall we break the harmony of the universal choir? Shall we not echo back their song, and reply, *To Him that loved us, and washed us from our sins in His own blood*, (which is more than He did for angels,) *to Him be glory and dominion for ever and ever, Amen*, Rev. i. 5, 6. Shall we not look to Him whose glory attracts the eyes of all the celestial armies, and congratulate His exaltation? We have cause indeed to rejoice in it; for O! He is exalted, that He may have mercy upon us, Isa. xxx. 18; He has ascended the throne, that He may thence scatter blessings on a guilty world beneath Him. He retains His usual love, and the tenderest bowels of compassion towards the meanest of His people. He is now pleading their cause in the court of heaven, and preparing a place for them. From thence He exhibits Himself to our intellectual view, and invites us to look to Him. And can we slight such glory and love united? Are our natures capable of such infernal ingratitude? O let us look to Him, especially since it shall not be in vain.

Hope of the Righteous in Death.

THE righteous man has an humble hope of *support in death*. He has repeatedly intrusted himself into the faithful hands of an almighty Saviour, for life and death, for time and eternity; and he humbly hopes his Saviour will not forsake him now—now, when he most needs His assistance. This was St. Paul's support, under the prospect of his last hour: 'I know whom I have believed, and am persuaded that He is able to keep that which I have committed unto him against that day,' 2 Tim. i. 12. As if he had said, finding my own weakness, I have committed my all into another hand; and I have committed it to one whose ability and faithfulness have been tried by thousands as well as myself: and, therefore, I am confident He will keep the sacred depositum, and never suffer it to be injured or lost. This was also the support of the psalmist, 'Though I walk,' says he, 'through the valley of the shadow of death, I will fear no evil; for Thou art with me; Thy rod and Thy staff they shall comfort me,' Psalm xxiii. 4. Yea, it was upon this support St. Paul leaned, when he braved death, in that triumphant language, 'Who shall separate us from the love of God? Shall tribulation, or distress, or persecution, or famine, or nakedness, or peril, or sword? No; in all these things we are more than conquerors, through Him that loved us: for I am persuaded,' says he, 'that death'—that separates our souls and bodies—that separates friend from friend—that separates us from all our earthly comforts, and breaks all our connections with this world, even death itself, 'shall never separate us from the love of God, which is in Christ Jesus,' Rom. viii. 35–39. What a faithful Friend, what a powerful Guardian is this, who stands by His people, and bears them up in their last extremity, and makes them more than conquerors in the struggle with the all-conquering enemy of mankind! How peculiar a happiness is this, to be able to enjoy the comfort of hope, in the wreck of human nature! How sweet to lean a dying head upon the kind arm of an almighty Saviour! How sweet to intrust a departing soul as a depositum in His faithful hand! O, may you and I enjoy this blessed support in a dying hour! and may we make it our great business in life to secure it! In that gloomy hour, our friends may weep, and wring their hands around our beds; but they can afford us no help—no hope! But Jesus can, as thousands have known by experience. Then He can bear home His promises upon the heart; then He can communicate His love, which is better than life; and, by His holy Spirit, bear up and encourage the sinking soul! Blessed Jesus! what friend can compare to Thee?—

> ' Jesus can make a dying bed
> Feel soft as downy pillows are;
> While on His breast I lean my head,
> And breathe my soul out sweetly there.'

Hope of a Happy Immortality.

OH, what a glorious hope is this! This has made many a soul welcome death with open arms. This has made them 'desirous to be with Christ, which is far better,' Phil. i. 23. And this has sweetly swallowed up the sensations of bodily pain. Indeed, without this, immortality would be an object of terror, and not of hope: the prospect would be insupportably dreadful. For who can bear the thought of an immortal duration spent in an eternal banishment from God and all happiness, and in the sufferance of the most exquisite pain? But a happy immortality, what can charm us more?

Christ Precious in His Instructions.

AS a prophet, how sweet are His instructions to a bewildered soul! How precious the words of His lips, which are the words of eternal life! How delightful to sit and hear Him teach the way of duty and happiness, revealing the Father, and the wonders of the invisible state! How transporting to hear Him declare upon what terms an offended God may be reconciled! a discovery beyond the searches of all the sages and philosophers of the heathen world. How reviving is it to listen to His gracious promises and invitations; promises and invitations to the poor, the weary, and heavy laden, the broken-hearted, and even to the chief of sinners! The word of Christ has been the treasure, the support and joy of believers in all ages. 'I have esteemed the words of His mouth,' says Job, 'more than my necessary food.' Job xxxiii. 12. It is this precious word the psalmist so often and so highly celebrates. He celebrates it as 'more to be desired than gold; yea, than much fine gold; sweeter also than honey and the honey-comb:' Psalm xix. 10. 'O how I love Thy law!' says he; 'it is my meditation all the day:' Psalm cxix. 97. 'How sweet are Thy words unto my taste! yea, sweeter than honey to my mouth:' ver. 103. 'The law of Thy mouth is better than thousands of gold and silver:' ver. 72. 'Behold, I have longed after Thy precepts:' ver. 40. 'Thy statutes have been my song in the house of my pilgrimage:' ver. 54. 'In my affliction Thy word hath quickened me:' ver. 50. 'Unless Thy law had been my delights, I should then have perished in my affliction:' ver. 92. This is the language of David, in honor of this divine Prophet, near three thousand years ago, when Christ had not revealed the full gospel to the world, but only some rays of it shone through the veil of the Mosaic dispensation. And must not believers now, who live under the more complete and clear instructions of this great Prophet, entertain the same sentiments of Him? Yes, to such of you as believe, even in this age, He is most precious.

Eternity.

'ETERNITY!' We are alarmed at the sound! Lost in the prospect! Eternity with respect to God, is a duration without beginning as well as without end! Eternity, as it is the attribute of human nature, is a duration that had a beginning but shall never have an end. This is inalienably entailed upon us poor dying worms: and let us survey our inheritance. Eternity! it is a duration that excludes all number and computation; days and months, and years, yea, and ages, are lost in it, like drops in the ocean. Millions of millions of years, as many years as there are sands on the sea-shore, or particles of dust in the globe of the earth, and these multiplied to the highest reach of number, all these are nothing to eternity. They do not bear the least imaginable proportion to it; for these will come to an end, as certain as day; but eternity will never, never come to an end. It is a line without end; it is an ocean without a shore. Alas! what shall I say of it! It is an infinite unknown something, that neither human thought can grasp, nor human language describe.

JOHN NEWTON.
1725–1807.

TRIALS.

NOTHING can harm us that quickens our earnestness and frequency in applying to a throne of grace; only trust the Lord and keep close to Him, and all that befalls you shall be for good. Temptations end in victory; troubles prove an increase of consolation; yea, our very falls and failings tend to increase our spiritual wisdom, to give us a greater knowledge of Satan's devices, and make us more habitually upon our guard against them. Happy case of the believer in Jesus! when bitten by the fiery serpent he needs not go far for a remedy; he has only to look to a bleeding Saviour, and be healed.

DEVOTION TO CHRIST.

I SHALL not always live this poor dying life: I hope one day to be all ear, all heart, all tongue; when I shall see the Redeemer as He is, I shall be like Him. This will be a heaven indeed, to behold His glory without a veil, to rejoice in His love without a cloud, and to sing His praises, without one jarring or wandering note, for ever. In the mean time, may He enable us to serve Him with our best. O that every power, faculty, and talent were devoted to Him! He deserves all we have, and ten thousand times more if we had it; for He has loved us, and washed us from our sins in His own blood. He gave Himself for us. In one sense, we are well suited to answer His purpose; for if we were not vile and worthless, beyond expression, the exceeding riches of His grace would not have been so gloriously displayed. His glory shines more in redeeming one sinner, than in preserving a thousand angels.

The Believer Safe.

BLESSED be God, we are in safe hands; the Lord Himself is our keeper; nothing befalls us but what is adjusted by His wisdom and love. Health is His gift, and sickness, when sanctified, is a token of love likewise. Here we may meet with many things which are not joyous but grievous to the flesh; but He will, in one way or other, sweeten every bitter cup, and ere long He will wipe away all tears from our eyes. O that joy, that crown, that glory which awaits the believer! Let us keep the prize of our high calling in view, and press forward in the name of Jesus the Redeemer, and He will not disappoint our hopes.

Assurance.

ASSURANCE grows by repeated conflicts, by our repeated experimental proof of the Lord's power and goodness to save: when we have been brought very low and helped, sorely wounded and healed, cast down and raised again, have given up all hope, and been suddenly snatched from danger, placed in safety, and when these things have been repeated to us and in us a thousand times over, we begin to learn to trust simply to the word and power of God, beyond and against appearances; and this trust, when habitual and strong, bears the name of assurance, for even assurance has degrees.

The Christian Soldier.

THE Lord has chosen, called, and armed us for the fight; and shall we wished to be excused? Shall we not rather rejoice that we have the honor to appear in such a cause, under such a Captain, such a banner, and in such company? A complete suit of armor is provided, weapons not to be resisted, and precious balm to heal us if haply we receive a wound, and precious ointment to revive us when we are in danger of fainting. Further, we are assured of the victory beforehand; and O what a crown is prepared for every conqueror, which Jesus, the righteous Judge, the gracious Saviour, shall place upon every faithful head with His own hand! Then let us not be weary and faint, for in due season we shall reap. The time is short; yet a little while, and the struggle of indwelling sin, and the contradiction of surrounding sinners, shall be known no more.

May the prospect of this blessed hope set before us revive our fainting spirits, and make us willing to endure hardships as good soldiers of Jesus Christ. Here we must often sow in tears, but there we shall reap in joy, and all tears shall be wiped from our eyes for ever.

Happy State of the Believer.

HOW happy is the state of a believer, to have a sure promise that all shall work together for good in the end, and in the mean time a sure refuge where to find present relief, support and protection! How comfortable is it, when trouble is near, to know that the Lord is near likewise, and to commit ourselves and all our cares simply to Him, believing that His eye is upon us and His ear open to our prayers. Under the conduct of such a Shepherd we need not fear; though we are called to pass through fire and water, through the valley of the shadow of death, He will be with us, and will show Himself mighty on our behalf.

Intercourse with Heaven.

HOW little does the world know of that intercourse which is carried on between Heaven and earth! what petitions are daily presented and what answers are received, at the throne of grace! O the blessed privilege of prayer! O the wonderful love, care, attention, and power of our great

Shepherd! His eye is always upon us; when our spirits are almost overwhelmed within us, He knoweth our path. His ear is always open to us; let who will overlook and disappoint us, He will not. When means and hope fail, when everything looks dark upon us, when we seem shut up on every side, when we are brought to the lowest ebb, still our help is in the name of the Lord who made heaven and earth. To Him all things are possible; and before the exertion of His power, when He is pleased to arise and work, all hinderances give way, and vanish like a mist before the sun. And He can so manifest Himself to the soul, and cause His goodness to pass before it, that the hour of affliction shall be the golden hour of the greatest consolation. He is the fountain of life, strength, grace, and comfort, and of His fulness His children receive according to their occasions: but this is all hidden from the world; they have no guide in prosperity, but hurry on as they are instigated by their blinded passions, and are perpetually multiplying mischiefs and miseries to themselves; and in adversity they have no resource, but must feel all the evil of affliction, without inward support and without deriving any advantage from it. We have, therefore, cause for continual praise. The Lord has given us to know His name, as a resting place and a hiding place, a sun and a shield. Circumstances and creatures may change; but He will be an unchangeable friend. The way is rough, but He trod it before us, and is now with us in every step we take; and every step brings us nearer to our heavenly home. Our inheritance is surely reserved for us, and we shall be kept for it by His power through faith. Our present strength is small, and, without a fresh supply, would be quickly exhausted; but He has engaged to renew it from day to day; and He will soon appear to wipe all tears from our eyes; and then we shall appear with Him in glory.

Prayer and Reading the Scriptures.

SECRET prayer and the good Word, are the chief wells from whence we draw the water of salvation. These will keep the soul alive when creature-streams are cut off; but the richest variety of public means and the closest attendance upon them will leave us lean and pining in the midst of plenty, if we are remiss and formal in the other two. I think David never appears in a more lively frame of mind than when he wrote the 42d, 63d and 84th psalms, which were all penned in a dry land, and at a distance from the public ordinances.

Faith's View of Christ Crucified.

O IF we could always behold Him by faith as evidently crucified before our eyes, how would it compose our spirits as to all the sweets and bitters of this poor life! What a barrier would it prove against all the snares and temptations whereby Satan would draw us into evil; and what firm ground of confidence would it afford us amidst the conflicts we sustain from the workings of unbelief and indwelling sin! I long for more of that faith which is the substance of things hoped for, and the evidence of things not seen, that I may be preserved humble, thankful, watchful, and dependent. To behold the glory and the love of Jesus, is the only effectual way to participate of His image.

The Sabbath an Earnest of Heaven.

THE Sabbath is a blessed day indeed, an earnest of heaven. There they keep an everlasting Sabbath, and cease not night or day admiring the riches of redeeming love, and adoring Him who washed His people from their sins in His own blood. To have such imperfect communion with them as is in this state attainable in this pleasing exercise is what alone can make life worth the name. For this I sigh and long and cry to the Lord to rend the veil of unbelief, scatter the clouds of ignorance, and break down the walls which sin is daily building up to hide Him from my eyes. I hope I can say, my soul is athirst for God, and nothing less than the light of His countenance can satisfy me. Blessed be His name for the desire; it is His own gift, and He never gives it in vain. He will afford us a taste of the water of life by the way; and ere long we shall drink abundantly at the fountain head, and have done with complaint for ever. May we be thankful for what we receive, and still earnestly desirous of more.

Divine Guidance.

WE see a highway through the wilderness, a powerful guard, an infallible Guide at hand to conduct us through; and we can discern, beyond the limits of the wilderness, a better land, where we shall be at rest and at home. What will the difficulties we meet by the way then signify? The remembrance of them will only remain to heighten our sense of the love, care, and power of our Saviour and Leader. O how shall we then admire, adore, and praise Him, when He shall condescend to unfold to us the beauty, propriety, and harmony of the whole train of His dispensations towards us, and give us a clear retrospect of all the way, and all the turns of our pilgrimage!

Blessed Fruits of Affliction.

BY affliction prayer is quickened, for our prayers are very apt to grow languid and formal in a time of ease. Affliction greatly helps us to understand the Scriptures, especially the promises, most of which being made to times of trouble, we cannot so well know their fulness, sweetness, and certainty, as when we have been in the situation to which they are suited, have been enabled to trust and plead them, and found them fulfilled in our own case. We are usually indebted to affliction as the means or occasion of the most signal discoveries we are favored with of the wisdom, power, and faithfulness of the Lord.

Afflictions are designed likewise for the manifestation of our sincerity to ourselves and to others. When faith endures the fire, we know it to be of the right kind; and others, who see we are brought safe out, and lose nothing but the dross, will confess that God is with us of a truth, Dan. iii. 27, 28. Surely this thought should reconcile us to suffer, not only with patience, but with cheerfulness, if God may be glorified in us. This made the apostle rejoice in tribulation, that the power of Christ might be noticed, as resting upon Him, and working mightily in Him. Many of our graces, likewise, cannot thrive or show themselves to advantage without trials, such as resignation, patience, meekness, long-suffering.

THOMAS SCOTT, D. D.
1747–1821.

MORNING PRAYERS FOR A FAMILY. I.

O MOST glorious and gracious God, whose kind providence has protected us through the night, and brought us in peace to meet together this morning; assist us, we earnestly beseech Thee, to present our unfeigned praises and thanksgivings, and to unite in fervent prayer and supplication before Thy mercy-seat.

But who are we, O thou high and lofty One, who inhabitest eternity, whose name is Holy, that we should venture into Thy awful presence? Even the seraphim veil their faces in deep humility, when they present their adorations before Thy throne—And we are not only immensely beneath them in our nature; but alas, we have been guilty of base ingratitude for Thy bounties, and of multiplied acts of rebellion against Thee, our Creator and Sovereign. 'We have forsaken Thee, the Fountain of living waters,' to seek happiness from the broken cisterns of earthly enjoyments and possessions! We have proudly rejected Thy easy yoke, and become slaves to divers lusts and pleasures! We have refused Thee that reasonable tribute of worship and love, which it would have been our privilege to render; We have broken Thy commandments in thought, word, and deed, and have abused Thy gifts to the dishonor of Thy name.

Thus we would with shame confess, we are fallen under condemnation and into bondage, from which we cannot deliver our own souls: and we may well be confounded, when we would lift up our hearts unto Thee. 'If Thou, Lord, shouldest mark iniquity, O Lord, who can stand? But there is forgiveness with Thee,' and plenteous redemption in Thy beloved Son. Through His atoning sacrifice, and prevailing intercession, we would approach Thy throne of grace; and while we smite on our breasts and say, 'God be merciful to us, vile sinners!' we would unite our penitent confessions with lively faith and hope, and bless Thee for these unspeakable benefits. Oh give us true repentance and living faith; convince us more deeply of our sinfulness; and discover to us every thing in our hearts and lives, which displeases Thee: that we may approach Thee in genuine poverty of spirit, and with sincere and fervent longings after those blessings which we ask with our lips. Enlighten our understandings, that we may more clearly perceive the nature and glory of Thy gospel: and more fully 'know Thee, the only true God and Jesus Christ whom Thou hast sent.' Teach us to count all things but loss, that we may win Christ, and partake of His salvation. May Thy holy Word, which we daily study, be treasured up in our memories, written in our hearts, and made legible in our tempers and conduct. Oh, do Thou rectify our mistakes, deliver us from prejudices, 'make us to be of good understanding in the way of Godliness,' and 'uphold our goings in Thy ways, that our footsteps slip not.' We beseech Thee, O Thou God of peace, that by faith in the blood of Thy beloved Son, we may enjoy the comfort of Thy reconciling grace, and sweet tranquillity in our hearts and consciences; and may our hope of forgiveness from Thee render us ready to forgive others, and form our dispositions to gentleness and love. Glorying in the Cross of Christ, may we be crucified to the world, and the world to us. May we be clothed with humility, walk before Thee with vigilance and circumspection, and serve Thee in the spirit of adoption. Enable us, we beseech Thee, for Thy sake, to 'do unto all men, as we would they should do unto us,' to live in peace one with another, and while we have time, to do 'good unto all men, but especially to them that are of the household of faith.' May Thy saving grace 'teach us to deny ungodliness and worldly lusts, and to live soberly, righteously, and godly in this present world:' may we be content with such things as we have; accommodate ourselves to the station allotted us; conscientiously attend to our proper duties; and watch against covetousness, anger, envy, and all other sinful passions. Oh, may we be indeed the followers of the lowly Jesus: may we walk as He walked; act in wisdom towards all around us; and improve our several talents to the glory of Thy great name: and thus may we 'wait for the mercy of our Lord Jesus Christ unto eternal life.'

Hear, we beseech Thee, these our prayers and supplications: be with us in all the employments and companies in which we may this day be engaged: may we act in them, as under Thine eye, and as it becomes Thy redeemed people: and may we be habitually prepared for death and judgment. These and all mercies we, unworthy sinners, humbly implore, for the sake, and through the merits and mediation of Thy Son, Jesus Christ; to whom, with Thee, O Father, and the Holy Spirit, we would ascribe co-equal and eternal praise and adoration. Amen.

II.

ALMIGHTY and everlasting God, we Thy unworthy creatures desire to bless and thank Thee, for Thy gracious protection, and the refreshment of sleep during the past night; and the renewed gift of life and a measure of health this morning. We would gratefully acknowledge likewise the conveniences of our dwelling and temporal provision; the comfort of kind friends and domestic peace, and all the security and tranquillity which we enjoy in this favored country. We confess, O Lord, that we are unworthy of the least of these Thy mercies: and we beseech Thee, enable us to show our unfeigned gratitude, by alacrity in every part of Thy service, and a proper use of all Thy benefits.

But we are bound especially to bless and praise

Thy holy name, O most gracious Father, for the salvation provided for us in Thy Son Jesus Christ our Lord. Without this inestimable benefit, no temporal peace or prosperity could have eventually profited us. By Thy righteous sentence we are doomed to die. Our present joys and sorrows, cares and pursuits, must soon vanish like the dreams of the past night; we shall shortly open our eyes amidst the important realities of the eternal world. And, Oh! if Thou shouldest, in that unchanging state, deal with us in strict justice according to our deserts, we could no more avoid final condemnation than we can escape the stroke of death.

But, blessed be Thy name, O Lord, our reprieves from the grave may now be improved as opportunities of seeking deliverance from the wrath to come, and of securing an incorruptible and eternal inheritance. Enable us, therefore, we humbly pray Thee, to regard with solemn attention Thy message of reconciliation, through the mediation of Christ, and by faith in His atoning blood. Enlighten our minds to a clear perception of the nature, glory, and inestimable value of Thy great salvation; and fill us with an admiring sense of Thy condescending and compassionate love to lost sinners, in this stupendous method of showing them mercy, and giving them eternal felicity. Here may we see the harmonious display of Thy justice and grace, Thy holy abhorrence of iniquity, and Thy tender love to condemned transgressors. Help us, we humbly beseech Thee, to discover, in some measure, that manifold wisdom, and all those glories, which fill the angelic hosts with admiring love, that we may learn on earth the worship of heaven, and here lisp our feeble praises 'to Him who loved us, and washed us from our sins in His own blood.' Oh, enable us to give such diligence in making our calling and election sure, that we may always be confident; knowing that when we shall be absent from the body, we shall be present with Thee in glory. And if any of us have hitherto neglected the one thing needful, resting in a form of godliness, or in any way deceiving ourselves; may we be stirred up without delay to seek first Thy kingdom and Thy righteousness, and to subordinate all other pursuits to this grand concern.

Teach every one of us, O merciful God, to serve Thee in our different employments; doing all in the name of our Lord Jesus Christ, and using our possessions, or improving our talents, as those who duly consider how soon it may be said, 'Give an account of thy stewardship, for thou mayest no longer be steward.' Enable us, we entreat Thee, so to act at all times and in all things, that we may joyfully anticipate the summons, and humbly hope to be received by the Saviour with that welcome, 'Well done, good and faithful servant, enter thou into the joy of thy Lord.' Grant us, O thou Fountain of Life, such consolations in communion with Thee, as may render us superior to the frowns and smiles of the world, and fix our affections on things above.

Teach us also to profit by all Thy rebukes and chastisements; that every painful feeling may serve to humble us, to wean us from earthly things, to embitter sin, to endear the love of our suffering Redeemer, to soften our hearts into compassion towards the afflicted, and to bow our wills into submission to Thine appointments. And as Thou, O glorious Lord of all, art pleased to permit us to call Thee our Heavenly Father, grant, we entreat Thee, that the lively exercise of all filial affections, by the sacred influences of the Spirit of adoption, may fully testify that we are indeed the children and heirs of God. Oh, let it be the ardent desire of our inmost souls, that Thy name should be hallowed, Thy kingdom established, and Thy will be done on earth, as it is by all the inhabitants of heaven.

Enable us now, we beseech Thee, to enter on our several employments, in submission and obedience to Thy will, and dependence on Thy grace. May we be preserved from the snares of the world, and defended against the assaults of Satan: may we watch over our hearts, govern our passions, and bridle our tongues, as under the inspection of Thine all-seeing eye; and be helped in all things to glorify Thy name, through Jesus Christ, Thy beloved Son, and our Mediator and Redeemer. Amen.

A FAMILY PRAYER FOR SATURDAY EVENING.

O THOU eternal God, in whom we live, and move, and have our being, enable us, we beseech Thee, to close this week in that manner which shall be most profitable to ourselves and most honorable to Thy name.

We have no occasion, O most righteous and holy God, to review the years which are past, in order to find cause of humiliation in Thy sight: every day and every week suggest abundant matter for painful reflections, and add to our conviction, that 'we are all as an unclean thing, and all our righteousnesses as filthy rags.' O Lord, if Thou shouldest mark iniquity, who could stand? Enable us, therefore, to confess our sins with ingenuous and unreserved sorrow and shame; to own that they are more in number than the hairs of our head, and a sore burden, too heavy for us to bear; and to present ourselves, in deep contrition at Thy throne of grace, in humble faith and reverent boldness, through our great and compassionate High Priest, that we may obtain mercy and find grace to help in time of need. Do Thou apply the atoning blood to our consciences this evening, to purge away the guilt of the past week; that we may go to rest in peace, and not carry the guilt of any unrepented, unpardoned sin, into the ensuing week, to mar our comfort, or blast our endeavors to glorify Thy name. O Thou Author and Finisher of faith, help us against all the incursions of unbelief: leave us not to a dead faith and presumptuous hope; and let us not be discouraged by needless fears and scruples. Grant us peace and joy in believing; and let the love of God shed abroad in our hearts by the Holy Spirit, assure us that our hope shall never cause us to be ashamed.

While we would thus seek forgiveness of all that is past, through the blood of sprinkling, enable us also to return Thee our unfeigned thanks for the mercies of the past week, and of our whole lives.

Another week hath now been added to the season of Thy long-suffering; and to our season of preparation for eternity! through another week we have obtained help of God, and been in some measure enabled to cleave to Thee! Accept our cordial thanks and praises for all Thine unnumbered mercies, and grant that our future lives may evince our sincerity.

Bless to us, we beseech Thee, the means of grace we have this week enjoyed: and grant that, through Thine assistance, we may remember and be edified by all we have read or heard from Thy holy Word. Sanctify also to us the dispensations of Thy providence: teach us to profit by all Thy chastisements; and to learn gratitude and confidence in Thee, by all Thy mercies: and may even the experience we have of our own weakness and folly, excite us to more fervent prayers for wisdom, strength, and grace, according to Thy precious promises.

And now, O merciful God, we beseech Thee to prepare our hearts for the approaching day of sacred rest: and teach us so to arrange all our temporal concerns that our thoughts may not be occupied, our attention distracted, nor our minds ruffled by them, when we would wait on Thee in Thy holy services. Let us not deem Thy sabbaths a weariness; but our delight, our privilege, and great advantage. May the care of our own souls, and of the souls of those who belong to us, sweetly occupy the hours of the day.

By self-examination and meditation on Thy Word, may we obtain increasing acquaintance with ourselves, our spiritual estate, the progress we have made, or the loss we have sustained, in this important concern. Enable us, we beseech Thee, to humble ourselves before Thee in true repentance, and cordially to renew our acceptance of Thy salvation; and while we wait on Thee, may our strength be repaired; may every grace be brought into vigorous exercise; and our knowledge of Thy truth and will in all respects enlarged. Assist us in Thy public worship, and favor us with Thy special presence and blessing. May Thy people, with whom we worship, be refreshed, comforted, and sanctified in Thy courts; and grant Thy special assistance and blessing to Thy ministers in their work and labor of love. Oh that increasing numbers may be added to Thy churches, of such as shall be saved; and many able and faithful laborers sent forth into the harvest; and may the Sun of Righteousness diffuse His healing influence, wherever the sun in the firmament enlightens the nations with his beams. Hear us, O merciful Father, in these our supplications; take us under Thy protection this night; fit us, both in body and soul, for the duties of the ensuing day, and by them prepare us for Thy eternal Sabbath, for the sake of Jesus Christ Thy Son our Lord, to whom, with Thee and the Holy Spirit, One God in three persons, even the God of our salvation, be glory and honor from all creatures, now and for evermore. Amen.

JOHN LOGAN, F. R. S.
1748–1788.

The Message which Jesus Brings.

THE message which he brought, was life and immortality. From the Star of Jacob, light shone even upon the shades of death. As a proof of immortality, He called back the departed spirit from the world unknown; as an earnest of the resurrection to a future life, He Himself arose from the dead. When we contemplate the tomb of nature, we cry out 'Can these dry bones live?' When we contemplate the tomb of Jesus, we say, 'Yes, they can live!' As He arose, we shall in like manner arise. In the tomb of nature, you see man return to the dust from whence he was taken; in the tomb of Jesus you see man restored to life again. In the tomb of nature you see the shades of death fall on the weary traveller, and the darkness of the long night close over his head; in the tomb of Jesus, you see light arise upon the shades of death, and the morning dawn upon the long night of the grave. On the tomb of nature, it is written, 'Behold thy end, O man! Dust thou art, and unto dust thou shalt return. Thou, who now callest thyself the son of heaven, shall become one of the clods of the valley;' on the tomb of Christ is written, 'Thou diest, O man, but to live again. When dust returns to dust, the spirit shall return to God who gave it. I am the resurrection and the life; he that believeth in me, though he were dead, yet shall he live.' From the tomb of nature, you hear a voice, 'Forever silent is the land of forgetfulness! From the slumbers of the grave shall we awake no more! Like the flowers of the field, shall we be as though we had never been!' from the tomb of Jesus, you hear, 'Blessed are the dead that die in the Lord, thus saith the Spirit, for they rest from their labors, and pass into glory. In my Father's house there are many mansions; if it were not so, I would have told you. I go to prepare a place for you, and if I go away, I will come again, and take you unto myself, that where I am, there ye may be also.'

Will not this assurance of a happy immortality and a blessed resurrection, in a great measure, remove the terror and the sting of death? May we not walk without dismay through the dark valley, when we are conducted by a beam from heaven? May we not endure the tossings of one stormy night, when it carries us to the shore that we long for? What cause have we to dread the messenger who brings us to our Father's house? Should not our fears about futurity abate, when we hear God addressing us with respect to death, as He did the patriarch of old, upon going to Egypt, 'Fear not to go down to the grave;

I will go down with thee, and will bring thee up again?'

The Christian's Victory over Death.

THIS, O Christian! the death of thy Redeemer, is thy strong consolation; thy effectual remedy against the fear of death. What evil can come nigh to him for whom Jesus died? Does the law which thou hast broken, denounce vengeance against thee? Behold that law fulfilled in the meritorious life of thy Redeemer. Does the sentence of wrath pronounced against the posterity of Adam sound in thine ears? Behold that sentence blotted out, that *handwriting*, as the apostle calls it, cancelled, nailed to thy Saviour's cross, and left there as a trophy of His victory. Art thou afraid that the cry of thy offences may rise to heaven, and reach the ears of justice? There is no place for it there; in room of it ascends the voice of that blood which speaketh better things than the blood of Abel. Does the enemy of mankind accuse thee at the judgment-seat? He is put to silence by thy Advocate and Intercessor at the right hand of thy Father. Does death appear to thee in a form of terror, and hold out his sting to alarm thy mind? His terror is removed, and his sting was pulled out by that hand, which, on Mount Calvary, was fixed to the accursed tree.

Well then may ye join in the triumphant song of the apostle, 'O death, where is thy sting? O grave, where is thy victory?'

Jesus Christ gives us victory over death, by yielding us consolation and relief under the fears that arise in the mind upon the awful transition from this world to the next. Who ever left the precincts of mortality without casting a wishful look on what he left behind,* and a trembling eye on the scene that is before him? Being formed by our Creator for enjoyments even in this life, we are endowed with a sensibility to the objects around us. We have affections, and we delight to indulge them: we have hearts, and we want to bestow them. Bad as the world is, we find in it objects of affection and attachment. Even in this waste and howling wilderness, there are spots of verdure and of beauty, of power to charm the mind and make us cry out, 'It is good for us to be here.' When, after the observation and experience of years, we have found out the objects of the soul, and met with minds congenial to our own, what pangs must it give to the heart to think of parting forever? We even contract an attachment to inanimate objects. The tree under whose shadow we have often sat; the fields where we have frequently strayed; the hill, the scene of contemplation, or the haunt of friendship, become objects of passion to the mind, and upon our leaving them, excite a temporary sorrow and regret. If these things can

---

* This sentiment is evidently borrowed from these inimitable lines of Gray:—

> For who, to dumb forgetfulness a prey,
> This pleasing, anxious being e'er resigned;
> Left the warm precincts of the cheerful day,
> Nor cast one longing, lingering look behind,

affect us with uneasiness, how great must be the affliction, when stretched on that bed from which we shall rise no more, and looking about for the last time on the sad circle of our weeping friends! How great must be the affliction, to dissolve at once all the attachments of life; to bid an eternal adieu to the friends whom we long have loved, and to part forever with all that is dear below the sun! But let not the Christian be disconsolate. He parts with the objects of his affection, to meet them again; to meet them in a better world, where change never enters, and from whose blissful mansions sorrow flies away. At the resurrection of the just; in the great assembly of the sons of God, when all the family of heaven are gathered together, not one person shall be missing that was worthy of thy affection or esteem. And if among imperfect creatures, and in a troubled world, the kind, the tender, and the generous affections have such power to charm the heart, that even the tears which they occasion delight us, what joy unspeakable and glorious will they produce, when they exist in perfect minds, and are improved by the purity of the heavens!

Jesus, thy Saviour, has the keys of death; the abodes of the dead are part of His kingdom. He lay in the grave, and hallowed it for the repose of the just. Before our Lord ascended up on high, He said to His disciples, 'I go to my Father and to your Father, to my God and to your God;' and when the time of your departure is at hand, you go to your Father and His Father, to your God and His God.

Enlightened by these discoveries, trusting to the merits of his Redeemer, and animated with the hope which is set before him, the Christian will depart with tranquillity and joy. To him the bed of death will not be a scene of terror, nor the last hour an hour of despair. There is a majesty in the death of the Christian. He partakes of the spirit of that world to which he is advancing, and he meets his latter end with a face that looks to the heavens.

Passing Away.

EVERY thing that you behold around you bears the marks of mortality and the symptoms of decay. He only who is, and was, and is to come, is without any variableness or shadow of turning. Every thing passes away. A great and mighty river, for ages and centuries, has been rolling on, and sweeping away all that ever lived, to the vast abyss of eternity. On that darkness light does not rise. From that unknown country none return. On that devouring deep, which has swallowed up every thing, no vestige appears of the things that were.

TIMOTHY DWIGHT, D. D., LL. D.
1752–1827.

THE BLESSINGS TO WHICH THE SAVIOUR INVITES US.

THESE blessings are noble, exquisite, and enduring, beyond the conception of finite minds. They extend alike to the soul and to the body; they fill time; they spread through eternity. In this world, they are formed of unceasing protection, guidance, support, consolation, holiness, peace which passeth all understanding, hope which is an anchor to the soul in the stormy sea of life and joy which the world can neither give nor take away. They include the best provision for our wants, the best conduct of our lives, and the perfect security of our well-being. They commence with our sanctification, they attend us through life, they accompany us in death, they follow us beyond the grave.

In the future world they assume a still brighter aspect. There our vile bodies will be refashioned like unto Christ's glorious body, according to that mysterious working, whereby He is able to subdue all things unto Himself. Adorned and invigorated with youth, strength, beauty and immortality, they will be reunited to our minds, made perfectly holy and excellent. In the highest heavens, the house of God, we shall dwell in His presence, be made members and brethren of His family; advance for ever in knowledge and virtue, in wisdom and loveliness, in peace and joy; meet the smiles of infinite complacency; commence a pure and perpetual friendship with the world of sanctified minds; become sons, and kings, and priests to God the Father, and joint heirs with the Redeemer to His immortal inheritance; shall be with Him where He is, and shall behold and receive the glory which He had with the Father before ever the world was. Are not these blessings great enough to fill the wishes even of an immortal mind? Could an angel ask more? Can we hope for the one half of these? Can we realize, can we believe that they will be given to such beings as we are? Yet these, and far more than human language can express, or human imaginations can conceive, He possessed from everlasting, and these He has of His own accord, unasked, undesired, proffered to our acceptance, declaring that all things in the universe, in time and through eternity, shall work together for good to them that love God.

Without an Interest in Christ.

WITHOUT the love, the atonement, and the intercession of Christ, how will you disarm death and triumph over the grave? Who will guide your lonely and anxious steps through the unknown world,—sustain your hearts before the last tribunal, acquit you of your immeasurable guilt, and redeem you from endless darkness and despair?

Who will conduct you to heaven? Who will provide for you immortal good; support you with self-approbation and peace; adorn you with beauty and excellency; inspire you with love; improve and refine you with wisdom; instamp on you the glorious image of God; and bring you to the general assembly of the first-born as their eternal friend and companion? Who will unlock for you the springs of life? Who will feed you with living bread? Who will clothe you with unfading robes of righteousness? Who will fix you in mansions of everlasting joy? Who, in a word, will be your light, your portion, and your friend for ever.

The Love of Christ.

THE love of Christ is immeasurably great. 'The love of Christ,' says St. Paul, 'which passeth knowledge.' It is a love which has proved itself to be stronger than death—a love which affliction could not quench, which sorrow could not drown. This is evident, with a lustre irresistible, in the things which He has done, which He is doing, and which He will do hereafter. It is unnecessary for me to recall on this occasion the things which Christ has already done. I need not exhibit Him to you on the cross, pouring out His blood for the salvation of men, nor present Him agonizing in the garden of Gethsemane, nor follow Him to the tomb. What must have been the intenseness of that benevolence which could bring the Son of God from the throne of heaven to shame and agony, to the cross and to the grave?

Less striking, I acknowledge, but scarcely less affecting, are the proofs of the same love in what He is now doing. There is something inexpressibly glorious to Him, and beyond measure interesting to us, in beholding the Saviour of mankind, who 'has ascended far above all heavens, that He might fill all things,' looking down, nay descending from this stupendous greatness to the miserable world which we inhabit, to blot out the transgressions and wash away the stains of a wretched sinner; to renew a polluted soul; to shed upon it peace passing all understanding; to reunite it to the favor of God; to chase away its fears of future woe; to pour the balsam of life into its wounds; to illumine it with the beams of hope; to conduct it safely through the trials and dangers of this melancholy pilgrimage; to bar the gates of perdition against its entrance; and to open for its reception the door of endless life.

The Saviour's Goodness to the Believer.

HE will in no wise cast you out. He will never leave you or forsake you. His eye, before which the night shineth as the day, will watch over you with unceasing care; and His hand, which nothing can resist or escape, guard you with infinite tenderness. In every sorrow He will comfort; in every danger He will deliver. The bed of death He will spread with down; the passage into eternity He will illumine with the light of His own countenance. In the judgment He will acquit you of all your guilt; and in His own house, the mansion of eternal light, and peace, and joy, he will present you to His Father as trophies of His cross and monuments of his boundless love.

The Sinner Invited to Return to God.

IS it not then infinitely desirable to know that you have a home to which you may go; plenty to which you may betake yourselves; friends from whom you may derive kindness and consolation; and a Father yet remaining, who, though so long forsaken, is still willing to acknowledge this relation to you? In His tenderness you may find an asylum; to His arms you may be welcomed? in His house you may find an everlasting residence. There all good things abound, are treasured up, and bestowed with unwearied as well as unlimited bounty.

Behold that Father advancing to meet you on your way! Hear Him calling to you with infinite compassion, Ho! thou starving, perishing prodigal, Return to me and to mine. Art thou hungry? I will feed thee with living bread. Art thou thirsty? I will lead thee to fountains of living waters. Art thou naked? I will clothe thee with the robe of righteousness. Art thou weary? I will guide thee to eternal rest. Art thou friendless? I will be to thee a Father, and an everlasting friend. Dead? thou shalt live again. Lost? I will restore thee to a universe of joy. Come; all things are ready. See, heaven is opened! Behold angels, and the spirits of just men made perfect, waiting for Thy arrival! See, the golden sceptre of forgiveness extended before thee! Approach, and touch and live for ever.

Advantages of Afflictions.

AFFLICTIONS, of course, if wisely improved and sanctified by God, yield the peaceable fruits of righteousness. If wisely improved by us, there is good reason to hope that they will be thus sanctified. Great multitudes of mankind are hopefully brought out of darkness into marvelous light during seasons of severe affliction. Then the first views begin, the first affections are cherished, the first resolutions are formed, which introduce all the succeeding happy train of conduct and character of the sanctified man. Eternal life is very often to be dated from the dying bed of our friends. Religion there sits kindly and constantly to persuade us to admit her as a future friend, a future and eternal inmate of our bosoms. Christ there solemnly and affectingly calls on us, as we dread death, to dread sin, the cause of death, and to be alarmed with the thought of dying for ever; to be reconciled to God, then waiting to receive us to His arms, and to believe in Himself, the resurrection and the life, that He may raise us up at the last day. Salvation here dawns like the day-star, rising out of a night of gloom and tempest, and anticipating a perfect and glorious day. The soul, here under a load of hopeless sorrow, finding no earthly friend or comforter able and willing to relieve its distresses, bows before its divine Redeemer, and turns to the Spirit of grace for heavenly and immortal consolation.

Consolation for the Afflicted.

TO the poor afflicted race of men religion is a heavenly messenger, who, like the angels sent to the Bethlehem shepherds to announce the birth of the Saviour, while she proclaims unceasingly, 'Glory to God in the highest,' sings also, 'Peace on earth, and good-will towards men.' Towards every sufferer, laboring under heavy sorrows, and in the midst of despondency casting around his eyes in vain to find consolation and relief, she approaches with her own serene and benevolent smile, and proffers herself as a comfort to mourners. In her hand she carries the word of God, and opening the wonderful book, points to lines written with the divine finger, and dictated by the voice of infinite compassion. 'Behold,' she cries, 'the testimonies of the Lord are the heritage of the afflicted for ever. They are the rejoicing of the broken heart.' In this sacred Volume read, and find all the relief which your sorrows need. Here the infinitely blessed Jehovah has portrayed Himself in characters of light, as the Father of all mercies and the God of all grace and consolation. Here He has disclosed Himself as the common, kind, and compassionate parent of men, and has taught them that all His chastisements are inflicted only for the good of the sufferers, that it is their frowardness which requires them, and their frowardness only which prevents them from being the choicest blessings. To cure your melancholy diseases, to overcome your dangerous and deadly passions, they have descended on you, that you may be a partaker of His holiness and live for ever. The boundless love which contrived the deliverance of this world from sin and ruin is here seen to watch with infinite tenderness over you. Hear the affectionate language in which is disclosed to you the glorious and benevolent character of Him who made you, 'The Lord is my shepherd, I shall not want. He maketh me to lie down in green pastures; He leadeth me beside the still waters. He restoreth my soul; He leadeth me in the paths of righteousness for His name's sake. Yea, though I walk through the valley of the shadow of death, I will fear no evil, for Thou art with me; Thy rod and Thy staff they comfort me. Thou preparest a table before me in the presence of mine enemies; Thou anointest my head with oil; my cup runneth over. Surely goodness and mercy shall follow me all the days of my life: and I will dwell in the house of the Lord for ever.

The Desire of Immortality.

IMMORTALITY is necessarily the object of earnest desire to every intelligent, and would be, if he could form the thought, to every percipient being. It was the actual and glorious lot of our first parents. It may be the lot of every one of *us*. A short period, a limited life, is the only period during which we can obtain it. This very consideration demands of us the utmost anxiety and diligence. The death, also, which we must all undergo enforces strongly, with its painful and distressing circumstances, this powerful argument. Like a beacon lighted up with an eternal fire, on a height visible to all the nations of men, it solemnly warns us of the evils to which we are exposed, and of which to all the impenitent it is itself the beginning. We need then to be warned. If we are wise we shall welcome the alarm, and, beholding the Sun of life hastening through the heavens, shall do, while the day lasts, whatsoever our hand findeth to do, with our might, and, to quicken our diligence, shall cast a constant and apprehensive eye toward the rapid approach of that night in which no man can work. Instead of wishing to live longer, we shall labor to live better. Instead of vainly panting for immortal being in a world of sin and sorrow, where we, together with others, should only sin and suffer, we should lend all our efforts to find it in that glorious world where it can be actually found, and where its ages roll on in the fullness of joy and pleasures for evermore.

Blessings of Prayer.

PRAYER will make you daily better, wiser, and lovelier in God's sight, by cherishing in you those views and emotions which constitute the character of a good man. It will soothe every tumult of your bosoms, allay your fears, comfort your sorrows, invigorate your hopes, give you peace in hand, and anticipate glory to come. It will restrain you from sin, strengthen you against temptation, recall you from wandering, give life and serenity to your consciences, furnish you with clearer views concerning your duty, alarm you concerning your danger, and inspire you with ardor, confidence, and delight in the Christian course.

In prayer God will meet you, and commune with you face to face, as a man with his friend. He will 'lift upon you the light of His reconciled countenance;' will 'put joy and gladness in your hearts;' and will awaken in you the spirit of 'thanksgiving and the voice of melody.' 'When you pass through the waters He will be with you; and through the rivers, they shall not overflow you; when you walk through the fire, you shall not be burned, neither shall the flame kindle on you: for He is the Lord your God, the holy one of Israel, your Saviour.' 'In an acceptable time He will hear you, and in a day of salvation will He help you.' 'The mountains will indeed depart, and the hills be removed; but' (if you seek Him faithfully) 'His kindness shall not depart from you, nor His covenant of peace be removed.' 'Seek, then, the Lord, while He may be found: call ye upon Him, while He is near.' 'When you call He will answer; and when you cry unto Him, He will say, Here I am.'

On Prayer for Revivals of Religion.

NO good descends from heaven to this world, except as an answer to prayer. 'Ask, and ye shall receive' is the great law according to which all blessings are given. Pray always with all prayer and supplication of the Spirit, therefore, for the restoration of mankind to the favor and the service of God. For this glorious end let the secret aspirations of the closet rise unceasingly to the throne of mercy. These let the morning and evening oblation of the household accompany every day to the presence of God, and call down the life-giving influence of the Spirit of grace upon this world of death and ruin. Finally, for the same delightful end, let the sweet incense of the sanctuary ascend in one vast cloud to heaven, from Sabbath to Sabbath, as the united and acceptable offering of all who love the Lord Jesus Christ, to Him who has not said to the house of Jacob, 'Seek ye my face in vain.' Thus shall the millions of your fellow-men, 'ransomed of the Lord, return and come to Zion with songs and everlasting joy upon their heads. They shall obtain joy and gladness, and sorrow and sighing shall flee away.'

Heaven Our Home.

HEAVEN is your proper home. Point your course to that glorious and happy world; and let every step which you take here advance you towards immortal life. Let angels behold your progress, and rejoice over your repentance, and the spirits of the just prepare to welcome you to their divine assembly.

Heaven in View.

CAN Christians fail to look often to that delightful world where their Saviour dwells, and where they are all finally to be assembled in His presence? Will not the remembrance of the fullness of joy, the pleasures which flow for ever in this region of immortality, awaken in the most ardent manner, their admiration, their love, their gratitude, and their praise to Him, who formed it in the beginning; who stored it with glory, life, and joy; who ascended the cross that He might open its everlasting doors for their admission to its infinite blessings.

Our Father's House.

'IN His Father's house,' Christ has told us, 'are many mansions.' To that happy residence 'He has gone before, to prepare a place for us,' nay, He has declared that He will 'create new heavens and a new earth,' for the reception of those who trust in Him and 'love His appearing.' In this new world, He has assured us, 'there shall be no more death, nor sorrow, nor crying, nor any more pain: for all these former evil things shall then have passed away.' In this happy region, the 'righteousness,' which the paradise below the sun was destined to reward, 'will dwell for ever.' There the tree of life blossoms, and bears anew; and there immortality flows again in 'the pure river of the water of life.' There 'the sun no more goes down; neither does the moon withdraw itself;' for Jehovah is 'the everlasting light' of His children, and 'their God their glory.' From that delightful world the Redeemer cries, 'Behold, I come quickly, and my reward is with me.' Oh that every heart may answer, 'Even so, come Lord Jesus.' Amen.

Heaven and Earth Compared.

Here also all things will live. Death and sorrow, disease and pain, crying and tears, will have fled for ever. There will be nothing to destroy, nothing to impair, nothing to lament. Everything will live; and not merely live, but grow, and flourish, and bloom, without interruption. Life, in a sublime and superior sense, life vernal and immortal, will impregnate the streams and trees, the leaves and fruits, and animate the bodies and minds of the firstborn.

As all things in heaven will be informed with life, so they will become universally means of joy. The present world is justly styled 'a vale of tears.' Distress awaits us here in a thousand forms. Within us it dwells, without it assails. We are sinners, are the subjects of ungratified desire, disappointment, discontent, reproaches of conscience, and distressing apprehensions concerning the anger of God. At the same time our frail bodies are subjected to the evils of hunger and thirst, of cold and heat, of weariness and languor, of sickness and pain, of decay and death. Our friends and families are in want, pain, and sorrow; they sicken and die; their sins disgrace them and wound us; and awaken excruciating apprehensions concerning their destiny beyond the grave.

War also frequently spreads wide the miseries of dismay, plunder, slaughter and devastation. To beings habituated to a state of existence so extensively formed of these distressing materials, how welcome must be the change which transports them from this world to heaven! When 'the ransomed of the Lord shall return, and come to' the celestial 'Zion with songs, everlasting joy shall be upon their heads; they shall obtain joy and gladness, and sorrow and sighing shall flee away.' Heaven is created to be the residence of happiness. Every thing which it contains will be beauty, grandeur and glory to the eye, harmony to the ear, and rapture to the heart; rapture which admits no mixture, and knows no termination.

Christ the Light of Heaven.

CHRIST is the light of heaven, as well as of earth. In this divine Person the Godhead will shine without a cloud, and be seen face to face. The splendor will be all intelligence and enjoyment, and the warmth, life and love. The happy millions will bask for ever in the benevolent beams; and, with the eagle's eye fixed on the divine luminary, will rise on eagle's wings with a perpetually invigorated flight, nearer and nearer to the Sun of Righteousness for ever.

ANDREW FULLER.
1754-1815.

Life of Faith.

GREAT and wonderful is the *consolation* that such a life affords. In all the vicissitudes of life and horrors of death, nothing can cheer and fortify the mind like this. By faith in an unseen world we can endure injuries without revenge, afflictions without fainting, and losses without despair. Let the nations of the earth dash, like potsherds, one against another; yea, let nature herself approach towards her final dissolution; let her groan as being ready to expire, and sink into her primitive nothing; still the believer lives! His all is not on board that vessel! His chief inheritance lies in another soil!

> 'His hand the good man fastens on the skies,
> And bids earth roll, nor feels her idle whirl!'

It will *make vision the sweeter*. It affords a great pleasure, when we make a venture of any kind, to find ourselves at last not disappointed. If a considerate man embark his all on board a vessel, and himself with it, he may have a thousand fears, before he reaches the end of his voyage; yet should he, after numberless dangers, safely arrive, and find it not only answer, but far exceed his expectations, his joy will then be greater than if he had run no hazard at all. What he has gained will seem much sweeter than if it had fallen to him in a way that had cost him nothing. Thus believers venture their all in the hands of Christ, persuaded that He is able to keep that which they have committed to Him against that day. To find at last that they have not confided in Him in vain—yea, that their expectations are not only answered, but infinitely outdone—will surely enhance the bliss of heaven. The remembrance of our dangers, fears, and sorrows will enable us to enjoy the heavenly state with a degree of happiness impossible to have been felt, if those dangers, fears, and sorrows had never existed.

Christ Crucified.

CHRIST crucified is the central point, in which all the lines of evangelical truth meet and are united. There is not a doctrine in the Scriptures but what bears an important relation to it. Would we understand the glory of the Divine character and government? It is seen in perfection *in the face of Jesus Christ*. Would we learn the evil of sin, and our perishing condition as sinners? Each is manifested in His sufferings. All the blessings of grace and glory are given us in Him, and for His sake. Practical religion finds its most powerful motives in His dying love. That doctrine of which Christ is not the sum and substance is not the gospel; and that morality which has no relation to Him, and which is not enforced on evangelical principles, is not Christian, but heathen.

Progressive Character of Heavenly Bliss.

BY the manner in which some have spoken and written of the heavenly state, it would seem not only as if all would possess an equal measure of blessedness, but that this measure would be completed at once; if not on the soul's having left the body, yet immediately on its reunion with it at the resurrection. But such ideas appear to me to have no foundation in the Holy Scriptures. There is no doubt that salvation is altogether of grace, and that every crown will be cast at the feet of Christ; but it does not follow that they shall be in all respects alike. Paul's crown of rejoicing, for instance, will greatly consist in the salvation of those among whom he labored; but this cannot be the case with every other inhabitant of heaven. And with respect to the completion of the bliss, there certainly will be no such imperfection attending it as to be a source of sorrow, but rather of joy, as affording matter for an endless progression of knowledge, and consequently of love, and joy, and praise. There is no sorrow in the minds of angels in their present state; yet they are described as looking with intenseness and delight into the doctrine of the Cross; which clearly indicates a progressiveness in knowledge and happiness. God is perfect, and immutably the same; but it is as He is *revealed* or *manifested* to us that we enjoy Him as our portion. If, therefore, He be gradually manifesting Himself through time, and thereby causing the tide of celestial bliss to rise higher and higher, it may be the same to eternity. Nay more, if heavenly bliss consist in knowing the love of Christ, and that love, when all is said and done, 'passeth knowledge,' it must be so; there must either come a period when the finite mind shall have perfectly comprehended the infinite, and therefore can have nothing more to learn, or knowledge and happiness must be eternally progressive.

Blessedness of Heaven.

IN what sense could Christ be said to 'prepare a place' for His followers, if His presence did not greatly tend to augment the blessedness of that world whither He went, and render it a sweet resort to them when they should have passed their days of tribulation? If heavenly bliss consist much in social enjoyment, the arrival of *any* interesting character must be somewhat of an acquisition. If our present conceptions, however, be any rule of judging, the being introduced to certain dear friends who have gone before us will be a source of pleasure inexpressible. In this point of view every one who goes before contributes in some degree to prepare a place for those that follow after; and as things continually move on in the same direction, the sum total of heavenly enjoyment must be continually accumulating. But if such be the influence arising from the accession of creatures, what must that have been which followed His entrance who is Life itself! His presence would render those blest abodes ten thousand times more blessed. Hence the grand motive to heavenly-mindedness in the New Testament is drawn from the consideration of Christ's being in heaven. 'If,' said Paul, 'ye be risen *with Christ*, seek those things which are above, *where Christ sitteth* on the right hand of God. And what the apostle recommended to others was exemplified in himself; for he had 'a desire to depart, and to *be with Christ*, which is far better.'

ROBERT HALL, A. M.
1764–1831.

REUNION OF GOOD MEN IN HEAVEN.

IF the mere conception of the reunion of good men, in a future state, infused a momentary rapture into the mind of Tully; if an airy speculation, for there is reason to fear it had little hold on his convictions, could inspire him with such delight, what may we be expected to feel, who are assured of such an event by the true sayings of God! How should we rejoice in the prospect, the certainty, rather, of spending a blissful eternity with those whom we loved on earth; of seeing them emerge from the ruins of the tomb, and the deeper ruins of the fall, not only uninjured, but refined and perfected, 'with every tear wiped from their eyes,' standing before the throne of God and the Lamb, 'in white robes, and palms in their hands, crying with a loud voice, Salvation to God, that sitteth upon the throne and to the Lamb for ever and ever.' What delight will it afford to renew the sweet counsel we have taken together, to recount the toils of combat, and the labor of the way, and to approach not the house, but the throne of God, in company, in order to join in the symphonies of heavenly voices, and lose ourselves amidst the splendors and fruitions of the beatific vision!

Friendship Founded on Religion.

FRIENDSHIP, founded on the principles of worldly morality, recognized by virtuous heathens, such as that which subsisted between Atticus and Cicero, which the last of these illustrious men has rendered immortal, is fitted to survive through all the vicissitudes of life, but it belongs only to a union founded on religion, to continue through an endless duration. The former of these stood the shock of conflicting opinions, and of a revolution that shook the world; the latter is destined to survive when the heavens are no more, and to spring fresh from the ashes of the universe. The former possessed all the stability which is possible to sublunary things; the latter partakes of the eternity of God. Friendship founded on worldly principles is *natural*, and though composed of the best elements of nature, is not exempt from its mutability and frailty; the latter is *spiritual*, and therefore unchanging and imperishable. The friendship which is founded on kindred tastes and congenial habits, apart from piety, is permitted by the benignity of Providence to embellish a world, which, with all its magnificence and beauty, will shortly pass away; that which has religion for its basis, will ere long be transplanted, in order to adorn the paradise of God.

How a Minister Should Preach.

DISPLAY the sufferings of Christ like one who was an eye-witness of those sufferings, and hold up the blood, the precious blood of atonement, as issuing warm from the cross. It is a peculiar excellence of the gospel, that in its wonderful adaptation to the state and condition of mankind as fallen creatures, it bears intrinsic marks of its divinity, and is supported not less by internal than by external evidence. By a powerful appeal to the conscience, by a faithful delineation of man in his grandeur and in his weakness, in his original capacity for happiness and his present misery and guilt, present this branch of its evidence in all its force. Seize on every occasion those features of Christianity which render it interesting, and by awakening the fears, and exciting the hopes, of your hearers, endeavor to annihilate every other object, and make it appear what it really is, the pearl of great price, the sovereign balm, the cure of every ill, the antidote of death, the precursor of immortality. In such a ministry, fear not to give loose to all the ardor of your soul, to call into action every emotion and every faculty which can exalt or adorn it.

The Pursuit of Salvation.

THE pursuit of salvation is the only enterprise, in which no one fails from weakness, none from an invincible ignorance of futurity, none from the sudden vicissitudes of fortune, against which there exists no effectual security, none from those occasional eclipses of knowledge and fits of inadvertence, to which the most acute and wakeful intellect is exposed. How suitable is it to the character of the Being who reveals Himself by the name of *Love*, to render the object which is alone worthy of being aspired to with ardor, the only one to which all may, without presumption, aspire; and while He conceals thrones and sceptres in the shadow of His hand, and bestows them where He pleases, with a mysterious and uncontrollable sovereignty, on opening the springs of eternal felicity, to proclaim to the utmost bounds of the earth, 'Let him that is athirst, come; and whosoever will, let him partake of the water of life freely.'

Funeral Obsequies of a Lost Soul.

WHAT, my brethren, if it be lawful to indulge such a thought, what would be the funeral obsequies of a lost soul? Where shall we find the tears fit to be wept at such a spectacle; or could we realize the calamity in all its extent, what tokens of commiseration and concern would be deemed equal to the occasion? Would it suffice for the sun to veil his light, and the moon her brightness; to cover the ocean with mourning, and the heavens with sackcloth; or were the whole fabric of nature to become animated and vocal, would it be possible for her to utter a groan too deep, or a cry too piercing, to express the magnitude and extent of such a catastrophe?

A Penitent on His Knees.

THE sight of a penitent on his knees, is a spectacle which moves Heaven; and the compassionate Redeemer, who, when He beheld Saul in that situation, exclaimed, 'Behold he prayeth,' will not be slow or reluctant to strengthen you by His might, and console you by His Spirit. When a 'new and living way' is opened 'into the holiest of all,' by the blood of Jesus, not to avail ourselves of it, not to arise and go to our Father, but to prefer remaining at a guilty distance, encompassed with famine, to the rich and everlasting provisions of His house, will be a source of insupportable anguish, when we shall see Abraham, Isaac, and Jacob enter into the kingdom of God, and ourselves shut out.

Preparation for Judgment and Eternity.

'AFTER death is the judgment.' What is to shield you in judgment from the stroke of vengeance? Have you been hearing the calls of the gospel without regarding them? Have you not applied the truth to yourselves? O, retreat now from the snares of the world; shut your eyes upon the scenes of time, on which they must soon be closed for ever. Converse with the world to come; endeavor to yield to the power of it; look at 'the things which are not seen;' walk, as it were, upon the borders of the ocean of eternity, and listen to the sound of its waters till you are deaf to every sound besides.

The blessed Saviour, who, when He was upon earth,

raised the dead and healed all manner of diseases, is able to heal your spiritual maladies, and to raise you from the dead. He is exalted for this purpose: the 'river of life' flows from His side; He invites you to partake of it; 'the Spirit and the bride say, Come. And let him that heareth say, Come. And whosoever will, let him come and take of the water of life freely,' Rev. xxii. 17. In the blessed Saviour are all the springs of pardon, grace and everlasting consolation: He will guide you through every scene, give you victory over death, admit you through the gates into the city, and there He will 'wipe away all tears from your eyes,' Rev. xxi. 4. He will dwell with you, and you with Him; and you shall be 'kings and priests unto God' for ever.

The Lamb of God.

AS our salvation from the effects of sin is a deliverance from a far worse than Egyptian captivity and misery, so its accomplishment required a far greater exertion of Deity than was required to arrest the billows of the Red Sea. Never did 'the mighty God' more fully display the greatness of His power, than when He showed Himself 'mighty to *save*, even to the uttermost.' He fixed the foundation on which we may build our hope of immortality, and find it to be 'a hope that maketh not ashamed,' founded on the Rock of Ages. He went into the shadow of death, into 'the lowest parts of the earth,' that He might lay *deep the basis of that edifice which was to rise as high as the throne of God!*

'He bore our sins in His own body on the tree,' that we might become partakers of His own divine nature. *This*, my brethren, is a view of 'the Lamb of God,' of the *last* importance to be taken by us all. If you see Him not in this character, you see *nothing* to any valuable purpose. You have taken hold of *nothing*, you have grasped only *shadows*, if you have not taken hold of *Christ*, your *Life*. Flee to Him: cleave to Him: say of Him in the sincerity of your heart, 'This is all my salvation and all my desire.'

The Eye of Faith.

TO the eye of Christian faith, which looks at what is seen and temporal by the light of what is unseen and eternal, the darkest clouds of present sufferings appear, as it were, irradiated with a reflection of that glory which will ere long break forth from their gloom, to shine and brighten through an endless day. One glimpse of that glory, we feel assured, would put out all these little clouds from our view or remembrance! Let us aim to walk by faith, and not by sight; and in our trials, to realize the well grounded conviction, 'these sufferings of time are not worthy to be compared with the glory that shall be revealed' when time shall be lost in eternity.

The Divine Promises.

WE should be much in meditation on the Divine promises. We should be mindful, indeed, of the threatenings of God; we should not be inattentive to the prophecies contained in His Word: but it is peculiarly the duty, as well as the privilege of Christians, to meditate upon His promises. If you would enter into the vital reality of religion, you must enter into these promises; into their pure and sanctifying consolations. Taste of the love of God! Review the riches of your inheritance! Look to the Saviour as the source of all fullness! Endeavor to let your mind be saturated with these promises! Oh, let us not be satisfied with a cold, a formal, legal obedience to the commandments: let us learn to feed upon the sweetness of the promises! And we shall need their support ere long: time is hastening from us all; man is but breath, but dust! soon you will be here no more. He that shall come, will come ere long! Happy they that hope and wait for His coming! Every day, if you are a Christian, you are nearer to heaven; less of toil and trial remains. And death, as well as life, is yours; to die is your exceeding gain. 'I heard a voice from heaven saying, Blessed are the dead who die in the Lord; for they rest from their labors, and their works follow them.'

Continual Virtue of Christ's Blood.

HIS blood, so to speak, is just as warm and fresh as when it was first shed: it has an undecaying virtue. The Lamb forever appears as newly slain, though millions have been already saved, and millions more remain to be saved. He was offered once for all; He is an eternal, unchangeable High Priest; for God's law has been once for all fully satisfied by Him. No generation can arise that will not equally want this Saviour, and none that will not equally find Him sufficient; for all the fulness of God dwells in Him, and He ever lives to make intercession for us!

Importance of the Christian Ministry.

VANITY is inscribed on every earthly pursuit, on all sublunary labor; its materials, its instruments, and its objects will alike perish. An incurable taint of mortality has seized upon, and will consume them ere long. The acquisitions derived from religion, the graces of a renovated mind, are alone permanent. This is the mystic inclosure, rescued from the empire of change and death; this is the field which the Lord has blessed; and this word of the kingdom, the seed which alone produces immortal fruit, the very bread of life, with which, under a higher economy, the Lamb in the midst of the throne will feed His flock and replenish His elect, through eternal ages. How high and awful a function is that which proposes to establish in the soul an interior dominion—to illuminate its powers by a celestial light—and introduce it to an intimate, ineffable, and unchanging alliance with the Father of spirits. What an honor to be employed as the instrument of conducting that mysterious process by which men are born of God; to expel from the heart the venom of the old serpent; to purge the conscience from invisible stains of guilt; to release the passions from the bondage of corruption, and invite them to soar aloft into the regions of uncreated light and beauty; 'to say to the prisoners, go forth, to them that are in darkness, show yourselves!' These are the fruits which arise from the successful discharge of the Christian ministry; these the effects of the gospel, wherever it becomes the power of God unto salvation; and the interests which they create, the joys which they diffuse, are felt in other worlds.

Salvation to the Uttermost.

THE blood of Jesus Christ is a deluge that drowns all the mountains of transgression; that pure ocean washes away all stains of guilt. It is a sacrifice whose odor fills all worlds! a satisfaction that extends to all the principles of the divine government. The apostle seems almost to single out himself as a selected and designed monument of the unlimited extent of Christ's atonement. 'This is a faithful saying, that Jesus Christ came into the world to save sinners, of whom I am chief. Howbeit for this cause I obtained mercy, that in me first, Jesus Christ might show forth all long-suffering, for a pattern to them that should hereafter believe unto life everlasting.' Some may think they have wandered too long in ways of sin, stifled too many successive convictions, and sinned away the virtue of Christ's blood. However long you may have sinned, yet if you will now repent, though at the eleventh hour, you shall be saved. Among the redeemed multitude, there will be found sinners of every extent and condition: some that early sought the Lord, and walked long with Him in grace; but others, also, called in their hoary hairs, after many years of rebellion.

Gratitude to the Saviour.

WHAT gratitude is due from us, to this dear Saviour! What shall we render to Him for all that He has suffered, in order that He might procure such benefits for us! What can be so shocking as that we should alienate ourselves from Him who bought us with His blood, lifted us up from the abyss of despair, beautified us with salvation, made us to sit with Himself in heavenly places! By what strict and tender ties are we bound to Him! especially when the faculties which we give to Him are dignified; and we receive ourselves back, as it were, purified and ennobled!

It should be our constant desire to gratify and honor Him; the uppermost feeling in our hearts should be, 'What can I do for Christ? How shall I make it appear that I have been with Him, that I have learned of Him?' If we are influenced by this spirit, He will come and make His abode with us; He will manifest Himself to us. 'Behold, what manner of love the Father hath bestowed upon us, that we should be called the sons of God!' Let every saint esteem all beside but loss, in comparison with the possession of His love! Let us live on Him as the bread of life, and live to Him as the Lord of conscience. Let His love be the commanding principle in all our hearts.

Come to the Saviour Now.

SEEK now an interest in 'the common salvation!' Now is the accepted time; now is the convenient season. While all around is mutable, unstable, and we can fix on nothing that does not escape from our eager grasp, lay hold on Jesus Christ, the Rock of Ages! While all beside is carried away by the irresistible tide of vanity and corruption, secure that inestimable deposit which will exist forever in the hands of Him who is able to keep it against the day of his appearance and glory! Come to the Saviour just as you are; if you were to wait to all eternity, you would be no better prepared, by any efforts of your own, for His acceptance. All power is given to Him; He is able to save to the uttermost all who come to God by Him: whosoever will, let him come to Christ; and thus be prepared, by His grace and power, to exchange the light affliction, which is for a moment, for an exceeding and eternal weight of glory!

A Prayer.

'O THOU, who art the Fountain of all good! we would approach Thee with that humility and reverence which become us in all our addresses to Thine infinite Majesty. Before the mountains were brought forth, or ever the earth and the world were created, from everlasting to everlasting Thou art God. As from Thee we have derived our existence, so on Thee we depend for every moment of its continuance: in Thee we live, and move, and have our being. Thou hast been the refuge of Thy people in all generations; our fathers trusted in Thee, and were holpen; they looked unto Thee, and were lightened, and their faces were not ashamed. As for man, his days are as grass; but the mercy of the Lord is from everlasting to everlasting upon them that fear Him. We bless Thee that we are permitted once more to appear in Thy presence, the spared monuments of Thy providential goodness. We beseech Thee to assist us in these sacred exercises; in singing Thy praises, and hearing Thy holy word. We serve Thee only with Thine own; and what we have received in mercies and blessings, we would render back to Thee in gratitude and love. Enable us to consider the operations of Thy hand in all things around, and all things within us; in the workings of Thy providence abroad, and of Thy Spirit upon ourselves. Let us make Thee the Omega as well as the Alpha, the end as well as the beginning, of all our undertakings; let all our works be begun, continued, and ended in Thee. May we put on the whole armor of God, be strong in the Lord, and in the power of His might; and, seeing that we are encompassed with so great a cloud of witnesses, may we lay aside every weight, and run with patience the race set before us, looking unto Jesus, the Author and Finisher of our faith. Since our adversary, the devil, walketh about, seeking whom he may devour, him may we resist, steadfast in the faith. May we rejoice as if we rejoiced not; weep as if we wept not; and, knowing that the end of all things is at hand, may we let our moderation be known unto all men. O Lord, hear us in these our supplications, and pardon and accept us, and wash us and our services in the precious blood of the dear and adorable Redeemer; for whom we bless Thee, as Thine unspeakable gift; and with whom, to Thyself and Holy Spirit, be undivided and everlasting praises.' Amen.*

* This beautiful prayer was offered immediately before Mr. Hall delivered his last sacramental lecture, and only a short time before his death. It was transcribed by the Rev. T. Grinfield, who says:
'It is a remarkable circumstance that, on this last opportunity alone, as though impelled by a prophetic sympathy, I preserved, at the same time, the following fragments of the prayer which preceded this farewell address. Simple, and almost purely Scriptural, as are the sentiments and expressions, they may be deemed interesting here, as they present, I believe, the only recorded relic of those prayers, in which, scarcely less than in his preaching, Mr. Hall excelled; and this so near to his death. I give it *verbatim*, as noted at the time: in all his prayers the impression was much enhanced by the utterance, which was eminently that of one 'praying in the Holy Spirit,' and 'clothed with humility.'

JOHN M. MASON, D. D.
1770-1829.

REDEMPTION THROUGH THE BLOOD OF CHRIST.

WHAT the atonement of Jesus is, in itself, and what His Father has expressly declared it to be, millions of sinners have found it to their eternal joy. All *the spirits of just men made perfect*, and all the believers at this hour upon earth, have *washed their robes, and made them white in the blood of the Lamb.* Search the records of the saved, and you will see names of the most atrocious offenders who were pardoned, and sanctified, and are now with God. Ask them how they escaped the wrath to come, and entered the everlasting rest? With one voice they will exclaim, *He loved us, and washed us from our sins in His own blood!* Ask all the family of grace, who shall speedily join the celestial throng, how they obtained deliverance from the curse, and access to that terrible God? With equal unanimity they will reply, *We are accepted in the Beloved!* There is, therefore, *redemption through His blood.*

Let the doubting, disconsolate sinner throw himself, with all his guilt and vileness, into the arms of this forgiving mercy. It never yet repulsed any who came in the faith of the Mediator's blood, and it will not begin its repulses with thee. Go without delay; go with all boldness in this blood; and thou shalt find as cordial a welcome as grace can give thee.

Death to a Child of God.

DEATH brings no *peril* to a child of God; and ought to be no more an object of his fear than the approach of sleep at the close of day. I speak not of the physical pangs of dying, which relate to our animal perceptions, and to which our animal part never can nor should be reconciled. I speak of death as affecting our *moral* being. In this view he is rightly named the '*king of terrors;*' because, to ungodly men he is the *wages of sin*. It is from guilt that he draws his terrifying power. He announces to the wicked the end of their respite; the filling up of their cup; *a certain fearful looking for of judgment and fiery indignation which shall devour the adversaries;* and if they be not alarmed, if their faces gather not blackness, and their bosoms horror, it is because they are *hardened by the deceitfulness of sin*. Their stupidity will only heighten the surprise and consternation of the eternal world. But Jesus, having delivered His people from the wrath to come, delivered them by the blood of His cross, has for them stripped death of his terrors, and given them authority to cry, as he hands them over the threshold of life, *O Death, where is thy sting? the sting of death is sin, and the strength of sin is the* law; but thanks be to God who giveth us the victory through our Lord Jesus Christ!* In such a case death deserves not the name. It is but a sleep; sleep in its most heavenly form; sleep in Jesus.

Blessed Effects of the Gospel.

'I HAVE *seen* this gospel hush into a calm the tempest raised in the bosom by conscious guilt. I *have seen* it melt down the most obdurate into tenderness and contrition. I *have seen* it cheer up the broken-hearted, and bring the tear of gladness into eyes swollen with grief. I *have seen* it produce and maintain serenity under evils, which drive the worldling mad. I *have seen* it reconcile the sufferer to his cross, and send the song of praise from lips quivering with agony. I *have seen* it enable the most affectionate relatives to part in death; not without emotion, but without repining; and with a cordial surrender of all that they held most dear, to the disposal of their heavenly Father. I *have seen* the fading eye brighten at the promise of Jesus, *Where I am, there shall my servant be also.* I *have seen* the faithful spirit released from its clay, now mildly, now triumphantly, to enter into the joy of its Lord.'

Forgiveness of Sins Final.

THE forgiveness of sins is final. In the justification of a sinner, God, the gracious One, pardons once for all—pardons forever! Pardon would be of no use to us, were it not irreversible: it would no sooner be gained than lost. The Lord doth not so deal with His pardoned ones; give them just to taste the sweetness of His mercy, that their own sinfulness may the next moment fill their mouths with the bitterness, and their hearts with the horrors of the curse. His bounty is of another order altogether. His gifts and His calling are without repentance, i. e. unchangeable. His love is everlasting, and so is the life which He bestows upon them. They are united with His dear Son; their lives entwine with His life. Whatever reaches them to destroy them, must first kill their Redeemer. *Because I live*, is His gracious promise, *ye shall live also.* They are kept by the power of God through faith unto salvation; therefore they shall never perish. There is, there can be, no condemnation for them—they shall have everlasting life.

Contemplation of the Love of Christ.

DRAW nigh, and contemplate *the love of* Christ; a love without parallel, and beyond comprehension. *Though He was in the form of God, and thought it not robbery to be equal with God, yet He made Himself of no reputation and took upon Him the form of a servant, and was made in the likeness of men.* Source of eternal wonder! Lo 'the Creator of the ends of the earth' descends into a tabernacle of flesh, and sojourns among men! And whence, blessed Lord, whence this condescension? It was for 'the good of His chosen.' He assumed their nature that He might occupy their place; might take their guilt; might become *a curse for them that they might be made the righteousness of God in Him.* Yes, dear Christian, He put His soul in *thy* soul's stead; He drank *for thee* the cup of trembling; it was *thy* guilt which nailed Him to the ignominious tree; *thy* guilt which rolled the billows of wrath in upon His sinless soul. It was in bearing *thine iniquity* that hell's blackest midnight thickened upon His spirit, and wrung from Him that agonizing cry, MY GOD, MY GOD, *why hast* THOU *forsaken me?* Hath He passed through the fires of the pit to *save* thee? and doth He 'stake all the glories of His crown to *keep* thee?' and wilt thou, canst thou, darest thou be backward in promoting the frequent commemoration of His love? O Saviour, if we forget Thee, let our right hand forget her cunning!

OUR DUTY AND HAPPINESS.

THE sum of our duty and happiness, O believer! is comprised in this precept—*As ye have received Christ Jesus the Lord*, SO WALK YE IN HIM. The blood of sprinkling, kept by faith in the conscience, is the sure preservative from guilt; the holy secret of a comfortable and familiar walk with God. In this privilege let us go *from strength to strength*, lifting up our eyes to the *hills from whence cometh our help; showing forth the righteousness and the salvation of Jehovah all the day long:* and waiting for that great consummation, when, all the sorrows of earth's pilgrimage ended, and all its defilements washed away,

> 'Heaven lifts her everlasting portals high,
> And bids the pure in heart behold their God!'

THOMAS CHALMERS, D. D., LL. D.
1780-1847.

CHOOSE CHRIST.

CHOOSE Christ, then, my brethren, choose Him as the Captain of your salvation. Let Him enter into your hearts by faith, and let Him dwell continually there. Cultivate a daily intercourse and a growing acquaintance with Him. Oh, you are in safe company indeed, when your fellowship is with Him! The shield of His protecting mediatorship is ever between you and the justice of God; and out of His fullness there goeth a constant stream to nourish and to animate, and to strengthen every believer. Why should the shifting of human instruments so oppress and so discourage you, when He is your willing Friend; when He is ever present, and is at all times in readiness; when He, the same yesterday, to-day, and for ever, is to be met with in every place; and while His disciples here, giving way to the power of sight, are sorrowful and in great heaviness, because they are to move at a distance from one another, He, my brethren, He has His eye upon all neighborhoods and all countries, and will at length gather His disciples into one eternal family! With such a Master, let us quit ourselves like men. With the magnificence of eternity before us, let time, with all its fluctuations, dwindle into its own littleness.

Human Life Perishable.

WHERE are the men who a few years ago gave motion and activity to this busy theatre? where those husbandmen who lived on the ground that you now occupy? where those laboring poor who dwelt in your houses and villages? where those ministers who preached the lessons of piety, and talked of the vanity of this world? where those people who, on the Sabbaths of other times, assembled at the sound of the church-bell, and filled the house in which you are now sitting? Their habitation is the cold grave, the land of forgetfulness. * * * And we are the children of these fathers, and heirs to the same awful and stupendous destiny. Ours is one of the many generations who pass in rapid succession through this region of life and of sensibility. The time in which I live is but a small moment of this world's history. When we rise in contemplation to the roll of ages that are past, the momentary being of an individual shrinks into nothing. It is the flight of a shadow; it is a dream of vanity; it is the rapid glance of a meteor; it is a flower which every breath of heaven can wither into decay; it is a tale which as a remembrance vanisheth; it is a day which the silence of a long night will darken and overshadow. In a few years our heads will be laid in the cold grave, and the green turf will cover us. The children who come after us will tread upon our graves; they will weep for us a few days; they will talk of us a few months; they will remember us a few years; when our memory shall disappear from the face of the earth, and not a tongue shall be found to recall it. * * * How perishable is human life, yet no man lays it to heart.

Hope of Immortality.

HOLD it firm and fast even unto the end; and the bed of death will be to you a scene of triumph—the last messenger will be a messenger of joy; and those bright images of peace and rapture and elevation, which, out of Christ, are the mere fabrication of the fancy, will, in Christ, be found to have a reality and a fulfilment, which shall bear you up in the midst of your dying agonies, with a joy unspeakable and full of glory. It is no longer an idle declamation now. There is many a minister of Christ who could give you experience for it. He can take you to the house of mourning—to the mansion of pain and of sickness—to the chamber of the dying man. He can draw aside the curtain which covers the last hours of the good man's existence, and show you how a Christian can die. He can ask you to bend your ear, and to catch the faltering accents of praise and of piety. What meaneth that joy in the midst of suffering—that hope in the midst of breathlessness and pain—that elevation in the midst of cruelest agonies? It is not his own merit which sustains him.—

It is the merit of a benevolent Saviour. It is not a sense of his own righteousness which gives intrepidity to his expiring bosom. It is the righteousness of Christ. It is the hope of being found in Him, and a sense of the grace and forgiveness which he has received through His hands. In a word, it is Christ who resolves the mystery. It is His presence which throws tranquillity and joy around the scene of distress. It is He who administers vigour to the dying man; and, while despair sits on every countenance, and relatives are weeping around him, He enables him to leave them all with this exulting testimony—O death, where is thy sting—O grave, where is thy victory!

Come to Christ.

O AVAIL yourselves, then, of the precious moment that is now passing over you. Christ is offered to you. Salvation is at your choice. Forgiveness, through the blood of a satisfying atonement, is yours if you will. God does not want to magnify the power of His anger—He wants to magnify the power of His grace upon you. Try to approach Him in your own righteousness, and you will find yourselves toiling at an impracticable distance away from Him. But come with the righteousness of Christ as your plea, and you will indeed be permitted to draw nigh. God will rejoice over you for the sake of Him in whom He is well pleased; and you may freely, and with all your heart, rejoice in God, through Him, by whom ye have received the atonement. Could we state the thing more plainly, we would. We want to bring you into the condition of a simple receiver of God's pardon—a simple holder on the truth of His promises. It is on this footing, and on this alone, that you will ever be clothed in the garments of acceptance; or stand firmly and surely on the ground of reconciliation before Him. O turn then into this peaceful haven; and, in the act of so turning, God will pour out His Spirit upon you. As the fruit of your faith, you will become a new creature; and, in stepping over to that region of sunshine, where all is gladness, you will be sure to experience also that all is grace—that the peace and purity of the gospel are ever in alliance—They who walk before God without fear, being they who walk before Him in righteousness and in holiness all the days of their life.

Death will Come.

I BESEECH you to think how certainly death will, and how speedily it may, come upon the likeliest of you all. The very youngest among you know very well that, if not cut off previously—which is a very possible thing—then manhood will come, and old age will come, and the dying bed will come, and the very last look you shall ever cast on your acquaintances will come, and the agony of the parting breath will come, and the time when you are stretched a lifeless corpse before the eyes of weeping relatives will come, and the coffin that is to inclose you will come, and that hour when the company assemble to carry you to the churchyard will come, and that minute when you are put into the grave will come, and the throwing in of the loose earth into the narrow house where you are laid, and the spreading of the green sod over it—all, all will come on every living creature who now hears me; and in a few little years the minister who now speaks, and the people who now listen, will be carried to their long homes, and make room for another generation.

A Christian's Love for the Sabbath.

EVERY Sabbath image, and every Sabbath circumstance is dear to him. He loves the quietness of that hallowed morn. He loves the church-bell sound, which summons him to the house of prayer. He loves to join the chorus of devotion, and to sit and listen to that voice of persuasion which is lifted in the hearing of an assembled multitude. He loves the retirement of this day from the din of worldly business, and the inroads of worldly men. He loves the leisure it brings along with it—and sweet to his soul is the exercise of that hallowed hour, when there is no eye to witness him but the eye of Heaven —and when in solemn audience with the Father, who seeth him in secret; he can, on the wings of celestial contemplation, leave all the cares, and all the vexations, and all the secularities of an alienated world behind him.

Our Great High Priest.

CONSIDER Him who is the High Priest of your profession. I call upon you ever and anon to think of this sacrifice—and to ward off the legality of nature from your spirits, by a constant habit of recurrence, upon your part, to the atonement that He hath made, and to the everlasting righteousness that He hath brought in. Without this, the mind is ever lapsing anon into alienation and distrust—and the habitual jealousy of guilt, when not met, at all times, by a sense of that blood which washes it away, will throw us back again to our wonted distance from God—and instead of breathing the free air of confidence in Him, or rejoicing in the sunshine of His reconciled countenance, there will be a flaw of suspicion in all our intercourse, and instead of loving Him as a friend, we shall still stand in dread of Him as an accuser. There may be the occasional recognition of Christ, and, perhaps, along with it a gleam of light and of liberty. But the general state will be, that of a mind which is overcast. And, therefore, to keep all clear, and habitually clear, would I advise a regular forth-going of your believing thoughts, to the great decease that was accomplished at Jerusalem. I would have you to look unto Jesus Christ, and unto Him crucified, and be lightened thereby. Forget not that for guilt there has been an appropriate remedy provided in the gospel—and the way for you to stand delivered from all your fears of its vengeance and its agony, is to think of the vengeance that has already been poured out, and of the agony that has already been endured for it. Be very sure, that when justice is satisfied, then mercy, set at large from this obstruction, is free to rejoice over you. And justice is satisfied. The sufferings of the Garden and the Cross, have absorbed it all—nor after Christ hath poured out His soul unto the death for you, will it seek, in the horrors of your condemned eternity, for a double redress, and a double vindication. O, come out then, from the prison house of despondency—and, when you think of your sins, think also of the ransom which has been paid for them. On the strength of this, do make your resolute stand against the spirit of bondage—and looking, and looking hourly unto the Victim who has already bled a full expiation, do uphold yourself in the confidence, that sin is made an end of, that transgression is finished, that reconciliation for iniquity is made, and that now the believer, released from captivity, may walk before God in the security and the triumph of an everlasting righteousness.

Omnipresence of God.

HIS eye is upon every hour of my existence. His Spirit is intimately present with every thought of my heart. His inspiration gives birth to every purpose within me. His hand impresses a direction on every footstep of my goings. Every breath I enhale, is drawn by an energy which God deals out to me. This body, which, upon the slightest derangement, would become the prey of death, or of woful suffering, is now at ease, because He at this moment is warding off from me a thousand dangers, and upholding the thousand movements of its complex and delicate machinery. His presiding influence keeps by me through the whole current of my restless and ever changing history. When I walk by the way side, He is along with me. When I enter into company, amid all my forgetfulness of Him, He never forgets me. In the silent watches of the night, when my eyelids have closed, and my spirit has sunk into unconsciousness, the observant eye of Him who never slumbers, is upon me. I cannot fly from His presence. Go where I will, He tends me, and watches me, and cares for me; and the same Being who is now at work in the remotest domains of nature and of providence, is also at my right hand to eke out to me every moment of my being, and to uphold me in the exercise of all my feelings, and of all my faculties.

Prayers. I.

O GOD, make me to live to Thy glory. May I be clothed with the armor of religion; may I grow more and more in the right principles and practice of Thy Son's gospel; and, as years roll over me, may I withdraw my affections from time, and feel that in moving through the world I am moving toward eternity.

II.

O God, may I number my days so as to apply my heart to wisdom. Grant me the guidance of Thy Spirit, and the joys of Thy salvation. May my delight, O Lord, be in Thy law, and may eternity be ever present to my recollection and my feelings. Time is short; and as years revolve over me, may I learn to prize as the truest of all wisdom, the wisdom of the gospel. I am in Thy hand, O God. If Thou pleasest to add another year to my pilgrimage below, may it witness my progress in the faith and charity of the New Testament. Make me to feel a clear union with Thee in Christ. May I taste the joys of Thy chosen, and rejoice in the contemplation of that everlasting crown which is laid up for all who love the Lord Jesus in sincerity and in truth. May I be faithful in the duties of my calling, and may the care of the souls of my people engross more of my time and prayers and strenuous application. All I ask is for the sake of Him to whom, with Thee and the Holy Spirit, I give all the praise and all the glory. Amen.

REGINALD HEBER, D. D.
1783-1826.

Life Like a River.

LIFE bears us on like the stream of a mighty river. Our boat at first goes down the mighty channel—through the playful murmuring of the little brook, and the willows upon its grassy borders. The trees shed their blossoms over our young heads, the flowers on the brink seem to offer themselves to our young hands; we are happy in hope, and grasp eagerly at the beauties around us; the stream hurries on, and still our hands are empty. Our course in youth and in manhood is along a wider, deeper flood, and amid objects more striking and magnificent. We are animated by the moving picture of enjoyment and industry passing us; we are excited by our short-lived enjoyments. The stream bears us on, and joys and griefs are left behind us. We may be shipwrecked, but we cannot be delayed; for, rough or smooth, the river hastens towards its home, till the roar of the ocean is in our ears, and the waves beneath our feet, and the floods are lifted up around us, and we take our leave of earth and its inhabitants, until of our further voyage there is no witness save the Infinite and Eternal.

Earth and Heaven.

I PRAISED the sun, whose chariot rolled
On wheels of amber and of gold;
I praised the moon, whose softer eye
Gleamed sweetly through the summer sky;
And moon and sun in answer said,
'Our days of light are numbered.'

O God! O good beyond compare!
If thus Thy meaner works are fair,
If thus Thy bounties gild the span
Of ruined earth and sinful man,
How glorious must the mansion be,
Where Thy redeemed shall dwell with Thee.

Christ is Ours.

HE lived as well as died for us; His prayers are ours; ours are His blameless innocence and purity; it was our nature which fasted with Him in the desert; it was our nature which was transfigured in the mount with Him; it was our nature in which, united with His person, and inseparable from Him for ever, the Almighty Father declared Himself well pleased! In Him we are the sons of God once more, and the heaven, whither He is gone to prepare a place for us, is henceforward not only His but our inheritance!

Fear of Death Removed.

OH, Saviour of the faithful dead,
With whom Thy servants dwell,
Though cold and green the turf is spread
Above their narrow cell,—

> No more we cling to mortal clay,
>   We doubt and fear no more;
> Nor shrink to tread the darksome way,
>   Which Thou hast trod before.

OUR SALVATION OF GRACE.

OUR salvation is of grace alone, inasmuch as our first admission into the covenant of peace is without any previous probation of virtue, and, in the case of adult converts, in spite of many previous sins. It is of grace inasmuch as the services which are afterwards required from us have no aptitude in themselves to call down reward from the Most High; and are, on the other hand, exclusively calculated to promote our own happiness and the happiness of those around us. It is of grace, since to the performance of these very services the strength is furnished from above, by Him who not only calls on us to hope, but bestows on us the spiritual gifts by which that hope is sealed and perfected. It is of free grace, above all, and as it respects the consummation of our Christian warfare, because we are not only *first* freely called and *afterwards* freely strengthened to perform the obligations of our calling; but, even where we have neglected and transgressed our duty, the repentance and the faith which were, at first, our only passports to Christianity, are still suffered to attend us and plead for us, and by the same merits of the Redeemer through which we were justified and sanctified we are accepted at length and glorified.

Hymn Before the Sacrament.

BREAD of the world, in mercy broken!
　Wine of the soul, in mercy shed;
By whom the words of life were spoken,
　And in whose death our sins are dead!

Look on the heart by sorrow broken,
　Look on the tears by sinners shed,
And be Thy feast to us the token
　That by Thy grace our souls are fed!

EDWARD BICKERSTETH.
1786-1850.

MEDITATIONS AND PRAYERS ON THE LORD'S SUPPER. I.

HEAVENLY Father! grant that Thy Holy Spirit may bring to my remembrance all that which Christ did for me, whenever I go to His table; so that by the eye of faith, I too may see the suffering and Glorified Redeemer. Blessed Redeemer! I desire to call to mind Thy glory before the world was, Thy love in undertaking the work of our redemption, Thy birth of a lowly virgin, Thy life of sorrow, Thy shame and contempt, Thy rejection by man, Thy bloody sweat and agony, Thy crown of thorns, Thy stripes, the nails in Thy hands and Thy feet, Thy cross and all Thy passion, Thy painful death, and Thy burial in the tomb, and the sin of man as the cause of these Thy humiliations and sufferings. O how unmeasurable is Thy love! *It is strong as death—many waters cannot quench it.* It was not the nails that fastened Thee to the cross, but something more firm and binding; Thy love fixed Thee and kept Thee there, till Thou gavest up the ghost; otherwise every fetter that man could have devised would have been utterly unavailing.

I call to mind yet farther, Thy glorious resurrection and ascension, Thy leading captivity captive, and receiving gifts for men, Thy sitting at the right hand of the Father, Thy meditation, the future judgment, and the glory yet to come; and recalling these things to mind, may I afresh learn to hate and flee from every sin, to trust in Thee, and prepare to meet Thee. Thus may my hope of being with Thee for ever, be enlivened and established, and thus may my affections towards Thee and man be afresh enkindled and enlarged.

II.

GOD has graciously promised, *Ask, and ye shall have.* I believe His promise, and while waiting on Him at His table, would now implore His grace.

Lord! I wait for the increase of FAITH. Lord, help me more clearly to apprehend divine truths, and to be more distinct and firm in my assurance of them. I desire to attend at Thy table with a lively faith in the merits of my Redeemer. I would look up to Jesus, and trust in Him with entire and full confidence, as having ransomed me from sin and death, and procured for me life and salvation with His own precious blood. O give me faith to trust solely in Thy mercy through Christ for acceptance, and earnestly to look for the aid of the Spirit, to teach and to purify me.

Lord, I wait to receive STRENGTH to overcome my spiritual enemies. I know myself to be weak, helpless, and insufficient for any good work. But if I abide in Christ, He has said that I shall bear much fruit. Through this ordinance let me be drawn near to Him, and led to abide more in Him, so that my affections to the world may be deadened, and my whole soul may be refreshed and strengthened.

Lord, I wait hungering and thirsting for Thy SALVATION, in all its grace and fullness. O that the blood of Christ may speak peace to my troubled heart! O that the gladdening light of Thy countenance may shine on me, and the sense of Thy peculiar presence be felt in my heart! O that here I may clearly see that Christ is mine and I am His—that the Holy Spirit may be largely given unto me, and I may have a full assurance of hope that my sins are pardoned and my soul is saved.

Lord, I wait for the SPIRIT OF ADOPTION. I would come to Thy table as a child goes to an affectionate and tender parent, feeling that Thou hast a father's love to me, and having the tempers and disposition of a loving child towards Thee. O give me a filial, even a confiding, reverential, loving and obedient spirit. Let me look up to Thee, my Heavenly Father, for the bread of life, in full assurance that Thou wilt not send me away empty.

Now Lord, *truly my hope is in Thee* for the supply of all my spiritual wants. Give me that which Thou seest would be good for me: and thus shall I be blessed not only now, but all my life long, and in death, and through eternity.

III.

HOW full of love, even to the end, was our adorable Lord! The last words sounding in the ears of His disciples was a blessing. He ascended to heaven blessing them, and is still the same yesterday, to-day, and for ever. O ascended Saviour, may my heart rise whither Thou art gone; and now Christ is gone to heaven, may my affections be set on things above. *I know that my Redeemer liveth.* This is a blessed confidence that can support the soul in the severest trials. He makes Himself known too *in the breaking of bread.* I would not then only remember His death; but looking at His ascension, see the power given to Him, mark the gifts which He has received, dwell upon the work which He is now carrying on, and daily come to Him, and hold communion with Him.

Remember, too, O my soul, *this same Jesus which* was thus *taken up into heaven,* shall *so come in like manner* as He was seen *going into heaven.* Now at His table, I profess my expectation of His coming again. O may I be always ready for that day. The Lord in mercy grant that this sacred Institution may raise my heart to my ascended Saviour, and lead me to look, and diligently prepare for, His second coming.

IV.

LORD Jesus, help Thou me to take up my cross and follow Thee; all blessings come in faith and self-sacrifice; all evils come in self-confidence and self-indulgence. My Saviour, then grant me Thy grace, for the residue of my days; be it many years, be it one year, or be it but the present day, to deny myself, and live to Him who has redeemed me with His blood, feeling my own weakness, and not looking to a season of rest *below*, but *above;* not calculating on a time of enjoyment on earth, but preparing for it in heaven.

Help me also to maintain to the end of the conflict; looking forward to that crown of life which Thou hast promised to Thy faithful soldiers.

I turn to Thee, Thou blessed Redeemer. I turn from myself where all is polluted and wretched, to that gracious Saviour, where all is compassion, and love, and tenderness; where is a full atonement for enemies and rebels, a rich provision of mercy for the sinful, a complete salvation for the lost. O Jesus, pity, save, and bless my soul. Strengthen me for every duty that lies before me. In nothing can I claim blessings, but in Thy free promises and Thy full redemption. May I then delight in Thee, and walk closely with Thee every day. Draw me, and I will run after Thee.

V.

WHERE can I fly, O Jesus! where, but to Thee? In Thy wounds I hide me. At Thy cross I shelter me. *There* iniquity is pardoned; *there* the transgression of the remnant of Thy heritage is passed by.

But now, O God, my Saviour, I entreat Thee, *sub-*

due my iniquities. Only Thine almighty arm can vanquish them. I look to Thee for victory. Fight for me, fight *in* me; that I may be more than conqueror, through Him that loved me.

VI.

O LORD, I would now, in the fullness of my heart, earnestly pray for the hallowing of Thy name, the coming of Thy kingdom, and the doing of Thy will on earth as it is in heaven. And O grant that, till the Lord come, His table may be crowded with believing and joyful guests. O when shall all the ends of the earth look to Jesus and be saved! Hasten it in Thy good pleasure, O Lord; that Christ Jesus may be known, loved, and obeyed, in every land, and the Lord's name be praised from the rising of the sun to the going down of the same. Thus glorify Thy great name, fulfill Thy gracious promises, and let Thy kingdom be fully established through Jesus Christ, our only Redeemer. Amen.

WILLIAM NEVINS, D. D.
1797–1835.

Heaven.

A REST remaineth to the people of God. The meanest saint shall enjoy it. The moment he shall put off this robe of mortality, the mantle of Elijah's God shall descend and cover him.

This world is to heaven, what the inn upon the road is to the home at the end of it.

God is everywhere, but not so manifestly in all places as He is in some select places. He is everywhere, but His Shekinah is not everywhere. He does not *reveal* Himself everywhere. The glory of the Lord filled the ancient temple, but it dwelt peculiarly and visibly above the mercy-seat, in the most holy place. The glory of God fills the earth, but there are localities in the universe where it shines forth with peculiar splendor. God is everywhere, but His 'presence, where there is fullness of joy,' is not everywhere. Heaven is not merely a state.

Grace is the infancy of glory—glory the maturity of grace. Grace is the head of glory—glory the ripe fruit of grace.

How glorious and happy a place heaven must be, into which there shall nothing enter that defileth. There we shall never, never sin. Oh! it is the grand recommendation of heaven, that there there is no sin. The cause not being there, none of the effects will be there—no natural evil, because no moral evil; no debility, deformity, disease, ache, pain, perturbation, fear, anguish, nor sadness. No tear shall fall, no blood be spilt, no separation occur, no bereavement be felt, no disappointment, no satiety, no death.

Heaven's Attractions

I HAVE been thinking of the attractions of heaven—what there is in heaven to draw souls to it. I thought of *the place*. Heaven *has* place. Christ says to His disciples, 'I go to prepare a *place* for you.' It is a part of the consolation with which He comforts them, that heaven is a place, and not a mere state. What a place it must be! Selected out of all the locations of the universe—the chosen spot of space. We see, even on earth, places of great beauty, and we can conceive of spots far more delightful than any we see. But what comparison can these bear to heaven, where every thing exceeds whatever eye has seen, or imagination conceived? The earthly paradise must have been a charming spot. But what that to the heavenly? What the paradise assigned to the first Adam, who was of the earth, earthy, compared with that purchased by the second Adam, who is the Lord from heaven? It is a 'purchased possession.' The price it cost the purchaser, every one knows. Now, having purchased it, He has gone to prepare it—to set it in order—to lay out His skill upon it. O what a place Jesus will make, has already made heaven! The place should attract us.

Then I thought of the freedom of the place from the evils of earth. Not only what *is* in heaven, should attract us to it, but what is *not* there. And what is not there? There is no *night* there. Who does not want to go where no night is? No night, no *natural* night—none of its darkness, its damps, its dreariness; and no *moral* night—no ignorance—no error—no misery—no sin. These all belong to the night; and there is no night in heaven. And why no night there? What shines there so perpetually? It is not any natural luminary. It is a *moral* radiance that lights up heaven. 'The glory of God doth lighten it, and the Lamb is the light thereof.' No need have they there of other light. This shines everywhere, and on all. All light is sweet, but no light is like this.

And not only no night there, but 'no more *curse*.' Christ redeemed them from the curse of the law, being made a curse for them. And 'no more *death*.' The last enemy is overcome at last. Each, as he enters the place, shouts victoriously, 'O death, O grave!' 'Neither *sorrow*.' It is *here*. O yes it is here—around, within. We hear it; we see it; and at length we feel it. But it is not there. 'Nor *crying*'—no expression of grief. 'Neither shall there be any more *pain;* for the former things are passed away.' And what becomes of *tears ?* Are they left to dry up ? Nay, God *wipes* them away. And this is a sure sign they will never return.—What shall cause weeping when He wipes away tears ?

I have not said that there is no *sin* in heaven. I have not thought that necessary. If sin was there, night would be there, and the curse and death and all the other evils—the train of sin. These are not there; therefore sin is not. No, 'we shall be *like* Him ; for we shall see Him as He is.'

What *is* there, then, since these are not ? *Day* is there; and there is the *blessing* that maketh rich ; and there is *life,* immortality ; and since no sorrow, *joy*—'fullness of joy—joy unspeakable,' and *smiles* where tears were : and there they *rest,* not from their labors only, but from cares and doubts and fears. And *glory* is there, an ' exceeding and eternal weight.'

Then I thought of the *society.* It is composed of the *élite* of the universe. The various orders of angels who kept their first estate—as humble as they are high—not ashamed of men. Why should they be, when the Lord of angels is not ashamed to call us brethren ? The excellent of the earth also—all the *choice* spirits of every age and nation; the first man; the first martyr; the translated patriarch; the survivor of the deluge; the friend of God, and his juniors, Isaac and Israel ; Moses the lawgiver, and Joshua the leader of the host ; the pious kings ; the prophets ;

the evangelists and apostles, Paul, John; the martyrs; the reformers; the Puritan fathers; the missionaries Swartz, Brainerd, Martyn—Carey and Morrison have just gone up; and the young brothers who ascended from Sumatra—and another connected with missions, Wisner, has been suddenly sent for to heaven.

Is that all? Where is he who used to lisp, 'father, mother'—thy child? Passing out of your hands, passed he not into those of Jesus? Yes, you suffered him. If any other than Jesus had said, 'Suffer them to come to me,' you would have said, No. Death does not quench those recently struck sparks of intelligence. Jesus is not going to lose one of those little brilliants. All shall be in His crown.

Perhaps thou hast a brother or a sister there; that should draw you towards heaven. Perhaps a *mother* —she whose eye wept while it watched over thee, until at length it grew dim, and closed. Took she not in her cold hand thine, while yet her heart was warm, and said she not, 'I am going to Jesus. Follow me there?' Perhaps one nearer, dearer than child, than brother, than mother—the nearest, dearest is there. Shall I say who? Christian female, thy husband. Christian father, the young mother of thy babes. *He* is not—*she* is not; for God took them. Has heaven no attractions?

Heaven is gaining in attractions every day. True, the principal attractions continue the same. But the lesser ones multiply. Some have attractions there now, which they had not but a few months ago.—Earth is losing. How fast it has been losing of late. But earth's losses are heaven's gains. They who have left so many dwelling-places of earth desolate, have gone to their Father's house in heaven. What if they shall not return to us, we shall go to them. That is better.

But the principal attractions I have not yet mentioned. There is our Father, our heavenly Father, whom we have so often addressed as such in prayer: He that nourished and brought us up, and has borne us on; He that has watched over us with an eye that never sleeps, and provided for us with a hand that never tires; and who can pity too. We have never seen our Heavenly Father. But there He reveals Himself. There He smiles; and the nations of the saved walk in the light of His countenance.

And there is He, to depart and be with whom Paul desired, as being 'far better' than to live. There is His glorified humanity. If not having seen, we love Him; and in Him, though now we see Him not, yet believing, we rejoice with joy unspeakable and full of glory, what will be the love and the joy when 'we shall see Him as He is?' There is He.

Heaven *has* attractions, many and strong—and yet who would think it? How few feel and obey the heavenly attraction! How much more powerfully earth acts upon us! How unwilling we are to leave it even for heaven.

The Saint Near to Heaven.

THERE shall be but a step between him and it. Some are as near as all that to heaven. It is not a day's journey there. It is but to take a step, and, follower of Jesus, thou art where no night is, and no sound of moaning is heard, and every tear is wiped away. So near to heaven! How frequent then and fond should be your thoughts of it. *All so near!* Then 'what manner of persons ought we to be in all holy conversation and godliness!' How carefully and circumspectly ought they to walk whose path lies along such a brink!

And since the end of all our opportunities is as near as death, whatever our minds meditate, or our hands find to do, for our own souls, for the good of others, or for the glory of God, let us do it with our might.

Christ's Love and that of the Christian.

O HOW different Christ's love to us, from ours to Him! We have not to ask Him if He loves us. If any one should ever ask that question of Jesus, He would say, 'Behold my hands and my feet.' He bears on His very body the marks of His love to us. But what have we to point to as proofs of our love to Him? What has it *done* for Him; what *suffered?* O, the contrast! His love so strong, ours so weak; His so ardent, ours so cold; His so constant, ours so fickle; His so active, ours so indolent. So high, so deep, so long, so broad His love, its dimensions cannot be comprehended, it passeth knowledge; while ours is so limited and so minute, it eludes research.

> 'Dear Lord, and shall we ever live
> At this poor dying rate;
> Our love so faint, so cold to Thee,
> And Thine to us so great?'

Sympathy of Christ for the Believer.

O THINK that He, in all thy sorrows, pities thee. Yes, thy God feels for thee. Thy sufferings go to His heart. There is One in heaven who, from that exaltation, looks down upon thee; and the eye that watches over you wept for you once, and would, if it had tears, weep for you again. He knoweth your frame. He remembereth that you are dust. He will not break the bruised reed, nor quench the smoking flax. It was He who, when His disciples had nothing to say for themselves, made that kind apology for them, 'The spirit is willing but the flesh is weak.' He can be touched with the feeling of all your infirmities. You may cast all your cares on Him, for He careth for you. All through this vale of tears, you may rest assured of His sympathy, and when the vale of tears declines into the valley of the shadow of death, not His sympathy only will you have, but His inspiriting presence and His timely succor. And after that, what will not his bounty be whose pity has been so great? When there is no longer any occasion for pity—when misery is no more, and sighing has ceased, and God's hand has for the last time passed across your weeping eyes, and wiped away the final tear, what then will be the riches of His munificence?

WILLIAM JAY.
1769–1853.

The Bible.

Love and study the Scriptures. He that avoids reading a portion of them daily, forsakes his own mercy; and is so far regardless of his safety, welfare, and comfort. Therefore 'bind them continually upon thine heart, and tie them about thy neck. When thou goest, it shall lead thee; when thou sleepest, it shall keep thee; and when thou awakest, it shall talk with thee. For the commandment is a lamp; and the law is light; and reproofs of instruction are the way of life.'

Precious Bible! like thy blessed Author, our sun and our shield, thou giver of grace and glory, thou conductor through all this gloomy vale to our everlasting home, how many advantages have we already derived from thee! Thou hast often solved our doubts, and wiped away our tears. Thou hast been sweeter to our taste than honey and the honeycomb. Thou hast been better to us, in our distresses, than thousands of gold and silver. Unless thou hadst been our delight, we should have perished in our affliction.

No wonder Job 'esteemed thee more than his necessary food.' No wonder David chose thee as his heritage forever, and found thee to be the rejoicing of his heart. No wonder the noble army of martyrs parted with their estates and with their blood, rather than with thee. May we value thee as our richest jewel; may we love thee as our dearest good; may we consult thee as our surest counsellor; may we follow thee as our safest rule!

Death of Christian Friends.

LET us remember that when no longer visible to us, they are not lost. They have reached their Father's house. They are disposed of infinitely to their advantage. And this should subdue the selfishness of our grief. If we love them, we ought to rejoice in their promotion.

We have no distinct assurance that they are acquainted with our circumstances, or can employ themselves for our welfare—yet for us they languish, and for us they die. We may improve their removal; it should draw us away from earth, and attach us the more to heaven. And thus their going away will be for our welfare. When we lose the lives of our friends, we should be careful not to lose their deaths too.

They will not come to receive us to themselves; but they will welcome us when we enter their everlasting habitations. The separation is temporary. A time of re-union will come. We shall see their faces, and hear their voices again in the flesh. O cheerful consolation! how suitable, and how sure! 'I would not have you to be ignorant, brethren, concerning them which are asleep, that ye sorrow not, even as others which have no hope. For if we believe that Jesus died and rose again, even so them also which sleep in Jesus will God bring with Him. For this we say unto you by the word of the Lord, that we which are alive and remain unto the coming of the Lord shall not prevent them which are asleep. For the Lord Himself shall descend from heaven with a shout, with the voice of the archangel, and with the trump of God: and the dead in Christ shall rise first: then we which are alive and remain shall be caught up together with them in the clouds, to meet the Lord in the air: and so shall we ever be with the Lord. Wherefore comfort one another with these words.'

On Prayer.

PRAYER is the breathing of the desire towards God. Words are not essential to the performance of it. As words may be used without prayer, so prayer may be used without words; He that searcheth the heart 'knoweth what is the mind of the Spirit;' and when we cannot command language like some of our fellow-christians, it is well to be able to say, 'Lord, all my desire is before Thee, and my groaning is not hid from Thee.'

The expediency, the necessity of prayer, results from our indigent and dependent state. We have enemies to overcome—and how are we to conquer them? we have trials to endure—and how are we to bear them? We have duties to accomplish—and how are we to perform them? We need mercy and grace to help us—and how are we to obtain them? God has determined and revealed the method in which He will communicate the blessings He has promised. 'For all these things will I be enquired of by the house of Israel. Draw nigh to God, and He will draw nigh to you. Ask, and it shall be given to you; seek, and ye shall find.' And, as He is a Sovereign, and under no obligation to favor us at all, He has surely a right to appoint the way in which He will be gracious; but, in this appointment, His wisdom appears as conspicuous as His sovereignty; and His goodness as clearly as His wisdom. Nothing can be so beneficial to us as prayer is, not only by the relief it obtains, but by the influence it exerts; not only by its answers, but by its energy. Beyond every thing else that is instrumental in religion, it improves our characters, it strengthens our graces, it softens and refines our tempers, it contributes to our spirituality, and promotes our holiness. The more we have to do with God, the more we shall resemble Him. 'It is therefore good for us to draw near to Him.'

A Family Prayer for the Morning.

O LORD! Thou art good, and Thou doest good. Thou hast revealed Thyself as nigh unto all that call upon Thee—to all that call upon Thee in truth. May we who now address Thee be found the heirs of this promise; nor suffer us to incur the reproach of drawing near to Thee with the mouth, and honoring Thee with our lips, while our hearts are far from Thee. Unite our hearts to fear Thy name; and grant that we may worship Thee in the Spirit, and rejoice in Christ Jesus, and have no confidence in the flesh. We remember that we are sinners, and acknowledge the multitude and aggravations of our offences. Conscious not only of the reality, but the greatness of our guilt, we could indulge no hope, hadst not Thou exhibited Thine infinite benevolence, and revealed a Mediator, in whom Thou art reconciling the world unto Thyself, not imputing their trespasses unto them.

Thou hast not left Thyself without witness, in that Thou hast been doing us good, and giving us rain from heaven and fruitful seasons, filling our hearts with food and gladness. But herein is love; not that we loved God, but that He loved us, and sent His Son to be the propitiation for our sins. Blessed be Thy name, we have all the certainty we could desire, that with Thee there is mercy. *That* mercy the publican sought, and—found : *that* mercy—has never disappointed any that trusted in it : *that* mercy —at this very moment cries to us, Ask and it shall be given *you*, seek and *ye* shall find. O Lord, we avail ourselves of Thine invitation, and plead Thy promise! According to the multitude of Thy tender mercies blot out our transgressions. Create in us also a clean heart, and renew a right spirit within us.

We hope we are convinced that while many things are desirable and some useful, *one* thing is needful;

and that instead of the inquiry, What shall I eat, and what shall I drink, and wherewithal shall I be clothed? the supreme anxiousness of our soul is, What must I do to be saved? O visit us with Thy salvation, in the illumination of the mind, and the sanctification of the life; in all the comforts of the Holy Ghost, and in all the fruits of the Spirit. May we willingly obey all Thy commands, and cheerfully submit to all Thy appointments. In the annihilation of self-will, and in the temper of implicit devotedness, may we as to every duty say: Lord, what wilt Thou have me to do? And as to every event: Here I am, let Him do what seemeth Him good. Grant us piety and wisdom to accommodate ourselves to the allotments of life; and enable us to maintain a Christian temper and behavior in all the changing scenes of providence, that all things may work together, if not for our gratification, yet for our good.

May we disengage ourselves from the present evil world, and be received and acknowledged as the sons and daughters of the Lord Almighty. May the righteous be our attraction and delight; and though few in number, and despised by the foolish and wicked, may we go with *them*, because God is with them; and, like Moses, may we choose rather to suffer affliction with the people of God than enjoy the pleasures of sin for a season.

May we walk by faith, and not by sight. May we weigh both worlds, and may the future and the eternal preponderate. May this be our growing experience as well as profession—As for me, I will behold Thy face in righteousness; I shall be satisfied when I awake with Thy likeness.

By Thy mercies we renew this morning the consecration of ourselves to Thy service. Go forth with us into the concerns of the day. Keep us in all our ways. Innumerable are our dangers; but the greatest of all is sin. Uphold our goings therefore in Thy word, and let no iniquity have dominion over us. May we abstain from all appearance of evil: and the very God of peace sanctify us wholly: and may our whole spirit, and soul, and body be preserved blameless unto the coming of our Lord Jesus Christ.

And to God only wise, the Father, the Son, and the Holy Ghost, be ascribed all honor and praise for ever and ever. Amen.

A Family Prayer for the Evening.

O GOD! Thy greatness is unsearchable. Thy name is most excellent in all the earth. Thou hast set Thy glory above the heavens. Thousands minister unto Thee, and ten thousand times ten thousand stand before Thee. We feel ourselves in Thine awful presence to be nothing, less than nothing, and vanity: nor do we presume to approach Thee because we are deserving of Thy notice—for we have sinned—we have incurred Thy righteous displeasure—we acknowledge that Thou art justified when Thou speakest, and clear when Thou judgest.

But our necessities compel us; and Thy promises encourage us. Thou art nigh unto them that are of a broken heart, and savest such as be of a contrite spirit. Thou hast provided and revealed a Mediator, who has not only obeyed, but magnified the law and made it honorable; and Thou hast made us accepted in the Beloved. And we behold an innumerable multitude returning from Thy throne successful, rejoicing and encouraging us to go forward. *They were not, though all guilt and indigence, refused nor upbraided; but freely obtained pardon and holiness and righteousness and strength, and were blessed with all spiritual blessings in heavenly places in Christ.*

O look Thou upon us, and be merciful unto us, as Thou usest to do unto those that love Thy name! Convince us of sin both in its penalty and in its pollution; and may we mourn over it with a godly sorrow. Give us that faith by which we shall be enabled to believe on the Lord Jesus Christ; and, believing, may we have life through His name.

And may we not only have life, but have it more abundantly. We often question the reality of our grace; but the imperfections of our religion are too obvious not to be acknowledged, and too aggravated not to be deplored. Our souls cleave unto the dust; quicken Thou us according to Thy word. Strengthen in us the things that are ready to die. May we not only live in the Spirit, but walk in the Spirit. By holy resemblances, may we put on the Lord Jesus Christ. May the same mind be in us which was also in Him; and may we feel it to be our dignity and delight to go about doing good.

And as He suffered for us, leaving us an example that we should tread in His steps, may we learn to suffer like Him. When reviled, may we revile not again, but commit ourselves to Him that judgeth righteously. Whoever may be the instrument of our grief, may we never lose sight of an over-ruling agency in preparing and presenting it; but be able to say, The cup which my Father giveth me shall I not drink it? In patience may we possess our souls. May we be calm to inquire, wherefore Thou contendest with us. Let not weeping hinder sowing; nor sorrow, duty.

We live in a world of changes, and have here no continuing city—may we seek one to come; and have our minds kept in perfect peace, being stayed upon God. Be with us to the end of our journey; and after honoring Thee by the life we have lived, may we glorify Thee by the death we shall die. When heart and flesh fail, be Thou the strength of our heart and our portion for ever; at death may we fall asleep in Jesus; and in the morning of the resurrection, may He change our vile body, that it may be fashioned like His own glorious body; and so may we be for ever with the Lord.

Who can understand his errors? Forgive, O God, the sins of the past day, in thought, word, and deed, against Thy divine Majesty. We bless Thee for our preservation in our going out and our coming in, and in all our ways: and we bless Thee for all the supplies and indulgences which Thy good providence has afforded us.

And now, O Thou keeper of Israel, we commit our souls and our bodies to Thy all-sufficient care. Suffer no evil to befall our persons, and no plague to come nigh our dwelling. May our sleep be sweet; or if Thou holdest our eyes waking, may we remember Thee upon our bed, and meditate on Thee in the night-watches.

And with the innumerable company who never slumber nor sleep, and who rest not day and night, we would join in ascribing blessing and honor and glory and power unto Him that sitteth upon the throne and unto the Lamb, for ever and ever. Amen.

A Family Prayer for Sabbath Morning.

O COME, let us worship and fall down; let us kneel before the Lord our Maker, for He is our God, and we are the people of His pasture and the sheep of His hand.

Yes, O Lord, we are Thine; and Thee we are bound to serve. We grieve to think how many of our fellow-creatures live without Thee in the world; and confess, with shame, that other lords have had dominion over *us;* but henceforth by Thee only will we make mention of Thy name. We hope Thou hast subdued the insensibility and indifference towards Thyself, so awfully natural to us; and awakened in us the inquiry: Where is God, my Maker, that giveth songs in the night? We hope we are disposed to acknowledge Thee in all our ways; but we feel our need of the exercises of devotion. We trust we hold communion with Thee every day; but we find week-days to be worldly days; and our allowed intercourse with secular concerns tends to reduce our heavenly impressions, and to make us forgetful of our work, and our rest. We therefore bless Thee for the return of a day sacred to our souls and eternity; a time of refreshing from the presence of the Lord; in which, by waiting upon Thee, our hearts are enlarged, and our strength is renewed; so that we can mount up with wings as eagles, run and not be weary, and walk and not faint.

This is the day which the Lord hath made; we will rejoice and be glad in it. O let our minds be withdrawn from the world, as well as our bodies. Let our retirement be devout. Let our meditation be sweet. Let our conversation be edifying. Let our reading be pious. Let our hearing be profitable —and on Thee may we wait all the day!

Afford us the supply of the Spirit of Jesus Christ. None can need Thy succors more than we. Thou knowest our infirmities; let Thy strength be made perfect in our weakness. Our duties are far above our own power—let Thy grace be sufficient for us. Our dangers are numberless, and we are utterly unable to keep ourselves from falling; hold Thou us up, and we shall be safe. The burdens we feel would press our lives down to the ground: lay underneath us Thine everlasting arms. Fears alarm us; cares corrode us; losses impoverish us; our very affections are the sources of our afflictions; surely, man walketh in a vain show; surely, we are disquieted in vain—all, all is vanity and vexation of spirit; while in the world we have tribulation, in Thee may we have peace; and in the multitude of our thoughts within us, may Thy comforts delight our souls!

Yet, O Lord, we would remember, that gratitude becomes us much more than complaint. Our afflictions have been light compared with our guilt; and few compared with the sufferings of others. They have all been attended with numberless alleviations; they have all been needful; all founded in a regard to our welfare; all designed to work together for our good. We bless Thee for what is past; and trust Thee for what is future; and cast all our care upon Thee, knowing that Thou carest for us.

Thou hast commanded us to pray for all men, that we may be bound by our very devotions, as we have opportunity, to do good unto all men, especially unto them that are of the household of faith. May we always cherish and display benevolent dispositions toward our dependents; forgiving dispositions towards our enemies; peaceable dispositions towards our neighbors; and candid dispositions towards our fellow-christians. May we be able to say with our Lord and Saviour, *Whosoever* shall do the will of my Father that is in heaven, the same is my brother, and sister, and mother; and pray with Paul, Grace be with *all* them that love our Lord Jesus Christ in sincerity!

May the goings of our God and King be seen this day in every Christian sanctuary. Go with *us* to Thy house, and give testimony to the word of Thy grace. May it have free course, and be glorified in the hearts and lives of those that shall hear it. May it enlighten the ignorant; awaken the careless; reclaim the wandering; establish the weak; comfort the feeble-minded; and make ready a people prepared for the Lord!

Remember those who are this day denied our advantages. Be a little sanctuary to them in the midst of their privations; and let them know that Thou art not confined to temples made with hands. And O forget not those who never enjoyed our privileges; never smiled when a Sabbath appeared; never heard of the name of a Saviour—and let Thy way be known on earth, Thy saving health among all nations! Our Father which art in heaven, hallowed be Thy name. Thy kingdom come. Thy will be done in earth, as it is in heaven. Give us this day our daily bread. And forgive us our trespasses, as we forgive them that trespass against us. And lead us not into temptation; but deliver us from evil: for Thine is the kingdom, and the power, and the glory, for ever and ever. Amen.

A Family Prayer for Sabbath Evening.

IT is a good thing to give thanks unto the Lord, and to sing praises unto Thy name, O Most High; to show forth Thy loving-kindness in the morning, and Thy faithfulness every night.

We have this evening to acknowledge the blessings, not only of another day, but of another Sabbath. We bless Thee that the Sabbath was made for man, and that Thou hast hallowed such a portion of our time, for purposes the most important, but which, alas! we are prone to neglect. Thus Thou art affording us opportunities to retire, and compare the objects which court our attention; to learn, among all the cares of life, that one thing is needful; and to hear the inquiry—'What is a man profited, if he should gain the whole world and lose his own soul?' Thus we have moments of abstraction and leisure in which we can more fully investigate our character, examine our condition, and ask for what purpose we entered this mortal stage, and what will become of us when the scene closes.

We thank Thee that the lines are fallen to us in pleasant places, and that we have a goodly heritage; so that we can add to private meditation and devotion the public ordinances of religion, and can sit under our own vine and fig-tree, none daring to make us afraid. We bless Thee that we have not only the Scriptures, but the ministry of the gospel; and have this day not only read, but heard the words of eternal life. We hope we have seen Thy power and Thy glory in the sanctuary, and have found the house of God to be the gate of heaven.

But, O God, the effects we experience while waiting upon Thee, though delightful, are as often transitory, and prove like the morning cloud and early dew. Before the lapse of a single day we are compelled to complain, My soul cleaveth unto the dust; and to pray, Quicken Thou me according to Thy word. Render therefore the impressions made upon us deep and durable; keep these things forever in the imagination of the hearts of Thy people; and let Thy word *dwell* in us richly in all *wisdom*.

May the instructions we receive attend us in every part of our ordinary life, and regulate and excite us in the discharge of all our relative duties, so that whether we are husbands or wives, parents or children, masters or servants, we may adorn the doctrine of God our Saviour in all things. May we be satisfied with no knowledge, no belief, no professions, no feelings in religion, while our hearts are void of Thy love, and we are strangers to that grace which bringeth salvation, and teacheth us to deny ungodliness and worldly lusts, and to live soberly, righteously, and godly in the present world.

We take shame to ourselves, not only for our open violations of Thy law, but for our secret faults, our omissions of duty, our unprofitable attendances on the means of grace, our carnality in worshiping Thee, and all the sins of our holy things. Our iniquities are increased over our head, and our trespass is gone up into the very heavens, and there *He* is gone also, who is our advocate with the Father and the propitiation for our sins. Behold His hands and His feet; and hear, O hear the voice of the blood of sprinkling that speaketh better things than that of Abel.

Pity those who have this day been deprived of the public means of grace by sickness or infirmity. Let them know that Thou art not confined to temples made with hands; be with them in trouble; and give them their vineyards from thence, and the valley of Achor for a door of hope.

And remember the millions who were never favored with the advantages we enjoy, and would be grateful for the crumbs that fall from our table. But they never smiled when a Sabbath appeared; they never heard of the name of Jesus; they feel guilt, but know nothing of the blood that cleanseth from all sin; they feel depravity, but know nothing of the renewing of the Holy Ghost; they are bleeding to death of their spiritual wounds, but no one proclaims among them the balm of Gilead and the Physician there! O send out Thy light and Thy truth! Let Thy way be known on earth, Thy saving health among all nations.

We now commit ourselves with all our connections into Thy hands. Guard us through the defenceless hours of sleep from every evil to which we are exposed. If, as life is always uncertain, it should please Thee to call us hence this night, may we awake in glory and be for ever with the Lord; or if Thou shouldst continue us in being, may we rise in health and comfort, to pay Thee the homage of a grateful heart in a course of cheerful obedience.

In Thy favor is life—Do *Thou* bless us, and we shall be blessed—safe from every evil, and assured of every good.

And prepare us, at length, for the rest that remains for Thy people; in which we shall join the general assembly and church of the first-born, in ascribing blessing and honor, and glory and power to Him that sitteth upon the throne, and to the Lamb, for ever and ever. Amen.

INDEX OF SUBJECTS.

Advice to the afflicted .... PAGE 405
Affections, on religious 411
Afflictions 463
" advantages of 486
" blessed fruits of 463
" consolation in 302
Assurance 247, 458

Backsliding, recovery from 203
Believer's possessions, the 388
Believer, happy state of the 457
" the, safe 459
Bible, the 359, 347
Blessed, no pain among the 380
Blessings to which the Saviour invites us 481
Bliss, perpetuity of 213
Blood of Christ, redemption through the 514
Blood of the cross, efficiency of .. 225

Celestial city, the 59
" glory, visions of 192
Choose Christ 519
Christ, beholding of, a transforming sight 89
" beholding the glory of 199
" communion with 133
" crucified 496
" crucified, faith's view of .. 461
" coming to God by 282
" devotion to 456
" filled with Spirit 267
" vision and enjoyment of .. 437
" fullness of 198
" glory of, at the last day ... 135
" grace of 280
" giving glory to 283
" is ours 530
" imitation of 300
" incarnation of 305
" love to, as our advocate... 262
" made sin for us 281
" meditations on the glory of 251
" our acceptance in 272
" our advocate 254
" prayer to, in seasons of distress 189
" precious in His instructions 453

Christ presenting the memorials of His death 257
" resurrection of 295, 307
" second coming of 158, 428
" sympathy of, for the believer 546
" the believing soul's address to 439
" the believer's joy at the revelation of 134
" the heavy laden invited to 441
" the light of the Christian .. 140
" the love of 483
" the only foundation 449
" the preciousness of 448
" the study of 228
" without an interest in 482
Christ's blood, virtue of 507
" intercession 282
" intercession, comfort in .. 288
" intercession, efficacy of .. 261
" intercession, perpetuity of 259
" invitations 413
" love, and the Christian's . 545
" love, as manifested in His death 271
" love, constancy of 248
" love manifested from the cross 235
" presence with believers at death 443
Christian's trials, end of the 350
" joys 328
Christian hope 317
" ministry, importance of 508
Church fellowship 284
Come to Christ 522
" to the Saviour now 511
Comfort in distress 90
" in the death of pious friends 333
" against death 276
Communion of believers in heavenly worship 190
" table, thoughts at the 44
" table, thoughts after the 47
Consolation 121
" for the afflicted 487
Covert from the tempest 197

INDEX.

Death and heaven — 211
" but a sleep — 51
" comfort in the hour of — 100
" fear of, removed — 530
" hope of the righteous in — 451
" meditation on — 32
" of pious friends — 212
" of a pious youth — 385
" of Christian friends — 548
" of Christian relations — 385
" spiritual desire of — 138
" the Christian's victory over 477
" the Christian in his — 55
" the night of — 63
" the soul's triumph over — 360
" to the believer — 404
" to the child of God — 515
" will come — 523
Devotion for the evening, a model
    of — 408
" the Christian in his — 54
Devout meditation — 398
Divine Being, excellency of — 445
" care — 230
" guidance — 463
" knowledge — 361
" love — 83
" mercy, the ocean of — 245
" promises — 506
Do this in remembrance of me — 46

Earth and heaven — 530
Earthly and heavenly joys — 294
" enjoyments, inconstancy of 329
Ejaculations, pious — 359
Eternal glory — 136
"   happiness — 291
Eternity — 59, 455
End of time — 380

Faith, the eye of — 506
" language and power of — 156
" life of — 495
" life by — 177
" steadfastness in the — 135
" triumphant in death — 198
" walking by — 426
Fly to the mercy seat — 372
Forgiveness of sins final — 516

Glorified Redeemer, the — 263
Glory of Christ, manifestation of
    the — 251
God, a life of communion with — 360
" all-sufficiency of — 390
" awake to — 373
" behold as really present — 42
" contemplation of — 178
" grace of — 237
" infinite compassion of — 268
" infinite goodness of — 181
" love of — 164, 265
" love in the gift of His Son — 446
" manifested in the flesh — 70
" omnipresence of — 526

God, our access to — 265
" our portion — 98
" our refuge — 96
" pleasures of communion with 355
" rest in — 66, 233
" thoughts of, in the devout
    person — 43
" the saint's delight in — 321
" the saint's love to — 412
" sinner invited to return to — 486
" spared not His Son — 271
" walking with — 153, 233
" the Word of — 163, 195
" visions of, in glory — 228
God's mercy — 123
" unchangeableness, faith in — 232
Gospel, the — 275
" blessed effects of the — 516
" substance of the — 264
Grace — 86, 285, 442
" and sanctification, the work
    of — 332
" free — 126, 236
" maturity of — 249
" opposing sin — 331
Great Physician — 306

Happy immortality, hope of a — 453
Happiness of the life to come — 140
Heaven — 539
" and earth compared — 493
" anticipation of the joys of — 312
" blessedness of — 4 8
" Christ the light of — 494
" everlasting joys of — 165
" foretastes of — 241
" in view — 492
" intercourse with — 459
" love to saints in — 175
" mutual joy of Christ and
    believers in — 406
" no night in — 381
" no sorrow in — 376
" our journey towards — 423
" our home — 402, 491
" on the joys of — 337
" reunion of good men in — 500
" the Christian hidden life in 389
" the felicity of — 68, 429
" the glory of — 75
" the Sabbath an earnest of — 462
" the saint near to — 545
Heaven's attractions — 540
Heavenly aspirations — 185
" and earthly things — 57
" bliss, progressive char-
    acter of — 497
" conversation — 209
" hope — 331
" joys — 63, 208
" rest — 331, 375
" rest, meditation on the — 357
" manna, the — 66
" mindedness — 72
" things, excellency of — 296

INDEX.

Heavenly things, meditating on -- 319
" recognition --------- 73, 173
Hiding place from the wind ------ 196
Holy breathings --------------- 369
" fortitude ------------------ 370
" Ghost, joy in the ------------ 239
" joy and praise, exercise of --- 356
" Spirit, our guide ----------- 87
Home, the happy return --------- 67
" the Christian's ----------- 56
Honey from the rock ------------ 64
How to die comfortably --------- 204
" a minister should preach --- 502
Human life perishable ---------- 520
Humility -------------------- 58, 314
Hymn before the sacrament ------ 532

Immortality, the desire of ------- 488
" hope of ------------ 521

Jesus, safe in ------------------- 405
Judgment and eternity, preparation for ------------- 504
" day, the saint's happiness at the --------- 447

Lamb of God ------------------ 505
Life a pilgrimage --------------- 81
" everlasting, the ------------ 310
" fountain of ---------------- 227
" how to live a pleasant ------ 167
" like a river --------------- 529
" the water of --------------- 397
" uncertainty of ------------ 372
Live with eternity in view -------- 327
Longing soul's reflection, the ---- 243
Lord, ever with the ------------ 214
" praising the -------------- 396
Lord's supper ----------------- 379
Lord's supper, institution and benefits of the -------------------- 436
Lord's supper, meditations and prayers on the 533, 534, 536, 537, 538
Lord's supper, meditations on the 341, 342, 343
Love of Christ, contemplation of the ------------------------- 517
Lost and found ----------------- 245
" soul, funeral obsequies of --- 503

Meditations on the eighth Psalm - 137
Mercy for the vilest ------------- 48
Message which Jesus brings ----- 475
My Father's house ------------- 402

New song in glory -------------- 289
Now or never ------------------ 187

On the length of the way -------- 82
Our duty and happiness --------- 518
" Father's house ------------ 492
" great High Priest ---------- 525
" great Intercessor ---------- 399
" our Life ----------------- 303
" pious departed friends ------ 377

Paradise ---------------------- 77
Pardon of sin ------------------ 329
" for the most guilty ------- 38
" for the most heinous sins- 237
" greatest sinner ---------- 418
Pardoning mercy --------------- 90
Passing away ----------------- 480
Penitent on his knees, a --------- 504
Pious friends, loss of ----------- 176
Pilgrims, all are ---------------- 50
" entering the celestial city 285
Poor in spirit, the -------------- 430
Praising God ------------------ 93
Prayer ---------------------- 52, 129
" advantages of ------------ 119
" and praise ------------- 91, 435
" and reading the Scriptures 461
" before a journey ---------- 113
" blessings of ------------ 489
" for one in affliction ------- 338
" for one in trouble -------- 111
" for one in sickness ------- 112
" for gospel blessings, a ---- 401
" for spiritualized affections- 46
" for the penitent ---------- 186
" in the hour of death ------ 155
" on committing the soul to Jesus ------------------- 404
" on, for revivals of religion- 490
" on --------- 117, 279, 439, 549
" privileges of ------------- 431
" the man of -------------- 492
" a, for Saturday evening --- 451
" a, for Sabbath morning --- 556
" a, for Sabbath evening ---- 559
" a, for the morning -------- 550
" a, for the evening -------- 553
" a, for faith and trust in God 349
" a, for God's gracious presence ------------------ 351
" a, for increase of grace ---- 350
" a, for submission of spirit- 364
" a morning ------------ 344, 365
" an evening ----------- 346, 367
" on going abroad ---------- 348
" on preparation for death -- 352
Prayers, 102, 103, 104, 105, 106, 107, 108
109, 143, 144, 145, 146, 147, 148
149, 151, 216, 218, 220, 223, 393
394, 395, 432, 433, 511, 527, 528
" morning, for a family- 465, 468
" evening ------------- 109, 110
" for pardon of sins ---- 115, 116
" on receiving the sacrament ---------------- 114, 115

Reconciliation, God to be praised in ------------------------- 277
Redeemed, joy of the ----------- 246
" in glory, the ---------- 171
Redemption ------------------- 53
" near ---------------- 427
" admiration of angels- 127
" the divine mercy in -- 36
" the covenant of ------ 266

INDEX.

Reflection of a growing Christian - 244
Religion, friendship founded on -- 501
" in the heart ----------- 425
Repenting sinner, the ------------ 124
Resignation to the Divine will ---- 442
Resurrection, joy at the ---------- 383
Righteous eternally secure ------- 340
" flourishing of the ------ 200
" glorified bodies of the - 293
" safe ------------------ 120
" willing to die ---------- 315

Sabbath, a Christian's love for the 524
Sacramental petition ------------ 362
Saint's joy ---------------------- 161
Saint's rest --------------------- 193
Salvation ----------------------- 125
" blessedness of ---------- 31
" near ------------------ 409
" of grace --------------- 531
" the pursuit of ---------- 502
" to the uttermost ------- 509
Saving grace -------------------- 200
Saviour, attractions in the -------- 420
" come to the ------------ 139
" gratitude to the -------- 510
" in Gethsemane ---------- 27
" in His exultation -------- 450
" on the love of the ------ 337
" received up into glory --- 71

Saviour's agony --------------- 47, 269
" ascension and glorification ----------------- 308
" condescension and love - 183
" goodness to the believer 484
" patience --------------- 364
" sufferings and glories -- 76
Scriptures, the ------------------- 128
Soldier, the Christian ------------ 458
Solitude ------------------------ 180
Soul, peace to the --------------- 238
" repose of the ---------- 166
" the departing ---------- 205
Spiritual decays in the Christian - 202
" desertion ------------- 97
" light ----------------- 416
Standfast, Mr., last words of ------ 287

Thanksgiving and praise --------- 169
" duty of ------------ 298
Trials -------------------------- 456
True Christian happy ------------ 60
" penitence --------------- 48
" pleasures --------------- 207
" rest --------------------- 131

Unchangeable duration ---------- 79

Warfare, the Christian ----------- 131
World, crucified to the ----------- 187

Other Puritan Reprints from Solid Ground Christian Books

A BODY OF DIVINITY: Being the Sum and Substance of the Christian Religion
Archbishop James Ussher

CLASSIC COMMENTARY ON THE NEW TESTAMENT
John Trapp

A COMMENTARY ON THE EPISTLE TO THE HEBREWS
Exegetical and Expository *William Gouge*

AN EXPOSITION UPON THE EPISTLE OF JUDE
William Jenkyn

HEAVEN UPON EARTH: Jesus, The Best Friend in the Worst Times
James Janeway

THE MARROW OF TRUE JUSTIFICATION
Benjamin Keach

THE REDEEMER'S TEARS WEPT OVER LOST SOULS
John Howe

A SHORT EXPLANATION OF THE EPISTLE TO THE HEBREWS
David Dickson

THE TRAVELS OF TRUE GODLINESS
Benjamin Keach

THE COMPLETE WORKS OF THOMAS MANTON
Thomas Manton

www.ingramcontent.com/pod-product-compliance
Lightning Source LLC
Chambersburg PA
CBHW031957220426
43664CB00005B/47